# The Political Structure of Early Medieval South India

# The Political Structure of Early Medieval South India

Kesavan Veluthat

Orient BlackSwan

THE POLITICAL STRUCTURE OF EARLY MEDIEVAL SOUTH INDIA

**ORIENT BLACKSWAN PRIVATE LIMITED**

*Registered Office*
3-6-752 Himayatnagar, Hyderabad 500 029, Telangana, India
e-mail: centraloffice@orientblackswan.com

*Other Offices*
Bengaluru, Chennai, Guwahati, Hyderabad,
Kolkata, Mumbai, New Delhi, Noida, Patna


First published 1993
Second Edition 2012
Reprinted 2025

042963

ISBN 978-81-250-4651-6

*Typeset in*
Bembo 10.5/13 by
Eleven Arts, Delhi

*Printed in India at*
Saurabh Printers, Greater Noida, UP

*Published by*
Orient Blackswan Private Limited
3-6-752 Himayatnagar, Hyderabad 500 029, Telangana, India
e-mail: info@orientblackswan.com

*For MGS*
*and the memory of my parents*

# Contents

# Preface to this Edition

This book has been out of print for quite some time. A reprint, work on which was begun in May 1995, did not materialise for some reason. The publishers recently came back to me but suggested that I revise the book for a second edition or write an afterword surveying the development in the field since its publication. They told me that at the very least a new Introduction was necessary. As I was too busy—a euphemism for 'too lazy'—, I agreed to the last suggestion.

In reality, to go back to a book one wrote about a quarter of a century ago should be interesting in many ways. Among the many temptations that it holds out is that one can detach oneself from the book, and look at it more critically with the benefit of the experience one may have gained with the passage of time. The wealth of knowledge that has since accumulated in the field can help in this. However, I do not claim to have made an alternative reading of the sources or revisited the field in any major manner. Therefore, I have not touched the text at all; nor do I seek to survey the ground afresh in the new Introduction. I do not pretend to present before the readers what could be described as my reconsiderations or even interim reflections on the subject. Instead, what I have presumed to do in the 'Introduction' to this edition is to dwell a little on certain points which were not treated sufficiently elaborately in the first impression, to which extent the discussion there, I have realised, was incomplete. That, I hope, will be apology enough for this reissue, even if it has been delayed.

I thank M/s. Orient Blackswan Private Limited, and their earlier *avatar*, Orient Longman, for the keen interest they have always shown in this book. I am also indebted to the reviews that the book got, some encouraging and some forcing me to rethink my formulations. I also thank my students, both past and present, who keep me going.

Delhi, Kesavan Veluthat
30 November 2011

# Preface to the First Edition

The following pages embody substantially the dissertation submitted by the author for the Ph.D. degree of the University of Calicut in 1987. The attempt here is to analyse the political structure of south India in the early medieval period, i.e. the centuries between the seventh and the thirteenth of the Christian era. For the purpose of this study, 'South India' is equated with the region known to early sources as Tamilakam, generally corresponding to the present day linguistic states of Kerala and Tamil Nadu. Whenever political powers from this region, e.g., the Cōḻas, extended their arm to other areas such as Karnataka, evidence from such regions is also considered. The present study seeks to bring together and integrate evidence from different parts of the region; aspects of polity in the different kingdoms within the region are considered together. The book is of an interpretive nature and the data has been largely collected from the information available in the rich secondary literature.

I am indebted to several individuals and institutions who have helped me in various ways, during the course of this study. While the errors of fact and/or judgement are my own, what little worth this study has is largely due to them. I thank every one of them most sincerely. I must make special mention of Professor M. G. S. Narayanan, my teacher, and the late Sri Veluthat Narayanan Nambudiri, my father. The Indian Council of Historical Research supported this study with a generous fellowship and Mangalore University by granting me leave of absence. To members of my family, especially my wife Parvathy, my debt is irredeemable.

8 January 1991 Kesavan Veluthat

# Abbreviations

| | |
|---|---|
| A.I. | Ancient India |
| A.R.E. | Annual Reports of (South Indian) Epigraphy |
| A.S.I. | Archaeological Survey of India |
| C.P. | Copper Plate(s) |
| E.C. | Epigraphia Carnatica |
| E.I. | Epigraphia Indica |
| I.A. | Indian Antiquary |
| I.H.Q. | Indian Historical Quarterly |
| M.AR. | Mysore Archaeological Reports |
| P.C.P. | Pāṇḍyar Ceppēḍugaḷ Muppatu |
| S.I.I. | South Indian Inscriptions |
| T.A.S. | Travancore Archaeological Series |
| T.A.S.S.I | Transactions of the Archaeological Society of South India |
| T.P.C.P. | Thirty Pallava Copper Plates |

# Introduction to this Edition

This new 'Introduction' to *The Political Structure of Early Medieval South India* seeks to raise questions concerning the origin of the state in south India which had not been addressed in the earlier edition. The questions raised here relate chiefly to the chronological point at which the process of state formation becomes visible–one of the markers of the early medieval phase of south India's history–as well as the causative factors behind the process. That the state emerged in different parts of the world at specific historic conjunctures in answer to specific needs is a matter of recent realisation, notwithstanding romantic and not-so-romantic ideas about a pre-state situation in constructions of the 'state of nature' existing from very early times. In the case of India, modern scholarship took for granted the existence of the state in the pre-modern period. This was partly because of an abiding obsession with the notion of Oriental Despotism and its Marxian variant, the Asiatic Mode of Production, and partly because the categories historians of India were familiar with were taken from nineteenth century European historiography. Accordingly, they thought in terms of territorial states with fixed boundaries, notions of sovereignty, ideas of jurisprudence and so on—features of the Greek City States, Roman Empire, early modern nation states, modern empires and so on. Kings, ministers, military commanders and bureaucrats were habitually looked for and seen in this scheme, from the age of the Vedas to the age of the Mughals whom the British 'replaced' in India. A non-state or pre-state society was beyond their imagination.

This was no different in relation to the history of south India. When epigraphists and historians interpreted and published the documents they had discovered, they wrote as if all the features of a state society were present in the political system of which these inscriptions and court literature were the products.[1] Even in relation to the earlier periods, the same scholars, such as Kanakasabhai[2] and Nilakanta Sastri,[3] were convinced that Tamil society was a state society even in the more remote periods of the 'Sangam Literature'. Accordingly, they wrote about the 'kingdoms' and 'empires' of the Cēras, Pāṇḍyas and Cōḷas, their 'capitals', their 'systems of government', their 'armies' and all the appertaining details of the states they presided over.[4] There promptly were 'assemblies' which assisted the 'kings', 'officers' who 'executed' their orders, a 'judiciary' which meted out justice and so on. The master narrative of south Indian history, contained in the works of K. A. Nilakanta Sastri,[5] presented this picture of an unchanging polity and those who followed him, such as T. V. Mahalingam[6] and C. Minakshi,[7] carried it forward somewhat uncritically. Thus, Mahalingam, in a monograph devoted exclusively to south Indian polity, gives us to understand that the state continued with only minimal changes from the earliest period to the sixteenth century![8] In relation to the earliest periods, namely, the 'Sangam Period', the picture of a society characterised by all features of a state stood confirmed in a study devoted exclusively to the 'Sangam polity'.[9]

It is understandable that, in the context of the politics of the 'Dravidian' movements in Tamil Nadu, the celebratory exercises around the perceived glories of the 'Sangam Period' continued well into the period of Independence and after. Apart from great empires, there was grandeur in other areas as well. For example, historians waxed eloquent about trade with the Roman Empire. However, a more realistic appreciation of the evidence from literature and other sources has been made by Sri Lankan scholars like K. Kailasapathy[10] and K. Sivathambi[11] who raised questions of a different nature. Subsequently, Indian and Western scholars have comprehensively reconsidered the evidence and we have a more dependable picture of society in the centuries immediately before and after the turn of the Christian era.[12] It has now been recognised, placing the problem within the combined perspective of the social sciences, that the sources from this period represent stages in the biography of a clearly recognisable social formation—its emergence, maturing and dissolution. Different forms of production and different ways in which man sought to relate himself to nature in his struggle for livelihood characterised this period. Considered formerly as constituting a single corpus called 'Sangam Literature', the early Tamil texts are now appreciated as composed over a period of more than a millennium and belonging to different strata. They are essentially bardic compositions exhibiting traits of oral poetry.[13] They were selected, thematically arranged and brought together at a much later date in a well-organised manner. Of the various groups of anthologies such as *Eṭṭuttokai*, *Pattuppāṭṭu* and *Patineṉkīḻkkaṇakku*, six anthologies of the first, excluding *Kalittokai* and *Paripāṭal*, are the earliest.[14] They use an interesting floral symbolism in the nomenclature of what is called *tiṇai*s, and this is standardised and theorised in the later poetic works. Each of these *tiṇai*s signifies primarily a poetic situation and context in the literature and its poetics, representing generally particular expressions of war and love. Of the *tiṇai*s, a grouping of five in the love songs is of particular interest to the historian.

These five *tiṇai*s represent a division of the physiographic region of the Tamil-speaking world into five different eco-zones. Thus, the five *tiṇai*s of *Kuṟiñci* (hills and forests), *Mullai* (pastures and thickets), *Marutam* (riparian plains), *Pālai* (parched lands) and *Neytal* (costal tracts) represented clearly distinguishable geographical zones. People who lived in these zones lived a life close to nature and in tune with their surroundings. The hunters and gatherers known as *Kuṟavar* in *Kuṟiñci* worshipped *Cēyōn*, the war god; the pastoralists called *Iṭaiyar* in *Mullai* had their bucolic god in *Māyōn*; the plough agriculturists or *Uḻavar* of *Marutam* prayed to *Vēntan*, the rain-god; the fierce robbers and fighters described as Maṟavar in *Pālai* propitiated the blood-thirsty *Koṟṟavai* and the *Paratavar* fishermen of *Neytal* knelt before *Kaṭalōln*, the sea god. Labour employed for production was largely kin-based. *Kuṭi*s or households and *ūr*s or clan settlements were the units of social organisation. To be sure, this division into different *tiṇai*s did not involve any watertight division of any kind: transitional situations indicating merger or overlap of more than one *tiṇai* are spoken of and these are called *tiṇaimayakku*.[15] So also, different forms of production can be seen in the same *tiṇai*, with one in a dominant position in a particular *tiṇai*. The resultant picture is of a society in which people pursued their livelihood by following different modes of production. Regarding the relations of production in these different eco-zones, the information is clear: the principle of organisation was kinship. This is visible in situations of both pastoralism and agriculture. In such a system of production, distribution of surplus to the various factors of production is irrelevant. In any case, production was largely for subsistence and hardly for surplus.[16]

The picture provided by archaeology is complementary. In the megalithic horizon,[17] which corresponds to this literature both chronologically and culturally, human settlements are sparsely distributed. Sites throwing up evidence of settled agriculture, if few and far between, are nonetheless seen to be continuously occupied from Neolithic levels.[18] Iron is present, but the implements show a marked bias towards hunting and fighting, to the point of a near-total exclusion of those for agriculture. Artefacts such as pottery, terracotta, beads, semiprecious stones, bronze objects, etc., besides the iron implements, point to a relatively high level of craft production. But it is questionable if there was any concern with surplus even here, for such exchange was not, as might be understood, a disposal of the surplus. The supplementary sidelight provided by the Tamil Brahmi cave labels illumines the picture further:[19] they speak of certain varieties of traders, who sold gold, cotton clothes, (?iron) ploughshares, salt, sugar and liquor, etc. There is a solitary reference to a goldsmith. One of the records refers to 'the men of the *nigama*'. The reference to the Sanskritic *nigama* and the fact that most of these labels are associated with Jain and Buddhist monks may indicate a north Indian connection for at least a section of the traders. It is interesting that the term used for trader in these documents is *vaṇikan*, derived from the Sanskrit *vaṇik*. It has been demonstrated recently, following a systematic analysis of names figuring in the pottery inscriptions in Tamil Brāhmi that 'both the pure Prakrit forms and Tamilised forms ... would make nearly fifty per cent of all names found.' Again, 'if we consider the proper names of persons ... the proportion of Tamilised Prakrit names comes to nearly fifty per cent in rock inscriptions, too.'[20] These tell us about the agency in the 'trade' that is spoken of, apart from putting to rest all the debates about the origin of the script. The find spots of these inscriptions is itself revealing: they are located on major routes within the Tamil country.

The anthologies, too, refer to exchanges of the products of different *tiṇai*s. That literature also makes occasional references to *cāttu* (? Sanskrit *sārtha*), translated as 'caravans'. Uṟaiyūr Iḷampoṉvāṇikanār and Madurai Aruvaivāṇikan Iḷavēṭṭaṉār, who figure in the literature as poets, are thought to be 'specialised traders' in gold and textiles respectively.[21] In any case, trade, oriented towards profit, is hard to come by. What can at best be seen is exchange based on reciprocity. Gift and redistribution were the other forms of exchange; but even there the basis was either reciprocity or patronage–not value or profit.

The evidence of 'Roman trade'—embodied in the Tamil songs, Greco-Roman accounts, archaeology of Roman settlements themselves and numerous hoards of Roman coins–tells a similar story. This was highlighted in the past to show that south India had reached a degree of civilization, high enough to rub shoulders with the Roman world, with the balance of trade in favour of this side. In discussing evidence of Roman trade, it is important to bear in mind that the items exported included pepper, ginger, cardamom, cloves and similar spices; faunal articles such as animal hides and ivory; beasts and birds like apes and peacocks; wild wood articles such as aloe, sandal and teak; precious stones like beryl and pearl, and some cotton fabrics. Gold and silver coins constituted the chief items of import, besides some copper, tin and arsenic. Significantly, a major share of the Roman coins discovered from south India come from hoards and very few from occupational levels. Most of these are yet fresh from the mint, showing no wear and tear. Some of them also have a hole at the edge, indicating their having been used as ornaments such as necklaces or pendants. This shows clearly that the Roman coins were used less as a medium of exchange than as 'primitive valuables' gathered for their socio-technic or ideotechnic value.[22] This points, once again, to a situation of exchange of goods where ideas of price and profit did not make much sense from the Indian point of view.[23] So also the ports and centres of exchange in the interior could be shown as urban centres; but they were rather enclaves brought into existence by what has been described as stimulus from outside and not any organic development from within.

Thus, the economy and society were characterised by subsistence production, redistribution, reciprocity and patronage. The literature of the period elaborates this further. Copious accounts of war, where the concern was plunder and cattle-lifting, illustrate the general ethos of society. The hero *par excellence* was the warrior-hero and the poets were never tired of singing the praise of his heroism in different ways.[24] The innumerable hero-stones as well as references to the elaborate procedure of raising and worshipping them in the literature are further evidence of the general ethos of war and the cult of the warrior-hero.[25] Redistribution of booty captured in war and communal feasts following the plundering raids, often approximating to potlatch-like destruction, are brought out vividly in the texts.[26] This went a long way in claiming prestige and status for the hero who went to war, and his kinsmen basked in the reflected glory. Along with this, we also see a number of bards and minstrels, known as *Pāṇa*s, sometimes accompanied by members of their families, singing the praise of the hero in the numerous poems of love and war contained in the anthologies. These bards and minstrels moved from one centre to another and were amply rewarded by the heroes with gifts. The munificence of the hero was often the subject matter of the songs, and such songs earned their composers further gifts from the patrons. This cycle, too, formed part of the process of legitimating the chiefs, apart from the redistributive and potlatch-like exercises mentioned above.

We come across a number of such chiefs in the literature. Wherever possible, they led plundering raids into the rich rice-producing *Marutam* plains and sought to control them. These raids and the booty captured in them enhanced the resources of those chiefs. They could now give more gifts and organise more potlatch-like ceremonies. This was a definite advantage which those chiefs who lived in the proximity of the riparian plains had over the others farther afield. Such chiefs, naturally, got greater legitimacy, commensurate to the more generous gifts they were able to give and the more elaborate feasts and other communal gatherings they were able to organise. Claims staked on the rice-producing plains in the form of occasional raids graduated to regular control once this potential was realised.

Control of the riparian plains meant control of the rivers. These were arteries which connected the hills and forests to the sea. The large number of ports frequented by the Roman traders lay largely at the mouths of these rivers. The hill-products, which formed the bulk of the merchandise, flowed to the ports and beyond through these rivers.

Thus, those chiefs who were privileged enough to have control over the *Marutam* plains and their produce also had control over the precious items brought in by the Roman traders. The 'primitive valuables' of ideotechnic value, which they were now able to flaunt and occasionally give away as gifts, enhanced their prestige and legitimacy as never before. This superiority, gained by the twin advantage of controlling the rice-producing plains and the transmarine trade, set them apart from the less fortunate chiefs. A distinction is made in the literature between two kinds of chiefs as *vēntar* and *vēḷir.* These were the Cēra, the Cōḻa and the Pāṇḍya constituting the *mūvēntar*, the 'three crowned kings', and the several *vēḷ*s known as the *kuṟunilamannar* or the 'lesser kings'.

The relatively insignificant distinctions of detail apart, the organisation and functioning of these chiefs were similar. Kinship, agnatic and affinal, formed the major principle of organisation while reciprocity and patronage were the basis of redistribution. Mobilisation of resource was largely through plundering raids. No regular mechanism of appropriating surplus as tax can be identified and nor does one come across any agency carrying out functions associated with the state, not to speak of a bureaucracy. Urban centres, such as they were, are presented as resulting from 'external stimuli' and not as products of an organic development from within. No trace of what could be described as monumental architecture has come down to us. There certainly is evidence of literacy, but how far it was used for purposes of communication is very questionable.[27] Its exotic character in the context of south India in this period is hard to miss. In any case, there is no 'administrative document' showing the presence of the state through these records. Again, even though the general ethos of society was centred on war and the cult of the warrior hero, an organised military arm of a state is not visible in the songs. Ferocious fighters do figure as individuals; and they attach themselves occasionally to this chief or that, or a caravan that needed defence from a plundering raid. In short, there is nothing in the sources which shows the presence of the institution of state in that society.[28]

There is some lack of clarity in the picture after the third century AD, as we do not have many precisely datable documents from this period. By the seventh century AD, however, the historical scene becomes brighter once again. Profuse light is shed from various angles.

A notable feature is the entirely different nature of the new sources in both form and content. Inscriptions, in their thousands, form the chief category of sources now. Literature remains an important category; but it is not any more the oral compositions of the wandering minstrel: it is the literature of the court and the temple, with all its stereotypical characteristics. There are other expressions of high culture, which include monumental architecture of stupendous proportions. It will be a truism to say that this sudden emergence of newer and richer sources, entirely different in form and content from those of an earlier period, is indicative of a transformation that society had gone through. The details of the passage from the one to the other are not as clear as what are available for study at either of its ends. Therefore, what the historian can do is to extrapolate the information from both sides with a view to constructing a meaningful picture of what lay between them.

When one goes deeper into the sources on either side and examines the world represented by them more closely, the transformation is brought home more clearly. The inscriptions of the latter age, for instance, demonstrate this in numerous ways. They record largely royal charters or proceedings of local bodies of various descriptions with the somewhat pompous statement that both the medium and the message were intended to last 'as long as the moon and the stars endure'. Both kinds of documents announce the presence of the state in an unmistakable manner, the royal charters directly and the resolutions of local bodies in an oblique manner. They are largely concerned with the grant of land or other arrangements related to the utilisation of land, showing the importance that agriculture had come to acquire in the economy. They also tell us how far the distribution of agrarian surplus had led to differentiation, bringing about a division of society into distinct, and mutually antagonistic, classes. There are also records related to urban centres and trade, artisans and their activities, and so on, all showing the sea change in economy and society by the time these records begin to make their appearance.

The single most striking change of all is perhaps the phenomenal expansion of agriculture. It is obvious that the transactions of land, in their thousands, appearing in the period are indicative of this expansion. We see a large number of peasant settlements in what are known as the *veḷḷānvagai* villages.[29] Groupings of such settlements constituted the *nāḍu*, about which a huge body of literature has become available in recent years.[30] Agrarian corporations managed by non-cultivating intermediaries such Brāhmaṇas and to a lesser extent Jains and others, are more visible in the records although these groups may not have been more numerous than others.

If the world of primary economic activity, namely agriculture, is shown to have undergone such phenomenal changes, the case of trade was not any different either. It has been shown that in the wake of the agrarian developments which were taking place under the Pallavas and Pāṇḍyas and which continued under the Cōḻas, trade and urbanisation became more elaborate and complex and showed signs of structural differences.[31] Trading centres acquired a certain degree of autonomy and were controlled by corporations of traders. What had been a need-based exchange, whose character was determined by principles of reciprocity and patronage, got replaced by the 'instituted process' of trade with clear notions of sale and purchase, pricing, profit and shares of profit going to different agencies. Along with trade, urbanism too developed considerably. The trade enclaves of an earlier period, which had grown in response to external stimuli, lost their place and new ones came up in trading nodes and administrative centres. Unequal distribution of surplus as well as the proliferation of trading and artisanal activities led to social differentiation, which expressed itself in the form of *jāti*. Literature and inscriptions of this period make clear references to not only the existence of numerous *jāti*s but the hierarchical relation in which they stood.

Along with these developments, particularly the growth of agriculture in the plains in a phenomenal manner, and not unrelated to them, we can see two other developments–namely the widespread use of literacy and the rise of what approximated to monumental architecture. The thousands of inscriptions indicate the former. These are different, in both quality and quantity, from the old 'cave labels'. They are expressly addressed to the 'men of the locality', which assumes literacy among a section of the population.[32] Elaborate accounting is done and equally elaborate administrative documents are kept. All this was related primarily to agriculture, because the business of most of the inscriptions is to record grants of lands or to place on record arrangements for cultivating the land so granted. There are documents related to trade as well, which rose to an altogether different level.

The emergence of monumental architecture too has its significance in this context. If the best of monumental architecture related to the earlier period we considered were the paltry megaliths, huge temples, both rock-cut and structural, begin to make their appearance now.[33] These temples were often centres of the agrarian settlements and, in most cases, a function of the surplus produced by those settlements. The management of the institution and its properties is a subject of separate study, a large number of monographs starting with the Śucīndram temple being already available. A few of them, such as the 'royal temples' of Kāñcīpuram or the ultimate, the Bṛhadīśvara temple of Tañjāvūr, came up as statements of royal power. The sum and substance of our argument is that monumental architecture began to announce itself as a new presence.

This new formation, with relatively advanced means of production, considerable agrarian surplus and its differential distribution leading to relations going well beyond kinship ties and bringing about distinct and mutually antagonistic classes, the instituted process of trade and the urban networks replacing the exchange of natural products for primitive valuables and the isolated urban enclaves, a hierarchically oriented society where clannish loyalties had broken down and caste identities had solidified and an overarching ideology which subsumed and legitimised all these, was ready to receive the state, as it were, on its arrival.

What announces this arrival in the most unequivocal way is the unmistakable presence of the sovereign. The kingdoms of the Pallavas and Pāṇḍyas had come up in the Tamil-speaking regions from the seventh century onwards. The west coast witnessed this process by the end of the eighth or early ninth centuries, and the Cōḻas had established themselves most authentically in the Kaveri valley by the middle of the ninth century AD. An elaborate self-image of royalty had been created in the royalist expressions and the details of this, as well as the way in which power and control had been articulated, demonstrate that these kings were not the clannish chiefs of an earlier period any more.

The state did not mean just the king. Various nodes of power existed, deriving their authority either from a delegation or from other sources. These nodes were integrated into the system at various levels. They included a large number of what an earlier fashion of historiography described as 'feudatories'.[34] Their role in the newly formed polities has been viewed differently in recent years;[35] but it is clear that they were incorporated in a subordinate way. Another feature of a state society is 'government'. Was it a case of 'the superior executive strength' on account of 'a highly organised and thoroughly efficient bureaucracy' which was both 'numerous and powerful'[36] or a total lack of anything that carried out any governmental work altogether?[37] Recent work on the massive epigraphical data with computer-aided analysis has shown that the state identified and co-opted a large number of landed magnates as its agents to carry out its functions.[38] Another good pointer to the nature of the state is its resource base and the mobilisation of the surplus. There has been considerable debate on this issue as well, with Nilakanta Sastri dwelling upon the 'myriad' revenue terms in Cōḻa inscriptions[39] and Burton Stein denying any such revenue.[40] However, following a computer-aided analysis and other systematic studies of what had been looked upon as 'revenue terms' in Cōḻa inscriptions, it has been convincingly suggested that a regular levy from the primary producer collected at an impersonal level reached the state.[41]

It needs hardly any emphasis that this new political form is eminently qualified for the description of state. It was in every way the expression of the new social formation, which had come up on the ruins of the old. Its ideological apparatus of legitimation, too, conformed to the new situation. A self-image of royalty was so elaborately constructed that it went a long way in gaining validation for the ruler. Further statements of the power of the ruler can be seen in the elaborate claims about the military expeditions and, of course, success, which the rulers are always credited with. The way in which even iconography and architecture, apart from whole genres of court poetry, were used for this purpose is phenomenal. Munificent endowments formed another aspect of this attempt at validation: Rajendra Cōḻa's Karantai Plates record the creation of a new settlement of as many as 1080 Brāhmaṇs.[42] The way in which a certain ideology was made use of for the legitimation of hegemony is indeed crucial; but it is important to realise that this hegemony was far from ritual. It was *real political hegemony.*

Thus, we have two formations, the one entirely different from the other, the former characterised by a clearly pre-state society and the latter, noted for the authoritative presence of the state. We believe that we can locate the causative factors behind the emergence of the state in this scenario in the passages from the one formation to the other. Unfortunately, however, there is some lack of clarity in the picture after the third century AD. It is, thus, only by extrapolating what is known from either side that the passage itself can be examined. One way in which the four centuries or so following the 'Sangam Period' is looked at by historians is as if it represented a dark age, caused by a 'Kaḷabhra interregnum'.[43] This perception, however, is not supported by evidence;[44] nor is it helpful for our purpose for the period before and during the so-called Kaḷabhras as they are presented as presiding over their own state!

Extrapolating from what is known on either side and using such evidence as is available, one can still seek to fill the gap, however tentatively, and see an epochal transformation there. Forces capable of dissolving a whole formation and bringing about a new one had been present even towards the close of the early historical period. These included the importance that plough agriculture was gaining in the riparian plains and the Brāhmaṇical element that was introduced into society and culture. The warriors who took part in the plundering raids for the chiefs start insisting that they would settle for nothing less than fertile paddy fields in return for their services.[45] Brāhmaṇas who work as priests and officials in sacrifices are granted land on a large scale.[46] The didactic texts attributed to the last phase of what is called the Sangam Age extol the virtues of agriculture as opposed to plunder, and almost simultaneously underline the superiority of the ethics of the Brāhmaṇical śāstraic texts.[47] In this context, the significance of that 'outstanding epigraphical discovery' of the Pulāṅkuṟicci inscriptions is brought home.[48] They record the creation of *brahmadeya*s with superior rights over cultivating tenants (*kārāḷa*) and earlier occupants (*kuṭi*). The process is shown to have begun at least from the fifth century AD. Thus we have, on the one side, the picture of an agrarian expansion and, on the other, that of the creation of a class of non-cultivating Brāhmaṇa landholders placed above the peasantry. This resulted in an unprecedented demand for labour, as the labour-intensive agricultural activities increased as never before. This huge demand could not have been obviously met by the family labour of earlier times. Labour from outside the kinship group became essential. This proved to be the thin end of the wedge[49] which brought about the eventual erosion of the earlier system of production and distribution based on kinship, reciprocity and patronage and the evolution of a new system based on the differential distribution of surplus. Needless to say, the whole process was slow, uneven and extremely complex.

In the light of the above pieces of evidence, it is possible to hazard a guess about the process that was at work. As agriculture developed and society felt the need for expanding it further, new agrarian settlements were gradually coming up. Social relations in these settlements were naturally more differentiated than in the earlier period, what with extra-kin labour, non-cultivating owners of land, and intermediaries placed between the two. The work of Noboru Karashima has shown the nature of these settlements.[50] Y. Subbaryalu had earlier brought out the pattern of the evolution of such agrarian settlements in the *veḻḻānvagai* villages.[51] These villages, as they grew more and more differentiated, also got spontaneously grouped into larger units of social and, should one say, political organisation in what are known as the *nāḍus*.[52] These *nāḍu* units are shown to have grown, both in their number and range of activities. In any case, they get incorporated into a new system. The increasing number of *brahmadeyas* and other eleemosynary grants that came to be created is another factor that has to be considered along with this.

In the process of agrarian expansion which characterised this period, such intermediary groups, both individuals and institutions, with untold command over the productive forces and the surplus produced came into existence and started exercising deep influence in economy and society. In fact, such groups are conspicuous by their absence in the earlier period; they are the most prominent in the inscriptions of the later period. Could one say, therefore, that it is they who make all the difference? Considering the role they played in the political structure of the period under consideration, such a statement may not be too wide off the mark. When the old chiefdom level organisation was not any more compatible with the new formation that had come into existence, new political forms, where these new elements had a major stake and role to play, began to emerge. Chiefs of old, such as the Pāṇḍyas, Cēras and Cōḻas as well as new ones such as the Pallavas, were conducting a new experiment when they tried on the habit of a king and changed their role into presiding over a monarchical state. Into the system that was so created, the newly developed intermediaries were gradually incorporated, both in the corporate units such as the *nāḍu* or *kōṭṭam* and the individual land-owners. They were recognised and enlisted into the service of the state, which had well and truly arrived.

The new elements in society and culture that show up in this period reflect and legitimise this new system. For one thing, we have the emergence and solidification of the institution of *jāti*. The change in religion, represented by the worship of *āgamaic* deities consecrated in temples, is another factor. But more important than all these is the emergence of what has been described as the Bhakti Movement in south India. Elements of devotion to personalised gods of the *āgamaic* tradition have been identified in the texts which formed part of the later strata of the 'Sangam literature' such as the *Kalittokai* and *Paripāṭal*.[53] But their north Indian, Brāhmaṇical, character is hard to miss. In a joint study that M. G. S. Narayanan and I have undertaken, we have argued that the Bhakti Movement represented an ideology which sought to reflect and legitimise the emerging socio-political order.[54] It is possible to imagine that the Bhakti Movement developed as an unpremeditated by-product of the new Brāhmaṇical agrarian settlements centred on temples, partly as a means of fulfilling their mission and partly as an antithesis. This antithetical aspect, represented by the elements of dissent and protest in the early phase of its development, however, gave in and helped in the consolidation of a new orthodoxy.

It is against this background that we have to see the emergence of the state in the Tamil South. The Pallavas in the northern parts of Tamilnadu, with their experience from the activities in the Andhra region, were coming up with an answer to the new demands. They got identified with a definite territory and a city after they moved to the Tamil region by the end of the sixth century AD. They were successful in integrating the newly developed agrarian and agro-pastoral sub-regions called *nāḍus* and *kōṭṭams*. Pre-existing chiefdoms, such as the Maḻavas and others, representing the 'feudatories' of an earlier historiography, were integrated at various levels. So also the *sabhās* of the brāhman groups and the temples were brought under the system. Patronage of the latter as well as their earlier record of performing sacrifices, claims to the *brahmakṣatra* status and a whole lot of other means went into legitimising the new polity in the context in which it emerged. It was an extremely complex and gradual process, the details of which have to be worked out. It is significant to remember that there were variations in relation to the integration of the agrarian and pastoral groups in the Pallavan case itself. It will be very risky, therefore, to suggest that the same model would explain the process of the formation of the state in the whole of south India. However, it may be suggested, at the risk of oversimplification, that factors such as the heavy use of non-kin labour, rise of huge agrarian corporations, the proliferation of Brāhmaṇical settlements and their control of economy and society through the institution of the temple, the religious ideology it represented and the attendant developments led to the rise of the state in south India.

It should not, however, be thought that the state that came into existence in south India in this way was a finished product. It was rather a process. The experiment under the Pallavas and Pāṇḍyas was carried forward under the Cōḻas. Even there, the state did not have a uniform character or structure all through the period of its existence, or throughout the territory it covered. It does not need any elaborate argument to show that the Cōḻa state before and after Rājarāja I was unrecognisably different from each other. Even in the post-Rājarāja I period, it can be seen, the changes that overtook the nature of the state were so far-reaching that they affected the very fabric of political structure. In a recent study, Noboru Karashima argues 'for the processes of state and social formation during the 200 years of upheaval between the collapse of the Cōḻa state in the thirteenth century and the establishment of the Vijayanagar institutions under *nayaka*s in the fifteenth century.'[55] I hope the pages that follow will prepare the necessary foundation for understanding the process that was the state in early medieval south India.

## NOTES

1. Thus, the dynasties of the Pallavas, Pāṇḍyas and Cōḻas were identified as ruling over kingdoms of their own when the copper plates and stone inscriptions were discovered and published in the late nineteenth and early twentieth centuries. This was done by the epigraphists such as Hultzsch and others who published the inscriptions as well as by the scholars such as Kanakasabhai who discovered and published the literary works. While this was indeed a correct perception, it is questionable whether it was the result of any

serious consideration of the character of these 'states'. When historians like Joveau-Dubrueil, R. Gopalan and Niakanta Sastri integrated the evidence to write the history of the Pallavas or the Pāṇḍyas or, later, the Cōḻas, this picture was carried forward.

2. V. Kanakasabhai, *The Tamils Eighteen Hundred Years Ago* (Madras, 1904).

3. K. A. Nilakanta Sastri, *The Pandyan Kingdom* (London, 1929).

4. *Ibid.* Sastri talks about the 'the first empire' and the 'second empire' of the Pāṇḍyas to denote the two formations represented in the 'Sangam literature' and the later inscriptions respectively.

5. *Ibid.*; idem., *Studies in Chola History and Administration* (Madras, 1932); *The Colas* (Madras, I Edn., 1934); *History of South India* (Oxford, 1955), etc.

6. T. V. Mahalingam, *South Indian Polity* (Madras, 1954).

7. C. Minakshi, *Administration and Social Life under the Pallavas* (Madras, 1938).

8. Mahalingam, *South Indian Polity*, *op. cit.*

9. N. Subramanyan, *Sangam Polity* (Second Edition, Madurai, 1980).

10. K. Kailasapathy, *Tamil Heroic Poetry* (London, 1968).

11. K. Sivathambi, 'Early South Indian Society and Economy: the Tinai Concept', *Social Scientist*, 29, 1974. A few of Sivathambi's seminal articles, including this one, are brought together in K. Sivathambi, *Studies in Ancient Tamil Society* (Chennai, 1998).

12. See, for instance, Kamil Zvelebil, *The Smile of Murugan* (Leiden, 1973); George L. Hart III, *The Poems of Ancient Tamil: Their Milieu and Their Sanskrit Counterparts* (Berkeley, 1975); idem, "Ancient Tamil Literature: Its Scholarly Past and Future" in Stein, ed., *Essays on South India*, (Delhi, 1975); R. Champakalakshmi, 'Archaeology and Tamil Literary Tradition', *Purātattva*, VIII, 1975–76; *idem*, *Trade, Ideology and Urbanization: South India 300 BC to AD 1300* (Delhi, 1996); M. G. S. Narayanan, 'The Mauryan Problem in Sangam Works in Historical Perspective', *Journal of Indian History*, Vol. 53, No.2, 1975; *idem*, 'The Vedic, Puranic, Sastraic Elements in Tamil Sangam Society and Culture', *PIHC* (Aligarh, 1975); *idem*, 'Cattle Raiders of the Sangam Age', *PIHC* (Bhubaneswar, 1977); *idem*, 'The Warrior Settlements of the Sangam Age', PIHC (Kurukshetra, 1982); *idem*, 'Peasants in Early Tamilakam', in H. V. Sreenivasamurthi, B. Surendra Rao, Kesavan Veluthat and S. A. Bari, eds., *Essays on Indian History and Culture: Felicitation Volume to Professor B. Sheik Ali* (New Delhi, 1990); J. A. Marr, The Eight Anthologies: A Study in Early Tamil (Madras, 1987); Rajan Gurukkal, *Social Formations in Early South India* (New Delhi, 2010).

13. Kailasapathi, *op. cit.*

14. Zvelebil, *op. cit.*, Gurukkal, 'Towards a New Discourse', in *Social Formations in Early South India* (New Delhi, 2010).

15. This was taken formerly as 'confusion by poets of the native habits of different regions': N. Subramanyan, *Pre-Pallavan Tamil Index* (reprint, Madras, 1990), p. 430 s.v. *Tiṇai-Mayakku*. For a different interpretation, Gurukkal, *Social Formations in Early South India.*

16. Gurukkal, *Social Formations in Early South India.* It is important to remember that surplus had no relevance in such a society and that surplus itself 'is in any case not an event but a process.' Romila Thapar, *From Lineage to State* (Bombay, 1984), p. 77.

17. B. K. Gururaja Rao, *Megalithic Culture of South India* (Mysore, 1972); A Sundara, *Early Chamber Tombs of South India* (Delhi, 1975); Leon S. Leshnik, *South Indian 'Megalithic' Burials: The Pandukal Complex* (Wiesbaden, 1974). It will be rewarding to read these with Champakalakshmi, *Archaeology ...*', *op. cit.*

18. Paiyampalli is a good case in point. *Indian Archaeology: A Review* (1964–65), pp, 22–23; (1967–68), pp. 26–30.

19. T. V. Mahalingam, *Early South Indian Palaeography* (Reprint, Madras, 1974); Iravatham Mahadevan, 'Corpus of the Tamil Brahmi Inscriptions' in R. Nagaswami, ed., Seminar on Inscriptions (Madras, 1966); *idem*, *Tamil Brahmi Inscriptions* (Madras, 1970). For an insightful analysis, Rajan Gurukkal, *op.cit.* pp. 166–81. For a most authentic compilation of the texts and translations of all hitherto known records and a competent study, Iravatham Mahadevan, *Early Tamil Epigraphy From the Earliest Times to the Sixth Century AD*, Chennai and Harvard, 2003.

20. Y. Subbarayalu, 'Pottery Inscriptions of Tamilnadu: A Comprehensive View', in *Airāvati: Felicitation Volume in Honour of Iravatham Mahadevan*, ed. by R. Kalaikkovan *et al.*, Chennai, 2008, pp. 209–248. See also Y. Subbarayalu, 'Visāki and Kuvaran: Historical Implications of Names in the Tamil Brahmi Inscriptions', in K. Indrapala, ed., *Early Historic Tamilnadu c. 300 BCE to 300 CE: Essays Commemorating Prof. K. Kailasapathy on the Twenty-fifth Anniversary of his Death*, Colombo and Chennai, 2009, pp. 95–122.

21. Gurukkal, *Early Social Formations, ... op. cit.* p. 21, n. 18. For more such names and useful details, Champakalakshmi, *Trade, Ideology and Urbanization ...*, p. 107.

22. Champakalakshmi, *Trade ..., op. cit.*, pp. 25–36.

23. For the Romans, however, what they paid was probably price money or a fee for protection. See Romila Thapar, 'Black Gold: South Asia and the Roman Maritime Trade', *South Asia; Journal of the South Asian Studies Association*, Armidale, New South Wales, Australia, 1992, Vol. XV, No. 2, (New Series), pp. 13–14.

24. Gurukkal, 'Towards a New Discourse ...', *op. cit.* He speaks of 'about thirty-five enunciative codes ... which may be grouped ... into five clusters of closely related meanings: those extolling individual heroism; the family tradition and heritage of heroes; the virtues of raids and plunder; the collective passion of the communities for raid; and the act of gift-giving.'

25. Narayanan, 'Peasants ...', *op. cit.* p.30; Subramanyan, *Sangam Polity*, Chapter VI, pp. 126–86.

26. Narayanan, 'Cattle Raiders ...', *op. cit.*; Subramanyan, *Pre-Pallavan Tamil Index*, p. 129 *s.v. Uṇḍāṭṭu*. These details may be profitably read with the insight provided by Romila Thapar, *From Lineage to State*, Chapter II, esp. pp. 31–33.

27. Gurukkal, 'Writing and Its ...', *op. cit.*

28. R. Champakalakshmi, 'Introduction', *Studies in History*, Vol. IV, No. 2, July–December 1982, pp. 161–67 suggested this for the first time in a fleeting manner. An alternative argument can be seen in the recent works of Rajan Gurukkal. See, for instance, his 'Antecedents of State Formation in South India' in R. Champakalakshmi, Kesavan Veluthat and T. R. Venugopalan, eds., *State and Society in Pre-modern South India*, (Thrissur, 2002), pp. 39–59 and 'Did State Exist in Pre-Pallavan Tamil Region?' in *Proceeding of the Indian History Congress*, Amritsar, 2002, pp. 138–150. For a different pattern, Kesavan Veluthat, 'Into the 'Medieval' and Out of It—Early South India in Transition', Presidential Address, 58th Session, Indian History Congress, Section II, Medieval Indian History, Bangalore, 1997, reproduced in Kesavan Veluthat, *The Early Medieval in South India*, New Delhi, 2009, pp. 19–60.

29. Noboru Karashima, *South Indian History and Society: Studies from Inscriptions* AD *850–1800* (Delhi, 1984), pp. 40–55; Y. Subbarayalu, 'The Place of Ūr in the Economic and Social History of Early Tamilnāḍu', paper presented at the ICHR Seminar on South Indian History, Madras University, February, 1977.

30. For a discussion, Kesavan Veluthat, 'The Role of Nāḍu in the Socio-Political Structure of South India (A. D,c. 600–1200) in H. V. Sreenivasamurthi, *et al.*, eds., *op. cit.*, pp. 85–100, reproduced in Kesavan Veluthat, *The Early Medieval in South India, op.cit.*, pp. 109–120

31. For the growth of trade and urabanisation in the period of the Pallavas and after, Champakalakshmi, *Trade, Ideology and Urbanization ..., op. cit.*, pp. 203–310; M. G. S. Narayanan, *Cultural Symbiosis in Kerala* (Trivandrum, 1972); Kenneth Hall, *Trade and Statecraft in the Age of the Colas* (Delhi, 1980).

32. The thousands of inscriptions that make their appearance in this period is evidence of a greater use of literacy. The formula in most copper plate charters, addressing the notables in the locality, shows that there was a section

of the population that was literate. So also, references to the revenue account books (*varippottagam*) are significant in this context.

33. There is such rich literature on the subject of architecture in south India that it would look pedantic to give a reference here.

34. K. A. Nilakanta Sastri, *The Pandyan Kingdom* (London, 1929), pp. 74–75; *The Cōḷas*, pp. 126–28; 187–89; 259–60; 347–48; 372–75; 400–408; 429–32; T. V. Mahalingam, *South Indian Polity*, pp. 321–28; M. S. Govindaswamy, *The Role of Feudatories in Pallava History* (Annamalainagar, 1975); *idem*, *The Role of Feudatories in Later Chola History* (Annamalainagar, 1979); M. Arokiaswamy, *The Kongu Country* (Madras, 1956); V. Balambal, *Feudatories of South India 800–1070 AD* (Allahabad, 1978). The information they provide is copious; but the feudal jargon has no conceptual rigour behind it.

35. See above, Chapter on 'Role of the Chiefs'.

36. Sastri, *Colas*, pp. 461 f.

37. Burton Stein, 'The State and Agrarian Order in Medieval South India', in Burton Stein ed., *Essays on South India* (Delhi, 1975); *idem*, *Peasant State ...*, *op. cit.*

38. Noboru Karashima, Y. Subbarayalu and Toru Matsui have undertaken a computer-aided analysis of personal names figuring in Cōḷa inscriptions. *A Concordance of Personal Names in Cola Inscriptions* (Madurai, 1978), 3 vols. Our own analysis is based on this.

39. Sastri, *Colas*, Chapter XIX: 'Taxation and Finance', pp. 520–45.

40. Burton Stein, 'The State and Agrarian Order in Medieval South India', in Burton Stein ed., *Essays on South India* (Delhi, 1975); *idem*, *Peasant State ...*, *op. cit.*

41. Karashima, *South Indian History and Society*, pp. 69–130; P.Shanmugam, *The Revenue System of the Colas, 850–1279* (Madras, 1987). We have followed the results of their analysis in our own formulations. Kesavan Veluthat, 'Labour Rent and Produce Rent: Reflections on the Nature of the Revenue System under the Colas', *PIHC*, Dharwad, 1988 reproduced in Kesavan Veluthat, *The Early Medieval...*, *op. cit.*, pp. 100–108.

42. K. G. Krishnan, ed., *Karandai Tamil Sangam Plates of Rajendrachola* (New Delhi, 1984). Stein uses this and other similar records to argue his point of ritual hegemony. *Peasant State ...*, pp. 343–61

43. Nilakanta Sastri, *History of South India*, p. 144; Stein, *Peasant State and Society ...*, p. 143; Rajan Gurukkal, 'Non-Brāhmaṇa Resistance to the Expansion of Brahmadeyas: The Early Pāṇḍya Experience', *PIHC* (Annamalaingar, 1994), pp.181–84; *idem*, 'Early Social Formation of South India ...', *op. cit.*; *idem, The Kerala Temple and Early Medieval Agrarian System* (Sukapuram, 1992.), p. 27. Gurukkal sees indications of a major social crisis

in these statements, reminding us the pathologically fearful descriptions of the Kali Age in North Indian sources. This association with Kaliyuga has lured a number of scholars. D. N. Jha, ed., *Feudal Social Formations in Early India* (Delhi, 1987), Introduction, p. 92. B. P. Sahu takes a more sober position, 'Conception of Kali Age in Early India: A Regional Perspective', *Trends in Social Science Research*, Vol. 4, No. 1.

44. For a rejection of the 'Kaḷabhra interregnum' and all that has been made of it, Veluthat, 'Into the 'Medieval' and Out of It ...', *op. cit.*

45. Narayanan, 'Warrior Settlements ...', *op. cit.*

46. Narayanan, 'Peasants ...', *op. cit.* p. 28, n. 20 on p. 40. A large number of instances where land is said to be gifted to Brāhmaṇas are given here.

47. Gurukkal, 'Towards a New Discourse ...', *op. cit.*

48. R. Nagaswami, 'An Outstanding Epigraphical Discovery in Tamilnadu', *Proceedings of the Fifth International Conference Seminar on Tamil Studies, Madurai*, 1981. I am indebted to Dr. M.R. Raghava Varier for allowing me to use his transcription of the record.

49. M. G. S. Narayanan proposes a 'wedge hypothesis' where the newly introduced Brāhmaṇical element is described as a wedge driven between the chiefs on the one side and the 'traditional Tamil society of the tribal-pastoral-agrarian type' on the other. 'Peasants ...', p. 35. We take this further and argue that land in the hands of Brāhmaṇas necessitated the use of non-kin labour and that this was responsible for the ultimate break-up of the old formation. Cf. Romila Thapar, *From Lineage to State, op. cit.*, p. 36.

50. Noboru Karahima, *South Indian History and Society*, pp. 40–55.

51. Y. Subbarayalu, *Political Geography of the Chola Country*, Madras, 1973.

52. *Ibid.*

53. R. Champakalakshmi, 'From Devotion and Dissent to Dominance: The Bhakti of the Tamil Alvars and Nayanars', in Champakalakshmi and S. Gopal, eds *Tradition, Ideology and Dissent: Essays in Honour of Romila Thapar*, New Delhi, 1996, pp. 135–163. See also Gurukkal, 'Towards a New Discourse ...' in *op. cit.*

54. M. G. S. Narayanan and Kesavan Veluthat, 'The Bhakti Movement in South India' in S. C. Malik, ed., *Indian Movements: Some Aspects of Dissent, Protest and Reform* (Simla, 1978), pp. 33–66.

55. Noboru Karashima, *South Indian Society in Transition: Ancient to Medieval* (New Delhi, 2009), pp. 2–3.

# Introduction to the First Edition

Among the better researched areas in the history of pre-modern India is the deep south in the seventh through the thirteenth century AD, which witnessed the rise, refinement and further elaboration of the monarchical form of government in the kingdoms of the Pallavas, Pāṇḍyas, Cēras and Cōḻas. One reason for this amplitude in research is the availability of a profusion of sources—inscriptions, monuments and literary works in both Sanskrit and Tamil. After the outlines had been generally drawn by the end of the 1930s in the twentieth century, there was a lull in the historiographical output for over three decades with only repetitions and rephrasings appearing in the countless monographs and dissertations. This is not to deny the wealth of new information brought out, for example, by the innumerable temple studies in terms of quantity.[1] It was only by the middle of the 1970s, however, that a qualitative change was effected on account of the entry of a few American and Japanese scholars into the field with tools of analysis and assumptions different from those available to Indian historians of an earlier generation. They have, quite naturally, thrown up a serious challenge which has been eminently responded to by scholars of our own generation. In the circumstances, it becomes necessary to take stock of the historiographical situation as a preface to adding one more essay to the existing corpus. In the first part of this chapter we survey the historiography on early medieval south India with special reference to the socio-political formations and structures.

## HISTORIOGRAPHY

In the nineteenth century, when Western scholars, both missionaries and administrators, initiated a search for sources of south Indian history, there existed only vague traditions about the different dynasties, social groups and institutions in south India.[2] By the second half of that century, thanks to the efforts of pioneering epigraphists like Rev. Thomas Foulkes, G. Bühler, Sir Walter Elliot, Robert Sewell, B. Lewis Rice, Jas Burgess, J. F. Fleet, R. C. Temple, F. Keilhorn and others, a number of inscriptions on copper and stone were deciphered, edited, interpreted and published from different parts of south India. Broad outlines of the history of south India were gradually revealing themselves: the Cōḻa dynasty for instance began to announce its presence from the copper plate records of the Eastern Caḷukya rulers, the picture getting wonderful confirmation from the legendary chronicles like the *Koṅgudēśarājākkḷ*.[3] Individual rulers were gradually identified, dated and placed in context as the search for and discovery of new inscriptions progressed. This search received systematisation by 1886 when the Government of Madras started the Department of Epigraphy with none less than Dr E. Hultzsch at its head.[4] That department initiated a more or less thorough combing of Madras Presidency. This was continued by Hultzsch's able successors like V. Venkayya and H. Krishna Sastri. The princely states of south India such as Mysore, Pudukkottah, Travancore, Cochin and Hyderabad joined the stream, thus bringing to light thousands of inscriptions of which many were published.

Simultaneously, there was research going on in another direction as well. Thanks largely to the efforts of Dr U. V. Swaminatha Iyer, the corpus of literature generally known as the 'Sangam Literature' was brought to light.[5] This literature contained a lot of information, hitherto unknown, concerning the very same dynasties whose epigraphical records were receiving scholarly attention. When, however, these literary texts were subjected to historical studies, not long after their discovery and publication, it was found that the information contained in these two categories of sources were mutually exclusive: the one category was clearly produced after the memories of the age which the other represented had faded off. Which came first was never a subject of debate—both categories were dated almost independently. Scholars like V. Kanakasabhai who studied these ancient literary texts themselves came upon and published other Tamil literary texts like the *ulās* and *paraṇis* which, however, had a close bearing on the history of the period with which the early inscriptions were concerned.[6]

Another corpus of literature, the *bhakti* hymns, had not been forgotten as they were something of a liturgical material in temples; and perhaps for that very reason they were the last to have received the historian's attention. Even when they were studied, the problems addressed did not go beyond the dates of individual saints together with a philosophical and literary appreciation of the texts.[7] Gradually, by the 1920s, outlines of the dynastic history of the Pallavas, Pāṇḍyas and Cōḻas emerged in a rather clear fashion, thanks to the efforts of M. Joveau-Dubruéil, S. Krishnaswami Aiyangar, R. Gopalan and others.[8] It was, however, at the hands of Professor K. A. Nilakanta Sastri that south Indian history received a definitive and exhaustive treatment, evidence of which was readily forthcoming with the publication of his *Pandyan Kingdom* (1929), *Studies in Chola History and. Administration* (1932), *The Colas* (Two vols., 1932 and 1935) etc. He also more or less standardised the historiographical tradition of early medieval south India, and his *History of South India* (1955) has not been replaced to this day.

Nilakanta Sastri's understanding of the past had a Rankean claim about it: he spoke of 'knowing them [i.e., our ancestors] as they were'[9] and 'a correct understanding'[10] of the past. Yet most of what he wrote had a tendency for idealisation and glorification.

He wrote:

> ... in its administrative system and in its literary and artistic achievement, Tamil civilisation attained its high watermark under the Cōḻa empire of the tenth to the thirteenth centuries. Under this empire also flourished in their greatest strength the sea-faring instincts of the people of Southern India which enabled them to add for a time an overseas empire to the more abiding prospects of a profitable trade with the states of the far east. The telling of a story which fills so large a place in the past of the land and is so full of colour and incident should not be unduly postponed.[11]

The eulogy he lavishes on Rājarāja[12] 'who was a great and good man as well as a far-sighted ruler' is another case in point. He shared with most Indian nationalist historians a nostalgia for the golden age that had to be placed somewhere in the 'dim distant past'. For him

> the history of the Cōḻa empire belongs, on the whole, to this earlier and happier phase of India's history, ... [when] much greater things were accomplished by corporate and voluntary effort, a greater sense of social harmony prevailed, and a consciousness of active citizenship was more widespread ... than in more recent times.[13]

Although Professor Sastri was given to this kind of idealisation, he was nevertheless successful in laying bare the details of nearly all aspects of the history of the period under study. He settled the problems of chronology in relation to the Pāṇḍyas and Cōḻas in a defensible manner; he reconstructed the complex political relations among the different major and minor dynasties; he brought out aspects of the central and local government in the kingdoms; and he also examined the various facets of the economic history including taxation, public finance and trade. It is to him, in fact, that we owe our knowledge of almost every detail of south Indian history. If, however, the resultant picture is somewhat exaggerated, that will have to be explained against the historiographical background. His writings were, as of most other Indian historians in the pre-Independence period, influenced by the knowledge of the Western experience in relation to polities with fixed boundaries and territorial administration, recognised sovereignty and centralised authority and a monopoly over coercive power—characteristics of the Roman empire or the state in the absolutist period or the modern nation states—and the reading of literature on jurisprudence and political economy again produced in the West.[14]

Nilakanta Sastri's writings became a model of historical writing in south India. Many scholars, starting with C. Minakshi, A. Appadorai and T. V. Mahalingam and a number of others followed this model, adding quantitatively to the existing corpus of knowledge but never questioning the basic assumptions of the Professor's historical method or philosophy. Thus, historiography in south India attained a conventional quality about it since it resisted changes of a qualitative nature.[15]

Although the publication of sources relating to the Cēra kingdom was going on almost simultaneously with developments similar to other parts of south India,[16] a historical treatment was undertaken only in the second half of the twentieth century. It was Professor Elamkulam P. N. Kunjan Pillai, a Malayalam pandit, who was responsible for the identification of a kingdom of the Cēras with Mahōdayapuram as its capital.[17] With the inclination for glorification typical of the nationalist writers, Kunjan Pillai chose to describe this kingdom as the 'Kulaśēkhara Empire' or the 'Second Cēra Empire',[18] attributing to it every one of the elements with which golden ages in history are made.[19] However, not long after Professor Pillai formulated his conceptions, they were taken up for a thorough critical examination and in this respect he could not share the position of Professor Sastri. As a result, fortunately, the model of Professor Pillai did not go unchallenged and hence did not become stereotyped. Professor M. G. S. Narayanan in his seminal work on the political and social conditions of Kerala under the later Cēra kingdom challenged most of Pillai's formulations while still acknowledging his debt to the latter.[20] A definitive and defensible chronological framework which substantially revises that of Professor Pillai, a reassessment of the place of the later Cēras in the larger context of south Indian politics, a conception of the various aspects of polity, society and economy which do not contradict each other—these distinguish Narayanan's work from that of Kunjan Pillai. In fact, further studies in the history of Kerala undertaken by scholars like Rajan Gurukkal, Raghava Varier, P. L. Chackochan and the present writer owe their inspiration to the writings of Narayanan.[21] Unfortunately, although much of the literature on the Cēra kingdom had been available in print since the early 1970s, this part of south India has been largely neglected in the writings on the region. Given the fact that even this part conforms to the general pattern of development in south India, this is surprising, especially because a conception different from what is conventional is available in relation to this part of the deep south.

An attempt to look at the history of south India from a frame of reference different from that of the Sastri school was made by the 1960s by Professor Burton Stein. He articulated a full length critique of the 'conventional' historiography in 1975.[22] He very effectively exposed the contradictions in the writings of Professor Nilakanta Sastri and his successors. While acknowledging Nilakanta Sastri's understanding of the economic history and the agrarian system as 'accurate', Burton Stein correctly pointed out that this system was incongruent with Professor Sastri's conception of a Byzantine royalty with a centralised bureaucratic state. Thus, he was disposed to describe even the accuracy in Sastri's understanding of the economic organisation as 'largely inadvertent'[23] and despite the historian. The papers of George Spencer on the Ceylonese expedition of Rājarāja and Rājendra describing them as a 'politics of plunder'[24] and on the temple building activities of the Cōḻas describing them as 'a system-maintaining mechanism of a weakly organised polity'[25] were in a similar vein. In this historiographical critique, which Stein himself described as a prolegomenon to an alternative model to explain polity, he argued that political evidence of the medieval period of south India would not fit into an alternative framework based on Indian textual traditions. Stein also dismissed the possibility of viewing the evidence in the framework of the feudal formation by way of a comparative approach. This critique awakened historians of south India from the lull of complacency by administering a veritable shock treatment.[26]

As a sequel to this critique, he came out with his alternative thesis on the nature of state in south India from the seventh to the sixteenth century AD, concentrating on the Cōḻa and Vijayanagar states. This was first presented in an article published in 1977 and later elaborated in a book in 1980.[27] Stein's work served the purpose of questioning existing assumptions and emphasising the need for a total reorientation of the historiographical tradition in south India and to that extent the importance of his work shall never diminish. After this, for example, no serious work in this area can follow the conventional pattern of treating dynastic/political history with chapters on 'economy', 'society', 'culture' etc., as uncomfortable appendages. In fact, not long after its publication, the work was lauded in the superlative by his own associates and colleagues. Thus, George Spencer described it as 'monumental' and 'by far the most penetrating analysis of the Cōḻa state'[28] and R. E. Frykenberg went even further:

> No contribution to the understanding of south India's history, or even of India's history as a whole, can compare with this piece of scholarship. Certainly not in our lifetime has any piece of such craftsmanship been produced. Such is its monumental scale and abiding worth, moreover, that we are not likely to witness another like it. In its depth, magisterial sweep and thoroughness, it reminds one of Marc Bloch's *Feudal Society.*[29]

However, his colleagues in Asia with a firmer footing in the world of empirical data were not nearly as ecstatic. The book evoked severe criticism at the hands of professors R. Champakalakshmi, Noboru Karashima, M. G. S. Narayanan, D. N. Jha, Y. Subbarayalu and Vijaya Ramaswami, not one of them agreeing with the empirical and theoretical aspects of Stein's thesis.[30] Our critique of Stein's thesis below draws largely on the various problems raised by these scholars, each one of whom has brought to bear on his/her critique a first hand experience of the data which Stein takes up or fails to take up.

Stein's conception of polity in south India during the age of the Cōḻas is based on the model of the segmentary state, constructed by Aidan Southall to explain the situation in East Africa in the Alur Society.[31] It assumes a world of 'peasants without lords' organised into a number of ethnically cohesive and spatially compressed units. Each of these units was a segment of the political system wielding actual political power and subject only to the ritual sovereignty exercised by one of the units which was a prime centre. There was no specialised administrative staff or bureaucracy as part of the prime centre above; nor was there a monopoly of coercive power which it enjoyed, not to speak of any central mechanism of revenue assessment and collection. Most of his assumptions, arising out of invalid theoretical underpinnings, an inadequate consideration or even misinterpretation of data, and a total reliance on speculation which is at best inspired guess and at worst mere fiction, are open to question.

To this group may be added the names of a few other scholars who, even when all of them may not agree with Stein in all the details, broadly follow his pattern. Among them perhaps the most important is the name of George W. Spencer whose articles on religious networks and royal influence and on the politics of plunder both pertaining to the weakness of the state and the near absence of a revenue mechanism follow the fashion of describing medieval south India as almost stateless.[32] The work of Kenneth R. Hall on trade and statecraft in the age of the Cōḻas[33] also, as Professor B. D. Chattopadhyaya has suggested, adheres to the same orientation in an unreasoned and tenacious manner.[34] A few articles published by Nicholas B. Dirkes, Friedhelm Hardy, Richard Kennedy[35] and others also more or less share the same tendency.

While studies with this kind of orientation are progressing on the one side, those with a clearly different one are increasing on another. The work of Professor Noboru Karashima,[36] and that of Professor Y. Subbarayalu, who though he began independently,[37] joined hands with Karashima's,[38] and a few of their associates[39] have a greater claim to endurance for they are based on the hard rock of empirical data and not the quicksand of speculation. Similarly, the work on the processes of urbanisation by Professor R. Champakalakshmi,[40] that on the temple economy by Professor D. N. Jha,[41] that on the agrarian system and state under the Pāṇḍyas by Professor Rajan Gurukkal,[42] on the ideology of *bhakti* as a projection of the temple centred society by Professor M. G. S. Narayanan and the present writer[43] etc., tries to project the data within a conceptual framework although all these scholars do not share the same perspective.

At this historiographical juncture, a fresh look at the problem of the nature of state in medieval south India would look both possible and necessary, both for the vastness of the data and the richness of theories. In the following pages, an attempt is made to examine the power structure of south India and the position of the monarch in it. This will, it is hoped, help in raising and answering of further questions about the nature and processes involved in the socio-political formation of this period. Plainly stated, the present essay is to test the validity of the concept of Indian feudalism as formulated by D. D. Kosambi and elaborated by R. S. Sharma and others in this context. It is true that a number of eyebrows have been raised with regard to this concept, some of them demanding further refinement of terminology and some, outright rejection of the concept altogether. Our position is that, since a concept only represents and does not present an actual situation, its use is always recommended in clarifying empirical data, in so far as in so doing the data are not distorted and manipulated. Thus, expressions like the 'medieval Indian system' (which, of course, is admittedly used for want of a better term)[44] fail to communicate anything.

In the case of north India in the Gupta and post-Gupta periods, in which context the concept of Indian feudalism has been systematically applied, information regarding the erosion of state power following the alienation of administrative, judicial and fiscal powers along with estates of land is available in the copper plate charters.[45] However, the 'operational' part of this formation, or its mechanics, is not clearly visible in those records. Similarly, the picture of a feudal polity, with its typical pyramidal structure, is not clear enough there. In the case of south India both these aspects can be clarified: the thousands of stone inscriptions record the transactions of either the *brahmadēya* assemblies consisting of those very groups who were granted the administrative, judicial and fiscal rights or similar bodies like the *ūr, nagaram, nāḍu*, etc., which had been enjoying an equal amount of these rights.

## SOURCES

Our sources consist mostly of inscriptions. They can be divided into two broad categories: (1) the copper plate grants with a Sanskrit *praśasti* in the beginning followed generally by a statement, in Tamil, of the objective of the record which in most cases is the grant of land to brahmans, temples or other religious institutions and (2) the stone inscriptions, mostly in Tamil (or old Malayalam in the case of the Cēra kingdom) generally recording transactions of temple committees and other local groups concerning the transaction of land and other forms of property. It is not as if these are mutually exclusive categories; thus the Kanyākumāri stone inscription of Vīrarājēndra[46] shows the typical features of a copper plate grant while the Vāḻapaḻḻi copper plate of Rājaśēkhara[47] and the Māmpalli plates of Srivallabhan Kōta[48] show characteristics of the stone inscriptions. Still the general categorisation is useful in so far as it helps us clarify certain broad general patterns. The typical copper plate charters, with the *praśasti*s of varying lengths, communicate, in typical Sanskritic idiom, an ideal of the dynasty and the ruler who makes the grant and assume an audience that can internalise these communications, generally the brahman *śiṣṭa*s who constituted the majority of the donees and perhaps their descendents. The terse, business-like, Tamil portion records the details of the gift in question, attention being paid to such matters as the boundaries, conditions and witnesses. These records are the title-deeds of property and hence preserved in the lockers of the owners and are not meant for the public. On the other hand, the stone inscriptions record transactions of property. This includes the assignment of land endowed to temples, the management of cattle endowed for the maintenance of 'perpetual' lamps in the temples and such other matters. Obviously, these records deal with the more important sections of society such as landowners both brahman and non-brahman, merchants and other notables. Thus, copious as the information is, they keep out certain other major aspects of social life, not covered by the scope of these records. It is not altogether unlikely that the historian is misled going religiously by the statements in the inscriptions: what is present there could be highly exaggerated vis-a-vis what is not present there. In fact, as N. Subrahmanian has observed, those records 'which were never inscribed could conceal more effective, crucial and clinching information than what the known ones provide.'[49] The sweeter melodies are the ones which are unheard! Thus, in studying society and economy as well even as the superstructures like polity, one has to look at the information provided by these records only as the narrow tips of the submerged ice-berg; but, nevertheless, they can serve as pointers to the real situation, if properly tackled. Our use of the inscriptional material, therefore, takes into consideration this narrow, one-sided, character of these documents and our attempts at generalisation on the basis of these records also follow an attempt to extrapolate from the known to the unknown. It has to be also stated that, in the case of the Cōḻa country, the historian is fortunate that the fabulously rich data contained in the numerous inscriptions have been subjected to conceptual analysis and systematic treatment has replaced the speculative one. The present work is indebted in large measure to the computer-aided analyses undertaken by N. Karashima, B. Sitaraman, Y. Subbarayalu and P. Shanmugham,[50] and especially to the three-volume *Concordance of Personal Names in the Cola Inscriptions* prepared by Karashima, Subbarayalu and Toru Matsui. In the case of the Cēra kingdom, the *Index to Cera Inscriptions* which forms a companion volume to M. G. S. Narayanan's doctoral thesis has been very handy and helpful.

The literary works of this period can be generally classified, again, into two groups: (1) the one centering on temples, and (2) the one centering on courts. The first category has been subjected to analysis by a number of pundits and historians, and a recent study undertaken by M. G. S. Narayanan and the present writer has demonstrated that this expressed the ideology of the emergent feudal formation in south India.[51] The court literature has not received the same amount of detailed treatment, although they too have striking parallelisms with the *bhakti* literature both in form and content. This, however, is a question that has to be looked into.

Architectural monuments form another major group of sources. They have received very scholarly treatment at the hand of historians, with the result that we possess a wealth of information in relation to their architectural details, iconography and other aspects.[52] What has not been studied, however, is their social function, i.e., the question of how the architecture symbolises contemporary social formation. Although we have not made any such study ourselves, it may be that the huge *sanctum sanctorum* in the middle, encircled by the many circumambulatory passages and the *prākāras*, as also the chief deity enshrined attended to by a number of lesser deities point to a hierarchical pattern in society.[53] This surmise may be supported with the elaborate parallelism drawn between services in the temples and the royal courts as brought out by our study of the *bhakti* literature.

## HISTORICAL BACKGROUND

The earliest known phase in the history of south India, known in established historiography as the Sangam Age, gives the picture of a society where tribal loyalties were fast disintegrating and social differentiation was solidifying. The literature of that age, by no means the product of a short span of time, provides useful information, which is supported by evidence from archaeology, numismatics and accounts of Greco-Roman travellers.[54] In this literature we have the picture of small peasant settlements coming into existence on the river valleys in the plains, with a concentration on the Kāvēri valley as attested by archaeology.[55] This must have naturally introduced an important aspect to the economy of this region; what was described as a tribal hand-to-mouth economy based on hunting, cattle-herding, etc. was getting transformed. The warrior-heroes who led the clannish warfare, chiefly on account of cattle-lifting, had already started claiming a place of pride in society with a major part of the booty from such raids kept for themselves.[56] Similarly, the communal gatherings, transferring eatables to a central place and from there effecting a redistribution of such wealth, known as *uṇḍāṭṭu*, also ensured this primary position of the warrior-chiefs.[57] Thus there came into existence in these basically acephalic, tribal, societies the notion of a 'chief'. A number of wandering minstrels went on singing the praise of these chiefs and provided the necessary legitimation in the newly emerging polities. In fact, a major chunk of what is known as the Sangam literature consists of their bardic poetry.[58] Another apparatus of legitimation, perhaps, was the performance of Vedic sacrifices.[59] A number of songs or their colophons of a later date refer to them.

The emergence of small peasant communities in the fertile river valleys on the plains, as suggested earlier, introduced a new element to this socio-political formation. The ecological region, known as *marutam* in the poetic conventions of the Sangam, was what was favoured by this social transformation. How far the initiative of the chiefly houses was responsible for this is not clear in the records, although late traditions attribute an irrigation work on the Kāvēri to one of the Cōḻas[60] and the construction of a number of tanks to a Pāṇḍya.[61] This process of transformation was accelerated by the evolution of trade in two different ways: (a) the inter-regional exchange of essential commodities and (b) long distance trade in luxury articles which were mostly 'primitive valuables.'[62] This trade led to the formation of urban enclaves in the interior where there was a concentration of potential consumers of these luxury articles as well as the emergence of a few major entrepots or emporia on the coastline. Those chiefs who were situated in the *marutam* region were largely to have had control over these interior trade enclaves as well as the coastal emporia apart from their control over the newly emerging peasant communities. As a result, their resource-base expanded. The literature of this period describes three of these chieftains as the *mūvēntar* (the three crowned kings), namely the Cēras of Vañji, the Pāṇḍyas of Madurai and the Cōḻas of Uṟaiyūr.

While their own seats in the headquarters were trade enclaves, they also enjoyed control over the coastal emporia of Muciri, Kōrkai and Pukār respectively. Naturally, the less fortunate of the chiefs could not participate in this transformation and remained in relative isolation in their old world of cattle-raids and hero worship.

This earliest known phase in the history of south India, which is generally taken to have come to a close by the third century AD is thought in the conventional literature to have been separated by the next known phase of the monarchies under our study, i.e. the early seventh century, by a 'long historical night.'[63] This disjunctive character of the age of Pallavas has been rightly questioned in recent years.[64] Continuity there certainly was, but what is equally important was a series of change that had been effected in the social and economic spheres which had reflected itself in the form and content of the political organisation. A totally new ideology, which suited the new social formation, had been developing, and this helped reinforce it in a big way. Thus, even when one does not agree with the conventional view of the disjunctive character of the age of the Pallavas and after in the history of south India, these sea changes should not go unnoticed.

As stated earlier, our information regarding the social and economic processes in the age of the Pallavas from the seventh century AD is to be gleaned from the very few epigraphical records, which present only a narrow, one-sided picture. A number of large scale agrarian settlements opened up on the river valleys of the Peṇṇār and Pālār. A distinctive feature of these settlements was the existence of a managerial class of non-cultivating intermediaries, superimposed over the cultivating peasantry and enjoying superior rights over the land and having direct links with the state. In fact, the majority of copper-plate records and stone inscriptions record the creation and maintenance of a number of brahman corporations in both settled and unsettled areas either subjecting the pre-existing peasantry or replacing them by new peasant settlers. As a result, the leadership of the brahman settlers from the north, with better organisational abilities and a more advanced calendar was made use of by the Pallava rulers and in expanding the base of their power and resources. This resulted in the integration of the agrarian order, not so much by forging a brahman-peasant alliance as by the subjection of peasantry by the brahmanical upper classes resulting, in the process, in a strong alliance between the brahmans and the rulers.[65] This secured a position for the brahmans in the ruling class. It was this new ruling class which shaped the character of the state, its legitimacy and the overall ideology of society. Naturally, the readily available framework existing in north India was borrowed and fitted into the situation in south India. This may have resulted in a number of loose ends, the reconciliation of which was not very simple. This explains in part a major gap between what is presented as the ideal and what is seen as the real.

The process that was going on in the northern districts of the Tamil country under the Pallavas was almost repeated in the southern districts under the Pāṇḍyas on the Vaigai-Tāmrapaṇi basin. In addition, we also see that a number of irrigation works were undertaken in this region by the Pāṇḍyas.[66] An excellent study of the agrarian system under the Pāṇḍyas made by Rajan Gurukkal brings out effectively the role played by such irrigation undertakings in the development of agriculture and the integration of society based on that.[67] The role of the brahman settlements in this region as the harbingers of change cannot be over-estimated. Perhaps the same process was at work here also as in the case of the Pallava kingdom in establishing the brahmanical sections as part of the upper class and identifying these as the ideologues of the newly emerging social formation.

This process can be seen to have extended from the nucleii of the Pallavas and Pāṇḍyas in Kāñci and Madurai respectively. The minor chiefs of an earlier period living in relative isolation in their own world of primitive organisation with cattle-raids and hero worship were subjugated and brought under the control of these new monarchical states. The process of granting land and opening up settlements in a big way continued wherever it was possible. It was, however, the extension of this practice in the Kāvēri valley in the Tañjāvūr and Tiruchirapally districts that was responsible for a major breakthrough. A rich resource-base, which was now tapped to a considerable extent, enabled that region to be the base of a much stronger state than under the other two houses, namely, the Pallavas and Pāṇḍyas.

Similar developments were taking place on the west coast in Kerala. Brahmanical settlements drawing through the Konkan and Canarese coast, with their tradition of Paraśurāma, had been firmly established in three clusters on the Ponnāni, Periyār and Pampā rivers by the beginning of the ninth century.[68] Although the extent of royal initiative behind the establishment of such settlements in Kerala is not known, it has been convincingly argued that the establishment of the Cēra kingdom on the west coast, following the sack of the Cēra capital Karūr by the Pāṇḍyas, was a by-product of these new settlements there. It gave political expression to the new social formation, given the character of the upper class. M. G. S. Narayanan's research on the history of this later Cēra kingdom and the present writer's work on the brahman settlements in Kerala have brought out this relation between the brahmanical upper classes and the rulers in this part of the country.[69]

The Tamil *bhakti* movement which was coeval with these developments in the economic, social and political spheres helps in the analysis of the ideology which legitimised and sanctified these developments.[70] It has been shown that the *bhakti* of the Tamil saints was devotion to Śaiva or Vaiṣṇava deities consecrated in the temples and not just to 'god' nor even Śiva or Visnu in the abstract. It is also seen that the earlier saints, both Vaiṣṇava and Śaiva, had their sphere of activity in the Pallava territory which got extended to the Kāvēri valley by the time of the later saints of the *bhakti* tradition. So also, an analysis of the distribution of temples sung about by the later *Āḻvār and Nāyaṇār* saints shows a concentration of the temples, both Vaiṣṇava and Śaiva, in the Cōḻa country on either side of the Kāvēri.[71] The temple in the south at this time was emerging as a huge landed magnate and also as the centre around which the brahmanical settlements revolved. When such centres became the rallying point of a social movement such as the *bhakti* movement, it was naturally the ideology of the brahmanical landed magnates that it carried with it as the leitmotif.

It has been brought out that the *bhakti* movement legitimised the entire gamut of relationships in the social, economic and political spheres. The graded hierarchy of economic relations with various shades of right in land, the equally graded hierarchy of social relations with different shades of ritual status and the corresponding graded hierarchy of political relations with different shades of power and authority—this was reflected and legitimised in the religious world. While the *bhakti* movement has been shown by earlier historians as representing a veritable social reform movement spearheaded against caste and other forms of inequality, our analysis shows that it helped in consolidating the new social and political order in south India in the early medieval period. It strengthened and gave support to the new monarchy; and by favouring the ideology of the brahmanised sections in society, it helped the entire upper class to send its roots deeper in society. As for the ruling class, the identification of the necessary apparatus of legitimation was indeed possible through this ideology. The socio-political milieu in which this ideology took shape in northern India had evolved a ready-made framework for itself and, once the ideological standards of that milieu were adopted, it was also easier to adopt the apparatuses of political legitimation as they had developed there.

All this should not, however, give the impression that society in south India in this period was dominated, in any physical sense, by brahmans. The large number of non-brahman peasant settlements, the number of individual land-owners and an equally impressive number of military lords point to this. To this group may be added the old locality chiefs, wielding political power in their regions but still living in the world of heroes, who were subjugated by the new monarchies. However, even these large sections of non-brahman population of importance were brought under the pale of the religious ideology of the *bhakti* even as these sections were subsumed within the emerging feudal structure of society.[72] Thus, by the time these monarchies came of age in the ninth century, a new social order, with an ideology to support it, had been firmly established in south India.

Once established, the growth and further refinement of these monarchies followed without much disturbance. The Pallavas fought the Cāḷukyas in the Deccan; the Pāṇḍyas and Pallavas fought each other in the Kāvēri delta. These wars also necessitated alliances among the different ruling houses. Not only were marriage alliances contracted (and broken!) among the major houses such as the Pallavas, Pāṇḍyas, Cēras and Cōḻas; but between one of them on the one side and one of the chiefly houses on the other also, there were matrimonial relations. The political alliances, cemented by military bonds, were thus reinforced by connubial ties. This complex network was a manifestation of the political culture of south India at this time. Thus if the Cēra king sent his forces against the Rāṣṭrakūtas to help the Cōḻas, it was not merely fulfilling a feudal military obligation; after all Cōḻa Rājāditya, who was at the head of the Cōḻa forces, was a cousin of the Cēra king. The Cēra intervention in the marriage of the Mūṣika prince to a Cedi princess would also fall in the same pattern.

The middle of the ninth century witnessed the emergence of the house of the Cōḻas from obscurity when Vijayalaya captured Tañjāvūr from the Muttarayar, one of the chiefs who stood in a kind of feudatory relationship with the Pallavas.[73] This marked the beginning of a meteoric rise of the Cōḻa dynasty for the next one century when under his successors, Āditya and Parāntaka, the house of the Cōḻas extended its sway to the north and south, bringing the Pallava territory under complete control and subjugating the Pāṇḍyas for a long time.[74] The causative factors behind this lay partly in the rich resource-base of the Kāvēri valley which opened up in a big way and partly in the war-like people who lived in these areas whom the Cōḻa state had enlisted into service in the process of expanding its power-base. In fact, even after the discomfiture in the battle of Takkolam at the hands of the Rāṣṭrakūtas, the power of the Cōḻas went on increasing in spite of a temporary setback.[75] Thus when Rājarāja I ascended the throne in 985 AD, he inherited a patrimony on which a relatively strong state, that would endure at least for a century, could be built. During the reign of Rājarāja I and his successors, the juggernaut of state rolled over the numerous feudatory chiefs, thus bringing the entire area of Cōḻamaṇḍalam and Jayaṅgoṇḍacōḻamaṇḍalam (Toṇḍaimaṇḍalam) under direct control. In this process, the chiefly territories were reorganised into *vaḷanāḍu*s, each of which was an artificial administrative unit in contrast to the pre-existing spontaneous local groupings called *nāḍu*s.[76] So also a large number of landed magnates in the country were pressed into the service of the state on whom were bestowed high-sounding titles and who were assigned either administrative or military functions. Part of this scheme was the elaborate survey and assessment of land for purposes of taxation.[77]

However, this state of affairs could not continue for long because of the deeply entrenched character of the centrifugal tendencies. From the time of Kulōttuṅga and Vikrama, one notices the reappearance of the chiefly rule in the regions, the tapering off of the officialdom and the general weakness of the revenue mechanism.[78] This process led to the re-assertion of the Pāṇḍyas in Madurai and the Cēras in

Mahōdayapuram even though the latter house itself was overwhelmed early in the twelfth century by similar feudal forces at home.[79] Even in the Cōḻa kingdom the state was completely eroded by the last quarter of the thirteenth century and thereafter that house disappears altogether. As for the Pāṇḍyas we hear of their continued existence not in Madurai but in Tenkasi, perhaps following what Nilakanta Sastri has described as dynastic drift.[80]

The present study tries to examine the political structure in the four kingdoms and the position of the monarch within the power structure there. A study of this problem helps raise questions about the character of the state and the mode of production in this region during the period under study. As noted in an earlier section in this chapter, there have not been many studies addressed to this problem. Historians like Nilakanta Sastri and Minakshi have, among other things, attempted a survey of the details available about the government under the Cōḻas, Pāṇḍyas and Pallavas. A. Appadorai has given a rather elaborate picture of the economic conditions of south India in the first half of the second millenium AD. Burton Stein, depending mostly on secondary writers, has presented the picture of a 'segmentary state' within a peasant society; Y. Subbarayalu has marshalled a lot of material with a heavy bearing on this problem, and has in a later paper tried to describe the Cōḻa state as an 'early state'; Noboru Karashima has fleetingly suggested that the pre-Rājarāja I period may be closer to Stein's segmentary state while the post-Kulōttuṅga phase may be described as largely feudal with a period of about a hundred years with its strong centralised state to intervene between the two phases. None of these scholars has, however, taken into account the situation on the western side of the Western Ghats, where information regarding a similar polity is available with clues to understand some obscure but important problems of south Indian history.[81] Our difficulties with the formulation and theoretical underpinnings of each of the writers mentioned above will be taken up in the appropriate context below.

Our study opens with an examination of the image of the monarch presented in the royalist literature.[82] A large number of elements taken from the Sanskritic stereotypes in the *kāvyā-śāstra-nāṭaka* literature went into the making of this image. They included origin myths, dynastic traditions and genealogy in order to claim ideological sanction for the ruler. Then there were the claims to the kṣatriya caste status, the emulation of the *cakravartin* model and the putting on the robe of the warrior-hero—all the three of which provided the justification for the military/political aspects of the monarch. Attributes of divinity about the person of the king were another means of legitimising the position of the monarch. The ideal of the donor which most rulers claimed for themselves, both added colour to their image and also underscored royal initiative in land grants and settlement of land. All in all, the image of royalty, however idealistic, served the major purpose of legitimising monarchy in the newly evolved polities in south India.

Against the background of this image, we examine the governmental structure which is taken as the expression of the surface reality of the power structures.[83] In the governmental structure hereditary monarchy is seen at the helm of affairs. It is seen as attended and assisted by a royal court of councillors and major functionaries. As part of the king's government we see a number of royal functionaries who were members of the major landowning groups. We see a number of locality chiefs with varying fortunes in different points of time. As for the character of military organisation it is noticed that the personal body-guards of the king and the specialists such as the archers, elephant riders and cavalry men constituted the central forces which were supplemented by similar forces, supplied by the mercenaries drawn from among the peasants and artisans and perhaps also brahman theoreticians in the art of warfare. This would show that there was not anything like a monopoly of coercive power which the state enjoyed. In the matter of judicial and fiscal administration, too, we notice the generally local and decentralised character, thereby suggesting that there was considerable erosion of state power.

In examining the deeper reality in social structure it could be seen that society consisted of numerous peasant settlements.[84] Some of these were the groupings of non-brahman peasant settlements while some others were brahmanical corporations of a class of non-cultivating intermediaries placed between the state on the one side and the cultivating peasantry on the other. Closely related to the second category and at times even synonymous with it were the temples which owned huge estates of land. Studding this landscape of peasant settlements were the *nagaram* marketing centres, whose organisation was also closely similar to that of the agrarian corporations. By the time we come to the closing years of our study we see the emergence of a number of landed magnates in the Kāvēri valley wielding great influence in society as brought out by the recent studies of Karashima.[85] This is in the pattern of the feudatory chiefs exerting great influence over the political sphere so that the weakening of the state was complete.

Old stereotypes such as Oriental Despotism and its Marxist variant, Asiatic Mode of Production, are inadequate to explain this formation. Even the highly qualified and modified version of the Asiatic Mode of Production, sought to be resurrected by Kathleen Gough, is not suitable to the situation.[86] So also the idea of a highly centralised imperial structure bulwarked by a numerous and powerful bureaucracy[87] cannot be sustained. Stein's idea of 'segmentary state',[88] based on untenable theoretical underpinnings, an inadequate understanding of data and speculation, too, will not hold much water. Similarly, the description of the Cōḻa state as an early state,[89] which does not explain much as the category includes a vast variety of political systems, fails to inspire confidence. On the other hand, the idea of Indian feudalism as elaborated by R. S. Sharma in the context of north India can be seen most suitable to this situation. The advantage in the context of south India is that not only are the social and economic aspects of the feudal formation clear in the records but also the entire range of political relations conforms to the typical feudal pattern. The ideology of this formation as expressed in the religious literature and symbolised in the religious architecture and sculpture would round out the picture.

## NOTES

1. M. G. S. Narayanan, Presidential Address, Section I, Indian History Congress, Hyderabad, 1978.

2. The most typical of these is the systematic collection of manuscripts undertaken by Colonel Mackenzie. Works of tradition like the *Koṅgudēśarājākkaḷ, Cōḻamaṇḍalaśatakam, Kēraḷōtpatti, Iḍaṅgai-Valangai Purāṇam* were among what was being discovered.

3. Jas Burgess, 'List of Chola Kings' *Indian Antiquary* (Hereafter *I.A.*), Vol. XIII, pp. 58–59; Walter Elliot, 'Note on the Family and Date of the Great Rajendra Chola of Tanjore' (S. 944), *I.A.*, Vol. XIV, p. 203.

4. The report of Hultzsch on his work from 21 November 1886 to 20 September 1887 was put up by a bureaucrat to higher authorities 'noting with satisfaction!' G.O. No. 1462, dt. 24 October 1887.

5. It was in the last decade of the nineteenth century and the first decade of the twentieth that Swaminatha Iyer discovered and published these literary works, later joined by C.W. Thamotharam Pillai, a Ceylonese scholar. Iyer's autobiography, *En Kathai* (in Tamil) is illuminating and inspiring.

6. Among the other scholars who discovered and published such texts were M. K. Narayanaswami, T. A. Gopinatha Rao and C. Rasanayagam.

7. M. G. S. Narayanan and Kesavan Veluthat, 'Bhakti Movement in South India' in S. C. Malik (ed.), *Indian Movements: Some Aspects of Dissent, Protest and Reform*, (Simla, 1978), p. 35. For a detailed bibliography on this literature, *ibid.*, pp. 61–6.

8. G. Joveau-Dubréuil, *The Pallavas*, English Translation, (Pondicherry, 1917); *Dravidian Architecture*, (Madras, 1917); *Pallava Antiquities*, Vol. I, (London, 1916); Vol. II, (Pondicherry, 1918); *Ancient History of Deccan*, (Madras, 1920); etc. S. Krishnaswami Aiyangar, *Early History of Vaishnavism in South India*, (Madras, 1920); *Evolution of Hindu Administrative Institutions in South India*, (Madras 1929, 1932); *Ancient India and South Indian History and Culture*, (Poona, 1941); R. Gopalan, *History of the Pallavas of Kanchi*, (Madras, 1928), etc.

9. K. A. Nilakanta Sastri, *Studies in Chola History and Administration*, (Madras, 1932), p. 98.

10. *Ibid.*, p. 97.

11. *Idem., The Colas*, Second edition, (Madras, 1955), p. 2.

12. *Ibid.*, pp. 168–69.

13. *Ibid.*, pp. 446–47.

14. Cf. Reinhard Bendix, 'Introduction', in *State and Society: A Reader in Comparative Political Sociology*, (Boston,1968), p. 7. quoted in Richard G. Fox, 'Introduction' in Fox, (ed.), *Realm and Region in Traditional India*, (Delhi, 1977), pp. x–xi.

15. This is excellently brought out by Burton Stein, 'The State and Agrarian Order in Medieval South India: A Historiographical Critique', in Stein (ed.), *Essays on South India*, (Delhi, 1975), esp. pp. 64–65.

16. A few records such as the Jewish Copper Plates and the Syrian Copper Plates were known to the world of scholarship in the eighteenth and nineteenth centuries. However, a systematic search for and publication of the epigraphical material began only in the early years of the twentieth century when the Government of Travancore established a Department of Archaeology with T. A. Gopinatha Rao as the Superintendent. *The Administration Reports* of that Department contain notices and the *Travancore Archaeological Series* (1910–35)

contain the texts and translations of several inscriptions. The good work begun by Gopinatha Rao was continued by K. V. Subrahmanya Aiyar and A. S. Ramanatha Aiyar, although by the time R. Vasudeva Pothuval took over, decay had set in. Similar developments were going on in the state of Cochin with scholars like A. Govinda Warrier and P. Aunjan Achan taking deep interest in epigraphical and archaeological studies. *The Bulletins of the Rama Varma Research Institute* published texts of a number of inscriptions.

17. Most of Pillai's articles and books are published in Malayalam. For a detailed list, see Bibliography. However, some of his more important formulations are available in English translation. Elamkulam P. N. Kunjan Pillai, *Studies in Kerala History*, (Kottayam 1971).

18. Elamkulam P. N. Kunjan Pillai, *Kēralam Ompatum Pattum Nūṟṟāṅtukaḷil* (Kottayam, 1968). Also *idem, Cila Keāḷacaritrapraśṇaṅṅal*, (Kottayam, 1963). The most popular and perhaps only text-book of the history of Kerala used at under-graduate and post-graduate levels in the Universities in Kerala, A. Sreedhara Menon, *A Survey of Kerala History* (Kottayam, 1969), repeats every one of Pillai' s formulations uncritically, as do the District Gazetteers which Menon has edited, thereby tending to make Pillai's conceptions stereotyped.

19. A good example is Pillai's Introduction to his *Cila Kerala Caritrapraśnaṅṅal, op. cit.*

20. M. G. S. Narayanan, *Political and Social Conditions of Kerala under the Kulaṣēkhara Empire, c. 800–1124* AD (Ph.D. Thesis, University of Kerala, Trivandrum, 1972). Three other books, which may be described as by-products of this work, are also published by Narayanan. *Cultural Symbiosis in Kerala* (Trivandrum, 1972); *Kēraḷacaritrattiṉṟe Atisthānasīlakal*, (Calicut, 1972), (in Malayalam); *Aspects of Aryanisation in Kerala* (Trivandrum, 1973).

21. The M.Phil. Dissertations of Gurukkal, Varier and Veluthat submitted to the Jawaharlal Nehru University, New Delhi, and the Ph.D. thesis of Chackochan to the Deccan College, Poona, are evidence of this inspiration, apart from several papers published by some of these scholars.

22. Above, n. 15.

23. *Ibid.*, p. 66.

24. George W. Spencer, 'The Politics of Plunder: The Cholas in Eleventh Century Ceylon', *Journal of Asian Studies*, Vol. XXXV, (1976), pp. 405–19.

25. *Idem*, 'Religious Networks and Royal Influence in Eleventh Century South India', *Journal of the Economic and Social History of the Orient*, Vol. XII, no. 1, (1969), pp. 42–56.

26. M. G. S. Narayanan, 'A Critique of the *History of South India* and a proposal for a New Conceptual Frame', paper presented to the 7th Session of The South Indian History Congress, Madras University, January, 1987.

27. Burton Stein, 'The Segmentary State in South Indian History' in Fox (ed.) *op. cit.*, pp. 3–51; *idem, Peasant State and Society in Medieval South India*, (Delhi,1980).

28. George, W. Spencer, '*The Politics of Expansion; The Chola Conquest of Sri Lanka and Sri Vijaya*', (Madras, 1983), p. 7.

29. This quotation from Frykenberg is from the typescript of a review of Stein's book which Professor Stephen F. Dale of the Ohio State University, Columbus, provided to me through my teacher Dr M. Gangadharan. I thank both Professor Dale and Dr Gangadharan.

30. R. Champakalakshmi, 'Peasant State and Society in Medieval South India: A Review Article', *Indian Economic and Social History Review*, Vol. XVIII, nos. 3–4 (July–December, 1981), pp. 411–26; D. N. Jha, 'Relevance of Peasant State and Society to Pallava-Cola Times', *Indian Historical Review*, Vol. VIII, nos. 1–2 (July 1981 to January 1982), pp. 74–94; Vijaya Ramaswami, 'Peasant State and Society in Medieval South India', a review article, *Studies in History*, Vol. IV, no. 2 (1982), esp. pp. 296–301; Noboru Karashima, *South Indian History and Society: Studies from Inscriptions, AD 850–1800*, (Delhi, 1984), pp. 25–28; M. G. S. Narayanan, Presidential Address to South Indian History Congress, V. Session, Mysore, February, 1985, Section on Socio-economic History.

31. Aidan Southall, *Alur Society: A Study in Processes and Types of Domination*, (Cambridge, 1956).

32. Above, nn. 24, 25, 28.

33. Kenneth R. Hall, *Trade and Statecraft in the Age of the Colas*, (Delhi, 1980).

34. B. D. Chattopadhyaya, Review of above, n 33, in *Indian Historical Review*, Vol. X, nos. 1–2; (July 1983–January 1984), pp. 186–89, esp. p. 187.

35. Nicholas B. Dirkes, 'Political Authority and Structural change in South Indian History', *Indian Economic and Social History Review*, XIII, no. 2 (1976); Richard S. Kennedy, 'The King in Early South India as Chieftain and Emperor', *Indian Historical Review*, Vol. XIII, no. 1, (1976); etc.

36. Most of Karashima's major papers written over the past two decades are brought together in Karashima, *op. cit.*, with a brilliant introduction.

37. E.g., Y. Subbarayalu, *Political Geography of the Chola Country*, (Madras, 1973).

38. E.g., Appendices in Y. Subbarayalu, *State in Medieval South India*, Ph.D. Thesis, (Madurai Kamaraj University, 1976); Noboru Karashima, Y. Subbarayalu and Toru Matsui, *A Concordance of the Names in the Cola Inscriptions*, 3 Vols., (Madurai, 1978); etc.

39. A few of the articles in Karashima, *op. cit.*, are co-authored by Indian scholars like B. Sitaraman and P. Shanmugham.

40. R. Champakalakshmi, 'Growth of Urban Centres in South India: Kudamukku-Palaiyarai, the Twin-city of the Colas', *Studies in History*, Vol. I, no. 1, 1979; *idem* 'Urban Processes in Early Medieval Tamilnad' in Sabyasachi Bhattacharya and Romila Thapar (eds.) *Situating Indian History*, (Delhi, 1986); *idem* 'Urbanisation in South India: the Role of Ideology and Polity', Presidential Address, Section I, Indian History Congress, 47th Session, Srinagar, 1986.

41. Some of his contributions are brought together in D. N. Jha, *Studies in Early Indian Economic History*, (Delhi, 1980).

42. Rajan Gurukkal, *The Agrarian System and Socio-political Organisation under the Early Pandyas, c. AD, 600–1000*, Ph.D. Thesis, Jawaharlal Nehru University, New Delhi, 1984 (unpublished).

43. Above, n. 7.

44. Irfan Habib, 'Classifying Pre-Colonial India', Journal *of Peasant Studies*, Vol. XII, nos. 2 and 3, (Jan–April, 1985), p. 49.

45. R. S. Sharma, *Indian Feudalism*, 2nd ed. (Delhi, 1980), *passim*.

46. *Travancore Archaeological Series*, (Hereafter *TAS*), Vol. III, No. 1. pp. 87–158.

47. *TAS*, Vol. II, no. 2, pp. 8–14.

48. *TAS*, Vol. III.

49. N. Subramanyan, 'A Review of Karashima', *op.cit.*, in *Indian Historical Review*, Vol. X, nos. 1–2, (July 1983–Jan. 1984), p. 185.

50. Above, nn. 37, 38, 39.

51. Above, n. 7.

52. A large number of studies are available on individual South Indian temples apart from works like P. V. Jagadisa Aiyar, *South Indian Temples*, (Madras, 1920); K. V. Soundara Rajan, *South Indian Temples*, (Delhi, 1966); S. R. Balasubrahmanyan, *Early Chola Temples*, (Delhi, 1974); *idem, Middle Chola Temples*, (Delhi, 1975); etc.

53. I owe this idea to the cover photograph on R. S. Sharma, *Indian Feudalism*, 2nd edn. (Delhi, 1980).

54. A few sites associated with Sangam literature have been excavated/ explored by archaeologists in south India. The discovery of Roman coins from different parts of the country both as surface finds and from excavations is also significant. Relevant Graeco-Roman accounts are contained in the works of Pliny, Ptolemy, and in *Periplus of the Erythrean Sea*, Nilakanta Sastri, (ed.), *Foreign Notices of South India*, (Madras, 1939). See also below n. 55.

55. R. Champakalakshmi, 'Archaeology and Tamil Literary Tradition', *Purātattva*, Vol. VIII, 1975–76, pp. 113 ff.

56. M. G. S. Narayanan, 'Cattle-raids in the Sangam Literature', *Proceedings of the Indian History Congress*, (Bhubaneswar, 1977).

57. I am indebted to M. G. S. Narayanan for the information on communal feasts in Sangam literature called uṇḍāṭṭu. The significance of this institution can be best understood in the light of the discussion in R. S. Sharma, *Material Culture and Social Formations in Ancient India*, (Delhi, 1983), p. 39. See also Karl Polanyi, 'The Economy as Instituted Process' in Polanyi, et al., *Trade and Market in Early Empires*, (Glencoe, 1957), p. 250; Emmanuel Terray, *Marxism and 'Primitive' Societies*, (London, 1972). p. 137 and p. 135, no.17; Romila Thapar, *From Lineage to State*, (Bombay, 1984); pp. 23–27; *idem, Ancient Indian Social History*, p. 105ff.

58. K. Kailasapathi, *Tamil Heroic Poetry*, (London, 1968). A recent study by T. M. Vijayan. *The Panas in Sangam Literature* (unpublished M.Phil. dissertation, Calicut University, 1986) brings out details of this aspect.

59. M. G. S. Narayanan, 'The Vedic-Sastraic-Puranic Element in Tamil Sangam Literature', *Proceedings of the Indian History Congress*, (Aligarh, 1975).

60. K. A. Nilakanta Sastri, *Studies in Chola History and Administration, op. cit.*, Chapter on 'Karikala'.

61. Below, Chapter II.

62. R. Champakalakshmi, 'Urbanisation in South India: The Role of Ideology and Polity', *op. cit.*

63. K. A. Nilakanta Sastri, *A History of South India*, 3rd edn, (1966), p. 144.

64. Stein, *Peasant State and Society*, pp. 65–67.

65. *Ibid.*, pp. 63–89 posits this brahman-peasant alliance. This has been rightly questioned by Jha, 'Relevance of 'Peasant State and Society', *op. cit.*, pp. 75–82.

66. Above, n. 42.

67. *Ibid.*

68. Kesavan Veluthat, *Brahman Settlements in Kerala: Historical Studies*, (Calicut, 1978).

69. Above, n. 20; n. 66; M. G. S. Narayanan and Kesavan Veluthat, 'A History of the Nambudiri Community in Kerala' in Frits Staal, (ed.) *Agni*. Vol. 2. (Berkeley. 1983), pp. 256–78.

70. Above, n. 7.

71. *Ibid.* and Kesavan Veluthat, 'The Temple-base of the Bhakti Movement in South India', *Proceedings of the Indian History Congress*, (Waltair, 1979), pp. 185–94.

72. This argument of ours (above nn. 68–69) is endorsed by D. N. Jha, above, n. 65, pp. 93–4.

73. In a slightly earlier period, there was a short-lived attempt on the part of one of the lines of the Cola family to eclipse the Pallava rule. T. V. Mahalingam.

'An Interregnum in Pallava History', *Journal of Indian History*, XLI. (1963). Also, *idem, Readings in South Indian History*, (Delhi, 1977), pp. 59–71.

74. K. A. Nilakanta Sastri, *The Colas*, Reprint, (Madras, 1975), pp. 110–139.

75. *Ibid.*, pp. 140–168.

76. Subbarayalu, n. 37.

77. *Ibid.*, Mahalingam. *South Indian Polity*, pp. 161–62; Karashima, *South Indian History and Society*. pp. 94–105.

78. Below, Chapter 3.

79. Narayanan, n. 20.

80. Sastri, *Colas*, p. 101. See also Clarence Maloney, 'Dynastic Drift: A Process of Cultural Universalization' in *Professor K. A. Nilakanta Sastri Felicitation Volume*, (Madras, 1971), pp. 89–107.

81. The Problems of the Companions of Honour taken up by M. G. S. Narayanan, *Reinterpretations in South Indian History*, (Trivandrum, 1977) and of the arms-bearing brahman militia of the *caṭṭa*s and *bhaṭṭa*s taken up by the present writer, 'The Caṭṭas and Bhaṭṭas: A New Interpretation', *Proceedings of the Indian History Congress*, (Aligarh, 1975) are two good cases in point. For an endorsement, Y. Subbarayalu, Presidential Address, Section IV, Indian History Congress, Burdwan, 1983.

82. Below, Chapter 1.

83. Below, Chapters 2, 3 and 4.

84. Below, Chapters 5 and 6.

85. Karashima, *South Indian History and Society*, pp. 21–31.

86. Kathleen Gough, 'Mode of Production in Southern India', *Economic and Political Weekly*, Annual number, February, 1980, p. 337–54.

87. Sastri, *Colas*, pp. 447, 461. This has been rightly challenged by Burton Stein. Above n. 15.

88. Above, n. 27. This is questioned by R. Champakalakshmi, D. N. Jha, Vijaya Ramaswami, Y. Subbarayalu, Noboru Karashima and M. G. S. Narayanan. See above n. 30.

89. Y. Subbarayalu, 'The Cola State', *op. cit.*

# One

# The Self-Image of Royalty

In most pre-modern Indian states, kingship was central to polity and, in spite of changing patterns in the socio-political formations, this central position was maintained at least in an outward form. In fact, this has resulted in two basic historiographical constructs about Indian civilisation: (1) the idea of a changeless political structure throughout the course of history in the pre-modern period and (2) the notion that state meant the king, postulates behind monoliths like Oriental Despotism and its Marxist variant, the Asiatic Mode of production. These constructs, however, have been questioned in recent years,[1] and it would take studies different in nature and scope from the present one to test their validity or otherwise. Nonetheless, we will be concerned here with examining the nature of kingship in early medieval south India. This would help in locating the institution within the changing power structure with the necessary mutations to suit such changes. It naturally would entail consideration of local differences in the character of royalty within the four states. In this chapter, we take up one aspect, i.e., the image of royalty projected in their official expressions. In discussing the image, we have to deal with the four states separately and, in the case of the Cōḻa state, the most durable and impressive of them, also the differences before and after Rājarāja I (985–1014 AD).

The structure of monarchy in early medieval south India saw the projection of an image carefully constructed by the king and his court, the contours of which were sharpened by several elements drawn from different sources. This image, which has influenced many a historian in our own times in describing the nature of monarchy,[2] is reflected in contemporary royalist literature in the main, preserved in the copious *praśasti*s and other forms of court literature, both in Sanskrit and Tamil. Several aspects went into the making of this image—origin myths, dynastic traditions, genealogies, etc., through which the dynasty in general sought legitimation as well as through the presentation of an individual king as having acquired the kṣatriya status, as a *cakravartin*, as a warrior-hero, as a protector and fountain-head of all *dharma*, as a munificent donor, as a divine figure, as of an attractive mien and finally as a patron of arts and culture. While most of these aspects were inspired by stereotypes presented in Sanskrit literature, there were aspects which had an equally local, Tamil, bearing which took into account traditions of the Sangam literature concerning dynastic connections and also myths about individual ancestors and culture centres.[3] The discussion in this chapter of the image of royalty will help raising and answering questions regarding the rationale behind such details in the context of the contemporary social formation.

## ORIGIN MYTHS

It is well-known that most early medieval dynasties of south India were revived from an earlier period, i.e., the Sangam Age. This is acceptedly so in the case of the Cōḻas, Cēras and Pāṇḍyas.[4] In the case of the Pallavas, there is the argument—which is not very convincing, though—that even they drew from the Toṇḍaimans of the Sangam Age.[5] This Sangam connection was, however, underplayed in all the cases. Thus each dynasty invented its own origin myths. These origin myths form part of the *praśasti*s and take the form of those drawing typically on the *itihāsa-purāṇa* tradition of northern India. They contain, in most cases, the elaborate accounts of a genealogy of the Sūryavaṁśa or Candravaṁśa lineage upto an eponymous founder of the dynasty in question and from him, through historically known figures, down to the contemporary ruler who makes the grant. Even here, figures up to and including the eponymous founder belong to the realm of mythology. After him, the figures may be historically known; but still, not necessarily do accounts of the same dynasty in different records tally in the matter of the sequence of rulers, etc., especially about the remote past, although there may be agreement in a general way about the more recent past. This may mean that these historical traditions record not so much what 'actually happened' but what the authors and their patrons believed or wanted themselves and others to believe to have happened.[6] However, what is clear in such traditions is a conscious attempt to link the historical reality of the ruling dynasty with the mythical lineages of the *itihāsa-purāṇa* milieu and thus claim origins which would validate the ruling dynasty within the existing system. This is clear in the case of the Pallava, Pāṇḍya and Cōḻa dynasties. In the case of the Cēras, owing to the absence of the conventional *praśasti*s (which absence is still an enigma),[7] we do not have any such details except faint claims to Sūryavaṁśa ancestry.

The Pallavas do not explicitly claim to be of either the Candravaṁśa or the Sūryavaṁśa although there is reference in a later literary work to their claim to belong to the Candravaṁśa.[8] Otherwise they claim to be of the Bhāradvāja *gotra*[9] and seek a curious validation through what they describe as *brahma-kṣatra*, a brahmanical lineage wielding the powers adjunct to kṣatriyas.[10] Accordingly, their genealogy starts from Brahman, the creator, and draws through Aṅgiras, Bṛhaspati, Śamyu, Bharadvaja, Drona and Aśvatthāman to the eponymous Pallava, with minor, almost negligible, variations in detail in the succession list.[11] In an inscription round the Kailāsanātha temple, Kāñcīpuram, however, Pṛthu is introduced as a son of Aśvatthāman and father of this eponymous Pallava.[12] The story of Pṛthu as the first righteous ruler is well-known[13] and his name being brought in is very significant in this context.

The founder of the Pallava dynasty is usually just stated as a son of Aśvatthāman but in two cases his mother is identified. In the Kāśākkuḍi plates of Nandivarman Pallavamalla she is Mēnakā, the *apsaras*[14] and, in the Rāyakōttai plates, where the founder's name is Skandaśisya, she is a Nāga woman (*dvijihvāṅganā*).[15] This Nāga connection, significantly, is once again looked for in the Vēlurpāḷaiyam plates of Nandivarman III where Virakūrca, one of the descendants of Pallava, acquired all royal insignia along with the daughter of a Nāga (*Phaṇīndrasutā*).[16] In most cases there is a wide gap after this founder which, ironically though, links the mythological past with the historical past by means of what Romila Thapar calls 'telescoping'.[17] In a few cases in this gap are seen floating figures like Aśōkavarman—obviously an attempt to claim greatness if this reference is to Aśōka Maurya and if indeed he was regarded as great by the Pallavan court in South India.[18]

The Pāṇḍyas make explicit claims to belong to the Candravaṁśa. The Daḷavāypuram plates of Parāntaka Viranārāyana trace the origins of the lords of Paṇḍyadēśa from the lotus in Nārayaṇa's (Viṣṇu's) navel through Brahmā, Atri and the Moon.[19] In the case of the record given in the Sivakāsi plates of Vira Pāṇḍya, everything else is the same as in the one given in the Daḷavāypuram plates except that it introduces an eponymous Pāṇḍya as the founder of the dynasty who had his origin from the Moon.[20] The Vēḷvikudi plates of Neḍuñjaḍaiyan use a sleight of words here: 'Pāṇḍya, who stood all by himself at the doors of the ocean, as it were, at the time of the flood in which all the three worlds had sunken, agreed to the request of Brahman to be the son of Moon and take the name, Budha.'[21] The clumsiness typical of most of Sanskrit *praśasti* poetry apart, this verse tries the same thing as all the instances quoted earlier in the case of the Pāṇḍyas. However, the only reference to the origin myth of the Candravaṁśa as it occurs in the Puranic sources or thereabouts[22] is found in the Tamil portion of the Daḷavāypuram plates—the story of Iḷā and her son Purūravas, from whom the *vaṁśa* issued.[23]

As stated earlier, in the absence of similar *praśasti*s, such a detailed examination is not possible in the case of the Cēras. However, they are stated to be of the Ravikula, Diptāṁśuvaṁśa, etc., in a contemporary astronomical treatise.[24] *Periyapurāṇam*, a near contemporary chronicle, speaks of Cēramān Perumāḷ, who was sitting in a temple, being brought to the city and crowned king.[25] In a tradition, embodied in the legendary chronicle called *Kēraḷōlpatti* of a much later date, there is the statement that the Perumāḷ was invited to accept the position by the representatives of the brahmans in Kerala.[26] In either case, there is no attempt at linking the dynasty with a mythological or even supposedly historical past. The only sanction behind its authority was, perhaps, that it was established by the brahmans and the temple committees (which, of course, was sanction enough!).

In the case of the Cōḻas, the claim is that they belonged to the Sūryavaṁśa. The story presented in the Kanyākumāri inscription of Vīra Rājēndra concerning the establishment of the Cōḻa rule in the Kāvēri area is an interesting case in point.[27] After presenting the origin of the Sūryavaṁśa and a number of rulers in that dynasty, an eponymous Cōḻa is introduced. He is stated to have gone on a hunt and been lured away southward by a demon in the guise of a deer. On reaching the Kāvēri valley, Cōḻa slew the demon and wanted to confer gifts on brahmans. Finding none, he invited a few from north India and settled them, thus opening the land by the Kāvēri. This is in the pattern of the *itihāsa-purāṇa*s, especially modelled on the Mārīca episode in the *Rāmāyana.* As usual, in this and other Cōḻa *praśasti*s such as the Tiruvālaṅgāḍ Copper Plates,[28] the Larger Leiden Plates[29] and the Anbil Plates,[30] there is a gap between the eponymous Cōḻa and the later figures. But curiously, even in the parts following this eponymous figure, there are names met with in mythology although names such as Karikāla, Rājakēsari, Parakēsari, Koccengaṇṇan, etc., are known in history. George W. Spencer has subjected these mythical genealogies to computer-aided analysis and has suggested that the function of this fiction was validation for the ruler.[31]

These origin myths suggest that in spite of the clear Tamil origins of these dynasts, they participated in a pan-Indian tradition of the origin of dynasties. This points to the commonness of the political culture that was evolving in early medieval India, which was sought to be emulated in the southern regions also. Perhaps the preponderance of the Sanskritic ideals indicates the influence of the brahmanical section of the population which wielded a large amount of power in the Tamil kingdoms as well, through the councillors in the court including the *purōhita*s of the royal families.

## DYNASTIC TRADITIONS

Apart from the origin myths, there are certain other traditions which each of the dynasties cherished. In some cases these traditions were universally applicable to all the dynasties which fitted into the *śāstra-kāvya-naṭaka* stereotype, but in some other cases there were traditions which, even though they conformed to the pattern, were used exclusively by certain dynasties. All these traditions together provide some of the more important contours in the image of royalty in early medieval south India.[32]

As for the Pallavas, there is nothing that they claim as an exclusive dynastic trait; they claim, like many other medieval Indian dynasties and their idealised versions in the *kāvyas* and *nāṭakas*, that both the Goddess of the Earth and the Goddess of Prosperity were wedded to them,[33] that they ruled the entire Earth covered on all the four sides by the oceans,[34] that they were the guardians of *varṇāśrama-dharma*,[35] that they were the destroyers of the evil of the Kali [age],[36] that they had performed several *yāgas*,[37] that they had accumulated merit by donating cows, gold and land,[38] and such other details that would be attending to such stereotypes. In short, nothing is wanting in the details given in the different Pallava *praśastis* to draw the picture of a dynasty which conforms to the ideal type obtaining in the *śāstra-kāvya-nāṭaka* literature in Sanskrit.

The case of the Pāṇḍyas is slightly different. Although the description contained in the different Pāṇḍyas *praśastis* too may yield a picture close to the one drawn by Pallavas with regard to their dynastic traditions, the points of variation appear more significant than those of convergence. Even those, to be sure, have an ostensibly Sanskritic character. Accordingly the Pāṇḍyas:

1. Caused the twin fish emblem to be engraved on the peak of Himālaya/Meru,
2. Were honoured by Indra by sharing with them his throne (*ardhāsana*),
3. Acquired Indra's garland/necklace,
4. Broke their bangle on Indra's crown,
5. Had Agastya as their family priest who anointed them and also taught them Tamil,
6. Built the city of Madurai and founded the Tamil *Sangam* there,
7. Had a number of irrigation tanks dug with the help of a *bhūta* and banished hunger from the country,
8. Had the *Dēvas* as messengers/played the role of messengers to the *Dēvas*,
9. Churned the ocean of milk,
10. Defeated the Kaurava army in the *Mahābhārata* war,
11. Had the *Mahābhārata* translated into Tamil,
12. Stopped the advancing ocean,
13. Crossed the ocean of knowledge by paying 40 million worth of gold (as fees),

14. Bathed in the waters of all the four oceans on the same day (i.e. commanded the entire earth covered on the four sides by the seas) and so forth.[39]

It is interesting to note that at least some of these traditions find a place in the post-Sangam epics like the *Cilappadikāram* and *Manimēkalai* and also in later works like the *Tiruviḷaiyādal Purānam*.[40]

It is equally interesting that the copper plates do not directly cherish many of the traditions of Sangam literature; they do not refer to any of the famous Pāṇḍyan kings mentioned in that literature as their ancestors nor do they participate in other traditions contained in the Sangam literature. However, the carving of the fish emblem on the Himālaya, the connection with Agastya, the establishment of the Sangam and the translation of the *Mahābhārata* into Tamil, referred to in items 1, 5, 6 and 11 above, echo the traditions of the Sangam Age. The case of Palyāgamudugudumi Peruvaḻudi[41] stands apart: it is not in the genealogy portion that he is referred to; the supplicant invokes a previous grant allegedly made by this ruler. Similarly, the statement in a couple of records, that one of the Pāṇḍyas established a Tamil Sangam does not in any case represent a tradition dating from the Sangam Age. On the other hand, it forms the core of the story contained in a late commentary, the *Iraiyanar Akapporuḷ Urai*. This is not to suggest that the Pāṇḍyas disowned their Sangam heritage; on the contrary, they did utilise such aspects of the heritage as were remembered in seeking as much validation by means of such locally rooted traditions. These aspects included a faint memory of the Battle of Talaiyālaṅgānam[42] or the victory over Atiyan.[43] This submergence of the Tamil, and preponderance with the Sanskritic, traditions might point to the changes more than the continuity in the royal tradition.

As in the case of the origin myths, so also in the case of dynastic traditions, the Cēras draw a blank owing to the non-existence of *praśasti*s. Perhaps the idea of courtiers like Śāṅkaranārāyana was that by latching the Cēras to the Sūryavaṁśa, this dynasty participated in the common traditions of the Sūryavaṁśa.

In the case of the Cōḻas, it can be seen that they claimed all typical kṣatriya traditions of the Sūryavaṁśa, sharing with the rest of the *vaṁśa* everything about the origins and the ancestors. This includes stories about Ikṣvāku and Rāma being the ancestors of the Cōḻas, about Manu punishing his son for inadvertently killing a calf, about Śibi who offered his own flesh equal in weight to that of a dove to save it and so on and so forth.[44] Especially claimed by the Cōḻa dynasty are such traditions remembered from the Sangam Age as that of Karikāla who built embankments on either side of the river Kāvēri and of Kocceṅgaṇān, the saint-king who built a number of temples for Śiva in various parts of the kingdom.[45]

Even these and other motifs occurring as part of the dynastic traditions may be seen as integrated to the pattern concerning origins. The ideals conform to the Sanskritic *kāvya-śāstra-nāṭaka* pattern, with some details taken from the earlier Tamil poetry. The motifs, such as the king being the protector of *varṇāśramadharma* taken up for discussion below, are especially significant from the point of view of the brahman ideologues, who created these motifs in an attempt to perfect the image of royalty which suited their own interests.

## GENEALOGY

Apart from the mythological aspect of the genealogies of the Bhāradvāja *gotra*, Candravaṁśa or Sūryavaṁśa, as the case may be, up to the eponymous founder of the concerned dynasty, there is another aspect which belongs to the historical past. There is often a gap between the point where the dynasty branches off, i.e., the eponymous founder and the historical figures. This gap both separates and links the mythological and the historical at the same time. To be sure, even in this portion of the genealogies there are discrepancies which have bewildered the historian in reconstructing the continuous history of a dynasty. Therefore, even when the chronological and dynastic-historical dimensions of these portions of the genealogies are not denied, it will be well to treat them as more than tools for such reconstruction; they provided for the contemporary authors and their patrons a strong means by which the authority of a dynasty or a ruler was strengthened with reference to worthy ancestors, a major and effective claim to authority and a significant use of the past.[46] This becomes clear when one remembers the *śāstra* prescriptions that when a charter granting land (which all our charters are) is drawn up, not only should the name of the donor be given, but also those of his ancestors be listed.[47] Here, along with the names of the ancestors, their achievement, mostly military, are given in inflated terms. This then shows that the purpose was precisely to project the picture of a dynasty where a number of heroes in succession ruled the state. While the details contained in the origin myths etc., are intended to provide ideological sanction, the genealogies relating to the historical past provide the necessary political validation, by projecting the image of a king with an ancestry most becoming of a valiant military hero and, through it, the necessary claims to authority. Both these conform to the general Indian faith in the inheritability of qualities in the family line.

The genealogy of the Pallavas during this period offers a very interesting case in point. The Prakrit and Sanskrit charters of the pre-Simhaviṣṇu period are not considered here for they fall chronologically into an earlier period and also because the genealogies there furnish very scanty information. In the records of the later rulers, the more remote period in the historical past, after the founder Pallava, is taken care of by vague expressions like a plain 'in that *vaṁśa*' or a more eloquent passage in which a few names are dropped—names attested in history like Virakūrca,[48] Siṁhavarmā,[49] Visnugopa,[50] *et al.*; names of otherwise historically famous personages like those of Aśōka;[51] and finally names with no basis such as Cūtapallava,[52] Kālabhartā,[53] Vimalakonkaṅaka,[54] *et al.* After that in most cases there is an account of three or four generations immediately preceding the donor, where there is general agreement among different records about the names. Here in several cases the 'achievement' of the ancestors is recounted. For instance, the Kūṟam Plates of Paramesvaravarman give the name of the grandfather, Narasiṁhavarman, who was a lion to the elephants or the enemy kings, who repeatedly defeated the Cōḻas, Kēraḷas, Kaḷabhras, Pāṇḍyas etc., who like the thousand-armed [Kārtavirya Arjuna] was triumphant in hundreds of battles and performed as if he had a thousand arms and who, in the battles of Pariyaḷa, Maṇimangala and Śūramara, had the letters 'Victory' inscribed on the back of Pulakēśin (when he was retreating showing his back) and who like Agastya had destroyed Vātāpi.[55] In the case of the father, the record is content with a double entendre on *suracitasampad* (*su-ractia* for the king and *sura-cita* for Indra) and the statement that he maintained the *Varṇāśramadharma* well.[56] This is followed by a twenty-two verse eloquent eulogy of the donor, Parameśvaravarman. Another interesting case is provided by the Paḷḷankōvil Plates of Siṁhavarman, which praise the son of the donor, Siṁhaviṣṇu, more than the donor himself.[57]

The copper plate grants of Nandivarman II Pallavamalla are very significant in this respect. The 'fact' of this king's 'election' as recorded in the sculpture and inscriptions of the Vaikuṇṭhapperumāḷ temple at Kāñci is too well-known to be repeated here.[58] But the genealogy portions of Nandivarman's records are interestingly silent about any such story. The Udayēndiram plates of his twenty-first regnal year trace his descent in the Pallava family from Siṁhaviṣṇu through Mahēndravarman, Narasiṁhavarman (who, again, like Agastya had destroyed Vātāpi and triumphed over the Vallabharāja in the battles of Pariyaḷa, Maṇimaṅgala, Śūramāra etc.), Mahēndravarman, Paramēśvaravarman (the victor of the battle of Peruvaḷanallūr), Narasiṁhavarman and Paramēśvaravarman, whose *son* Nandivarman is the donor of the grant.[59] There is absolutely no reference to either Paramēśvaravarman's death without a male issue to succeed on the throne or to Nandivarman's being chosen on account of other reasons. The Kāśākkudi Plates of his twenty-second year are more elaborate in the genealogy portions. They give a long (and necessarily confused) list of ancestors in relation to the historical past to get anchored on Siṁhaviṣṇu from whom the unbroken descent is traced through Mahēndravarman, Narasiṁhavarman, Mahēndravarman, Parameśvarapōtavarman, Narasiṁhavarman upto Paramēśvaravarman, *after* whom came Nandivarman. Significantly, the exact relationship between Paramēśvaravarman and Nandivarman is not given here.[60] Moreover, immediately after the name of Nandivarman, the poet suddenly goes back to the sixth ['generation'] and another genealogy is given from Siṁhaviṣṇu's younger brother, Bhīmāvarman, through Budhavarman, Ādityavārman, Gōvindavarman, upto Hiraṇya[61] and Nandivarman is described as Hiraṇya's son (Hairaṇya) and of pure descent from the mother's line (*śuddhamātranvavāyah*).[62] There is, however, no explanation for this apparently irrelevant insertion, nor is there any statement that he was chosen or elected or at least that his succession was unusual, unless the statement 'honoured by the subjects'[63] (*prajābhih mānyah*) indicates such an incident. This is the earliest record tracing the ancestry of the ruler from both the 'main' and 'collateral' lines of the dynasty. If indeed the purpose of the genealogy is just to record the pedigree of the donor then the descent through the 'collateral' line would have been sufficient. Since both these are given, it appears that there was a purpose beyond this, and the fact that we get from this record more detailed information about the main line than about the collateral line to which the ruler may have belonged shows that the claim to authority through the main line is held as the more important than a truthful account of biological ancestry.

Similarly the Pullūr Plates of his thirty-third year do not give any genealogy at all except stating that he was born into the *vaṁśa* of the Pallavas.[64] The Taṇḍantōṭṭam Plates of his fifty-eighth year, whose earlier portions have not come down to us, first give his father's name as Hiraṇyavarman.[65] Even the Paṭṭattāḷmaṅgalam Plates of his sixty-first year give the name of the *vaṁśa* and that of his father Hiraṇyavarman.[66] Does the statement in this record, that he acquired with his renowned strength the realm even as a youth (*ādhatta prathitabalō yuvaiva rājyam*) all by himself with his sword-wielding hand and destroying all his enemies (*prōdghātasphuritakṛpaṇirēkah ... hatvā sakalaripūn*), reflect the statements in the Vaikuṇṭhapperumāl record?[67] If it does, then, what appears is that Nandivarman's records used those aspects of his autobiography which were flattering and that too, late in his reign. Even in the Vēlūrpāḷaiyam record of his grandson, Nandivarman III, the genealogy is traced through the 'main' line, with nothing stated about the 'collateral' line although Nandivarman II (Pallavamalla) is introduced 'after' Paramēśvaravarman (*tadanantaram*) not stating the relationship between the two.[68] By the time we reach the period of Nṛipatuṅgavarman, in whose Bāhūr Plates the genealogy is traced only from Dantivarman, the entire succession list is normalised once again, with a mythological past and a historical past, punctuated by the usual gap in which floats an ageless figure, Vimalakoṅkaṇaka.[69] It then becomes clear that the purpose of even those portions of the genealogy dealing with the supposedly historical periods is not so much to keep an exact record of the pedigree of the ruler as to pin him down to a family of established political tradition and with purity of lineage which goes a long way in the process of legitimation. Expressions like *ubhayakulapariśuddhar* in the Vaikuṇṭhapperumāḷ temple record and *śuddhamātranvavāya* in the Kāśākkudi Plates too may indicate this obsession with purity of lineage from both the sides. So do perhaps the statements in the records of the post-Nandivarman period about the marriages of each of the kings, showing that the ruler of the next generation was of respectable lineage on both the sides.

The records of the Pāṇḍyas of the 'First Empire' are equally interesting. Each of their copper-plate charters is bilingual, with a Sanskrit portion followed by a Tamil portion. Curiously, at least in some cases, the names do not tally and, therefore, the historian of the Pāṇḍyan kingdom had to indulge in exercises of fixing the identity, etc.[70] Thus, while the Sanskrit portion of the Vēḷvikuḍi plates gives a genealogy of the donor starting with Māṟavarman (who was born into the *vaṁśa* of Pururavas) and drawing through Raṇadhira and Māṟavarman to Jaṭila Parāntaka (the donor) in lineal descent,[71] the Tamil portion gives a lengthier list. It begins with Kaḍuṅgōn (who established the Pāṇḍyan rule replacing the Kaḷabhras) and proceeds through Māṟavarman, Cēntan, Māṟavarman, Koccaḍaiyan and Tērmāran up to Neḍuṅjaḍaiyan, the donor of the charter.[72] While the military achievements are detailed in the Tamil portion, the Sanskrit portion which is generally brief is not so eloquent about them. But it takes care to establish that the mother of the donor was also of respectable descent, being the daughter of a Maḻava chief. In the Śrivaramaṅgalam Plates of the same ruler, the Sanskrit portion speaks of the donor's father as Māṟavarman and describes his victory over the Pallavas before dealing with the donor himself in a beautiful verse.[73] The Tamil portion, unlike in the Vēḷvikudi Plates, just goes on describing the donor further with a reference to the Sanskrit portion (*aṉṉaṉākiya*).[74]

The Smaller Śinnamanūr Plates of the same ruler do not give any genealogy at all in the Sanskrit portion.[75] The Tamil portion does give one, starting with Jayantavarman through Arikēsari.[76] But immediately after Arikēsari and some of the achievements of his son are described, a plate or two in which his name and those of his successors probably figured are missing in the surviving body of the inscription. It, however, is clear that the Tamil portion had originally given a genealogy. When we come to the Daḷavāypuram Plates of Parāntaka Vīranārayaṇa, we find that there is some disagreement between the Sanskrit and Tamil portions. The Sanskrit portion speaks of the line (*anvaya*) in which, after kings like Sundara had joined the gods by virtue of their acts,

## Fig. 1.1: The Family Tree according to the Sanskrit portion of the Larger Śinnamanūr Plates

- Pāṇḍya Vamśa in which Sundara Pāṇḍya and other countless Rājas were born
  - Arikēsari
    - Jatila
      - Rājasimha
        - Varaguṇa
          - Śrimara Śrivallabha
            - Varaguṇa
            - Parantaka
              - Rājasimha (the donor)

## The Family Tree in the Tamil Portion

- Parāṅkuśan
  - Rājasimha (Grandson)
    - Varaguṇamahārajan
      - Paracakra Kōlāhalan
        - Varaguṇavarman
        - Parāntaka Caṭaiyan
          - Rājasimha (the donor)

was born Māra, a son of Parāntaka. Of him was born Varaguna and his younger brother Viranārāyaṇa, the donor of the grant.[77] The Tamil portion speaks of Sri Parāntakan Kōccaḍaiyan and his son Śrivallabhan whose elder son was Varaguṇa, the devotee of Śiva and younger son was Sri Parāntaka Mahārāja Viranārāyana, the donor of the grant. It is in the Tamil portion that the military achievements of the earlier rulers are given.[78]

Similarly in the Larger Śinnamanūr Plates of Rājasimha,[79] the family trees look different in the Sanskrit and Tamil portions (see Fig. 1.1). Some of the achievements of Śrīmaran Śrīvallabhan, such as his victory over a Māyā Pāṇḍya, Kerala, Simhaḷa, Pallava, and Vallabha are given in the Sanskrit portion and so is the name of Rājasimha's mother, Vānavan Mahādēvi.[80] In the Tamil portion which yields another family tree,[81] some of the achievements of the characters are given.

The Sanskrit portion of the Śivakāsī Plates of Vira Pāṇḍya gives a rather lengthy genealogy. It starts from a certain Tivrakōpa, who was born in 'that' line (*anvavāya*) and progresses in lineal descent through Śrīvallabha, Manakulācala and Mānābharaṇa, who begat Vira Pāṇḍya, the donor, through a daughter of Ravi, the pride of the Kēraḷa *vaṁśa*. It is significant that after describing Vīra Pāṇḍya, an elder brother is introduced, Sundara Pāṇḍya who was related to Vīra Pāṇḍya in the same manner as Indra was to Viṣṇu.[82] The Tamil portion of the Śivakāśi Plates is less elaborate about the genealogy portion: it speaks of the lineage of the Pāṇḍya Paramēśvaras into which was born Mānābharaṇa, the father of Rājasiṁha, the donor.[83] It does not speak of any of their achievements.

This examination of the Sanskrit and Tamil portions of the Pāṇḍya *praśasti*s leads us to the same inference. Those portions of the genealogy concerning the more recent past of the donor served the purpose of providing the king with a lineage entitling him to all the claims his ancestors had, as well as qualifying him eminently for the office he was holding. In such cases when the younger brother is praised more than the elder (Parāntaka Viranārāyana and Varaguṇa and Vira Pāṇḍya and Sundara Pāṇḍya) it is likely that the younger brother, due to some reason, ascended the throne and that this had to be explained.

In the case of the Cōḻas, the genealogies present a similar pattern as regards the recent past. The confusion in Cōḻa chronology, especially in relation to the period between the end of Parāntaka's reign (955 AD) and the beginning of that of Rājarāja I (985 AD) is, in fact, a result of the conflicting information in the genealogies. This means that the Cōḻas too had appreciated the use of genealogy as the other houses in south India. However, what strikes one in the case of the Cōḻa records in the period from the eighth year of Rājarāja and after, is the lack of any genealogical information in the celebrated Tamil *meykkīrttis*. They refer more to the military achievements of the individual ruler and address, unlike the Sanskrit charters, the Tamil magnates, especially as they form part of the stone inscriptions exhibited in public rather than the copper plates which were kept in private custody.

It can be seen that even in the bilingual charters of the Pallavas and Cōḻas, the *praśasti* portion which includes the genealogy is in Sanskrit, with only the operational part of the grant in Tamil. This may point to the source of inspiration. The Tamil portions in the Pāṇḍyan records, which are sometimes even more elaborate than the Sanskrit portions in relation to genealogy, etc., point to a greater local bearing of this royal house. However, it is interesting that even in these Tamil portions, although the language is Tamil, many of the motifs are inspired by Sanskrit literature and Sanskritic traditions.

The Cēras of Makōtai cannot be studied in respect of their genealogy either. The donor in a post-Cēra copper plate record, however, claims descent from the Cēra lineage which is traced from Vira Kērala, a Śrī Bhūpālanarapati. This, however, does not lead us anywhere.

## CASTE STATUS

While the origin myths, dynastic traditions and genealogies deal with the dynasty as a whole, there were means by which the individual ruler was elevated and accorded a status unique in society. These were among the major components of the image of royalty in these kingdoms. One of them was the claim of the kṣatriya caste status.[84] It is neither suggested, nor probable, that there was any physical migration of the category of kṣatriyas from north India to the south either in times of peace or following the expansion of northern Indian states under the Mauryas, Guptas or other powers. Moreover, all the four dynasties discussed here are of a clear south Indian origin. The Pāṇḍyas, Cēras and Cō̤ḻas in the Sangam period did not explicitly claim this kṣatriya status, even if the idea of caste was known to south India in that period. In the case of the Pallavas, whose origins are less clear, even their *praśasti*s do not claim a kṣatriya origin for them. As noted earlier, theirs is a *brahmakṣatra* lineage, tracing descent through well-known brahman heroes like Drōṇa and Aśvatthāman but claiming kṣatriyahood in a clear manner in the period of their rule in south India. The unequivocal claim to kṣatriyahood, then, is found from the period of our study.

This was advanced in several ways. Among these, explicit claims that individual rulers were kṣatriyas may be taken up first. The statement in many early Pallava *praśasti*s that an ancestor of the Pallavas had acquired treasures of *kṣatra* and *tapa*s by the prowess of his own arms indicates this acquisition of the kṣatriya status by assertion. So also does the statement in the Pa̤ḻlankoil Plates of Siṁhavarman, that Siṁhaviṣṇu had cultivated the qualities of a kṣatriya (*ksātraguna*);[85] Nandivarman II Pallavamalla is described in the Kāśākkudi Plates as *kṣatriyamalla*;[86] Rājarāja called himself *Kṣatriyaśikhāmani*.[87] Examples like this could be multiplied. The linking of the dynasties with the Candravaṁśa and Sūrayavaṁśa lineages of Puranic fame discussed above itself has the obvious purpose of claiming kṣatriyahood for these dynasties.

Another means by which the rulers claimed kṣatriya status was the adoption of names ending with the *varman* suffix. It is well-known that the brāhmaṇa, kṣatriya, vaiśya and śūdra *varṇa*s were identified by the suffixes *śarman*, *varman*, *gupta* and *dāsa* added respectively to their names.[88] In northern India, at least by the time of Manu, this practice was standardised.[89] Of these, we begin to find the adoption of the kṣatriya caste suffixes in the case of the Pallavas and notice it spreading to the south among the Pāṇḍyas, Cēras and Cō̤ḻas. Thus we have Siṁhavarman (Pallava: 550–560 AD), Mahēndravarman (I Pallava: 580–630 AD; II Pallava: 668–670 AD; III Pallava: 720–728 AD), Nṛpatungavarman (Pallava: 850–899 AD), Māṟavarman (Pāṇḍya: 620–645 AD), Varaguṇavarman (Pāṇḍya: 862–885 AD), Ādityavarman (Cō̤ḻa: 871–906 AD), Parāntakavarman (Cō̤ḻa: 707–755 AD) Sthāṇu Ravivarman (Cēra: 844–883 AD), Bhāskara Ravivarman (Cēra: 962–1021 AD) Rāmavarman (Cēra: 1189–1124 AD), *et al.*, to take only a few examples. There was also the practice of adopting coronation names or *abhiṣēkanāmans* or titles or *birudas*, ending with the suffix *varman*.[90] It is stated that Nandivarman was an *abhiṣēkanaman* that Pallavamalla was given at the time of his consecration.[91] The royal Cēra playwright called himself Kulasekharavarman, who has been identified with Sthāṇu Ravivarman.[92] The Cōḻas adopted the coronation titles of Parakēsarivarman and Rājakēsarivarman in an alternating fashion. Rājarāja (Cōḻa: 885–1014 AD) had the name Arumoḻivarman, a curious addition of the Sanskritic suffix to a purely Tamil name.[93]

Besides, there are a few other cases where, even though the suffix *varman* is not used, the names clearly indicate the kṣatriyahood of the bearer amply. They included Śēndan (Jayanta—the Victor, Pāṇḍya: 654–670 AD), Arikēsari (Lion to the Foe, Pāṇḍya: 670–700 AD) Kulaśēkhara (Crest Jewel of the Race; a number of rulers in the Pāṇḍya and Cēra dynasties and all the Travancore kings bore this title), Manukulāditya (Sun in the Race of Manu, Cēra: 962–1021 AD) etc. These and other names and titles are significant in other respects also; they will be taken up for discussion below.

Apart from these claims and names, there were some rituals which were clearly meant for conferring the kṣatriya caste status to the ruler. The most significant among these was the *hiraṇyagarbha*. This was often preceded by another ritual *tulābhara* or *tulāpuruṣadāna* and less often by *gōsahasra*. *Tulābhāra* involved the gift of gold equal in weight of the donor and *gōsahasra*, a thousand cows. Many of the Pallava rulers are stated to have performed these rituals.[94] There is even the statement that Viramahādēviyar, the queen of Nṛpatuṅgavarman (859–899 AD) performed the *hiraṇyagarbha* and *tulābhara* ceremonies.[95] In the Pāṇḍyan kingdom Arikēsari Māṟavarman (670–710 AD)[96] and Rājasimha (740–765 AD)[97] are said to have performed these rituals. There are similar references in the records of the Cōḻa empire where Parāntaka (907–955 AD) and even a queen of Rājarāja (985–1014 AD)[98] are said to have performed these rituals. Although in the Cēra kingdom there is no contemporary evidence about the performance of these rituals, rulers in the erstwhile kingdom of Travancore who claimed direct descent from the Cēras there performed these rituals.[99]

The details of the ritual of *hiraṇyagarbha*, which is included in the list of *mahādānas*, are clearly described in the *Purāṇas* as well as in *dharmaśāstra* literature.[100] The aspirant to kṣatriya status was inserted into a large gold vessel, doubled up like a foetus in the womb (*hiraṇyagarbha* or 'golden womb'). This was followed by all prenatal sacraments prescribed for the 'twice-born' castes. When the performer emerged from the 'golden womb', sacraments such as the *jātakarman* followed. He was then deemed to have been symbolically reborn into the kṣatriya caste. (It goes without saying that the gold vessel was shared among the brahman priests who administered the ceremony!).[101]

Another significant ritual, which was slightly different in nature and content, was the *abhiṣēka* or coronation ceremony. There are statements in contemporary epigraphical and literary texts that rulers of south India performed this ceremony. The Pāṇḍyas had the dynastic tradition that they got this ceremony performed by none less than Agastya himself.[102] Certain rulers claim to have performed this ceremony on more than one occasion. References to land given as *dakṣiṇā* or fees to brahman priests for officiating in this ritual called *abhiṣēkakkāni* are also found in inscriptions.[103] So also, a reference to what is read by Noboru Karashima as *abhiṣēkakkāṇikkai*,[104] is taken to mean a tax, understandably levied on the occasion of the ritual, perhaps to meet its expenses. We have a few cases where detailed accounts of this ceremony are available. The one pertaining to Nandivarman II Pallavamalla (732–769 AD) is all the more interesting for the sculptural representation of the various scenes with descriptive labels below each of them and also for the different interpretations it has yielded in the hands of historians. The record as such is not contemporary to Nandivarman Pallavamalla. It is part of a series of sculptured panels purporting to depict the history of the Pallava dynasty from its mythological origins to the construction of the temple on the walls of which these panels occur, a veritable *praśasti in* sculpture. The question, however, is not so much whether the record offers a running commentary, as it were, of the coronation of this ruler or that, as whether it contains the details of the *abhiṣeka* ceremony as understood and perhaps even performed in the Pallava kingdom. The portion relevant to our problem could be summarised as follows:[105]

When following the death of Paramēśvaravarman II (728–732 AD) the Pallava throne at Kāñci fell vacant and the kingdom was reduced to a state of anarchy, the *mātras*, *mūlaprakṛtis* and *ghaṭikaiyār* approached Hiraṇyavarman mahārāja of the family of the Pallavas (Kāṭavēśa-kula) and requested him to become the king, he being capable of bearing the burden of the kingdom and being of pure descent on both sides. After some consideration, Hiraṇyavarman sent his youngest son, Pallavamalla, along with them. Pallavamalla was duly received with great honour at Kāñci and taken to the palace there. Now the *mantrimaṇḍala*, *mahāsāmantas*, the two *gaṇattār* and *ghaṭakaiyār* jointly anointed him (*abhiṣēkañjeydu*) as Nandivarman and invested him with the royal umbrella (*chatri*) called *karivai*, the Samudraghōṣa and Kaṭumukha-vāditra, the flag with the *khaṭvāṅga* as the symbol and the bull crest (*vṛsabhalāñchana*) and proclaimed his authority to issue royal command (*tiruvāṇai*) under the title Viḍelviḍugu. The record is badly damaged beyond this section and what could be made out suggests that he was made the *Perumān aḍigaḷ*.

The *Periyapurāṇam*, a twelfth century Śaiva hagiology composed in the Cōḻa court, too, gives some details of the coronation ceremony of Cēramān Permāl.[106] Again, this source too is separated from the hero by about three centuries. But the details in the account are reliable for our purpose on account of the close association that Cēkkiḻār, the author of *Periyapurāṇam*, is said to have had with the Cōḻa court. Here also the ministers invite Kaḻaṟiṟṟarivāṟ who was meditating in the temple of Tiruvañjaikkaḷam to become the Cēra king, take him to the palace and enthrone him, investing him with the insignia of royalty such as the umbrella and the chowry (*cāmarai*) and showering flowers on him. It is stated that on coronation he formed one of the three crowned monarchs, the two others being the Cōḻas (Vaḷavar) and the Pāṇḍyas (Ceḻiyar), whose duty it was to carry out justice according to the canons laid down by Manu. Further, all services befitting gods, such as ritual bath, incense smoke, ceremonial lamp, food-offerings, etc., were offered to him. Similarly the *kūttar* performed their dance before him.

The Pallavarāyanpēṭṭai inscription of the eighth year of Rājādhirāja II also throws some light on the same aspect.[107] The indispensable scholarly disputes concerning the identity and dates of the hero/heroes involved in the record notwithstanding, the information regarding the coronation is interesting. It states that on the death of Rājarāja II, Pallavarāyar, described as a major functionary in the Cōḻa court, protected the young children of the deceased king aged one and two, removing them from the *paḍaivāḍu* at Āyirattaḷi, to another. There is a gap in the record after this portion and what follows refers to an incident which had taken place in the life-time of Rājarāja II himself. On account of the lack of a successor to the throne, the king had made enquiries into the rights of possible claimants and the choice had fallen on a grandson of Vikramacōḷa Edirili Perumāl and son of Naṟi-uḍaip-Perumāḷ. Apparently Pallavarāyar was commissioned to fetch the newly chosen heir apparent to Rājarāja's presence so that he could be installed in his new place; four years later he was anointed under the title Rājādhirājadēva with the consent of the *uḍankūṭṭam* and the *nāḍu.*

The *abhiṣēcaniya* or the ritual of anointment had two major aspects about it.[108] One of them was the declaration of the title, as it were, to the throne and the other was the reiteration of the kṣatriya caste status. This latter aspect is clear from the fact that the *abhiṣēcanīya* is a ritual which forms part of the *rājasūya* in the *Dharmaśāstra* texts, the eligibility for the performance of which belongs exclusively to the kṣatriyas. In a similar manner the numerous references to the performance of the *aśvamēdha* and other *yajña*s by the rulers furthered their claims to the kṣatriya status, along with serving other purposes which will be taken up for discussion below.

## THE CAKRAVARTIN IDEAL

Another significant aspect of the image of royalty was the ideal of the Universal Emperor which it always looked forward to approximating. This ideal, however, was not exactly that of a *vijigīsu*, that aggressive conqueror idealised in the *Arthaśāstra*, but the *sārvahhouma*, the universal ruler, who was suzerain over other rulers: the *rajādhirāja* or later, *kōkōnmaikoṇḍān.* Thus, the image of the king projected in the records of early medieval south India is that which conformed to the above ideal: the one who relieved Ādiśēṣa of his burden of holding the earth, i.e., the one who bore the burden of the entire earth,[109] the one whose lotus feet are illuminated by the rays emitting from the jewels bedecking the crowns of the innumerable kings prostrating at his feet,[110] the one who ruled over the entire earth covered by the oceans on all the four sides,[111] and so on. In fact, nothing is wanting in the descriptions of the ruler to present him as the overlord of all the kings on earth. Pictures of kings such as the Vallabha, Kaḷabhra, Kēraḷa, Pāṇḍya, Cōḻa, Tuḷu, Gongaṇa (*sic*) and others waiting upon Nandivarman for audience and similar ones are many in the records.[112] The general picture is that of an overlord of other kings. The royal Cēra playwright, Kulaśēkharavarman, called himself Mahōdayapura Paramēśvara (Supreme Lord of Mahōdaya) and Kēraḷādhināthа (overlord of Kerala) at the same time.[113] The decree of Rājarāja is said to be celebrated by the [bowing] heads of the series of kings of earth. A later Sanskrit work describes the king of Mahōdayapura as being hailed as Rājā by the other Rājās. Examples of this kind could be multiplied to show the ideal of *cakravartin* or *sārvabhouma* that was sought to be emulated by the monarch in this period.

## THE HERO IDEAL

Closely related to that of the *cakravartin* is the Hero Ideal which all the rulers cherished about themselves. If the *cakravartin* was one whom all the other kings paid obeisance to, the Hero was a belligerent ruler, capable of vanquishing all his enemies.[114] This ideal is expressed in 'conventional expressions' like 'the one who subdued the circle of enemy kings', 'lion to the foe' (Arikēsari and Parakēsari—regular Pāṇḍyan and Cōḻa titles respectively) victor in battles, Jayanta, Āhavamalla, Śatrumalla, etc. There are, however, statements to the effect that almost every one of the rulers subdued the neighbouring kings like the Kēraḷa, Pāṇḍya, Cōḻa, Kaḷabhra, Tuḷu, Koṅkaṇa, Karṇāṭaka and so on, including sometimes the Kaliṅgas and Māgadhas of whom the authors of the *praśasti*s may have vaguely heard.[115] Historians have tried to 'reconstruct' the history of wars and alliances from such statements although they were uncertain as to whether descriptions like '*pratāpōpanata rājamaṇḍala*' in some records are only conventional glorifying terminology or convey any specific meaning'.[116] But even in cases where specific engagements are described, this uncertainty should apply, for there are well-known instances of conflicting statements from the opposite sides, the hero in a *praśasti* never losing a battle. Nilakanta Sastri, speaking about the statement in the Madras Museum Plates (Śrivarmaṅgalam Plates) about the Pallava king being deprived of his splendour at Kuḷumbūr where the Pāṇḍya, Māṟavarman Rājashimha I, captured innumerable elephants and horses from his enemy's forces, had with his characteristic brilliance pointed out that, that was the 'Pāṇḍyan version of the campaigns which led to the siege of Nandivarman Pallavamalla in Nandigrāma by the Tamil princes which was raised by the victorious general of the Pallava King....'[117] But even he does not go beyond that and raise the question whether such statements were nothing less than open flattery or whether they had any other purpose. It appears that rather than keeping an account of the military achievement, these statements served to create the ideal of a military hero, always valiant and successful in battles, an ideal which went a long way in the creation of the image necessary for political validation.

## THE PROTECTOR

Another major aspect of the portrait of the ruler in contemporary records is that he was the protector *par excellence.*[118] 'Protection' did not just mean the physical protection of subjects as a fee for which the king collected taxes (*rakṣābhōga*). This was too obvious to be stated. But 'protection' meant something more, the protection and maintenance of the ideal social order. This ideal social order was expressed in what is stated as the *dharma* of the caste, of the station. Quite clearly, it was the maintenance of the existing class structure, which was beneficial to those occupying the upper rungs of society. Moreover, by expressing this structure with its ideology in the paradigm of *varṇāśramadharma* and by presenting the ruler as protecting it, not only was he made out the protector of the existing class structure but, from the point of view of those ideologues, of the entire world. This, then, was another aspect of the validation of secular power at the hands of the priestly upper class.

The fact that the king was invariably presented as a kṣatriya with all the details attendant to that caste itself was in conformity with this ideal: for in the ideal social order kingship could be enjoyed only by kṣatriyas. Then, there was the express statement that the king looked after the *varṇāśramadharma.*[119] Statements using figures of speech, such as *varṇasāṁkarya*[120] (mixing of colours/*varṇas*) obtained only in painting, are numerous in the records. A common theme is that the king followed the canons laid down by Manu, that brahman protagonist of the *varṇāśramadharma* ideology.[121] This role of the king was often seen as a corollary of his role as the one who prevented the evils of Kali.[122] In fact, one of the records even puts these as complementary: 'causing the River of Manu to prosper and the River of Kali to dry up: *Manuvāṟuvaḷara, Kaliyāṟu vaṟuppa*'.[123] Again, this aspect of the king as protector is expressed by stating that he 'held' the kingdom, which expression means holding (*dharaṇa*) in order. The same idea is conveyed by expressions like *śāsana* (*v.*, to rule, different from *n.*, a charter or decree), *pālana* (to protect), *bharaṇa* (to govern), etc.[124] In all these cases, the two aspects of protection, i.e., the physical protection of the subjects and the protection of the ideal social order, are so beautifully mixed that the one shades off into the other, with optimum results. The king is portrayed as the wielder of *daṇda*, the rod which symbolises coercive power used for protection through the maintenance of law. The Pallavas are said to be always resorting to the *daṇda* in the right procedure.[125] Even the collection of taxes, which as *rakṣābhōga* was ideally the fee for protection, is justified by equating the king with the sun whose rays (*kara*, which expression in Sanskrit also means tax) although unbearable, are after all for the benefit of others.[126] Here we get a close relative of Kalidasa's description of Dilipa in the *Raghuvamśa:* 'For the prosperity of the subjects alone he collected tax from them. It is verily for repaying thousandfold that the sun takes away water.'[127] Incidentally, this and other points of contact between the *praśasti* literature on the one hand and the stereotypes in classical Sanskrit literature on the other, point to the source which inspired the ideals.

It may be seen that these three aspects—the claims to kṣatriya caste, the emulation of the *cakravartin* model and the approximation of the hero ideal—have a military emphasis about them as well. This seeks to validate the political position of the ruler, by lending legitimacy to his wielding coercive power for purposes of both aggrandisement and defence. Even this legitimacy is, in most part, sought through a borrowed idiom, namely the one already available in the stereotype about the king in north India in the Gupta and post-Gupta periods.

## THE DONOR IMAGE

A recurring theme in the documents of early medieval south India about the monarch is that he is a generous and munificent donor. The Udayēndiram Plates speak of the Pallavas having twigs (*pallava*) of hands which bow with the weight of water [accompanying] gifts.[128] The Kūṟam Plates say in two different places that the family of the Pallavas had not heard of one who was not a generous donor.[129] Speaking about individual rulers, the documents say that they gave away gifts generously to brahmans and the destitutes,[130] that they donated numberless *brahmadēya*s, and *dēvadāna*s[131] and so on. In fact, the picture of the king as a creator and patron of *brahmadēya*s is frequently repeated.[132] Similarly, most rulers are described as increasing their merit day by day by gifts of cows, gold and land.[133] The major *mahādāna*s discussed earlier such as the *gōsahasra*, *tulābhāra*, etc., are also to be considered here.

It is significant that in the above cases, except marginally, the gifts are not donations of charity, since they are not stated to be given to the poor, or those without property. Generally, it is given to 'deserving' brahmans, *śiṣṭas*, following the prescriptions in the *śāstra* literature.[134] Romila Thapar has discussed the significance of *dāna* and *dakṣiṇa* as forms of exchange in relation to the pre-Christian era of north Indian history with some incidental digression to the centuries of the Christian era as well.[135] It is possible to follow this line in the case of south India as well during our period. It can be seen that these *dāna*s here also served the function of gift exchange; what was received in return being explicitly stated as *puṇya* or merit and implicitly understood as recognition and legitimacy, the donor and the recipient both conferring status and material benefit on each other. Our records give us concrete evidence only of gift of land; there these two aspects are very clear. The Śivakāśi Plates of Vira Pāṇḍya expressly state that the donee composed a *praśasti* in praise of the donor and that the latter, pleased by the 'beauty of those *anuṣtups*' granted him the benefice in question.[136] Similarly, a highly fragmentary grant of Vira Cōḷa states that the king was shown by his moral preceptor (*dharmōpadēṣṭa*), a brahman Nīla, that giving away *brahmadēya*s to brahmans would clear the way for all his ancestors to heaven and the king, accordingly, promised a village, with an express request for blessing.[137] The debate concerning the 'real' purpose and effects of the land grants in early medieval India notwithstanding, what the donors and their panegyrists wanted to make the world (and perhaps even themselves) believe is clearly this: the exchange of wealth for merit and legitimacy. In the case of other forms of wealth gifted, such as gold, cattle, money, etc., of which we do not naturally have any records except statements in *praśasti*s that the king donated cows and gold apart from land, the same argument may be made. The recipients had to quality for the gifts, i.e., they had to be in a position to repay it in the form of merit and legitimacy. It may be recalled that the donation of the *mahadānas*, of which the *hiraṇyagarbha*, *tulābhāra* and *gōsahasra* form a part, is an achievement with which a number of south Indian rulers are credited.

This ideal of the monarch as a donor, especially of land, has its significance going beyond lending another hue to the image of royalty. This also indicates the monarch's positive role in accelerating social change and economic development through transformation of unsettled land to agrarian settlements or organising the peasantry in a more efficient manner. In a social formation which owed its existence primarily to this transformation, an image of the king highlighting his positive role in that transformation would convey a message more meaningful than just another aspect of royalty in conformity with an existing stereotype.

What is stated in the records about the munificence and generosity need not be taken literally. They at best wanted to project the picture of a patron. Even if they are taken literally, our analysis shows that rather than acts of charity, these gifts were investments of a discerning nature.

## DIVINE ATTRIBUTES

During the period under discussion, the monarchs were attributed divinity by several means.[138] This, to be sure, should not be confused with the 'divine right' as it was understood in the West.[139] This was achieved by equating the king with one of the gods by certain figures of speech, by adopting certain titles which are synonyms of the gods, by linking the king in kinship with the gods or heroes of the Puranic accounts, by stating in so many words that the king is god himself, by employing a pun on certain words so that descriptions of kings can deliberately sound like descriptions of gods, by identifying the role of gods in kings and so on and so forth.

Thus the king was always referred to as the husband (*bhartā*) of the Earth and of Prosperity.[140] This is a clear attribute of Viṣṇu, who is described as the husband of the Goddesses of the Earth and of Prosperity. The descriptions often take the stereotypical poetic forms in Sanskrit: the king acquiring these spouses in the typical kṣatriya form of marriage by capture or alternatively, these goddesses choosing the king as their spouse again in the typical kṣatriya form of marriage known as *svayamvara*. In more than one place the Pāṇḍya *praśasti*s describe the Pāṇḍyan king as 'undoing the commonness of the Earth',[141] which implies that the king abolished her polyandrous nature, i.e., that he made her his own. It is this role of being the husband of the Earth and of Prosperity that is expressed in the sharp and brief beginnings in the Tamil *meykkīrti* of Rājarāja: *Tirumagaḷ pōla perunilaccelyiyuntankkē urimai pūṇḍamai manakkoḷa*, and elaborated in the more ornate and involved passages in the *meykkirti*s of later rulers of the Cōḻa dynasty and of the Pāṇḍyas of the 'Second Empire'.

Then there was the use of figures of speech such as similes in which the king was equated with one of the gods or Puranic figures. Pallava Paramēśvaravarman is equated with Śiva,[142] Narasiṁha is stated to be the very human incarnation of Narasimha (Viṣṇu) himself,[143] Mahēndravarman is equated with Mahēndra.[144] Among the many exclusively Pāṇḍyan dynastic traditions discussed above are their participation in the Mahābhārata war,[145] sharing the throne with Indra,[146] acting as messengers to gods,[147] negotiating peace with Rāvaṇa[148] etc., which, through the Puranic connections, accord a certain amount of divinity to those rulers. The Vēḷvikuḍi Plates speak of the bewilderment of the Pallava king about Māṟavarman as to whether the latter was 'a human, a demon, Śiva, the Supreme Being (*Para Pūrusa*—Viṣṇu) or Indra.'[149] The same record speaks of Jaṭilavarman as equal to the son of Śiva (*Harasūnukalpaḥ*).[150] The Srīvaramaṅgalam Plates liken the birth of Jaṭilavarman, who was equal to Indra, from Māṟavarman to that of Budha from the Moon, of Pradyumna from Viṣṇu and of Subrahmaṇya from Śiva.[151] Speaking about Śrīvānavan Mahādevi, the wife of Parāntaka Viranārāyaṇa, the Larger Śinnamanūr

Plates say that she was what Śri was to Śrinivāsa and Paulōmi to Indra.[152] Similarly Sundara Pāṇḍya, the elder brother of Vīra Pāṇḍya, is described in the Śivakāśi Plates as standing in the same relation that Indra did to Viṣṇu.[153] In a passage which is as clumsy as it is lengthy, the Udayēndiram Plates describe Nandivarman having the qualities of different divine and Puranic figures, by employing figures of speech like the double entendre.[154]

The titles that many of the rulers adopted or were conferred on too had this effect. Many of them were names of gods or indicated divine qualities. In certain cases, the concrete achievement of a ruler is, again by some poetic technique, presented as one which was achieved earlier by a god or Puranic figure. Thus Narasiṁhavarman is described as the destroyer of Vātāpi, the city, even as Agastya had killed Vātāpi (the demon).[155] Rājarāja is described as *Ulakaḷanda Perumāḷ* (the Great One Who Measured the Earth—the so-called land survey of Rājarāja (1001 AD) being likened to the achievement of Trivikrama) and as none less than Śiva for conquering the land created by Bhārgava Rāma.[156] Kulaśēkhara, the Cēra king (844–883 AD) is compared to Viṣṇu for his victory over Mallaimānagar.[157] In a Kāñcipuram inscription, Raṅgapatākā, the queen of Narasimhavarman, is described by epithets whereby her husband is presented as Śiva himself.[158] In another verse in the same record she is said to have put an end to the boastfulness of Lakṣmī by having had Narasiṁha-Viṣṇu (*sic*) as her husband.[159] Examples like this are many which go to show the eagerness of the court poets to 'divinise' the king. The origin myths of the dynasties, which try to establish a connection between the dynasty on the one side and one of the gods on the other, is significant in this respect also. The construction and consecration of a large number of temples by the kings, the naming of these temples after the names of the kings themselves, etc., too are interesting in this regard. Especially noteworthy is the way in which 'Uḍaiyār Śrī Rājarājadevar' proudly boasted of the temple he built for 'Śrī Rājarājēśvaram Uḍaiyār' (the deity).

These divine attributes of royalty were again in conformity with the *Dharmaśāstra-purāṇa*s and *Kāvya-nāṭaka*s in Sanskrit. Manu says that the Creator created the king with the essential parts taken from Indra, Vāyu, Yama, Sūrya, Agni, Varuna, Candra and Kubera.[160] This idea in fact goes back to the *Dharmasūtra*s of Gautama and Āpastamba. The

*Nāradasmṛti* goes to the extent of stating that it is verily Indra who moves about on the earth in the guise of the king.[161] Statements like 'the king is none other than Viṣṇu (*nāviṣṇuh pṛthivīpatih*)' and 'king is god in his visible form (*rājā pratyaksa daivatam*)' which became a commonplace in premodern India actually derive from these ideas which were sought to be practised in actual situations.

This dimension of the image of royalty, namely, the divine attributes, has another significance. As the kingdom presided over by the king is presented as a microcosm of the universe presided over by god, the power and authority of the king is given a religious sanction. This equation of the king with god and concomitantly of treason with sacrilege went a long way in securing a place for the monarchical state within the political culture, given the character of the upper classes in society. This invocation of the religious symbols was resorted to in the process of legitimising the state and monarchy in it.

## SCHOLARSHIP AND PATRONAGE

Every ruler is presented both as a scholar and a patron of scholarship as also of the other arts.[162] Mahēndravarman is said to have been a painter (*Citrakārappuli*[163]), adept in music (*Saṅgītadhanah*),[164] a composer, a builder—in short, a curious mind (*Vicitracitta*).[165] Whatever the truth behind such claims, almost all the rulers of south India claimed greatness in scholarship. Moreover, it is stated that they were surrounded by a court of scholars and panegyrists. In fact, even this appears to be a replication of the court-style portrayed in the *kāvya-nāṭaka* literature in Sanskrit, a court of sycophants and poets such as *sūtas*, *māgadhas*,[166] etc. This too added colour to the portrait of the king as presented in court literature.

## ATTRACTIVE MIEN

Every ruler is described as of an attractive mien. In beauty he is invariably equated with Kāmadeva, the god of love.[167] On more than one occasion he is described as being coveted by beautiful damsels. Even in the so-called 'portrait' sculptures and paintings of the kings, we have the representation of iconographically perfect figures. The same is true of descriptions of rulers in literature. Nilakanta Sastri laments that 'no eyewitness has rendered to Rājarāja the service which Nuniz and Paes did to Kṛṣṇa Dēva Rāya' and states that[168] we have no 'authentic description' of Rājarāja. He is also inclined to reject the Tanjore bronze sometimes taken to be of Rājarāja as late and spurious, although he believes that 'a sculptured representation of a king (and queen) at Tiruviśalur may be of this king.' The conventional description, in a later commentary to one of the *nāṭakas of Kulaśekhara*, too does not appear to be a true account.[169] The *Ulās* and the *Piḷḷait tamils* also contain similar descriptions; in the cautious words of Nilakanta Sastri, they form 'a monotonous account of the amorous looks and the tell-tale acts of the women of the city who, at the sight of the king, become agitated and love-sick.'[170]

The foregoing examination brings together the different aspects which went into making the self-image of royalty sought to be projected in royalist literature, *praśastis* and court literature. One notices that this self-image is the result of a conscious attempt on the part of the ideologues in these polities to project a picture which was best suited to the cultural milieu of those ideologues. We saw that the first three aspects of the origin myths made a deliberate effort to identify the dynasties in question with well-known *kṣatriya* lineages of the North Indian *itihāsa-purāṇa* tradition in Sanskrit, thus underplaying the clearly south Indian origin of these dynasties. This is not to suggest that indigenous traditions about these dynasties were altogether disowned; indeed the Cōḷas and the Pāṇḍyas did faintly remember some of the more flattering events described in Sangam literature. By stressing, among other things, the lineages of a dynasty and the origin of individual rulers from pure descent on either line, it also accepted and propagated the idea of inheritability of virtues, typical of a caste society. Among the other aspects, the *kṣatriya* caste status, the *cakravartin* image and the hero ideal served the purpose of presenting the military character of kingship, which is primarily the king's claim to power. This military-political aspect of kingship is justified in presenting the king as wielding coercive power, both for defence and aggrandisement, the power which is also presented as the instrument of protection. Protection means the protection of the ideal moral order, apart from mere physical protection of the subjects. The positive role of the king in economic and social transformation is brought out by the donor image, especially in relation to land. Again the attributes of divinity invoke religious symbolism in an attempt to legitimise political power while attributes such as scholarship and patronage, beauty, etc., are meant to provide a cultural dimension to the image. Thus the king is presented not merely as a political figure; he had social and cultural roles to play as well. He was as much an organiser, a symbol of unity in society within the existing structure, as he was the pillar of the state.

It does not require any laboured argument to show that this image is of an ideal type and not at all of an individual. Even the ideal type could be seen to have adopted a readily available framework. It is this 'royal mystique', as Thomas R. Trautmann has put it, that emerges when an image of royalty is projected in the manifold ways discussed above.[171] When such tall claims are made by rulers and court poets of otherwise humble states like the Cēra and Pāṇḍyan kingdoms, then naturally one may ask the question, why such an image was presented. For, there definitely is a gap between the ideal and the actual. The poet's task in the courts may have been simple in presenting the silliest of skirmish as a very serious military engagement and the humble ruler of a small kingdom as the emperor of the three worlds; but the historian, in trying to 'dismantle the poet's edifice' will have to go beyond exposing the real face covered by this golden mask; he will also have to ask questions like why the suffering face of reality was so masked. It is only then that he can understand the nature of kingship and its position in the power structure of early medieval south India. Simplistic 'materialist' interpretations like those of shameless sycophancy being directly rewarded by vainglorious kings carried away by such flattery will not lead us too far. On the other hand, one will have to go beyond the court and see the amount of power exercised and authority enjoyed by the monarchy in the given power-structure. That is what is attempted in the following chapters.

## NOTES

1. In spite of the 'decent burial' given to the idea of Asiatic mode of production by scholars such as Perry Anderson, *Lineages of the Absolutist State*, (London, 1974); B. Hindess and P. Q. Hirst, *Pre-Capitalist Modes of Production*,

(London, 1975); R. A. L. H. Gunawardana, 'The Analysis of Pre-Colonial Social Formation in the Writings of Karl Marx', *Indian Historical Review*, Vol. II, no. 2, 1969; Bipan Chandra, 'Karl Marx: His Theories of Asian Societies and Colonial Rule' in Marion O' Callaghan, (ed.), *Sociological Theories, Race and Colonialism*, UNESCO, 1980; it is sought to be revived at a theoretical level by authors like Lawrence Krader, *The Asiatic Mode of Production*, (Budapest, 1979), and in the specific context of south India at an empirical level by scholars like Kathleen Gough, 'Mode of Production in Southern India' *Economic and Political Weekly*, Annual Number, 1980, and interestingly, Burton Stein, 'Politics, Peasants and the Deconstruction of Feudalism in Medieval India', *Journal of Peasant Studies*, Vol. XII, nos. 2 and 3,1985, esp. pp. 83–86. For the last mentioned author, any stick is good enough to beat the concept of feudalism in the Indian context.

2. The writings of C. Minakshi, *Administration and Social Life under the Pallavas* (Madras, 1938, 1977) and T. V. Mahalingam, *South Indian Polity* are good examples of this influence.

3. Below, n. 42 and 43. John Marr is quoted by Thomas R. Trautmann to have pointed out aspects of the Tamil bearings in the image of royalty: 'Traditions of Statecraft in Ancient India', in R.J. Moore (ed.), *Tradition and Politics* in *South Asia*, (New Delhi. 1979), p. 102.

4. This is taken for granted in standard works like K. A. Nilakanta Sastri, *History of South India*, 3rd edn. (London. 1966).

5. The origin of the Pallavas has been a free-for-all fishing pond for scholars with a number of red herrings. For a summary, see Minakshi. *op. cit.*, pp. 3–11 and Appendix III (by K. K. Pillay), pp. 35–38.

6. Cf. Romila Thapar, 'Origin Myths and Early Indian Historical Tradition', in *Ancient Indian Social History*, (New Delhi, 1978), p. 295.

7. M. G. S. Narayanan believes that the later Cēras of Makōtai (with whom we are concerned) followed the matrilineal system of succession and hence did not keep a genealogy. *Political and Social Conditions of Kerala under the Kulasekhara Empire, AD 800–1124*), Chapters on 'Chronology' and 'Nature of Monarchy'.

8. *Nandikkalambagam*, verse 43; see also C. Minakshi, *op. cit.*, p. 29. Does v. 2. II 4–6 in Kūṟam Plates of Paramēśvaravarman imply this by a *double entendre*? T. N. Subrahmanyan (ed.), *Thirty Pallava Copper Plates* (hereafter *TPCP*), (Madras, 1966), p. 46. Nṛipatungavarman is called *Kuruvaṁśavivardhana* in the Bāhūr Plates: *TPCP*, p. 268, 1.31. There is the statement in the *Suruci Jātaka* that king Bharata of the Candravaṁśa adopted the son of Bharadvāja. R. Thapar, *Ancient Indian Social History, op. cit.*, p. 340. See below, n. 9 for the Pallava claim to belong to the Bhāradvaja *gotra*. However, the Pallankōil Plates

describe Siṁhaviṣṇu as adorning the Śūryavaṁśa (*TPCP*, p. 27, and 12), which would suggest that Pallavas were not quite sure yet as to which line they should affiliate themselves.

9. This is usually found in the earlier Sanskrit charters such as the Ōmgōdu I Plates, *TPCP*, p. 279,1.1, Uruvappalli Plates, *TPCP*, p. 286, 1.15; Māṅkalur Plates, *TPCP*, p. 293, 1.14; Pikira Plates, *TPCP*, p. 299, 1.12; Neduṅgarāya Plates, *TPCP*, p. 306, 1.20; Vesānta Plates, *TPCP*, p. 311, 1.16; Viḷaveṭṭi Plates, *TPCP*, p. 316, 1.12; Cēntalur Plates *TPCP*, p. 325, 1.12; Ōmgōdu II Plates, *TPCP*, p. 344, II. 15–16; Śūra Plates, *TPCP*, p. 344, 1.15; Udayēndiram Plates of Nandivarman I, *TPCP*, p. 352, 1.10; Hirahaḍagaḷḷi Plates, *TPCP*, p. 363, 1.2, etc. The later records of the post-Siṁhavarman period trace the genealogy of the dynasty in which sage Bharadvāja has a prominent place.

10. J. C. Heesterman has pointed out that power and authority in Indian tradition are represented by *kṣatra* and *brahman* respectively: 'Power and Authority in Indian Tradition', in Moore, (ed.), *op. cit.*, esp. p. 65. In that case, the *brahmakṣatra* idea of the Pallavas stakes a claim to both power and authority. The inclusion of such kṣatriya-like brahmans as Drōṇa and Aśvatthāman in the Pallava genealogies is, thus, of great interest.

11. Some of these names are available in the damaged first plate of the Paḷḷankōil Plates: *TPCP*, pp. 26–27, II.3–6. For fuller lists, Kuram Plates, *TPCP*, p. 46, II. 9–11; Rāyakkoṭṭai Plates, *TPCP*, p. 103, II.3–10; Udayēndiram Plates, *TPCP*, p. 125, II. 8–12; Kāśākkudi Plates, *TPCP*, p. 157, II. 17–37; Pullūr Plates, *TPCP* pp. 186–87, II.1–3; Paṭṭattāḷmaṅgalam Plates *TPCP*, pp. 240–41, II. 5–10; Velūrpāḷaiyam Plates, *TPCP*, pp. 252–53, II. 6–8.

12. *South Indian Inscriptions*, (hereafter S.I.I.) Vol. I, p. 12.

13. *Viṣṇu Pūrāṇa*, 1,13. Earlier texts like the *Atharvaveda* VIII, 10; *Śatapatha Brāhmaṇa*, V, 3.5.4; *Mahābhārata*, Drōṇaparvan, 69, also remember this story. See also Romila Thapar, *Ancient Indian Social History, op. cit.*, pp. *307–08; idem, From Lineage to State*, (Bombay, 1984), pp. 118–19.

14. *TPCP*, pp. 158–59, II. 30–31.

15. *TPCP*, p. 103, II. 9–10.

16. *TPCP*, p. 253, II. 11–12. For a discussion of other details of this Nāga connection, T. V. Mahalingam, *Kancipuram in Early South Indian History*, (Bombay, 1969), pp. 17, 47; K. Gopalan, *History of the Pallavas of Kanchi*, (Madras, 1928), p. 50; ff. 196. For an interesting discussion, J. G. de Casparis, 'Inscriptions and South Asian Dynastic Traditions', in Moore, (ed.), *op. cit.*, pp. 106–8.

17. Thapar, *Ancient Indian Social History*, *op. cit.*, p. 280.

18. *TPCP*, p. 159, I.34, pp. 252–53, II. 6–8, and possibly p. 27,1.8. It is interesting that Aśōka is claimed as an ancestor by other dynasties in India as well. E.g., *Rājataraṅgiṇi*.

19. Tamil Varalātruk, Kaḻagam, (ed.), *Pāṇḍyar Ceppēdukal Pattu* (hereafter *PCP*), (Madras, 1967), pp. 95–96, II. 6–11.

20. *PCP*, 187, l.4.

21. *PCP*, pp. 19–20, ll.5–7.

22. *Viṣṇu Pūrāṇa*, IV, see Thapar, *Ancient Indian Social History*, *op. cit.*, pp. 294–325.

23. *PCP*, pp. 101–02, ll. 71–81. There are general statements in other records about the Candravaṁśa origin of the Pandyas. Śrī Varamaṅgalam Plates, *PCP*, p. 56–57, ll. 10–16; Smaller Śinnamanur Plates, *PCP*, p. 75), ll. 2–3; larger Śinnamanur Plates, *PCP*, p. 147, l.1, pp. 152–53, ll. 77–83; Śivakāśi Plates, *PCP*, p. 196, 1.46. The descriptions in the post-Sangam epic, *Cilappadikāram*, of the moon as the originator of the family of Pāṇḍyas (*tennavar kulattōr mudalvan* and *tennavar kula mudal*), of the Pāṇḍya as a successor of the moon (*mālaittiṅgal vaḻiyōn*) and of their family as that of the moon (*tiṅgaṭcelvan tirukkulam*) are also interesting in this respect.

24. Śankaranārāyaṇa, *Laghu Bhāskarīya Vyākhā*. See Narayanan, *op. cit.*, chapter on 'Nature of Monarchy'.

25. *Periya Purāṇam*, *Kaḻariṟṟarvār Nāyanār Purāṇam*.

26. Hermann Gundert, (ed.), *Kēraḷōtpatti*. See also Narayanan, *op. cit.*

27. *Travancore Archaeological Series*, (hereafter *TAS*). Vol. III, part 1, pp. 87–158.

28. *S.I.I.*, Vol. III, pt. 3, pp. 382–439.

29. *Epigraphia Indica* (hereafter *TAS*), Vol. XXII, pp. 213–66.

30. *E.I.*, Vol. XV, pp. 44–72.

31. George W. Spencer, 'Heirs Apparent: Fiction and Function in Chola Mythical Genealogies' in *Indian Economic and Social History Review*, Vol. XXI, no. 4, (1984), pp. 415–32.

32. The article of de Casparis, *op. cit.*, contains an illuminating discussion of the dynastic traditions cherished by ancient Indian rulers in their inscriptional records.

33. See, e.g., Pullur Plates, *TPCP*, p. 186, ll. 6–7; Taṇḍanōṭṭam Plates, *TPCP*, p. 207, ll. 6–8; Pattattāḷmaṅgalam Plates, *TPCP*, p. 240, ll. 8–9, etc.

34. See, e.g., Kāśākkuḍi Plates, *TPCP*, p. 160, ll. 44–5; Taṇḍantōṭṭam Plates, *TPCP*, p. 227, 1.2; Paṭṭattālmaṅgalam Plates, *TPCP*, p. 241, ll. 11–12; Velūrpāḷaiyam Plates, *TPC*, p. 254, l.22; Bāhūr Plates, *TPCP*, p. 266, ll. 12–13, etc.

35. This figures in all the early Sanskrit Charters. See also Kūṟam Plates, *TPCP*, p. 47, l.18; Kāśākkudi Plates, *TPCP*, p. 159, ll. 35–36, etc.

36. See, e.g., Unne Guravaya Pāḷaiyam Plates, *TPCP*, p. 71, ll. 8–9; Rēyūr Plates, *TPCP*, p. 84, ll. 8–9; Udayēndiram Plates of Nandivarman II Pallavamala, *TPCP*, p. 127, l.29; Kāśākkudi Plates, *TPCP*, p. 160, ll. 46–7; Bāhūr Plates,

*TPCP*, p. 267, ll.15–16; Uruvappalli Plates, *TPCP*, p. 286, ll. 12–13; Pikira Plates, *TPCP*, p. 299, 1.10, etc.

37. See, e.g., Unne Guravaya Pāḷaiyam Plates, *TPCP*, p. 71, ll. 1–2; Rēyūr Plates, *TPCP*, p. 84, l.6; Ōmgōḍu Plates, *TPCP*, p. 279, l. 2; Māṅkaḷūr Plates, *TPCP*, p. 293, ll. 15–16; etc. It is significant that this claim is rarely if ever made in the bilingual charters, in the post-Paramēśvaravarman period, perhaps indicating that the *yāgas* had gone out of fashion following the popularity acquired by the temple, *bhakti* cult. M. G. S. Narayanan and Kesavan Veluthat, 'Bhakti Movement in South India' in S. C. Malik (ed.) *Indian Movements: Some Aspects of Dissent, Protest and Reform*, (Simla), (1978).

38. Unne Guravaya Paḷaiyam Plates, *TPCP*, p. 71, ll. 6–7, Ōmgōdu Plates, *TPCP*, p. 279, ll. 6–7; Uruvappaḷḷi Plates, *TPCP*, p. 286, ll. 6–7; Pikira grant, *TPCP*, p. 299, ll. 5–6, etc. Even this claim in the compound *anēka-gō-hiraṇya-bhūmy-ādi pradānaih pravṛddha-dharmasañcaya*, is met with only in the early Sanskrit charters although the later, bilingual, charters are all grants of land.

39. *PCP*, p. 6, p. 85, p. 87, p. 182, et. *passim*.

40. *PCP*, editor's comments, *passim*. See also K. Kailasapathy, *Tamil Heroic Poetry*, (London, 1961).

41. Vēḷvikuḍi Plates, *PCP*, p. 22, 1.32. He or a namesake figures in some Sangam works as well. *Puṟanāṉūru*, 6, 9, 12, 15 etc.

42. Daḷavāypuram Plates, *PCP*, p. 103, 1.98; Larger Śiṉṉamaṉūr Plates, *PCP*, p. 154, II. 100–101.

43. Śrīvaramaṅgalam Plates, *PCP*, p. 57, II. 25–6.

44. K. A. Nilakanta Sastri, *The Colas*, 2nd edn. (Madras, 1975), p. 8. A reference to the Śibi story occurs, e.g., in *Puram*, 46.

45. *Ibid.* and the Larger Leyden Grant, above n. 29; Anbil Plates, above, n. 30, etc. These names figure in the Sangam literature.

46. Thapar, 'Genealogy as a Source of Social History', in *Ancient Indian Social History*, *op. cit.*, esp. p. 326.

47. Sastri, *Colas, op. cit.*, pp. 7–8; Thapar, '*Dana* and *Daksina* as Forms of Exchange', in *Ancient Indian Social History*, *op. cit.*, p. 118.

48. Paṭṭattāḷmaṅgalam Plates, *TPCP*, p. 241, l.12.

49. Paḷḷankōil Plates, *TPCP*, p. 27, 1.10.

50. Vēlūrpāḷaiyam Plates, *TPCP*, p. 253, l.14.

51. Above, n. 18.

52. Vēlūrpāḷaiyam Plates, *TPCP*, p. 253, l.11.

53. *Ibid.*, 1.10.

54. Bāhūr Plates, *TPCP*, p. 266, l.10.

55. *TPCP*, p. 46, ll. 14–16.

56. *Ibid.*, l.17.

57. *TPCP*, p. 27.

58. T. V. Mahalingam, *Kancipuram in Early South Indian History*, (Bombay, 1969), pp. 140–41; Minakshi; *op. cit.*, pp. 47–48, *idem, The Historical Sculptures of the Vaikunthapperumal Temple, Kanchi*, (Memoirs of the Archaeological Survey of India, no. 63), Sastri, *A History of South India*, p. 154.

59. *TPCP*, pp. 125–7, ll. 11–37.

60. *TPCP*, pp. 161–2, ll. 51–64.

61. *Ibid.*, ll. 64–6.

62. *Ibid.*, ll. 70–1.

63. *Ibid.*, l.63.

64. *TPCP*, p. 186, ll. 6–8,

65. *TPCP*, pp. 207–8.

66. *TPCP*, pp. 20–21, ll. 11–13.

67. *Ibid.*, ll. 13–14.

68. *TPCP*, pp. 253–54, ll. 13–30.

69. *TPCP*, pp. 265–8, ll. 2–24.

70. K. A. Nilakanta Sastri, *The Pandyan Kingdom*, (London, 1929).

71. *PCP*, pp. 20–21, ll. 12–26.

72. *Ibid.*, pp. 23–28, ll. 45–103.

73. *PCP*, p. 57, ll. 15–18.

74. *Ibid.*, l.19.

75. *PCP*, p. 75, ll. 1–3.

76. *Ibid.*, p. 76, ll. 14–28.

77. *PCP*, p. 97, ll. 23–29.

78. *Ibid.*, pp. 105–06, ll. 15136.

79. *PCP*, p. 146. (Editor's reconstruction)

80. *PCP*, p. 148, ll. 20–21; p. 149, ll. 28–29.

81. Above, n. 79.

82. *PCP*, pp. 187–88, ll. 71–12.

83. *Ibid.*, pp. 190–91, ll. 46–53.

84. For a detailed treatment in the south Indian context, Kesavan Veluthat, 'The Status of the Monarch: A Note on the Rituals Pertaining to Kingship and their Significance in the Tamil Country (600–1200 AD)' in *Proceedings of the Indian History Congress*, (Kurukshetra, 1982). For an analysis of the use of the claims to ksatriya *varṇa* in political validation, Romila Thapar, 'Legitimation Politique et Filiation: Le Varna Kshatriya en Inde du Nord', in *Annales*, no. 4, July–August, 1984, pp. 783–97.

85. *TPCP*, p. 27, 1.14.

86. *TPCP*, p. 164, p. 78.

87. Sastri, *Colas*, *op. cit.*, p. 186.

88. Kullūka on Manu II, 32. See also the appendix III added by K. K. Pillay to the revised edition of Minakshi, *Administration ..., op. cit.*, pp. 35–38.

89. Manu, II, 31, 2. See also R. S. Sharma, *Sudras in Ancient India*, 2nd edn., (Delhi, 1980), pp. 219–20.

90. Mahalingam, *South Indian Polity, op. cit.*, p. 46.

91. Minakshi, *Historical Sculpture ..., op. cit.*

92. Narayanan, *Political and Social ..., op. cit.*

93. Mahalingam, *South Indian Polity, op. cit.*, p. 46.

94. Minakshi, *Administration ..., op. cit.*, pp. 177, 1834.

95. *Ibid.*, pp. 185, 198.

96. Sastri, *Pandyan Kingdom* (reprint, 1975), pp. 47, 52, 149,150, *et passim.*

97. *Ibid.*

98. Sastri, *Colas*, pp. 125, 186. Also S.I.I., II, p. 383, v. 7; no. 42 of 1907.

99. See, e.g., Galetti, *The Dutch in Malabar*, p. 110, P. Shangoonni Menon, *A History of Travancore*, etc.

100. The *hiraṇyagarbha* and *tulābhara* form part of the celebrated sixteen *mahādānas.* P. V. Kane, *History of Dharmaśāstra*, Vol. II, part 2, pp. 870–72, *Matsyapurāṇa*, Chapters 274–89, devote more than 400 verses to detail the procedure of the *mahādānas.* Aparārka quotes not only these verses but adds further material from the *Bhaviṣyōttarapurāṇa.* Hemādri's *Dānakhaṇḍa* is more elaborate, and still more so is the *Dānamayūkha.* For details of *hiraṇyagarbha* see Kane, *op. cit.*, p. 872, and for a detailed analytical study, N. N. Bhattacharya, *Ancient Indian Rituals and their Social Content*, (Delhi, 1975), pp. 71–72.

101. D. D. Kosambi, *An Introduction to the Study of Indian History*, (Bombay, 1975 ed.), p. 318; Kosambi, *The Culture and Civilisation of Ancient India in Historical Outline*, (Delhi, 1972, ed.) p. 171 even observes that this ritual rebirth ensured for the chieftain entry into the world of caste society.

102. See above, n. 40.

103. S. I. I., IV, no. 537, XIII, nos. 44, 46.

104. Noboru Karashima, *South Indian History and Society*, (Bombay, 1984), p. 74, Table 9.

105. Above, n. 58.

106. *Periyapurāṇam*, Kaḻaṟiṟṟārivaṟ Nāyanār purāṇam, M. G. S. Narayanan, *Political and Social ..., op. cit.*

107. *ARE*, 1924, Part II, para 19–21; *E.I.*, Vol. XXI, pp. 184–93. See Sastri, *Colas, op. cit.*, pp. 354–60.

108. Kane, *op. cit.*, pp. 1215–18.

109. E.g., Vēlūrpālaiyam Plates, *TPCP*, p. 253, ll.8–9.

110. E.g., Paḻḻankōil Copper Plates, *TPCP*, p. 27, ll.91–10; Udayendiram Plates, *TPCP*, p. 126, II.24–5.

111. Above, n. 34. Also n. 39.

112. E.g., Paṭṭattāḷmaṅgalam Plates, *TPCP*, p. 241, II.17–8.

113. The plays of Kulaśēkhara, viz. *Tapatīsamvarana* and *Subhadrādhanañjaya* make this statement. M.G.S. Narayanan, *Political ...*, Chapters on Chronology and Arts and Literature.

114. Burton Stein, *All the King's Mana*, (Madras, 1984), pp. 31–3 believes that the hero ideal in Tamil kingship, like the one he quotes from the Kūṟam Plates of Paramēśvaravarman, 'might have been taken from a *puram* poem of the classical poetry'. While we do not deny the *Puram* or for that matter of any of the old Sangam traditions, this exclusiveness will have to be questioned. In fact, this is the stereotypical war-hero ideal of any early Indian king.

115. Above, n. 112; Pullur Plates, *TPCP*, p. 186, ll. 8–10; Kūṟam Plates, *TPCP*, p. 47, l.15. Burton Stein, *op. cit.*, p. 40 presents the statements in the Paṭṭattāḷmangalam and Pullūr Plates as evidence enough to show that the Kaḷabhras were 'among the allies' of Nandivarman. This is not the case. In fact, several generations before Nandivarman was Paramēśvaravarman who makes in his Kuram Plates a similar claim to have subjugated some of these houses including the Kaḷabhras. This is a clear case of misrepresenting evidence to support one's argument: in this case to 'show' that the idea of 'moral kingship' derived from the Jains, the Kaḷabhras being identified as Jains!

116. T. V. Mahalingam, *Kancipuram ...*, *op. cit.*

117. Sastri, *Pandyan Kingdom*, *op. cit.*, p. 51.

118. For a treatment, B. D. Chattopadhyaya, 'Political Processes and Structure of Polity in Early Medieval India' Presidential Address, Section I, Ancient India, Indian History Congress, Burdwan, 1983.

119. Almost all the Sanskrit charters of the Pallavas make this claim. Even in the bilingual charters, this is met with, *TPCP*, *passim*. This is true of records of the Pandyas and Cōḻas.

120. *TPCP.*

121. The *Periyapurāṇam* account of the coronation of Cēramān Perumāḷ, *above*, n. 106, makes a reference to this. So do records of the Pāṇḍyas like the Śrīvaramaṅgalam Plates, *PCP*, p. 59, l. 48; Larger Śinnamanūr Plates, *PCP*, 155, l. 115.

122. Above, n. 36.

123. *P.C.P.*

124. See details in J. D. M. Derrett, 'Bhū-bharaṇa, Bhū-Palana, Bhū-bhojaṇa: An Indian Conundrum', in *Bulletin of the School of Oriental and African Studies*, Vol. XXII, no. 11 (1959), pp. 108–23.

125. Kūṟam Plates, *TPCP*, p. 46, 1.7.

126. Kāśākkudi Plates, *TPCP*, p. 160, 1.43.

127. Another instance of almost bodily lifting Kālidasa's lines occurs in a fragmentary *praśasti of Vīra* Cōḻa where, speaking of Manu, it is said that Manu 'was born as the first king like *praṇava* in all *chandas*', IA, IX, p. 47, II.7–8; *Āsit kṣitibhṛtām ādyah pranavaḥ chandasāmiva.* This substitutes *kṣitibhṛt* for Kalidasa's *mahikṣit* in *Raghuvamsa*, I, 2.

128. *Dānāmbhu=bhāra=vinamat=kara=pallava: TPCP*, p. 125, l.7.

129. *TPCP*, p. 46, II. 7–8; 12–13.

130. E.g. *PCP*, p. 21, pp. 22–3; 61; p. 77, ll. 26.7, etc. But, in most grants, it is expressly stated that the donees were brahman worthies (*śiṣṭa*) versed in Vedas, Śāstras and rituals.

131. Cf. Daḷavāypuram Plates, *PCP*, p. 105–06, ll. 33–34; 122–23.

132. E.g. The Kanyākumari inscription of Vīra Rājēndra, *TAS*, III, p. 143.

133. Above, n. 38.

134. Above, n. 130.

135. R. Thapar, '*Dāna* and *Dākṣiṇa* as Forms of Exchange', *Ancient Indian Social History*, *op. cit.*, pp. 105–21.

136. *PCP*, p. 192, II. 63–64.

137. *I.A.*, IX, (1880), p. 47, Plate Va, ll. 1–7.

138. For an elaborate treatment, Kesavan Veluthat, 'Royalty and Divinity: Legitimisation of Monarchical Power in South India', *Proceedings of the Indian History Congress*, Hydrabad, 1979, pp. 241–39.

139. R. S. Sharma, *Aspects of Political Ideas and Institutions in Ancient India*, (3rd ed. Delhi, 1991) p. 307.

140. Above, n. 33, Also. Vēḷvikuḍi Plates, *PCP*, p. 20, II. 18–19; Larger Śinnamanūr Plates, *PCP*, p. 147, 1.4.

141. E.g., Smaller Śinnamanūr Plates, *PCP.* p. 75, l.11.

142. Kūṟam Plates, *TPCP*, p. 46, ll. 4–6.

143. *Ibid.*, p. 47, ll.14–15.

144. *Ibid.*, ll. 17–18.

145. Above, n. 39.

146. *Ibid.*

147. *Ibid.*

148. *Ibid.*

149. Vēḷvikuḍi Plates, *PCP*, p. 21, ll. 21–23.

150. *Ibid.*, l. 25.

151. Śrivaramaṅgalam Plates, *PCP*, p. 57, ll. 16–19.

152. Larger Śinnamanūr Plates, *PCP*, p. 149, ll. 28–29.

153. Śivakāśi Plates, *PCP*, p. 188, l.12.

154. *TPCP*, pp. 126–27, ll. 19–29.

155. Udayēndiram Plates, *TPCP*, p. 125, l.14.

156. Tiruvālaṅgāḍu Plates, above, n. 28.

157. T. A. Gopinatha Rao, *History of Srivaisnans*, (Madras, 1917).

158. S. I. I., Vol. I, i. no. 29.

159. *Ibid.*

160. Manu, V, 96; VII, 4,9. See Heesterman's interpretation, *op. cit.*, p. 74.

161. Kane, *History of Dharmasastra*, *op. cit.*, Vol. III, pp. 23–27.

162. See, e.g., Udayēndiram Plates, *TPCP*, p. 126, 1.27.

163. Minakshi, *op. cit.*, pp. 50–51 for this and other *birndas.*

164. *Ibid.*

165. Maṇḍagappaṭṭu inscription.

166. In fact even these words are used as such in *Periyapurāṇam*, Tirunagaracciṟappu, v. 21.

167. See e.g., Udayēndiram Plates, *TPCP*, p. 127, 1.30; Kāśākkudi Plates, *TPCP*, p. 163, II. 67–8; S.I.I., Vol. I, no. 24.

168. Sastri, *Colas*, *op. cit.*

169. Narayanan, *Politcal* ..., *op. cit.*

170. Sastri, *Colas*, *op. cit.*

171. Trautmann, *op. cit.*

Two

# The King and 'His Men'

Against the background of the image of royalty examined in the previous chapter, the nature of monarchy can be examined meaningfully by looking at, on the one side, the governmental organisation of the kingdoms and, on the other, its power base in society. The present chapter proposes to analyse the form and organisation of the king's government in early medieval south India. There is, to be sure, a spate of literature on the 'administrative system' in the different kingdoms; but in most of such writings there is a mixing up of the actual and the ideal, of the reality and the image. This results in a highly blurred picture of the governmental structure.[1] Hence the position of the monarch within the power structure does not emerge with clarity. This approach has been rightly exposed by Burton Stein.[2] But his alternative[3] suffers from the fact that it does not stand the test of evidence. The present discussion does not follow the conventional pattern, assuming an administrative system with typical divisions into 'central', 'provincial', 'local' etc., nor does it take the other position of rejecting governmental machinery with its system of control over the resource base and coercive power. In this chapter, we will examine how the king functioned in his governmental system, with his court of advisers and ministers and a large number of royal functionaries. So also, there will be a concern with the different titles assumed by, or conferred on, the governmental functionaries and their correlation with the powers they exercised, with a view to bringing out the nature of 'bureaucracy' in the state. The frequency with which these functionaries figure in the records over different periods of time points to the degree of the king's direct involvement in the administration. It would also clarify the changing mechanism of the king's government in the process of exercising its power and authority in the kingdoms from time to time.

## THE KING

The royalist literature of early medieval south India presents the picture of a polity presided over by the typical kṣatriya monarch at the centre, attended by the entire paraphernalia adjunct to such a system.[4] But the numerous other documents, when examined carefully, yield a picture which is not as brilliant, thus conflicting with this image of royalty. This contradiction contained in the contemporary sources was lost sight of by the conventional historians;[5] it has also made a number of scholars in this generation working on south Indian history discredit both the royalist literature and the conventional historiography.[6] In our approach, we believe that a careful analysis of the sources relating to the governmental organisation will yield a somewhat realistic picture that will enable raising and answering questions about the gulf between the image and the reality as well as about the necessity on the part of the rulers to have created an image so far removed from reality.

The form of government in the states under discussion from the seventh century onwards was doubtless monarchical. This is clear from the fact that the thousands of inscriptions acknowledge the authority of the king in various ways. Whatever the area of their provenance, the inscriptions of the king, the chiefs and the local bodies in most cases are dated in the regnal years of the Pallava, Pāṇḍya, Cēra or Cōḻa dynasts. This indicates that the authority of the respective ruler was acknowledged within the boundaries of the kingdom, in the core as well as the periphery, and even in areas under the rule of a chiefly family. This authority, which the records acknowledge, cannot be brushed aside as just 'ritual' because it is reflected in the actual processes of the administration.

In fact, a point raised over and over again in the writings of Burton Stein and George W. Spencer is that monarchy was weak and concomitantly that polity in the Cō̤ḻa state (with which they are concerned) was weakly organised.[7] While we do not endorse the conventional view of a top-heavy monarchical state, it is not possible to favour this position either. In Stein's understanding of the segmentary state, the Cō̤ḻa house exercised authority only in the core region of Kaveri valley.[8] In other areas they enjoyed at best a ritual hegemony. Spencer accepts this assumption implicitly and argues, following the anthropological model presented by David Kaplan, that the huge monuments like the great temples of Tanjavur and Gaṅgaikkoṇḍacō̤ḻapuram which the Cō̤ḻas had built were part of a 'system-maintaining mechanism' in a 'weakly organized polity'.[9] The Cō̤ḻa conquest of Śri Lanka and Śri Vijaya are looked upon by him as raids of plunder with which the state was sustained in the absence of a regular revenue system. His views are echoed by Venkat Raghottam.[10]

Neither of these arguments holds much water. In the case of the monuments, both the huge ones taken up as well as the not-so-huge ones and the additions effected to existing ones, both far and near, represent in concrete terms the power of the ruler. They indicate the resources the ruler could mobilise both in physical and economic terms and, as Stein has himself said elsewhere, catches the imagination of the onlooker 'like the pyramids'.[11] Moreover, since the temples had a greater role to play in society than just being architectural monuments, they communicate with those sections of society which mattered in the existing social structure, thus coming to terms with them. Again, while the significance of plunder in warfare is not denied and the role of war as a means of holding together the military chiefs is recognised, the view that this plunder made up for the slender resources of the Cō̤ḻa state is not acceptable. We have positive evidence of revenue from agriculture and marginally trade and plunder may at best have supplemented these. It has been shown that even if these campaigns were plundering raids, they helped maintain the armies and their fighting spirit. This necessarily would have led to a great amount of co-operation among the soldiers, the locality chiefs who led them and the overlord, thereby strengthening the state and adding prestige to it.[12]

In most cases the rule of succession to the throne is clear. It was hereditary and generally of patrilineal descent. In a few cases there is evidence to show that primogeniture was overlooked for considerations not clear to us. Even in the Vaikuṇṭhapperumal temple record, which is presented as evidence to show the elective character of monarchy, the position is that of an obsession on the part of the 'king-makers' with an incumbent of pure descent, and hence the choice of a member of one of the 'collateral' lines of the same dynasty to the throne when the 'main' line became extinct.[13] In the case of the Cēras, however, there is no direct evidence to show the rule of succession. It was certainly hereditary, and it has been convincingly argued that it was matrilineal in character, conforming to the system of succession prevalent among the non-brahman upper castes in Kerala.[14]

The fact of hereditary succession made it necessary to ensure—at least in the claims—an heir worthy of the throne and hence the concern in the documents with the purity of lineage. The diplomatic and military considerations involved in the complex system of matrimonial alliances among the royal families and between the royal families on the one side and the chiefly families on the other may have been real enough; but the concern with an offspring of a worthy ancestry on both sides would appear to be an equally possible factor especially because the records make explicit statements to this effect.[15]

If, thus, the form of government was hereditary monarchy, the question as to how the government of the king functioned will have to be raised. Burton Stein does not appear to recognise this basic fact. For him the Cōḻas (as he is taking up that state for detailed study) were only the leaders of the *nāṭṭār* of the deltaic portion of the Cōḻamandalam which formed, according to him, their *nāḍu*.[16] This suppresses all evidence which shows the hereditary, monarchical, character of the Cōḻa dynasty. Our reservations about the image of royalty as discussed in the previous chapter notwithstanding, we see from other records that the king exercised a considerable amount of power. He is generally referred to in the inscriptions as *kō* (the king), *perumāḷ, perumān aḍigaḷ* (the great one); and at times by high-sounding expressions like *rāja-rājādhiraja* and *kō-kōnmai-koṇḍān* (king of kings) and *kō-nērinmaikoṇḍān* (the unmatched king). He issued royal orders which are generally called *āṇai* (Sanskrit *ājñā*). There is a statement in the Vaikuṇṭhapperumāḷ temple record that when Nandivarman was crowned, he was invested with all royal insignia together with the right to issue royal commands (*tiruvāṇai*) under the Pallava title, Viḍelviḍugu.[17] The Jewish Copper Plates of Bhāskara Ravivarman describe their contents as the *prasāda* of the king.[18] The Bṛihadiśvara Temple inscriptions claim themselves to be the *śāsana* of Rājarāja.[19] It is stated in the *Dharmaśātra* literature that secular grants issued by the king are called *prasāda*, while religious ones are called *śāsana*.[20]

Rājarāja I referred to his own *āṇaai* (*nam āṇai*).[21] The temple authorities of Tiruvallam were required to make an account of the income and expenditure of the temple as per the royal order and the royal writ (*tiru-āṇaikkum tiru-ōlaikkum uriya vaṇṇam*).[22] If the order was the *āṇai*, the writ was the *ōlai*, literally the palm leaf on which the order was inscribed. The *ōlai* was often described ceremoniously as the *tirumandira ōlai*, 'the *ōlai* of the sacred word'. A letter communicating the royal orders was generally called *śrimukam* or *tirumukam*, there being practically no distinction between the *tirumandira ōlai* and *tirumukam*. The statement in the records, put into the mouth of the men of locality, that '[we] rose to welcome it [the *śrimukham*], saluted it and placed it on our heads before taking it and reading it', may be the highly formal and deferential official formula[23] for recording the receipt of royal orders; but even there it is clear that at least such an official formula was demanded. It would also show that the king appropriated the right to grant land both settled and unsettled and that the local magnates acquiesced. This is clear from the large number of instances granting land in the Pallava, Pāṇḍya and Cōḻa kingdoms, which most of the copper plates and some of the stone inscriptions record. In the case of the Cēra kingdom, however, we have only one instance of a royal grant, viz., the Jewish Copper Plates of Bhāskara Ravi.[24] In fact, as stated earlier, many royal inscriptions on copper have not come down to us from that kingdom. Two other records, the Syrian Christian Copper Plates[25] and the Mānypalli plates[26] are granted by the chiefs of Vēṇāḍu, Ayyan Aḍigal and Śrivallabhan Kōta respectively. The former acknowledged the authority of the Cēra overlord by both dating the record in his regnal year and making the grant in the presence of one of his deputies (*kōil adhikārigal*) while the latter appears to be relatively independent. This may be explained by the fact that, at the time of this grant, the Cēra sovereign, Bhāskara Ravi, was still a minor and had not assumed full powers,[27] and that the locality chief asserted himself in this situation, thereby suggesting that this is one of those typical exceptions which prove the rule. That this practice was repeated in case after case shows that the monarch's authority in this matter was hardly questioned. The process of the order issuing from the king and getting reduced to writing and communicated to the addressees such as the locality groups of the *nāḍu, sabhā* and *ūr* is too well known to be repeated here.

## THE ROYAL COURT

There is reference in the records to show the existence of a royal court. Although the evidence is slender and not sufficient to tell us the exact nature of its function, it would appear that this court consisted of the more important functionaries of the king's government, his advisers and priests, those who were close to the king as the captain of body-guards and perhaps even ministers. Mention of such councils of ministers is made at least in the cases of the Pallavas and Cēras and references to individual *mantrin*s in the Pāṇḍyan court also may indicate the same. This, of course, should not be confused with the highly idealised and necessarily confused picture presented by Mahalingam about the royal court,[28] nor with that projected by Minakshi in relation to the situation obtaining in the Pallava kingdom with a couple of epigraphical references sought to be 'supported' by statements from the *śāstra* literature and the much later *Periyapurāṇam* with a singular lack of chronological and spatial sense.[29] Our understanding of the court is, on the other hand, of something of a *darbār* with the figures referred to above attending it. The Vaikuṇṭhapperūmaḷ temple record speaks of the *mantrimaṇḍala, mātras, mūlaprakṛtis, ghaṭikaiyār* and *ubhayagaṇattār* as constituting the delegation to Hiraṇyavarman to petition for a worthy incumbent to the Pallava throne.[30] The same set of people are stated in the record to have performed the anointment of Pallavamalla. Although this seems to be the only record from that kingdom apart from the *praśasti*s to mention the court, it is clear enough that there was a body consisting of important men who were concerned with royal succession and related problems.

A similar situation is met with in the case of the Cēra kingdom in the near contemporary work, *Periyapurāṇam*.[31] There, Cēramān

Perumāḷ, who was meditating in the temple of Tiruvañjaikkaḷam, was invited by the Cēra ministers (*Cēramaiccar*) to take up the reigns of the kingdom. Perhaps a *double entendre* employed by the astronomer in the court of Sthāṇu Ravi Kulaśēkhara suggests that he had a council with eight members.[32] There is a statement in a medieval chronicle in Malayalam that in the Cēra capital of Mahōdayapuram was a council of eight celibate brahmans, two each from four different village settlements of the brahmans near the capital, and having their seats in four temples in the city. These villages are Iruṅgāṭikkūṭal, Mūḻikkaḷam, Airāṇikkaḷam and Paṟavūr and the temples in the capital associated with them are Ciṅgapuram Taḷi, Mēlttaḷi, Kīḻttaḷi and Neṭiya Taḷi respectively.[33] This body, known as the *nālu taḷi*, is mentioned at least in two inscriptions, both presenting it as forming part of the Cēra king's entourage.[34] Another character figuring in one of the records as part of this entourage is what is called 'The Thousand' or the *Āyiram*.[35] It has been convincingly shown that this was the captain of the king's personal body-guards, his companions of honour.[36] Yet another figure who is explicitly stated as a member of the council of ministers (*amaiccuḷḷurutti*) was the *kōil adhikārikaḷ* who is shown as a junior member of the Cēra royal house and with considerable power.[37] Occasionally, the locality chiefs who stood in subordinate relationship with the Cēra overlord also attended such councils. This is clear from at least two instances: a Kollam Ramēśvarasvāmin temple inscription records the convention of a Cēra court in Quilon at the capital of the chief of Vēṇāḍu and the Jewish Copper Plates is witnessed by six of the locality chiefs.[38] They present the picture of typical feudal courts, held in both the king's headquarters and that of the feudatory chiefs.

In the case of the Pāṇḍyas, although there is no direct mention of such a court or council, we notice the presence of *mantrins*. The Ānamalai records speak of Māṟan Kāri as the *uttaramantrin*.[39] The larger Śinnamanūr Plates speak of a *mantrin* who was a *dharmōpadēṣṭā*.[40] The Śivakāsī Plates also refer to a certain *Dramiḍa mahārāja*, the *uttaramantrin*, who was in charge of *sandhivigraha*. He is called *Tamiḻppēraraiyan* in the Tamil portion, and is said to have held the important office of the *mandira-ōlai-nāyagam*[41] At least in the case of a certain Raṇakīrtti, who is described as the *uḷviṭṭu-sēvaka* in an inscription of Māṟan Caṭayan from Viḻiñjam,[42] the evidence is to suggest that he was a companion of honour to the king. To the same group may be added the *Tennavan āpattudavidgaḷ* or their chief.[43] We also come across a certain Sāmantan Gaṇapati, who is called Pāṇḍi Amritamaṅgalavaraiyan and described as a *mahāsāmanta* of the king.[44] Thus even though there is no explicit mention of a council or a court in the case of the Pāṇḍyan kingdom, almost all its constituents are found there, much in the same pattern as in the other two cases taken up earlier.

Again in the case of the Cōḻas, the inscriptions do not help us identify a council of ministers there. There is, however, the mention of a *purōhita* who was the *dharmōpadēṣṭā* of a Cōḻa king.[45] To this group may be added the *rājagurus,* a number of whom are found in Cōḻa records, especially as their role is seen to be similar to that of the *dharmōpadēṣṭā*.[46] A large number of senior functionaries, such as *adhikāri, vāyil keṭpār, tirumandira-ōlai,* etc., are found in the records, who in all probability moved in the closest quarters of the king.[47] Nilakanta Sastri takes the body called *uḍankūṭṭam* mentioned in Cōḻa inscriptions as 'the nearest approach to a council of ministers' in itself.[48] But M. G. S. Narayanan has demonstrated that this constituted a group of body-guards of the king, answering to the *Tennavan āpattudavigal* in the Pandyan and the *Āyiram* of the Cēra records.[49] *Uḍankūṭṭam* may have been represented by its captain and we do get a few references to *adhikāris* of the *uḍankūṭṭam*. This picture may be supplemented by details available in the *Kaliṅgattupparaṇi* about the court of Kulōttuṅga in Kāñcīpuram with all the pomp and heraldry there.[50] So also, references in *Periyapurāṇam* are useful in this respects.[51]

It would appear, therefore, that the monarchs in the four states taken up for consideration maintained a court. This court, with the brahman councillors, priests and preceptors, with official functionaries such as the *adhikāris, tiru-mandira-ōlai-nāyagams, vāyil kētpār,* etc., with the chief of the king's retainers who was also a close confidant and sometimes with the major *sāmantas* perhaps conformed to the one envisaged in the *dharmaśāstra* literature. It is interesting to note that at least in the case of Vēṇādu which was held by hereditary chiefs under the overlordship of the Cēras there is a record to show that such courts were simulated if in miniature in the centres of the chiefly rule.[52]

## THE ROYAL FUNCTIONARIES

### I. Preliminaries

Closely related to the question of the king and his court is the problem of the nature of the bureaucracy, if any existed, and its role in the government. We have seen that the royal court or council itself contained personages holding high offices of the state. Whether they can be described to have constituted a bureaucracy or not, what the mode of their recruitment and payment was and in what relation they stood to the king—these are questions, the answers to which can throw light on the reality of the power structure and the nature of the state in general. Such a detailed analysis is possible in the case of the Cōḻa state with its incomparably large number of records though not in other cases. This state has been described in the past by historians like Nilakanta Sastri as a centralised imperial structure distinguished by 'the superior executive strength it was able to develop by bringing into existence a highly organised and thoroughly efficient bureaucracy.'[53] In recent years, however, there has been some controversy about this position, with scholars rejecting and endorsing this view, depending upon the methodological orientation and frame of reference of each scholar.[54] The rejection, by Burton Stein, is based on an impressionistic study of the sources[55] as much as its positing, by Nilakanta Sastri, was. Subbarayalu makes use of a statistical study of the inscriptions[56] and Karashima brings to bear on it further refinement.[57] We do not accept Nilakanta Sastri's idea of a strong, centralised, state bulwarked by a 'numerous and powerful' bureaucracy; nor do we reject the role of any state or royal functionary altogether. At the same time, we are not confident enough to use the expression 'bureaucracy' in describing the large number of royal functionaries or agents found in the records and analysed systematically by Karashima and Subbarayalu. Hence we prefer a less committed, if less colourful, term, 'functionaries'. This section may be devoted to an examination of the various functionaries and their role in the king's government.

Before taking up a thorough examination of the king's government and the role of his functionaries there, a few preliminary remarks about our sources and our method of using them may be necessary. The most important category of sources for this purpose are the stone inscriptions from the temples and other centres of importance. These inscriptions contain a large number of personal names in various capacities. In fact, the functions and other details of a large number of offices and functionaries can be delineated from a full analysis of these personal names. The systematic statistical analysis which they have been subjected to helps in a more scientific tackling of the problem[58] than could have been made by both the conventional historians like Nilakanta Sastri and their critics like Burton Stein.

## II. The Titles and Their Significance

The inscriptions strike us with a number of persons holding different titles in a regular pattern. This starts increasing from the time of Parāntaka and reaches the height in the post-Rājarāja I period.[59] These title-holders are seen to be directly linked with the affairs of the king's government, for there is a striking correspondence between what may be presumed as royal offices and these title-holders.[60] One also notices a gradation in the various titles and also in the different offices and, significantly, a correspondence between the titles and offices of a comparable rank.[61] This point is entirely lost sight of by Burton Stein. As pointed out earlier, not only does he miss the gradation among the different titles, but he also brackets them together and thus roughly identifies the title-holders with the locality chiefs discussed below.[62] This leads to a major misunderstanding, which forms one of the bases of Stein's thesis on the Cō̤la state.[63]

In spite of differences in length ranging from just one word or segment to as many as five or even more, there is a strikingly regular pattern in the way in which the personal names appear in the Cō̤la inscriptions.[64] If a name consists of just one segment it is generally either the name of the person (ego) or a title he bears. If it is a name with two segments, the former would represent the father's name and the latter, the ego's. It is also seen in a few such two-segment names, that the former segment shows the identity of the *ūr* or *nāḍu* division to which the person belongs and the latter, his title, e.g., Ciṟṟiṅgan-uḍaiyān=Iṅgānāṭṭū-Pallavaraiyan.[65]

In most three-segment names, the pattern is a place name (*ūr* or *nāḍu*) along with a term indicating possession or belonging such as *uḍaiyān, kiḻān, kiḻavan* in the first segment, the father's name in the second segment and the ego's name in the third.[66] Cases with the variation of place name+possessor followed by the ego's name and a title are also common.[67] So are a *gotra* name + father + ego in such three-segment names of Brahmans.[68] In the case of names with more than three segments there is invariably a title which in most cases is an *alias.* Thus we have Ciṟṟiṅgan-uḍaiyān = Paṭṭan = Kaṇṇan-āna = Iṅgānāttu-Pallavaraiyan.[69] Even though this is normally the order, cases such as, for example, Iṅganāṭṭu-Pallavaraiyan = Ciṟṟiṅgan-uḍaiyān = Paṭṭan = Kaṇṇan, or even with the less important segments dropped off, are found.

About twenty per cent of the total population figuring in inscriptions bear names with the place name + possessor segment, the expressions *uḍaiyān, kiḻān* and *kiḻavan* signifying possession.[70] Since we find more than one who 'possesses' the same village, the term should be taken to mean one who possesses some land in a village.[71] It cannot certainly mean simply a resident of the village for not all the residents of the village bore this segment in their names. This inference is supported by a large number of instances quoted by Subbarayalu and Karashima in their separate studies.[72] To take just one instance, a Kuḍumiyamalai inscription of 1232 AD records the sale of land by the *ūr* of Viśalūr,[73] where the new owner of land is permitted to enjoy all privileges due to the holder of the title *kiḻavan* (of a village). If it was a brahman landholder he was by the same standards a *brahmadeyak-kiḻavan*; but the relative infrequency of names with segments like this, in spite of the large number of brahman landowners, may be explained as a result of the preference of brahmans to identify themselves by either their *gōtra* or ancestral village. That the *uḍaiyān* title indicated landownership is proved further by the fact that of the 119 members of the *ūr* assembly identified by names in the Cōḻa inscriptions more than 60 per cent bore the *uḍaiyān* title;[74] and that the *ūr* consisted of only the chief landholders of the village is an accepted fact. Even in the case of the remaining 40 per cent, it is suggested that the *uḍaiyān* title is omitted to avoid repetition when two or more *uḍaiyār* of the same village are mentioned in quick succession.[75] When the significance of segments with the *uḍaiyān* suffix is thus recognised as related to landownership, the increase in names with this segment as the Cōḻa rule progressed in time may be explained as indicating the growth of private property in land and the growing importance of landowning groups.

A similar title indicating ownership of land together perhaps with the caste status was *vēḷān*, which is generally substituted for the father's name in a multi-segment name.[76] Segments with *vēḷān* suffixed to the name of a village or *nāḍu* or some other title also occur, e.g., Kōnilam-uṭaiyan=Vēḷān-ana Amparattu-vēḷān.[77] Closely related to *vēḷān* but superior in status is the title *mūvēndavēḷān* which is one of the most important titles found in the personal names in Cōḻa records.[78] Of the names ending with this title, which is always a suffix in an *alias,* about 94 per cent prefix the name or the title or a Cōḻa king e.g., Rājarāja-*mūvēndavēḷān* or Rājakēsari-*mūvēndavēḷān*, which indicates that the title was conferred by the king.[79] In fact, there is at least one record which states in so many words that the name Rājakēsari-*mūvēndavēḷān* was a conferred title (*paṭṭam kaṭṭiṇa peyar*).[80] The title *mūvēndavēḷān* is an exclusively Cōḻa title and it begins to make its appearance only from the time of Parāntaka.[81] Most *mūvēndavēḷān*s also bore the *uḍaiyān* title in an earlier segment in their names (118 out of 307) or other titles such as *kiḻān, kiḻavan* (12 each) or else prefixed the name of a *nāḍu* (34).[82] This suggests that they too were prominent landowners in the Cōḻa kingdom. The conferment of this title on these landed magnates would therefore point to the eagerness of the Cōḻas in their imperial phase to come to terms with the prominent landed magnates. This will be clearer when the strong association of those who bore this high title with offices of some importance is, as brought out below, borne in mind, demonstrating that the major Veḷḷāla landed magnates were enlisted in the service of the king, by which process they became an integral part of the state system.

Burton Stein fails to recognise this point altogether.[83] He fails to recognise the Cōḻa, and especially post-Parāntaka, character of this title and is carried away by the literal meaning of *mūvēnda* (of the three kings). He likens this suffixing title with the expression *mummuḍi* (misspelt by B. Suresh and repeated by Stein as *mummaḍi*) which forms a prefix in royal titles such as Mummudicōḻa which some of these and other title-holders prefixed to their names.[84] He argues that their loyalty to all the three houses was just formal and dated from the age of the Sangam. Further, he confuses these prominent landholders with the locality chiefs, thereby missing the importance of both the chiefs and the title-holders. In fact, one of the bases on which he rejects the existence of a bureaucracy in the Cōḻa state is this confusion. The same confusion mars his understanding of the other titles as well.

Another title which may be looked at along with that of the *mūvēndavēḷān* is *araiyan,* either standing independently or with a prefix such as *ādi-araiyan, pēr-araiyan, mārāyan* or even as a suffix in cases such as *Brahma-araiyan, Pallava-araiyan* and Viḻuppu+ *araiyan.*[85] It is noted below that *araiyan* is generally a title used by members of the chiefly families. It is in fact this apparent chiefly nature of this title which probably misled Stein.[86] At the same time this title could be seen to have been used by others as well, constituting about 13 per cent of the total names figuring in the Cōḻa inscriptions (1069 out of 8353).[87] There is a definite increase in this proportion as we come to the period of Rājarāja I and after, with an average percentage of 13.65 and in the post-Kolōttuṅga III period, with an average of about 20.50 per cent.[88] It may appear paradoxical that, although the century following the middle of the reign of Rājarāja I is marked by a conspicuous absence of chiefs and chiefly rule in the Cōḻa country, still the number of *araiyan* title holders should be on the increase. This is explained by the fact that *araiyan* was an honorific title assumed by or conferred upon important people and not exclusively a marker of membership of the chiefly families. This will be clear from the cases of Brahma + *araiyan,* Pallava + *araiyan* and Viḻuppu + *araiyan,* which together account for more than 40 per cent of the recognised chiefly titles ending with *araiyan* during the entire period covered by the Cōḻa rule.[89] In the century following the accession of Rājarāja I this reaches a startling proportion of 70 per cent. It is known that these three titles in particular were not related to any of the known chiefly families. Thus the Pallava *araiyan* need not be thought to have been related to the Pallava dynasty of an earlier period. Similarly, although there is a Viḻupparaiyanāḍu in the Cōḻa kingdom,[90] a chief of this *nāḍu* is not known by the name or title Viḻupp[u] + *araiyan.* Moreover, it is unlikely that such an inconsequential *nāḍu* should have produced so many chiefs as we meet with in the records, while other more prominent *nāḍus* are not known to have produced any at all. Therefore, one has to take them to be standing at par with or on a scale slightly higher than the *mūvēndavēḷān* and hence constituting the more important sections of the landed magnates in the Cōḻa empire, especially in the period after Rājarāja I. By the time we reach the post-Kulōttuṅga III period, there is a retardation in the proliferation of holders of these titles.[91] They are also found in association with what has been described below as the *pāḍi-kāval* system of land tenure and protection.[92]

Even in cases where we have the *araiyan* title which are identifiably of known chiefly families, such as Vāṇa*rāyan* and Noḷamba*rāyan,* it is seen that they were no longer chiefs in the post-Kulōttuṅga I period, for they figure in records from places far afield from the territories of the Banas or Nōḷambas as the case may be.[93] This has been explained as resulting from the erstwhile chiefs being reduced to a position of mere agriculturists.[94] What is likely in that case is that when the restructuring through a certain amount centralisation of the state bulldozed the chiefs, they lost their power, such as it was, and in the game of revival in the post-Kulōttuṅga I period, these chiefs failed to catch up and had just the title to live on.[95] Alternatively it is also possible that under Rājarāja and his successors a military displacement was effected and the erstwhile chiefs were assigned new lands so that they still maintained their position as landed magnates while they lost their political power.

Apart from these major titles borne by the major chunk of the population figuring in inscriptions and a sizeable section of the owning groups in society, there are other titles as well which, like the above ones, are indicative of the caste status of the holder. Thus we have the title *kōn,* associated with the *iḍaiya* or *manṟāḍi* caste (cattle-herders).[96] They are said to have enjoyed a relatively influential position in society, for they were charged with very responsible aspects of business in relation to temples, such as looking after endowments meant for burning lamps in the temples.[97] The association of a king's title with the *kōn* title, or even that of the king's title and name of a *nāḍu* + the *kon* title, would in any case show the influential position these title-holders enjoyed. Another similar instance is that of merchants with the title *ceṭṭi.*[98] We have instances of this title being prefixed by the adjectival *perum* (great). Thus we have a Cēramān Lokapperuñceṭṭi even in one of the immediate post-Cēra copper Plates.[99] Among the merchants themselves are holders of two other more distinguished titles, namely *mayilāṭṭi* and *pālan.*[100]

These two titles are found prefixed by a king's title, and important positions like that of the accountant and *sēnāpati* are seen to be occupied by holders of such titles.[101] Similar to the *peruñceṭṭi* are the artisanal titles with *perum* prefixed to the name of the caste, e.g., *peruntaccan, peruntaṭṭān, peruṅkollan*. Sometimes these titles are found prefixed, as in the earlier cases, by a king's title although we do not find these king's name + *perum* + artisan title-holders in any influential position except in the palace establishments and temples associated with them. There are two similar titles, i.e. *peruṅ-kāviḍi* and *peruntiṇai,* both borne by accountants, but there is no indication of caste about these titles.[102]

Similarly there are titles indicating the territorial identity of the person as well. Prefixed to the titles *āḻvān, vēḷān, mūvēndavēḷān, araiyan, bhaṭṭa, Viḻupparaiyan, Pallavaraiyan, uḍaiyān,* etc., is the name of a *nāḍu* which indicates the *nāḍu* from which the bearer of the title hailed or in which he had some landed interest.[103]

The above discussion of the occurrence and distribution of titles of a graded nature is necessary for understanding the functioning of the Cōḻa state, especially in the post-Parāntaka period. The Cōḻa state, by recognising the importance of the landed magnates, appears to have come to terms with them by conferring on them such royal titles. The occurrence of a king's name or title along with these titles of the notables, at least from the time of Parāntaka I and its unprecedented proliferation from the time of Rājarāja I, would indicate this attempt on the part of the state at consolidating itself by wooing the more powerful sections of society and integrating them to the state system. This is clear from the fact that in the case of the king's functionaries under the Cōḻas, especially in the period during and after Rājarāja I, there was a striking correspondence between the offices they held and the titles they bore in terms of the position in the hierarchy.

## III. The Offices and Officials

As stated earlier, conventional historiography has presented a neatly tailored fabric of the 'administrative system' of early medieval south India.[104] Alternatively, the writings of Burton Stein plainly reject this altogether, saying that there was no scope for any 'administration' at all.[105] Stein underplays the importance of the numerous functionaries figuring in the documents and dismisses these as local scribes at best.[106] This follows a literal translation of expressions like the *tiru-mandira-ōlai* and *vāyilkēḷvi*. In reality, however, they may compare with the modern 'registrar' or 'secretary', holding relatively high positions, still bearing ordinary labels to denote their office. (Our analogy is not meant to be extended further.) Stein does not notice the varying distribution of these functionaries as shown below with the result that its implication for the power structure is totally misunderstood and underestimated. Although we are not nearly as confident as either, it appears to us that there were a number of functionaries working in the service of the king's government in early medieval south India. The number of such functionaries is limited in the case of the Pāṇḍyas of the 'First Empire' and the Pallavas. So was the case of the Cēras, although it differed in details from the above two. As we come to the age of the Cōḻas, there is a gradual increase in the number of offices corresponding perhaps to the growth in the range of 'government'. This is more noticeable in the period of and after Rājarāja I: there is a proliferation in the number of offices and officials obviously indicating a greater amount of centralisation of state power. In the period after Kulōttuṅga, however, there is a steady decline in the number both of the officials and the offices which conversely points to the weakening of state power during this period. This fits neatly into the pattern of the eclipse of the chiefly rule during and immediately after the reign of Rājarāja I and its reappearance with renewed vigour in the post-Kulōttuṅga period, as is shown below.

The Kāśākkudi plates of Nandivarman II Pallavamalla mention three types of officials, viz., *nilaikkaḷattār, vāyikkēṭpār* and *adhikārar.* The *nilaikkaḷattār* (those of the *nilaikkaḷam*) are suggested to have been survey officials or related to the land department.[107] *Vāyil keṭpār* were literally those who took down the king's orders; and this was a relatively important office. This is an office which is frequently met within Cēra and Cōḻa records. *Adhikārar* were 'those who wielded authority', anticipating the *adhikāri*s *under* the Cōḻa empire. The Pallava records do not mention many more royal officials, which indicate that the state machinery had not grown to an extent comparable to the later Cōḻa period as to have had an elaborate organisation of officialdom. In the case of the Pallavas the two most important functions that we come across in the copper plate records are the *viṇṇappam* (Skt. *Vijñāpa*) and *āṇatti* (Skt. *ājñapti*).[108] The former was one who proposed or mooted a grant and the latter, one who executed it. This is seen in the case of the records of other dynasties as well. In most cases, these functions were carried out by state functionaries attached to different offices, suggesting that these did not constitute offices in themselves.

As we come to the Pāṇḍyas of the 'First Empire', we come across a few more officials and with titles conferred on them. Sāmantan Gaṇapati, a military 'General' of Varaguṇa I, is described as Pāṇḍi-Amṛitamaṅgalavaraiyan and a *mahāsāmanta* of the king.[109] An inscription dated in the twenty-seventh year of Māṟan Caṭaiyan from Viḻiñjam speaks of an *Uḷvīṭṭu-sēvaka* (household guard), Raṇakīrti by name, who laid down his life fighting the Cēra forces.[110] He may have been a companion of honour of the Pāṇḍya king. There is the mention of an Eṭṭi Śāttan being honoured with the title *Iruppaikuḍi-kiḻavan*.[111] An *uttaramantrin* of Vira Pāṇḍya is referred to in the Tamil portion of the Śivakāśi plates as Tamiḻppērariyan which is translated as Dramiḍamahārāja in the Sanskrit portion.[112] Tamiḻppērariyan is exactly in the same pattern as the titles we come across in the later records of the Cōḻas. We also have a reference to Kaṇaiyarpaḷḷi *mannina* Tennavan Uttaramantri *āyina* Iyakkan Celvan holding the office of *mandira ōlai nāyakar,* reminiscent of the similar offices under the Cōḻas.[113] Thus, even though the information concerning the offices and officials in the Pāṇḍyan kingdom is meagre, it does point to a system of a hierarchically arranged group of the king's functionaries with titles conferred on them according to the rank and position of each of them.

As we come to the case of the Cōḻas, we are in a much safer position, thanks to the incomparably larger number of inscriptions and also to the systematic analysis which they have received at the hands of Karashima and Subbaraya.[114] We have a fairly clear picture of the number and rank of a variety of functionaries who worked for the king's government in the Cōḻa country. Here, as a result of the computational analysis available, it is possible to check the frequency with which a particular title occurs along with the name of the person holding a particular office.

Perhaps the most numerous office in the Cōḻa kingdom is that of the *adhikāri,* literally the one who wields *adhikāram* (power, authority).[115] He is clearly stated in the records to be exercising power for or on behalf of the Cōḻa king (*Cōḻapperumāṇaḍigaḷukku adhikāram ceykiṟa*).[116] In the words of the Cōḻa kings themselves, they 'look after our business' (*nam karumam ārāyum*).[117] Therefore, it is clear that the *adhikāris* were functionaries in the king's government. The term *adhikāri* may be translated as 'an officer' and can signify an officer of any rank. But the instances that we have are clearly of officers of a relatively high position. Hence this may be taken as an important office. Prior to the period of Uttama Cōḻa (971 AD), we have very few references to *adhikāris* but from his reign on the number increases gradually and goes up to the unusual figures of eighty-six for the reign of Rājēndra.[118] During the reign of Virarājēndra, the downward trend sets in with a negligible figure for the reign of Kulōttuṅga. Beyond the reign of Vikrama, we do not come across any *adhikāri* at all.

Y. Subbarayalu has undertaken a detailed analysis of the personal names of the *adhikāris* in the Cōḻa records.[119] Of the 228 *adhikāris* figuring in the entire corpus of published Cōḻa inscriptions, four date from the period between Vijayālaya and Sundara, four from that of Uttama, twenty-five from that of Rājarāja I, twenty-six from that of Rājēndra I, five from that of Rājādhiraja I, eighty-six from that of Rājēndra II, sixty-eight from that of Virarājēndra, one from that of Adhirajendra, eight from that of Kulōttuṅga III and none after him. These 228 *adhikāris* had, among them, the holders of the following tides: *uḍaiyān* (70), *kiḻān/kiḻavan* (11), *vēḷān* (2) *mūvēndavēḷān* (123) *Brahma* (8), *Pallavaraiyan* (16), *Viḻupparaiyan* (17) and other chiefly titles (17). In some cases an individual uses more than one title, e.g., *uḍaiyān* and *mūvēndavēḷān*. In as many as 183 cases we notice that the name or a title of a Cōḻa king was used by the *adhikāri* as a prefix to his name or title.

Another significant office that we come across in the Cōḻa records is that of the *tiru-mandira-ōlai,* of which a passing mention has been made earlier.[120] The earliest reference to this office comes from the period of Uttama Cōḻa and from then on, this office is found more or less evenly distributed throughout the Cōḻa period. The work of this functionary appears to have been to commit to writing the orders of the king. But, as stated earlier, this is not to be confused with mere scribal function. He was a high official, in view of the confidence that the ruler had in him, his trustworthiness, the relatively secret nature of the documents in his custody and, above all, the safety of the person of the king himself. Up to the time of Vikrama Cōḻa we come across superintendents of this office, namely *tiru-mandira-ōlai-nāyakam*.

While the *tiru-mandira-ōlai* compares favourably with the *adhikāri* in the matter of titles with a preponderance of the *mūvēndavēḷān,* the *tiru-mandira-ōlai-nāyakam* is an office dominated by persons holding a *brahma* prefix to their title. This would imply that in the case of the superintendents to the office which was concerned with the *rāja-śāsana*s, there was a preference for brahman incumbents perhaps because of the highly entrenched nature of the *śāsana*s in the *Dharmaśāstra* tradition.

Another office of some interest, although not as numerous as either the *adhikāri* or the *tiru-mandira-ōlai,* was the *nāḍuvirukkai* otherwise known as *nāḍuvirukkum.*[12] Although it is tempting to identify this office with that of the *madhyastha* of contemporary records, in view of the fact that the latter is related to the locality groups and the former, to the king's government in the centre, we are not in favour of this identification. One significant aspect about this office is that the *nāḍuvirukkai* is always found mentioned in association with an *adhikāri*. The incumbents to this office were brahmans, with the title of *bhaṭṭa* except in one case where he was a *brahmādhirajan.*[122.] The references to this office are too few and far between to afford any more generalisation about it. We find them as a link between the king and officialdom.[123]

Among the other more important offices of the king's government was that of the *sēnāpati,* obviously a military office.[124] This was, as the name itself suggests, the office of the commander of forces. Curiously, in the entire period from the revival of the Cōḻas (850 AD) to the accession of Rājarāja (985 AD) we have reference to this office but once, while in the reign of Rājarāja I there are four, Rājēndra I, three, Rājādhirāja I, two, Rājēndra II, three, Virarājēndra, four, Adhirājēndra, two and Kulōttuṅga I, five. After him, the *sēnāpati*s again disappear from the records altogether.[125] The pattern of the distribution of the titles among those who held this office is interesting. Among the twenty-two known cases, sixteen bear the name or title of a Cōḻa king. There are four *uḍaiyān*s, six *brahma* and thirteen *araiyan* title-holders.[126] Significantly, *mūvēndavēḷān*s and even *vēḷān*s are absent among *sēnāpati*s.[127] Would it mean that the huge landed magnates did not take up military service? Lesser ones such as the *uḍaiyāns, kiḻāṇs*, etc., however, figure among the *sēnāpatis*.

An office related to that of the *sēnāpati* is *daṇḍanāyakam*.[128] *Daṇḍanāyakam* begins to appear from the reign of Rājarāja I and continues to figure in the subsequent reigns upto that of Rājēndra II, after which we have a solitary reference to this office each in the reigns of Kulōttuṅga I and Kulōttuṅga III. There is the mention of *daṇḍanāyaka-kaṇkāṇi* in a record of the time of Rājēndra II and another of the time of Kulōttuṅga I. Most *daṇḍanāyakams*, including the *daṇḍanāyaka-kaṇkāṇis*, are Pallava-araiyans. Again, as in the case of *sēnāpatis*, this office also does not have any *mūvēndavēḷāns* in it. There are at least two cases of persons holding the office *daṇḍanāyakam* becoming *sēnāpatis* and another becoming an *adhikāri*. Subbarayalu considers the former two as examples of upward mobility in the military hierarchy and the latter as an instance of a military officer being promoted and transferred to a civil office.[129]

Apart from these important offices in the king's government concerned with the central government, there were a few offices which looked after the affairs of the local *nāḍu*.[130] But even these offices functioned for and on behalf of the king's government and not as an organ of the local groups. They are the *nāḍu-vagai, nāḍu-kaṇkāṇi-nāyakam, nāḍu-kūṟu* and *kōṭṭam-vagai*.[131] *Nāḍu-vagai* is expanded as *nāḍu-vagai ceyvār* in certain records.[132] As the expression *vagai* literally means 'to order', 'to settle' etc., the *nāḍu-vagai ceyvār* or *nāḍu-vagai* may be taken as a settlement officer with duty assigned in a *nāḍu* unit. The *kōṭṭam-vagai* officers, naturally, were the counterparts of the *nāḍu-vagai* in the Toṇḍaimaṇḍalam region under the Cōḷas, where *kōṭṭam* was a territorial unit answering to the *nāḍu*. The *nāḍu-kaṇkāṇi-nāyakam* appears to have been an officer superior to the *nāḍu-vagai:* the two known cases, both dating from the reign of Rājarāja I, are seen to be exercising authority over more than one *nāḍu* at the same time. The *nāḍu-kūṟu* was an office of the rank of the *adhikāri*. There are two instances available: one is from the reign of Virarājēndra and the other from that of Kulōttuṅga III.[133] It may be noted that none of the twenty-five cases of *nāḍu-vagai* suggests that this office was equal to that of the *adhikāri*.[134] As regards their titles, six of them were *araiyans* (Viḻuppu, Pallava and Brahma: two each), fourteen of them *uḍaiyāns* and one (the *nāḍu-kūṟu* of the *adhikāri* rank), *mūvēndavēḷāns*.[135] Significantly, none of them had a title associated with the name of a *nāḍu,* much less that of the *nāḍu* where he is met with, which itself shows that they were not officials of the *nāḍu* group but king's functionaries employed at the *nāḍu* level.

The one 'department' about which we have the most detailed information is the land revenue department.[136] The impressive data on this department, discussed below, will be sufficient to dispel the misunderstanding created by recent scholarship contained in the writings of Burton Stein and George W. Spencer that the medieval south Indian states did not have any mechanism for the assessment and collection of revenue at all.[137] The exhaustive analysis of the revenue terms in Cōḻa inscriptions undertaken by Karashima and Sitaraman[138] would go to prove the falsity of Stein's position. In fact, Karashima has himself pointed this out.[139] Another study made by Karashima on the land revenue assessment during the Cōḻa rule illumines this point further.[140] Stein also ignores the well-known fact of the extensive land survey and assessment undertaken under Rājarāja I (1001 AD) following which the entire Cōḻa country was reorganised into *Vaḷanāḍu*s and similar surveys undertaken twice under Kulōttuṅga I in his sixteenth and thirty-eighth regnal years.[141] All this would suggest the existence of a systematic assessment and collection of revenue under the Cōḻas and it is natural that they had an elaborate land revenue department under them.

References to this 'department' begin to occur from the reign of Uttama Cōḻa.[142] This department grew into an elaborate affair with several sections each under a hierarchy of officers. After the reign of Rājarāja I this department came to be known as *puṟavu-varittiṇaikkaḷam*. The expression *triṇaikkaḷam* gets replaced by *srikaraṇam* in the reign of Kulōttuṅga II. In the case of areas covered by the chiefly rule, too, we have references to *tiṇai, tiṇaikkaḷam,* etc., evidently the same as *puṟavuvari tiṇaikkaḷam*. This 'department' under the chiefs, however, was a simple, relatively undifferentiated affair.

As stated above, this department in the king's government under the Cōḻas acquired its elaborate character with the hierarchy of officials from the reign of Uttama Cōḻa. Two of Uttama's copper plate grants give us a list of functionaries related to this department: *puṟavu-vari, varip-pottagam, mugaveṭṭi, varip-pottagak-kaṇakku, variyil-iḍu* and *paṭṭōlai* in that order.[143] This hierarchy gets further elaborated by the time of Rājēndra I. This agrees perfectly with the pattern brought out by Karashima that the frequently used revenue terms in Cōḻa records gain greater currency in the post-Rājarāja period.[144] The hierarchy becomes the most elaborate by the time of Rājēndra II with as many as ten on the scale, the additions being *puṟavu-vari-tiṇaikkaḷak-kaṇakkar, puṟavu-varit-tiṇaikkaḷam* and *puṟavu-vari-tiṇaikkaḷanāyagam,* all figuring in the place of the simple *puṟavu-vari* in Uttama's records. From the time of Kulōttuṅga I onwards, however, we see that the number of officers in this department tapers off. The two officers who find mention in the records of his reign and after are the *puṟavu-vari-śrikaraṇa-nāyagam* and *mugaveṭṭi,* the others being generally absent. In the records of the successors of Vikrama, a blanket term *variyilār,* evidently an abbreviaton for *puṟavu-variyilār,* is used to denote the department. It is possible that the *variyilār* constituted an undifferentiated group of functionaries which replaced the hierarchy of officials in the land revenue department or, less probably, this blanket term denoted the entire hierarchy.

The order of the hierarchy mentioned above, as reconstructed from the order in which the different offices find mention in the records, is supported by a comparison of the titles held by the incumbents. More than 50 per cent of the top four in the hierarchy bore the *uḍaiyān* title and about 30 per cent, the *mūvēndavēḷāns* title.[145] In *puṟavu-varit-tiṇaikkala-nāyagam*, however, there are very few *mūvēndavēḷāns*, but even this can be explained by the fact that the proportion of *mūvēndavēḷān* towards the later period of the Cōḻa rule becomes less, and it is during this period that the office *puṟavu-varit-tiṇaikkala-nāyagam* acquires currency. As we go down on the scale, for instance to *Varippottagam* and *mugaveṭṭi*, the proportion of the *uḍaiyān* title-holders goes up to as much as 70 per cent and that of the *mūvēndavēḷān* title-holders goes down to as few as 10 per cent. Further down, there are still fewer *mūvēndavēḷāns* among the lesser officers like *variyil-iḍu* and *paṭṭōlai* while the number of *uḍaiyān* title-holders are more numerous. In a similar manner, it can be noticed that the custom of using a king's name or title along with the name or title of an officer is less in the case of officers at the lower rungs of the hierarchy and more in the case of those at the upper rungs.

Another variety of functionaries are related to temples, known as the *śrīkaryam.*[146] They are described as performing or looking after the sacred business (*śrīkāryam ceykiṉṟa* or *śrīkāryam ārāykiṉṟa*). Although this office pertained to temple affairs as its name suggests, it did not include priestly duties. The evidence we have is definite as to the fact that this office was manned by the agents of the king's government. In fact, it is from the records related to this office that a major aspect of the functioning of the king's government under the Cōḻas can be reconstructed. We have instances of a few *adhikāris* in charge of the *śrīkāryam* office;[147] a few other instances where the *śrīkāryam* was in a subordinate position to that of the *adhikāri* and *sēnāpati,* but the bulk of evidence suggests that *śrīkāryam* was an independent office, the incumbents holding it in an exclusive manner. During the period between Vijayālaya and Sundara, we see as many as thirteen *śrīkāryam* officers, and nine under Uttama, twelve under Rājarāja I, seven under Rājēndra I and two under Rājādhirāja.[148] Under Rājēndra II, Virarājēndra and Adhirājēndra this office is not mentioned at all. Under Kulōttuṅga I we have five, under Vikrama and Kulōttuṅga III, two and under the others one each for the reign of every ruler upto Rājēndra III. As for the titles twenty-one of the total fifty-five *śrīkāryam* officers were *uḍaiyāns*. The distribution of other title-holders in this office is as follows: *kiḻān/kiḻavan* (5), *vēḷān* (0), *mūvēndavēḷāns* (9), *brahma* (1), *bhatta* (7), *kōn* (3), *Pallavaraiyan* (3), *Viḻupparaiyan* (2), a title associated with *nāḍu* (5) and a title associated with a king's name or title (14).[149] This break-up would testify further to (a) the secular character of the office and (b) its relation to the king's government rather than to the local group or temple committee.

Another functionary mentioned in the records of Rājarāja I, Rājēndra I and Rājēndra II is *paṇimagan.*[150] Strictly speaking this term did not indicate an office in particular; it was generally used to denote an officer of a lower rank. Thus a *varip-pottaga-nayagam* is referred to as a *paṇimagan.* This may be compared to *adhikaram-ceykiṟa* or *karumam-ārayakiṟṟa* used in relation to the *adhikāri.* But *paṇimagan,* literally a servant, is generally used to mean functionaries of a lower rank.

The general hierarchy and the ranking among the various offices discussed above can be determined to an extent with reference to a few cases involving the vertical mobility in the offices. Y. Subbarayalu has identified about twenty-five such cases, taking an assumption that this mobility is always upward involving only promotion and no demotion.[151] Thus in the *puṟavu-vari* or land revenue department alone, a ladder with about a dozen steps has been envisaged. There are cases of the *mugaveṭṭi, variyil-iḍu, paṭṭōlai* and *kiḻmugaveṭṭi* climbing two steps each and becoming *varipottagam, mugaveṭṭi, varipottaga-kaṇakku* and *variyil-iḍu* respectively. There are seven cases where the *mugaveṭṭi* climbs five steps to become *puṟavu-varittiṇai-kkala-śrīkaraṇa-nāyagam*. All these cases are, significantly, of the period after Kulōttuṅga I. There are at least four cases where an officer of the *puṟavuvari* department moves out of the department to become *adhikāris:* a *puṟavuvarit-tiṇai-kaḷam,* a *puṟavuvarit-tiṇai-kalam-nāyagam, a puṟavu-varit-tiṇai-kkaḷak-kūṟu* and a *puṟavu-vari-tiṇai-kkaḷa-kaṇkāṇi.* There are at least a couple of cases where the officers go down on the scale contraverting Subbarayalu's suggestion. They are (a) one *varippottaganāyagam* becoming a *varippottaga-kaṇakku* and (b) an *adhikāri* becoming a *puṟavuvarit-tiṇai-kaḷam.*[152] One comes across cases of 'transfers' also which involved inter-departmental mobility. Thus we have the following instances: (a) a *śrīkāryam* becomes an *adhikāri* (b) two *daṇḍanāyagam*s become *sēnāpati*s and another becomes an *adhikāri* and (c) a *daṇḍanayaga-kaṇkāṇi* becomes a *nāḍu-kūṟu* who may be of the rank of an *adhikāri.*[155] There are also cases which may be described as instances of horizontal transfer. One interesting case is of a certain Nārākkan Krishnan Irāman.[154] He was a *sēnāpati* in 1002 AD, an *ōlaināyagam* in 1008 and 1009 AD, again a *sēnāpati* in 1015 AD and once again, an *ōlaināyagam* in 10I5 AD. He served under both Rājarāja and Rājēndra. This suggests that the *sēnāpati* discharged civil duties as well, especially during times of peace. It may also show that these magnates were enlisted in the service of the king and did whatever the king bade them to do. This also points to the flexibility of work assigned to the different functionaries and to the fact that although a legion of servants and offices existed, a bureaucracy in the strict sense of the term did not exist The inheritability of offices,[155] titles and status is another significant point in this respect, and so is their unmistakable connections with land-ownership. This surmise gets support from a few other instances. In 1006 AD we find a *sēnāpati* collecting fines at Tirunāmanallūr.[156] Another *sēnāpati* was looking after the copying of the inscriptions in the central shrine of a temple under renovation in Tirumaḻapāḍi.[157] There is another record in the same temple stating that Uttama Cōḷa Brahma*mārāyan*, a *daṇḍanāyagam,* sent an order to the *śrīkāryam* of the temple concerning the copying of the inscriptions from the central shrine.[158]

Much of the discussion on the bureaucracy in early medieval south India with special reference to the Cōḻa state centres on an attempt to identify and locate the *Perundaṉam* (*Perundaram*) and *Ciṟudaṉam*.[159] These are generally taken to indicate the opposing bipolarities of the bigger and smaller grades, following a literal translation of the words. Accordingly, the officers are sought to be sorted in a horizontal division, those of the *perundaṉam* being assigned to the upper divisions and those of the *ciṟudaṉam*, to the lower divisions. But a contextual examination of the evidence does not warrant this. Although we have noted a relative grading of the offices where incumbents of corresponding ranks could be identified, there is nothing on record to show that those on the upper rungs belonged to *perundaṉam* and those on the lower rungs, to *ciṟudaṉam*. *Perundaṉam* figures mostly in the Tanjavur temple inscriptions of Rājarāja I although a few instances in a few earlier and a few later records are noticed. After Rājādhirāja I, however, we do not come across this category at all. As for *ciṟudaṉam*, we do not find the variant *ciṟudaṉam* and hence, on the face of it, the binary opposition is questionable.[160] Moreover, we have *ciṟudaṉattu perundaram* which means *perundaṉam* of the *ciṟudaram*. Nilakanta Sastri has unconvincingly explained this as of an 'intermediary status' between the two 'grades'.

In the inscriptions referring to *perundaram*, we have only two cases where the designation identifiable as of a civil office is given; an *ōlaināyagam* and another *ōlai*.[161] Another individual, who is described as of the *perundaṉam*, Uttaraṅkuḍaiyan kōn Vītiviṭaṅkan, is identified with his namesake who figures as an *adhikāri* in a record dated twenty-three years earlier.[162] On the other hand evidence is ample to show the military character of this category. There are three *daṇḍanāyagam*s and two *sēnāpati*s who are clearly stated to belong to the *perundaram*.[163] Further, in the Tanjavur temple inscriptions we have reference to a large number of army divisions of the *perundaram* assigned to the temple.[164] About the *ciṟudaṉam*, the information we have is far more meagre. It finds mention for the first time in the reign of Rājarāja I and disappears by the time of Rājādhirāja I.[165] We see certain army divisions categorised under *ciṟudaṉam*.[166] It would appear, therefore, that the presentation of the two categories as of the upper and the lower grades respectively must be left open in the present state of our knowledge.

Y. Subbarayalu has suggested that all the officers, whatever their rank, acted upon the bidding of the king.[167] These officers certainly derived their authority from the king. His suggestion that the officers were all relatives of the king is not very convincing. He bases this argument on an extended translation of the expression *kōyiṟṟamar* (*kōyil* = the king, the palace; and *tamar* = relatives) and a statement of Rājādhirāja I describing the officers as *nam tamar* (our relatives). This need not be really so. *Tamar* means literally 'men' with a possessive marker prefixed. Hence kōyiṟṟamar means 'men of the *kōyil*' and *nam tamar*, 'our men'. This identification of the royal functionaries as the king's men, however, is significant because it would have inspired a certain sense of belonging in the officers, taking them into confidence in the process of integrating the important sections of the landowning groups in the state system.

The above examination of the royal court and the royal functionaries in the case of the four states taken up in the present study has very interesting implications. The kingdoms of the Pallavas, Pāṇḍyas and Cēras and the pre-Rājarāja Cōḻas present in the records the picture of a governmental system without a very impressive officialdom. But as the resource base of the Cōḻas expands and that state reaches imperial dimensions, it is seen that a larger number of men were pressed into the service of the state system. Important and influential people in a certain locality were bestowed high-sounding titles, often prefixed by a king's name, and what are seen as major royal functions were discharged by such people. These facts not only point to the high correlation between the magnates favoured by the king and the royal officers but also suggest that what was done in integrating the governmental structure was to identify, tame and sublimate the powerful landed aristocracy and make use of them as the functionaries of the state. Hence, even if a centralised bureaucratic structure is not envisaged, our position is that what was obtaining in the early medieval south Indian political structure with its system of revenue management and coercive power, was far from being a stateless polity, as Stein would have us believe.

The discussion in this chapter will help us understand a major aspect of the surface structure of polity in early medieval south India:

of the king, his court and his functionaries. It was not certainly a top-heavy state, with the monarch concentrating all power and control in his hands. In the kingdoms of the Pallavas, Pāṇḍyas and Cēras, and of the pre-Rājarāja I Cōḻas, the power of the king appears to have been limited to the capital city and the areas surrounding it. At the same time his authority as an overlord was acknowledged in other areas as well in various ways such as dating the records in his regnal years and, more important, receiving orders from him. It is also seen that even when an act of some importance was undertaken in such peripheral areas, the concurrence of the king was obtained, represented perhaps by a deputy of the king himself. This monarchy is found assisted by a typical court of councillors, secretaries, priests, body-guards, *sāmanta*s and other major functionaries of the state. As we come to the period of Rājarāja I and afterwards in the Cōḻa empire, we see that monarchy gets strengthened with an officialdom consisting of the major landed elements growing in number. However, even this officialdom and the range of its activities is seen to be weakening in the twelfth century, when the local chiefs begin to reassert themselves. For a detailed examination of the problem of these locality chiefs we shall turn to the following chapter.

## NOTES

1. Examples are to be seen in Minakshi. *Administration and Social Life ..., op. cit.*, Mahalingam. *South Indian Polity, op. cit.*

2. Stein, 'The State and Agrarian Order....', *op .cit.*

3. Stein. *Peasant State and Society ..., op.cit.*, esp., pp. 255–64.

4. Above. Chapter 2.

5. Above, n.1.

6. Stein. 'The Segmentary State ...', *op. cit., idem, Peasant State and Society ..., op. cit.*

7. Stein, *Peasant State and Society ..., op. cit.*, pp. 254–365, *et. passim*; George W. Spencer, 'Religious Networks and Royal Influence in Eleventh Century South India', *Journal of the Economic and Social History of the Orient,* XII, I. (1969), pp. 42–56; *idem,* 'The Politics of Plunder: The Cholas in Eleventh Century Ceylon', *Journal of Asian Studies,* Vol. XXXV, (1976) pp. 405–19; *idem, The politics of Expansion: The Chola Conquest of Sri Lanka and Sri Vijaya,* (Madras, 1983).

8. Stein, *Peasant State and Society ..., op. cit.*, pp. 285–88.

9. Spencer, 'Religious Influcnce and....', *op. cit.*

10. Venkat Raghottam, 'Rajendra Cola's Raid on Sri Vijaya in A. D. 1025: A Study of the Political and Economic Dimensions of the Plunder Dynamic in Eleventh Century Tamilnadu', *Tamil Civilization.*

11. Burton Stein (ed.), *South Indian Temples,* (Delhi, 1975), p. 1.

12. M. G. S. Narayanan, 'The New Plunder Theory and the Nature of Cola Imperialism', Paper presented to the 45th session of the Indian History Congress, Annamalainagar, 1984.

13. Above, Chapter 1.

14. Narayanan, *Political and Social Conditions .... op. cit.*, Chapter on Chronology.

15. Above, Chapter 1.

16. Stein, *Peasant State and Society ..., op .cit.*, p.286.

17. Minakshi, *The Historical Sculptures of the Vaikunthapperumal Temple, Kanchi, op. cit.*

18. M. G. S. Narayanan, *Cultural Symbiosis in Kerala,* (Trivandrum, 1972), pp. 23–30 and Appendix.

19. *S.I.I.*, Vol. II, i. no. 1. 1.1.

20. R. S. Sharma, *Indian Feudalism*, 2nd edn., pp. 8, 11.

21. *E.I.*, Vol. XXI, p. 27, 1.4.

22. *S.I.I.*, Vol. III, no. 49.

23. *E.I.*, Vol. XV, pp. 44–72; II.174–75; *S.I.I.*, Vol. III, no. iii, pp. 382–439, ll. 143–44, etc. for a discussion, Sastri, *Colas*, p. 469.

24. Above, n. 17.

25. *TAS*, Vol. II, pp. 85–86.

26. *TAS*, Vol. III.

27. There are two series of records dated in the regnal years of Bhāskara Ravi, one indicating his reign to have commenced in 962 AD and the other, in 978 AD, but both drawing up to 1020–21 AD. These two series doubtless are of the same ruler, and the discrepancy is explained by suggesting that the first series reckons his reign to have commenced from the date of his succession when he was still a minor and the second series, from his actual coronation and assumption of full powers sixteen or seventeen years later when he attained maturity. Narayanan, *Political and Social Conditions ...*, Chapter on 'Chronology of the Ceras'. The present record, dated 973 AD, falls within the period when Bhāskara Ravi was still a minor.

28. Mahalingam, *South Indian Polity*, pp. 104–52.

29. Minakshi, *Administration and Social Life ...*, pp. 59–66.

30. Above, n. 17.

31. *Periyapurāṇam*, Kaḻaṟiṟṟārivār Nāyanār Purāṇam.

32. *Laghu Bhāskariya Vyākhyā*, v.1.

33. Hermann Gundert, (ed.) *Keralotpatti*, (reprint, Trivandrum, 1961) p. 26.

34. Narayanan, *Political and Social Conditions* ..., pp. 211–14; 299; 238–43.

35. *T.A.S.*, Vol. V, p. 45, II. 44–45. The inadequate reading of the Travancore government epigraphist is corrected by M. G. S. Narayanan, *Reinterpretations in South Indian History*, Trivandrum, (1977) pp. 107–08, n.17.

36. *Ibid.*, also M. G. S. Narayanan, 'The Hundred Groups and the Rise of Nayar Militia in Kerala', *Proceedings of the Indian History Congress*, (Burdwan, 1983).

37. Narayanan, *Political and Social Conditions* ..., Chapter on 'Nature of Monarchy'.

38. Narayanan, *Cultural Symbiosis in Kerala, op. cit.; idem, Political and Social Conditions* ..., Chapter on 'Divisions of the Kingdom', Section on Venadu.

39. Sastri, *The Pandyan Kingdom*, p. 53, n.2.

40. *PCP*, p. 151, 1.66.

41. *Ibid.*, p. 189, II.345; *Ibid.*, p. 193. 1.77.

42. K. V. Raman, *Some Aspects of Pandyan History in the Light of Recent Discoveries*, (Madras. 1972), p. 7.

43. See below, Chapter 4, under Military and Police.

44. K. G. Krishnan, 'Two Pandyan Inscriptions from Tirupparamkunram', *E.I.*, Vol. XXXVI.

45. *I.A.*, Vol. IX, p. 47, Plate Va, II.1–2.

46. Sastri, *Colas*, p. 452.

47. *Ibid.*, pp. 462–63.

48. *Ibid.*, p. 473.

49. Narayanan, *Reinterpretations* ..., pp. 99–112.

50. *Kalingattuparani*, XI, vv. 314–42.

51. *Periyapurāṇam*, Tirunāvukkaraśu Purāṇam, vv. 90–92; Siṟuttoṇḍa Nayānar Purāṇam, vv. 2–3.

52. *T.A.S.*, v. p. 45.

53. Sastri, *Colas*, p. 462.

54. Among those who contest the proposition of the existence of bureaucracy is Stein, 'The State and Agrarian Order ...', *op. cit., idem*, 'The Segmentary State ...', *op. cit., idem, Peasant State and Society, passim*; among those who support the idea are Y. Subbarayalu, *The State in Medieval South India, AD 600–1350*, (Ph.D. thesis, Madurai Kamaraj University, 1976); *idem*, 'The Cola State', *Studies in History*, Vol. IV, no. 2, (1982), pp. 265–306; Noboru Karashima, *South Indian History and Society*, (Bombay, 1984), Introduction.

55. Stein, *Peasant State and Society* ..., pp. 112–17. In this particular case Stein bases himself heavily on the work of B. Suresh, *Historical and Cultural Geography and Ethnology of South India (with Special Reference to Cola Inscriptions)*, (Ph.D. Thesis, Deccan College, Poona, 1965). This is another case of Stein's way of arriving at sweeping generalisations based on the work of others.

56. Subbarayalu, *The State ..., op. cit.*

57. Karashima, *South Indian History and Society.* Here the author interprets the results of the computational analysis within a theoretical framework.

58. Noboru Karashima, Y. Subbarayalu and Toru Matsui, *A Concordance of the Names in Cola Inscriptions*, 3 vols., (Madurai, 1978) (Hereafter *Concordance*). Most of the analysis below is based on this *Concordance* unless otherwise stated.

59. *Concordance*, Appendix 3.

60. *Ibid.*, pp. xlix–l.

61. *Ibid.*, see table on p. xlix.

62. Below, Chapter 3.

63. Stein, *Peasant State and Society* .... pp. 112–17. Perhaps this is a calculated misunderstanding, in order to support the idea of a stateless polity. See below, n. 84.

64. *Concordance*, p. xlii. n. 2.

65. *Concordance*, 4419; 4421.

66. *Concordance, passim.*

67. *Ibid.*

68. *Ibid.*

69. Above. n. 64.

70. *Concordance*, Appendix 3. pp. xlv–xlvii.

71. *Ibid.*, p. xlvi.

72. *Ibid.* Subbarayalu. *State ...*, pp. 115–18.

73. *Inscriptions of Pudukkottai State*, 30l.

74. *Concordance*, names associated with SB 230 (*Ur* assembly).

75. Subbarayalu. *State ...*, p. 118.

76. *Ibid.* p. 119.

77. *Concordance*, 4092.

78. *Ibid.*, Appendix 3, pp. xlvii.

79. *Ibid.* Tables on pp. xlix.

80. *S.I.I.*, Vol. III, no. 147.

81. Subbarayalu. *State ...*, p. 12l.

82. *Concordance*, Appendix 3, table on p. xlix.

83. Stein. *Peasant State and Society ...*, pp.111–17.

84. See Subbarayalu's comment. 'The Cola State', *op.cit.*, p. 296, n. 90.

85. *Concordance*, Appendix 3, table on p. Iii. .

86. Above. n. 82.

87. Subbarayalu. *State* .... p. 122; and Appendix 8, p. 284.

88. *Concordance*, Appendix 3, table on p. liii.

89. *Ibid.*

90. Y. Subbarayalu, *Political Geography of the Chola Country*, (Madras. 1973). Appendix IV. Nadu. no. 213.

91. *Concordance.* Appendix 3, table on p. liii.

92. Subbarayalu, *State* ..., p. 123.

93. See for example, the distribution of Vāṇa-rāyan (in its various forms). *Concordance*, nos. 0272, 0402, 0489, 0852, 2052, 2120, 2197, 2942, 3349, 3960, 4660, 4827, 5225, 5308, 5673, 6348, 7373, 7660, 7937, 8258, 8538, 8753, 8770.

94. Subbarayalu. *State* ..., p. 126.

95. This would remind one of the descriptions of the Kuru-Pāñcalas in a later period as 'living on the title of raja' *-rājaśabdōpajīvinaḥ: Arthaśāstra*, XI. 1.5. See also Romila Thapar, *From Lineage to State*, p. 69.

96. *Concordance.* Appendix I. Title group B. TB 050, 051, 052, 053, 054, For *Manṟādi* as a title, TB 060.

97. Subbarayalu, *State* ..., p. 127. See also a discussion of the significance of this caste on p. 87 and table on p. 86. The fact that the largest number of people identifiable by caste in inscriptions belong to this community is no index to their importance. This is one of the traps of statistical analysis. In fact, this prolific occurrence of the cattle-herders will have to be explained in the light of the fact that a majority of the Cola inscriptions are concerned with the endowment of what is described as 'perpetual lamps', for the maintenance of which cattle or sheep are granted to temples. Their maintenance would certainly involve the cattle-herders in large numbers. In an age when the maintenance of fire was achieved largely through lamps which were not allowed to go out, lamps burnt with clarified butter, with the minimum amount of soot formed on the wicks, are quite natural and hence this concern with perpetual lamps.

98. *Concordance*, Appendix I, TB 190.

99. *E.I.*, IV. pp. 290–7.

100. *Concordance*, 3213 and 3843 for *mayilāṭi* and 5970, 6729, 7293, 7313 and 7409 for *pālan*.

101. Subbarayalu, *State* ..., p. 127.

102. *Ibid.*

103. *Ibid.*, pp. 128–9.

104. Sastri, *Colas*, pp. 445–519; Minakshi, *Administration and Social Life* ..., pp. 45–175; Mahalingam. *South Indian Polity, passim*; Sastri. *Pandyan Kingdom*, pp. 76–84; Mahalingam, *Kancipuram* ..., *passim*; etc.

105. Stein, 'State and Agrarian Order ...', *op.cit. idem*, 'Segmentary State ..., *op. cit., idem*, Peasant State and Society .... *passim*.

106. *Idem*, 'The Segmentary State ...,' *op. cit.*, pp. 12,15–17.

107. *TPCP*, p. 168. See also Minakshi, *Administration and Social Life* ..., pp. 67, 75.

108. Minakshi, *ibid*. pp. 164–66, 182, 375. It is interesting that a 'motion' in the 'republics' in the time of the Buddha was known as a *natti, i.e. Jnāpti*. K. P. Jayaswal, *Hindu Polity*. 5th edn. (Bangalore, 1978). p. 87. *Ājñapti* and *Vijñapti* may well have had their roots in this.

109. Above. n. 44.

110. Above. n. 42.

111. No. 334 of 1929–30. Raman, *op. cit.*, p. 7.

112. Above. n. 41.

113. *PCP.*, p. 193, ll.75–6.

114. Above. n. 57.

115. The significance of this office was brought out by Sastri, *Colas*, pp. 462–43. The researches of Subbarayalu and Karashima have corroborated this further. *State* ... pp. 134–37; *Concordance*. Appendix 3. table on p. xlix. However, Stein does not accept this. He asserts that this 'title' was often used without personal names (which, as a matter of fact, is not the case). He also misquotes Nilakanta Sastri to sustain his point that it was in the sense of a person of personal merit and not official precendence that the *adhikari* was important. This is another case of his way of generalising on the basis of a faulty understanding. *Peasant State* ..., pp. 112–3.

116. *S.I.I.*, Vol. XIX, no. 218.

117. *S.I.I.*, Vol. II, no. 205, II. 37–49. For an identification of these as *adhikāris*, see *ibid.*, II.487–94. Also Subbarayalu, *State* ..., Appendix 14, nos. 12, 13, 23, 32, 37, 52.

118. Subbarayalu, *State* ..., Appendix II, p. 287.

119. *Ibid.*, and Appendix 13, p. 289.

120. *Concordance*, Status Group SB 031.

121. *Concordance*. Status Group SB 050.

122. Subbarayalu, *State* ..., p. 289, App. 13.

123. P. Venkatesan, "A study of the office called Naḍuvirukkum in the Central Administration under the Colas, *Tamil Civilization*, Vol. III, nos. 2 and 3, pp. 68–70.

124. *Concordance*, Status Group SB 040.

125. Subbarayalu, *State* ..., p. 287, Appendix II, p. 287.

126. *Ibid.*, p. 289, App. 13, p. 289.

127. See also *Concordance*, Appendix 3. p. Ii.

128. *Concordance*, Status Group SB 060.

129. Subbarayalu, *State* ..., pp. 141–56.

130. *Ibid.*, pp. 141–43.

131. *Concordance*, Status Group SB 213, 214, 215, 216 and 218.

132. Subbarayalu, *State* ..., p. 141.

133. *IPS*, 126, Also Subbarayalu, *State* ..., p. 142.

134. This is also suggested by the titles borne by the incumbents. below, n. 134.

135. Subbarayalu, *State* ..., Appendix 13, p. 289.

136. Mahalingam, *South Indian Polity*, pp. 143–46; Subbarayalu, *State* ..., pp. 143–52.

137. Above, nos. 7–9.

138. Noboru Karashima and B. Sitaraman, 'Revenue Terms in Chola Inscriptions', *Journal of Asian and African Studies*, no. 5, (1972), pp. 87–117. This is reproduced in Karashima, *South Indian History and Society*, pp. 69–94, to which references are made here.

139. Karashima, *South Indian History and Society*, Introduction, p. xxiii.

140. *Ibid.*, pp. 94–105.

141. *S.I.I.*, Vol. VIII, no. 223; 44 of 1907; M.E.R., 1913, Para 21; 199 of 1917; *ARE*, 1918, Para 25; 125 of 1896; 84 of 1897; 272 of 1907. Also Mahalingam, *South Indian Polity*, pp. 161–2.

142. Subbarayalu, *State* ..., p. 145.

143. *S.I.I.*, Vol. III, nos. 142 and 151.

144. Karashima, *South Indian History and Society*, pp. 72–73, Table 8.

145. Subbarayalu, *State* ..., Appendix 13, p. 289. The hierarchy could be reconstructed with the help of the following records: *S.I.I.*, Vol. III, no. 142; 151, 205, Vol. IV, no. 529, *E.I.*, Vol. XXI, no. 38, Vol. XXII, no. 34, *E.C.*, Vol. X, K1, 19, iii, *T.A.S.*, Vol. I, pp. 164–67, *ARE* 1931–32, pp. 51–54.

146. *Concordance*, Status Group SA 070, 071.

147. A certain Ciṟṟiṅkan-Utaiyān=Kōyil-āna-Madurāntaka-Muvēntavēḷan is found as both a *Śrīkaryam* and *adhikāri* in at least two records: *S.I.I.*, Vol. XIX, no. 92; 181.

148. Subbarayalu, *State* ..., Appendix 11, p. 287.

149. *Ibid.*, Appendix 13, p. 289. Of the seven instances of the *bhaṭṭa* title-holders, four come from the same temple, Maṇimangalam. Even otherwise, there is a domination of *uḍaiyāns and mūvēndaveḷāns* in this office.

150. Subbarayalu, *State* ..., p. 154. The *Concordance* does not code this item.

151. Subbarayalu, *State* ..., p. 155 and Appendix 14, pp. 290–306.

152. *Ibid.*, p. 156.

153. *Ibid.*

154. *Ibid.*, Appendix 15, pp. 307–08. Incidentally, the occurrence of a large number of incumbents from this family in different offices over the generations shows the hereditary nature of offices in the state.

155. *Ibid.*

156. *S.I.I.*, Vol. VII, 998.

157. *S.I.I.*, Vol. V, 652.

158. *Ibid.*, 651.

159. Mahalingam, *South Indian Polity*, pp. 136–37. This is generally the view held by historians, although Hultzsch had not been misled into this understanding. *S.I.I.*, Vol. II, p. 95, n. 2.

160. Mahalingam's distinction that *Karumigaḷ* of *perundaram* stood as a superior grade in relation to *paṇimakkal of ciṟudanam*, based on the epigraphist's report, is at best imaginary.

161. Subbarayalu, *State* ..., p. 159.

162. *S.I.I.*, Vol. XIII, 149; *S.I.I.*, Vol. II, 95, p. 459.

163. Subbarayalu, *State* ..., Appendix 14, nos. 5, 6, 62, 70, 71.

164. *S.I.I.*, Vol. II, Introduction, p. 9.

165. Subbarayalu, *State* ..., p. 160.

166. Above. n. 163.

167. *State* ..., p. 161.

Three

# The Role of the Chiefs

A significant factor in the power structure of monarchical rule in south India during the period of our study is the existence of a number of local chiefs in areas outside the heartland of the respective kingdoms. In this chapter, we take up for discussion the role of these chiefs in the political structure of the Pallava, Cēra and Cō̤la states. In the case of the Pāṇḍyan kingdom, however, one does not come across many such chiefs excepting the Āys in the southernmost tip of the peninsula, who had themselves been shifting their allegiance between the Cēras and Pāṇḍyas. A section of the existing historiography has described these chiefdoms as 'divisions' or 'districts' of the kingdoms and the chiefs who ruled these territories have been correspondingly called 'governors'.[1] This assumes too much of centralisation and an artificial character for these divisions. This is unacceptable because, for one thing, we have evidence to show the existence of most of these units in an earlier period, as also their chiefs such as the Adigamāns, Bāṇas, Gaṅgas, Muttaraiyar, Mūṣikas, Āys, *et al.* Secondly, this assumption cannot be sustained by an examination of other aspects of polity in these states. Therefore, rather than treating these chiefdoms as artificial divisions of the kingdom and the chiefs as owing their authority to the Pallava, Cēra or Cō̤la king's appointing them, we will have to take an altogether different view.

Alternatively, these chiefs have been described as 'feudatories'.[2] This 'feudatory approach', the 'fruitfulness' of which has been recommended by R. Sathianathaier,[3] has actually only obscured the role of these chiefs in south India. For, these writings, with their crude application of terminology, without any conceptual rigour, do not concern themselves with the entire range of meaning that the expression 'feudatory' carries about it. For instance, when M. S. Govindasamy speaks of the role of feudatories in Pallava history or in the later Cō̤ḻa history, one does not actually hear about the nature of 'feudal' relations between these 'feudatories' on the one side and their Pallava or Cō̤ḻa 'suzerains' as the case may be on the other. The same difficulty besets the more widely read writings of Nilakanta Sastri and Mahalingam and the less celebrated writings of scholars like Arokiaswamy and Balambal. In fact, there has been no detailed study of the nature of relationships between these lesser chiefs on the one hand and the more powerful rulers who enjoyed some hegemony over them on the other, much less in the framework of a feudal formation. Strangely, however, these crude formulations appear to stand the scrutiny of evidence, for that is what seems to be the relation in which these chiefs stood to their Pallava, Cēra or Cō̤ḻa overlords. In this connection, aspects such as the military obligation they had to their overlord, the attendance of these *sāmanta* chiefs in the royal court of the overlord whether in the headquarters of the overlord or one of the chiefs, the protective umbrella of the overlord under which they stood, the suggestions about payment of annual tribute to the overlord, and the complex network of alliances involving political and matrimonial terms among these chiefs are all worthy of consideration, within the context of an overall feudal socio-economic milieu. However, in the present chapter we use the less committed term 'chiefs' in preference to the perhaps more correct term 'feudatory', in view of the fact that that term has nearly lost its sharp edge.

Burton Stein, too, rejects this crude 'feudatory approach' to the chiefs in the case of the Cō̤ḻa state;[4] but his alternative understanding is clouded by a major confusion.[5] For him there is no distinction between these 'chiefs' who exercised authority over large areas of territory and the landed magnates on whom titles such as *mūvēndavēḷān, araiyan, udaiyān*, etc., were conferred. As a result, not only does Stein fail to appreciate the significance of these chiefs but he also attributes a higher status to the landed magnates than what they enjoyed. For, following this, Stein postulates the existence of a political chief in each of the 550 *nāḍu* units and thus each of them is represented as a replica of the centre in accordance with the segmentary pattern.[6] In reality, this is not the case. There is nothing on record to show that these title-holders were political chiefs of the locality; and there is indeed evidence to show that there were more than one *araiyan* or *mūvēndavēḷān* title-holders in the same *ūr* or *nāḍu*.[7] Again, this identification wrongly leads Stein to the rejection of the role of these title-holders as state functionaries. Thus we are not in favour of the position taken by Burton Stein in bracketing the chiefs together with the title-holders.

At present, no general statement can be made about the origin of these chiefs. We meet with some of these chiefly houses in Sangam literature in the early Christian or even immediate pre-christian centuries. Thus we have the Āys, Vēḷs, Mūvas or Mūṣikas, the chiefs of Koḍumbāḷur, the Adigamāns in that literature.[8] The Jambai inscription[9] helps in the identification of the Satiyaputo of Aśōkan edicts with the Atiyamān of Sangam literature which, among other things, attests to the antiquity of that house. Certain other houses are clearly of a later origin as they are not found in Sangam literature. However, most of them share the same characteristics. In Sangam literature itself, we see that these chiefs had largely failed to participate in the major socio-economic changes brought about by the expansion of agriculture and the resultant growth of peasant communities on the plains in the fertile river valleys as well as the trade that was developing on the coastal emporia and the urban enclaves in the interior.[10] The major houses such as the Cēras, Cōḻas and Pāṇḍyas benefited from these developments and came to be known as the *mūvēntar.* They were able to take off, as it were, to what may be called state systems while their less fortunate cousins in the chiefly houses remained in relative isolation and stunted their growth, continuing to be in the old world of cattle-raids and hero-worship.

It is this picture that we get of the chiefs in the beginning of the period of our study. Most of our evidence in this early period relating to these chiefs such as the Perumbāṇa-araicar, Gaṅga-araicar, Vāṇakō-araicar, Adigamāns, etc. occur in the hero-stones in South Arcot and Dharmapuri districts of the sixth and seventh centuries AD.[11] These records show that they continued to live in their own world of petty feuds over cattle-lifting and the worship of heroes fallen in such skirmishes. The relative isolation in which these chiefs stood from those better developed areas and their chiefs such as the *mūvēntar* may have been responsible for this. At any rate, there were continuous feuds among or within the different chiefly lineages, many of them on account of cattle-raids. Some of them are explicitly stated to be erected in memory of heroes described to have fallen defending the cattle of the villages under their rule,[12] which implies the involvement of a certain amount of territorial interest, one of the basic features of a state society. In fact a few records contain the phrase *nāḍu paviya*[13] (extending the limits of the territory) which clearly signifies this. However, none of these records is helpful in identifying the exact territory of any chief; neither the names of the territory nor its boundaries are discoverable from the records. Most records are dated in the regnal years of Simhaviṣṇu and Mahēndravarman, showing that these chiefs recognised the hegemony of these Pallava rulers.[14] Some records of the Bāṇas even speak of the *sēvakā* (servant, soldier) of the junior chief: *Perumbāṇa iḷavaraiyar sēvakan.*[15] A couple of records from Oddapatti in the Dharmapuri district, which are hero-stones dedicated to Adigamāns, mention Gaṅga Śripurusa,[16] suggesting a three-tier relationship with the Pāllavas at the top, the Gaṅgas in the middle and the Adigamāns at the bottom. At any rate, the records are far from complete to indicate the process by which this recognition or acknowledgement of subordinate and super-ordinate relationship among these chiefs and their overlords was articulated.

As one comes to the eighth and ninth centuries, one has more references to the chiefs and the picture is therefore, clearer. Among those about whom we have information are the Bāṇas sporting the title Mahābali-Vāṇa-rājan (Chittoor and the northern portions of North Arcot district); the chiefs of Koṇḍanāḍu or Vēṭṭuva-ādi-araiyan (Tirukkoyilur Taluk, South Arcot district); Vāṇa-ko-araiyar (Chengam Taluk, North Arcot district and Tirukkoyilur Taluk, South Arcot district); Viṇṇa-ko-araiyan (Gingee Taluk, South Arcot district); Ganga-araiyar (Wandiwash and Vellore Taluks, North Arcot district); Muttaraiyar (Kulattur Taluk, Tiruchirapalli district and Tanjavur Taluk, Tanjavur district) and Adigamāns (Dharmapuri district). We have information from records in the regions about their acknowledgement of the overlordship of the Pallavas in different ways. This goes to suggest that the statements in the *praśasti* portions of Pallava charters are not altogether empty claims.

In the early records of the Bāṇas, the level of their political development is not very clear. Characteristically, they figure as subordinates or allies in the praśasti literature composed in favour of the Cāḷukyas, Pallavas, Rāṣṭrakūṭas, and even of the Gaṅgas. This has been taken by historians to mean their shifting allegiances.[17] But given the nature of the *praśasti* literature, these conflicting claims are not so much of an enigma. However, the role of the house of the Bāṇas is interesting on account of the very important locale of their existence. In a record dated in the twenty-third year of Nandivarman (II Pallavamalla), a certain Vikramāditya Māvēli Vāṇarāyar is mentioned.[18] This is interesting because the record is dated in the regnal year of the Pallava ruler but the chief sports a Cāḷukyan title at the same time. Perhaps it is that earlier in his life he was subject to the hegemony of the Cāḷukyas but later on he had to acknowledge the authority of the Pallavas. Govindasamy has proposed the identification of this Bāṇa chief with Jayanandivarman figuring in the genealogies of the Gudimallam, Udiyendiram and Mudiyanur plates.[19] If this is correct, it would also mean that at a later stage he even adopted a Pallava name and this alone was remembered by later generations for purposes of genealogy.[20] In the ninth century, when the Rāṣṭrakūṭas rose to power in the Deccan, the Bāṇas were seen in some of their records in the position of subordinate allies. The Nandi copper plates are stated to have been granted by the Rāṣṭrakūṭa king at the request of the Kṣatriya Mahābali Bāṇāraja.[21] The Chikkaballapur plates too suggest Rāṣṭrakūṭa overlordship over the Bāṇas.[22] There is at least one reference to a princess of the Rāṣṭrakūṭa family being married to one of the Bāṇa princes.[23] Even in the latter half of the ninth century we find these chiefs fighting on account of cattle-raids. A number of inscriptions, for example, speak of the hostilities between the Bāṇas and Nōḷambas (another minor chiefly family) on account of cattle-raids.[24] A hero-stone at Jodi Dalasigere refers to Mahēndra, a Nōḷamba chief.[25] Another record dated to the twenty-sixth year of Pallava Nṛipatuṅga (875 AD) records a cattle-raid in which a 'servant' of the Gaṅgas was killed by a Nōḷamba chief.[26] By the close of the ninth century, when Pallava power declined, the Bāṇas started dating their records in their own regnal years and eras such as the Śaka era which is indicative of their relative independence.

Similarly, the records of the Gaṅgas too are very interesting. It is stated that some of the Gaṅga chiefs were consecrated by, or at least in the presence of, their Pallava overlords. Thus Harivarman was consecrated by Siṁhavarman, Madhava III by Skandavarman and Śivamāra II jointly by Rāṣṭrakūṭa Govinda III and Pallava Nandivarman.[27] This may suggest that both the Pallavas and Rāṣṭrakūṭas had claimed some hegemony over the Gaṅgas. However, the presence of an overlord on the occasion of the consecration of the Gaṅga chief is clearly indicative of the nature of relationship between them, and other records show that this was one of super-ordinate and sub-ordinate alliances. There is at least one instance to show the matrimonial ties which existed between the Gaṅgas and the Rāṣṭrakūṭas.[28] Similar relations may have existed between them and the Pallavas as also between them on the one side and other chiefly houses on the other.

Another significant case of chiefs subject to Pallava authority is that of the Muttaraiyar. Historians and epigraphists have tried to interpret the name Muttaraiyar variously.[29] This house controlled the territory on the fertile plains of Kāvēri in the Kulattur and Tanjavur taluks. Since both the Pāṇḍyas and the Pallavas in the seventh and eighth centuries were eager to control this rich resource base, the role of the Muttaraiyar chiefs was rather crucial. As the Muttaraiyar threw in their lot in favour of the Pallavas, which is clear by the dating of their records in Pallava regnal years as well as their adoption of Pallavan titles such as Viḍēlviḍugu and Perumbiḍugu, it was the Pallavas who were ultimately able to control this region. However, the process by which the Pallavas enlisted the allegiance of the Muttaraiyar or, conversely, by which the Muttaraiyar chose the Pallavas as their overlords, is not clear. But after the Kāvēri valley around Tanjavur was opened up in a big way under the initiative of the Pallavas, the Cōḷas, who were able to wrest that region from the Muttaraiyar, came into prominence so much so that, in a matter of a century, not only the Muttaraiyar chiefs, but even their Pallava overlords, were compelled to submit to their authority.

These chiefs, though subject to the overlordship of Pallava rulers, were relatively independent. There are records which could be described as their own *praśasti*s. At least in the case of the Gaṅgas and the Bāṇas, there were faint claims to kṣatriyahood; a Bāṇa chief even made it explicit.[30] But there were other chiefs who enjoyed a less exalted position. Thus, we have the Telugu Cōḍas, the Adigamāns, the Vēṭṭuva-ādi-araiyar, the Vāṇakō-araiyar, etc. The Telugu Cōḍas adopted the names of the Pallavas such as Nandivarman, Siṁhaviṣṇu, Mahēndravarman, etc. T. V. Mahalingam has ably brought out the career of an illustrious scion of this family, Rājakesari Śrīkanṭha Cōḍa of the Telugu Pottāpi line, who caused a veritable interregnum in Pallava history.[31] Incidentally, a daughter of this chief was the wife of Pāṇḍya Śrimāṟa Śrivallabha, thus indicating the network of matrimonial relations that existed among the chiefly families and royal houses in that period. Mahalingam has even suggested that the wife of Śrikanṭha Cōḍa and the mother-in-law of Pāṇḍya Śrīmāṟa Śrivallabha may have been a daughter of Pallava Dantivarman. The Adigamāns, whose house is known to have existed at least from the third century BC, too are known to have stood in a subordinate relation with the Pallavas.[32] In this case also a three-tier relationship is brought out with the Pallavas at the top, the Adigamāns in the middle and the Maḻavas at the bottom. The marriage of a Maḻava princess to Pāṇḍya Māṟavarma[33] is significant in the context of the rather unfriendly relations that existed between the Pallavas and Pāṇḍyas. A Vēṭṭuva-ādi-araiyan is described as 'possessing' Koṇḍanāḍu whose 'servant' made a fairly handsome gift to a temple.[34] Similar references to Vāṇakō-araiyan are there in one of which a chief of that house, Vairamēgha by name, is explicitly stated to be ruling Vāṇakopadi, Ilāḍip-aḍi, Milāḍu and all [other territories] lying to the north of the Kāvēri.[35] Towards the middle of the ninth century, however, we see that these chiefs were relatively independent, which suggests the intrinsic weakness of the Pallava authority which in any case was threatened by the Cōḻa house at about the same time.

An interesting aspect about the situation in the Pāṇḍyan kingdom proper, is the absence of such chiefly families except the Āys. The confusion which mars the understanding of Burton Stein, in treating the title-holding landed magnates on a par with the local chiefs, is shared by the otherwise excellent study of Rajan Gurukkal.[36] The only chiefly house that we come across to be continually under the over-lordship of the Pāṇḍyas is that of the Āys in the southern tip of the peninsula. Of course there were the Adigamāns and Muttarayar over whom they tried to claim some ascendancy.[37] Both of them were, as we saw, successfully enlisted by the Pallavas, although in the case of the Muttaraiyar there are at least two records dated in the Pāṇḍyan regnal years.[38]

The Āys, like many other chiefs of south India in the period, are known from the earliest phase of known history in the Tamil country and are mentioned in the Sangam literature.[39] Even in that literature they are presented as now subject to the Pāṇḍyas and now to the Cēras.[40] This shifting of allegiance can be seen to have continued in the changed socio-political context of the period of our study as well. The Āy chiefs such as Karunantaḍakkan and Vikramāditya adopted Pāṇḍyan titles such as Śrīvallabha and Varaguṇa respectively. Statements in Pāṇḍyan inscriptions to the effect that the Pāṇḍyas subjugated the Āys over and over again have been interpreted by historians in the context of the entry of the Cēras of Makōtai on the scene, with interest in that region and perhaps offering a helping hand to the Āy chiefs.[41] There are at least three of their copper plates, one of which is dated both in terms of the number of days expired in the Kali era and the regnal year of the Āy chief,[42] another in terms of the Kali days only[43] and a third one in the regnal year of the chief and giving a lot of astronomical details[44]—that is, none of them was dated in the regnal year of the Pāṇḍyan overlords. But the adoption of Pāṇḍyan names as titles by the chiefs is significant. The history of the Āys after Vikramaditya Varaguna is not known. What is likely is that their territory, at least in the north, went into the hands of the chiefs of the adjoining Veṇāḍu, who were subject to the Cēras of Makōtai while the rest remained directly under Pāṇḍyan control.

In the case of the Cēra kingdom, we have reference to a large number of chiefly houses. Since most of the information pertaining to the situation in the west coast is not yet available in print[45], we shall give greater details here. From the records we have information about at least thirteen such chiefdoms. These chiefdoms were known as *nāḍus*, clearly to be distinguished from units known by that name in the rest of south India. In the context of Kerala, *nāḍu* was a counterpart of Tamil *pāḍi* and Sanskrit *rāṣṭra*. This is clearly brought out by an inscription from Tiruvoṟṟiyūr near Madras, which, referring to Vaḷḷuvanāḍu in the Sanskrit portion, speaks of Vallabha-rāṣṭra.[46] These *nāḍus* in Kerala differed widely in size and political and social status.

Among the chiefdoms, Kōlattunāḍu stood at the northern edge of the Kerala country. A few inscriptions available from this territory, some of them dated in the regnal years of Cēra rulers and some others referring to a regulation concerning the conduct of village bodies all over the Cēra kingdom, attest clearly to the political status of this chiefdom vis-a-vis the Cēra kingdom.[47] But we know more about the history of this region from the *Mūṣikavaṁśakāvya*, a Sanskrit historical romance composed by a poet who describes himself as Atula.[48] The *kāvya* has all the qualities of both court poetry and a *mahākāvya* in Sanskrit, but at least from the later cantos, we get information which is borne out by other sources such as inscriptions. The founder of this chiefly house is stated to have been a certain Rāmaghata Muṣika, and that title and its Tamil form, Irāmakuṭa-mūvar, are known to have been used by later chiefs of this house. M. G. S. Narayanan identifies the second in the line, Nandana, with Nannan of the Sangam literature which, if correct, would go a long way in establishing the antiquity of this house from the fourth or third century BC.[49] By the time we come to the later periods, from the twelfth canto on in the *kāvya*, we have details which could be considered historical. Although the *kāvya*, typically, does not speak in so many words about the subordinate position of this house to that of the Cēras, there are many indications to that effect. In fact there is a detailed description in the *kāvya* of how the king of Kēraḷa imposed his overlordship over the Mūṣika chief.[50] Jayarāga, identified with Cēra Kōta Ravi Vijayarāga (883–913 AD), was married to a Mūṣika princess, daughter of Kuñcivarman and sister of Īśānavarman. Īśānavarman got married to Nandini, the daughter of a Cēdi ruler, who had lost his throne. Following this marriage, the Mūṣika chief helped his Cēdi father-in-law to recapture the lost territory. This apparently provoked the Cēra king, who is described in the very next verse of the *kāvya* to have marched to Mūṣika territory at the head of an army. A fierce battle followed which, according to the poet, was indecisive. When the royal brothers-in-law decided to settle the issue by single combat, Gōda, a Cēra prince, intervened between his father and maternal uncle. Both returned to the respective camps and, reflecting on their hostilities, were ashamed and sorry. The poet obviously does not want to say that the Mūṣika submitted to the Kēraḷa, but the descriptions of the honours with which the latter was received by the former in the capital, the tributes they paid him and such other things are clearly indicative of the subordinate status to which the Mūṣikas submitted themselves vis-a-vis the Kēraḷas. Perhaps, it was as a sequel to all this, that Īśānavarman married a Cōḻa princess.

The whole episode acquires significance against the background of the configuration of power politics in contemporary south India. In the beginning of the tenth century, the two most important factors in south Indian politics were the growing powers of the Rāṣṭrakūṭa and Cōḻa empires, every other power having had to define its position in relation to one of these two potentates. The Cēras were friendly, if in a subordinate position, to the Cōḻas at least since the middle of the ninth century and a daughter of Vijayāraga Cēra, Kiḻān Aṭikal *alias* Nīlī, was the wife of Parāntaka Cōḻa.[51] On the other hand, the Cēdis at the end of the ninth and early in the tenth centuries, under Kōkkāla and his son Śaṅkaragaṇa, were subordinate to the Rāṣṭrakūṭas.[52] Thus, when a Mūṣika brother-in-law of the Cēra ruler, who was a subordinate ally of the sworn enemy of the Rāṣṭrakūṭas, went into the latter's camp by marrying into the house of a Rāṣṭrakūṭa ally, the loyal Cēras could not simply ignore it. The happy ending of the whole episode, in which the Mūṣika chief took a Cōḻa princess in marriage, completes the picture of the political nature of the Cēra-Mūṣika relationship within the context of the Cōḻa-Rāṣṭrakūṭa bid for mastery over south India.

Another interesting aspect of this relationship is represented in the descriptions of another episode stated to have taken place about a century later.[53] Valabha, the junior chief of the Mūṣika house, was despatched at the head of a Mūṣika army to help the Kerala king against the Cōḻas. Valabha had to return home in the midst of the battle as he heard of the death of the ruling chief and an ensuing *coup*; but he did so expressly after notifying the Kēraḷa king through a messenger. On his way back home, he is described to have worshipped at [the *vihāra* of] Śrīmūlavāsa, which is known from documents to have been in the Cēra kingdom.[54] In fact, there is an earlier reference in the *kāvya* to the effect that Vikramarāma, the then chief, had protected Śrīmūlavāsa from inundation by raising embankments.[55] This shows a change in the relationship. The relationship that had been cordial between Cēra and Cōḻa was now strained. But even there, we see that the Mūṣikas continued to be allied with the Cēras, giving them military support. Finally, local tradition embodied in the late Malayalam chronicle has it that Udayavarman, the first of the independent Kōlattiris, owed his authority to the sanction of the last of the Cēramān Perumāls.[56] All this goes to suggest the subordinate status of the chiefs of Kōlattunāḍu.

Immediately to the south of Kōlattunāḍu were Puṟakiḻānaḍu and Kuṟumpoṟaināḍu, which together consisted of modern Waynad and parts of Calicut districts of Kerala. A copper plate record dated in the forty-sixth year of Bhāskara Ravi (1008 AD) speaks of a certain Śaṅkaran Kōta Varman who styled himself as Aṭikal Puṟakiḻār and is described Puṟakiḻānāṭṭu=mudu=kūṟu=vāḻumavar, i.e., the senior chief of Puṟakiḻānaḍu,[57] suggesting that the practice of identifying a younger member of the house to succeed to the position obtained there. There is another reference in the Tiruvalla copper plates from south Kerala where the chief of Puṟakiḻānaḍu, Ēṟan Śaṅkaran, makes a gift to the Tiruvalla temple.[58] M. G. S. Narayanan has suggested that Śaṅkaran Kota of the Tirunelli record could have been the immediate successor of Ēṟan Śaṅkaran, that Ēṟan Śaṅkaran was in south Kerala fighting for his Cēra overlord fulfilling his military duty and that he may have been killed in battle. To perform his ancestral rites Śaṅkaran Kōta went to Tirunelli.[59] The chief of this territory maintained a company of retainers, called the Five Hundred.[60]

In the case of Kuṟumpoṟaināḍu lying further south, there is very little information. From another copper plate record from Tirunelli we learn that Kuñcikkuṭṭavarman *alias* Aṭikal Vīrakkuṟumpuṟaiyār was holding the position of the senior chief of Kuṟumpoṟaināḍu (*Mūtta-kūṟu-vaḻkiṇra*)[61] as in the case of Puṟakiḻānaḍu. He had a band of retainers, the Seven Hundred and a number of functionaries such as *adhikāran, paṭanayān, mēnāyan* and *peruntaṭṭān* as we learn from the record. A band of retainers, the Three Hundred, is stated to have been attached to the junior chief of this territory. Both these chiefly houses followed hereditary succession, and used the *varman* suffix to their names indicating their claim to kṣatriya caste. But in the territory immediately to the south, Rāmavaḷanādu, we hear of chiefs belonging to two different houses, both of whom did not claim the kṣatriya caste status.[62] A company of retainers called the Six Hundred, was attached to these chiefs.

Immediately to the south of these territories was that of Ēṟāḷanāḍu which was to become the medieval principality around Calicut ruled by the Zamorins.[63] A chief of this territory figures as one of the witnesses in the famous Jewish copper plates of 1000 AD.[64] Again, a chief of

Ēṟāḷanāḍu, Mānavikrama by name, figures as the foremost *sāmanta* of the last Cēra king, attending the royal court convened at Kollam.[65] An undated inscription from Pulpatta near Manjeri speaks of a company of Six Hundred of Ēṟālanāḍu and Three Hundred of Eḍattaṟanāḍu.[66] Eḍatrāḷpad or the chief of Eḍattaṟanāḍu was the fourth prince in the Zamorin's family in late medieval and modern times;[67] hence this Three Hundred of Eḍattaṟanāḍu may have been attached to a junior chief of Ēṟāḷanāḍu, much in the same way as in the case of Kuṟumpoṟaināḍu. Later traditions, embodied in the *Kēraḷotpatti* as well as the palace chronicles of the Zamorin, have it that the chief of this territory owed his authority to a donation of the Cēramān Perumāḷ.[68] So also there are traditions recorded in the same chronicles about the involvement of these chiefs in the wars that the Perumāḷs of Kerala fought.

Vaḷḷuvanāḍu, to the south of Ēṟāḷanāḍu, was another important chiefdom. The chiefs of this territory bore the hereditary title Rājaśēkhara or Rāyiran, its Malayalam form.[69] A chief of this territory figures as witness to the Jewish copper plates dated 1000 AD.[70] A member of this chiefly family named Veḷḷan Kumaran distinguished himself in the battle of Takkōḷam,[71] fighting it on the Cōḷa side on behalf of the Cēras. Incidentally, it was this Veḷḷan Kumaran who became famous as the ascetic Caturānana Paṇḍita and got attached to the *maṭha* of Tiruvoṟṟiyūr. This chiefly house also maintained a company of Six Hundred as retainers.

Further south were the Neḍumpuṟaiyūrnāḍu and Neduṇkālāi-nāḍu, small territories in the Ottappalam and Palghat taluks of Palghat district. We have a few records which speak of these chiefdoms.[72] There is one record in which two officers called *Neḍumpuṟaiyūrnāṭṭu=paṭai=nāyar* regulated the affairs of the temple of Neḍumpuṟm Tali on behalf of the chief of this *nāḍu*,[73] showing the role of the chiefs and their officers in local government. A Rājādityēśvaram inscription speaks of a certain Malaiyālan Neḍunkālāināṭṭu=Iśānamaṅgalattu= Mānavallan=Kaṇṇa as one of the soldiers from the Cēra country who helped the Cōḷas.[74] This shows the military character of the relation between the chiefs and the Cēra overlord and also the Cēras and the Cōḷas, a typical case of a three-tier feudal relationship in military hierarchy.

Kālkaraināḍu, another chiefly territory around Eḍappaḷḷi near Ernakulam, was ruled by hereditary brahman chiefs.[75] Immediately to its south was Vempalanāḍu. In the late medieval period, there were two principalities of Tekkumukūr and Vaḍakkumkūr, literally the southern and northern divisions of this territory.[76] At least in one of the Cēra inscriptions, the southern division is referred to,[77] implying thereby the existence of both these divisions as early as that period. Even in the late medieval period, these chiefs were described as belonging to the Nāyar caste although in modern times they claimed kṣatriya status.[78]

Kīḻmalaināḍu, Muññināḍu and Naṉṟuḻaināḍu were three chiefdoms to the south and southeast of Vempalanāḍu. The chiefs of Kiḻmalaināḍu bore the hereditary title Māḷuvakkon.[79] A member of this chiefly family was probably among the Malayāḷi soldiers in the Cēra forces which helped the Cōḻa prince Rājāditya in the battle of Takkōḷam.[80] There is reference to the Six Hundred of this *nāḍu*.[81] Information regarding Muññināḍu is scanty except that the chiefs of this territory claimed kṣatriya status and that there was hereditary succession.[82] Naṉṟuḻaināḍu offers a curious case of chiefs being 'appointed' by the Cēra rulers. Thus Gōvardhana Mārtāṇḍa, who was the chief of Veṇāḍu and a witness of the famous Jewish Copper Plates of 1000 AD, is appointed as the chief of Naṉṟuḻaināḍu. He is known to have maintained this dual capacity.[83] In another case, a certain Maṇalmaṉṟattu Yakkan Cirikaṇḍan is mentioned as the chief of this division[84] and we know that from the Maṇalmaṉṟattu family hailed a chief of Neḍumpuṟaiyūranāḍu.[85] There is reference to the Three Hundred of this *nāḍu*.

Veṇāḍu, which developed into the big kingdom of Travancore in medieval times, was the southernmost *nāḍu* in the Cēra country. It had its headquarters in Kollam or modern Quilon, where a trading centre was founded in 825 AD along with a Syrian Christian settlement.[86] Veṇāḍu was under the rule of hereditary chiefs. A junior chief of this house is mentioned in the Syrian Christian Copper Plates of the chief of Veṇāḍu.[87] These plates were issued by Ayyan Aḍigaḷ, the chief of Veṇāḍu, but are dated in the fifth regnal year of the Cēra king, Sthāṇu Ravi (849 AD). Similarly, there is the signature of Gōvardhana Mārtāṇḍa, the chief of Veṇāḍu, as a witness in the Jewish Copper Plates of 1000 AD.[88] A member of this chiefly family, viz., Vēḷkula-sundaran, figures in the Rājadityēśvaram record as one of the Malayāḷi soldiers in the army of Rājāditya Cōḻa.[89] All these indicate the subordinate position of the chiefs of Veṇāḍu to the Cēra king. A palace called Paṇaiṅkāvil palace is mentioned at least in two records as the residence of the chiefs of Veṇāḍu.[90] One of them is very significant as it is stated that Ramavarma Kulasekhara, the Cēra king, resided at the Panaiṅkāvil palace and held his court there in 1102 AD.[91] This is significant because it shows that Kollam was something of a second capital of the Cēras during the Cōḻa wars. It also brings out the fact that the overlord could convene his court or council at the headquarters of the feudatory chiefs also.

The situation with regard to the chiefs in Kerala presents an interesting phenomenon. There were chiefs who were hereditary rulers of territories. Some of them claimed a kṣatriya status while some others belonged to the Nayar caste. There is at least one case where the chief was of a brahman family. In the case of another chiefdom, the ruler owed his authority to the appointment by the Cēra king himself. The Jewish Copper Plates reveal that at least the more important chiefs assembled at the court of the Cēra sovereign in situations of emergency, which is confirmed by the Kollam Ramēśvarasvāmin temple inscription where the only difference is that the court is held at the headquarters of one of the chiefs. The military obligation of the chiefs to the overlord is also borne out by the Rājādītyēśvaram inscription where a number of soldiers belonging to the different chiefly families in Kerala figure. The same picture is presented by the statements in the *Mūṣikavaṃśakāvya*, cited above. So also, the references to matrimonial relations between the chiefly houses and the Cēra royal house, as exemplified in the *kāvya*, may be representative of the situation existing in relation to other chiefly houses as well.

One sees three clear stages in the fortunes of these chiefs under the Cōḻas. Till the close of the tenth century, i.e. about the middle of the reign of Rājarāja I, the situation was almost as if affairs continued relatively unchanged from the time of the Pallavas. For about another century from the beginning of the eleventh, one is struck by the absence of references in the records to the chiefs ruling in the localities. Members of the chiefly families, however, figure as state officials in the records. Towards the end of the eleventh century, we see that the chiefs reassert themselves, as it were, with a vengeance, for there is an unprecedented profusion of references to both the number of the chiefs and the range of their activities. This pattern fits in neatly with the relatively weak officialdom of the central government in the pre-Rājarāja I period, its unprecedented elaboration in about a century following Rājarāja I, and then the tapering off of such officials after that. These two would together support the idea of an attempt at centralisation under Rājarāja I and his successors which, however, was thwarted towards the twelfth century by the centrifugal tendencies typical of a feudal formation.

Among the more powerful chiefs under the Cōḻas in the pre-Rājarāja phase were the Paḻuvēṭṭaraiyar, the Vēḷs of Koḍumbāḷur, the Maḻavas, the Milāḍu chiefs, the Bāṇas and the Gaṅgas. During this period, the records where they figure show clearly that they represented a logical development from an earlier period in history. The Paḻuvēḍu chiefs are referred to as the Kēraḷa kings.[92] They exercised authority within the region of Kuṉṟa-Kūṟṟam which was a single *nāḍu*. A few records show the extent of their authority within this territory. Permission from the ruling Paḻuvēḍu chief is sought in 884, 893 and 968 AD for reclaiming land.[93] They had their own department of land revenue (*puṟavu-vari*), as is clear from the expression *tiṇai* or *peruntiṇai* figuring in their records.[94] An 'army division' of the Paḻuvēḍu chiefs is known from an inscription of Rājarāja Cōḻa.[95] An officer of the Perundiram (i.e., *Perundaram*) is found in a record.[96] A record of the grant of land as life tenure (*janma-bhumi*) to an officer states that the *nāḍu* assembly was required, besides executing the grant, to concur with the chief's decision concerning the assessment of the land granted.[97] Another record claims to follow the standard prevailing in Nandipuram in the matter of assessing fines and other dues from the two *nagaram*s and twelve *kaḻaṇai*s (castes) of Paḻavūr.[98] This indicates, in another way, the subordination of the territory under Paḻuvēṭṭaraiyar to the Cōḻas, for Nandipuram was another name of Āyirattaḻi or Paḻaiyṟai, the royal residence of the Cōḻas.[99] In the records of the post-Rājarāja period, we do not come across this chiefly line at all.

While the Paḻuvēṭṭaraiya chiefs exercised authority over a single *nāḍu*, the Vēḷs (the Irukku- and Iḷaṅgō) did so over a larger territory. They patronised temples on a munificent scale.[100] A number of tax-free *dēvadāna* gifts were made by the Vēḷ chiefs.[101] Even in the case of the Vēḷ chiefs, the land revenue department appears to have been active as we gather from a reference to the *tiṇai* as an official title[102] and also to a register (*pottakam*) in which entries regarding tax remission were made.[103] Even in the same way that the Cōḻa king would do, a Vēḷ chief addressed a *śrīmukam* to the *brahmadēyakkiḻavar* and the local *nāḍu*.[104] There is at least one case where a Vēḷ chief receives an order from the Cōḻa king and acts on it,[105] bringing out the subordinate position in which he stood to the Cōḻa overlord. A daughter of Tennavan Iḷaṅgōvēḷār was married to a son of Parāntaka while one of his daughters, Anupamā by name, was married to a Koḍumbāḷur chief.[106]

The fortunes of the Koḍumbāḷūr chiefs in this period and after Rājarāja I is interesting. They lost their political power and authority as local chieftains following the centralisation of the empire by Rājarāja I. Instead, we see members of their chiefly family in important positions in the Cōḻa officaldom. Thus we have a certain Madhurāntakan Sundara Cōḻa *alias* Rājarāja-Iḷaṅko-vēlān who is described as a *sēnāpati* under Rājarāja,[107] a Madhurāntakan Rājādhirāja Iḷaṅkovēlān, a *daṇḍanāyagam* under Rājādhirāja,[108] a Vira Cōḻa Iḷaṅkovēlān and another Rājarājan Jayaṅgonda Cōḻan *alias* Irukkuveḷān, both under Adhirājēndra.[109] However, after 1070 AD, we do not hear much about this chiefly house, either as political chiefs or as royal functionaries.

As in the case of the Paḻuvēṭṭaraiyar, there is a reference to a Maḻava chief who regulated the collection of fines according to the standard of Nandipuram.[110] A Viṇṇakō chief is stated to be in possession of a *nāḍu*, who, in association with the *nāḍu* group, decides about certain paddy contribution for the maintenance of a local tank.[111] We have references to Viṇṇakō, Milāḍu, Munaiya and other chiefs in the same period.[112] In the case of the Milāḍu chiefs, there are at least two instances where they are referred to as belonging to the Bhārgava *gōtra* and one of them sports a *varman* suffix in his name.[113] When a Gaṅga chief donated some land to a *brahmadēya*, he did so, significantly, with the consent of the Cōḻa king.[114] There the local *nāḍu* group was required by the chief to fix the boundaries. Similarly, another Gaṅga chief sought the permission of Uttama Cōḻa before he created a tax-free *dēvadāna* in his *nāḍu*.[115] There are other clear instances of feudal subordination and the political hierarchy in which they were placed. All these references are to the period before Rājarāja I.

It follows that in the pre-Rājarāja phase of Cōḻa history, the areas peripheral to the central Cōḻa territory or Cōḻamandalam (Tañjāvūr and parts of Tirucciṟāpalli district) were under the control of these different chiefs. The 'expansion' of the Cōḻas in that period did not mean much more than having these chiefs' acceptance of their hegemony; uprooting or replacing the chiefs did not really take place. Even this acceptance or recognition of the Cōḻa hegemony expressed itself in the relatively few but significant instances where these chiefs are stated to have received 'orders' from the Cōḻa king apart from the Cōḻa titles which some of them took and the Cōḻa regnal years in which they dated their records. These instances clarify the lord-vassal relationship of varying degrees consequent on the super-ordination of a higher political authority over these pre-existing chiefly families. The evidence brought together by Nilakanta Sastri on Parāntaka I's relation with the Bāṇas and Vaidumbas on the eve of the battle of Takkōlam is significant in this respect.[116] M. G. S. Narayanan has thrown significant new light on the character of the alliance between the Cēras and Cōḻas in this war, a number of chiefs in the Kerala country offering military support to the overlord of the Cēras, thereby bringing out the feudal hierarchy with the Cōḻa suzerain at the top, his Cēra vassal below him and the feudatory chiefs of the Cēras still lower.[117]

These chiefs cultivated a complex network of matrimonial relations among themselves as well as between them on the one hand and the Cōḻa royal family on the other, thereby creating a sort of integrated community. Thus Parāntaka Cōḻa had a Paḻuvēṭṭaraya princess by name Arumoḻinaṅgai for his wife.[118] Ariñjaya, the Cōḻa prince, was her son. Pañcavan Mādēvi, the queen of Rājarāja I, was a Paḻuvēṭṭaraya princess, probably a daughter of Kaṇḍan Maṟavan.[119] Another Paḻuvēṭṭaraya princess married a Cēra prince.[120] Yet another princess of the house of Paḻuvēṭṭarayas married an Irukkuvēḷ chief.[121] Similarly, Parāntaka, a son of the Koḍumbāḷur chief Bhuti Vikramakēsari, married a Cōḻa princess, perhaps a daughter of Parāntaka.[122] He had other wives as well, including a daughter of a Muttaraiya.[123] Another Parāntakan Kuñjaramallan, a Koḍumbāḷur chief, married a sister of Sundara Cōḻa.[124] The complex matrimonial relations involving the Cēras, Mūṣikas, Cēdis and Cōḻas have been referred to earlier in this chapter. We have also information about matrimonial ties among Vāṇa-ko and Ilāḍa,[125] Vēḷ and Paḻuvēḍu,[126] Vāṇa-ko and Gaṅga,[127] etc. However, one notices that on the basis of this complex endogamous network and the common social function, these chiefs did not surprisingly arrogate to themselves the kṣatriya caste status which the Cōḻa overlord was claiming for himself. The only exception was of the Milāḍu chiefs who fleetingly claimed to belong to a brahman *gotra* and sported the kṣatriya caste suffix. This fact of the kṣatriya status being claimed almost exclusively by the Cōḻas may be taken as illustration of the process by which the more important ruling houses elevated themselves to a higher ritual status with the help of priests and court poets while their kinsmen in the chiefly families were kept inferior in ritual status to correspond to their political and social status vis-à-vis those of the overlords.

A major change in the political situation is noticed during the reign of Rājarāja I (985 to 1014 AD). The Cōḻa records from about the middle of this reign are curiously silent about these chiefs or the chiefly rule. Wherever they are mentioned it is as officials of the king's government. Again, it is seen that many of the members of such chiefly families, who were now reduced to officials of the state, functioned in areas far afield from their home territory.[128] Thus, in an inscription dated 1085 AD we have a Bāṇa, Ceṅgēṇi Cāttan Vīra Cōḻan *alias* Vāṇaṟājar, acting as a *sēnapāti* in the Chingleput district.[129] Another Bāṇa, Arumoḻi Vikrama Cōḻa *alias* Vāṇātarājan functioned as an *olainayagam* in 1063 AD,[130] and still another Vāṇātirājan as an *ōlaināyagam* in the reign of Virarājēndra in 1068 AD.[131] A large number of members of the Bāṇa, Nōḷamba, Pallava, Kāḍava, Cēdi, Gaṅga, Vaidumba and other chiefly houses are seen to be carrying out functions of the king's government in several capacities.[132] We have seen similar situations in relation to the Paḻuvēṭṭaraiya chiefly house. What is more, the territories covered by the chiefdoms hitherto were reorganised and resettled as *vaḷanādus* during Rājarāja's reign. In these *vaḷanādus*, officials of the king's government replaced the chiefs, thereby restructuring the entire polity of the Cōḻa state. In fact, evidences of this kind of an attempt at imperial centralisation under Rājarāja are manifold. This state of affairs in relation to the chiefs appears to have continued for about a century and by the post-Kulōttuṅga I period the chiefs begin to reappear in a subdued manner. This would suggest that the chiefly families were not obliterated but only made to surrender their political power in favour of the overlord.

The records of these chiefs are few and far between under Kulōttuṅga and Vikrama Cōḻa. In the period that followed, however, there was a proliferation of these chiefs on a scale unequalled in the earlier periods of south Indian history.[133] As usual they are found donating land to temples. When they do that they certainly acknowledge the suzerainty of the Cōḻa king by dating their records in Cōḻa regnal years and prefixing a Cōḻa title to their names. But there is a qualitative difference in the nature of the role of these chiefs. They are no longer the heroes of the old world that they had been in the pre-Rājarāja period. They get more and more integrated into the system of the Cōḻa state, if in a subordinate position. A significant difference in the post-Kulōttuṅga III phase is that in the records of this period which are more numerous and more copious than those of the earlier phase, there is no reference to the chiefs receiving orders from the Cōḻa king nor is there an indication of the chiefs seeking permission from the Cōḻa king before making a grant or issuing an order. This clearly suggests an increase in the power and authority of the chiefs who were asserting their independence once again. It is interesting and significant that by this time the chiefs return to their original territories.

This is further found in what is called the *pāḍi kāval.*[134] *Pāḍi kāval* literally means the protection (*kāval*) of the territory (*pāḍi*). This involved the policing of the country. The remuneration on account of this protection was also known by this expression. A record of 1160 AD speaks of the holder of land as *pāḍi kāval kāṇi* in the local *nāḍu*,[135] which indicates that land was assigned on service tenure in lieu of the remuneration for *pāḍi kāval*. From a few inscriptions mentioning the gift of the *pāḍi kāval* dues, it can be seen that even land owned by temples was not free from this levy. Subbarayalu has computed the rate of the *pāḍi kāval* as between five and ten per cent of the total produce, which was considerable.[136] He has also suggested that the chiefs seemed to have collected other dues as well. An interesting aspect about the *pāḍi kāval* is that out of the thirty-seven references to this in the published Cōḻa inscriptions, nine are from the Chittoor district, four from Chingleput, five from North Arcot and nineteen from South Arcot, suggesting that this in no time obtained in the heartland of Cōḻamaṇḍalam.[137] Further, it is also significant that all these records date from the post-Kulōttuṅga period.[138]

Another pointer to the changed nature of the chiefs in the post-Kulōttuṅga period of Cōḻa history are the numerous pacts known as the *nilamaitfīṭṭu* concluded between two or more chiefs.[139] *Nilamaitfīṭṭu* literally means the 'document of *status quo*', and the contents also attest to this meaning. Generally two or more chiefs agreed to respect their territorial boundaries as well as help each other against a common, specified enemy. In some cases, we see interesting 'diplomatic' changes, for who was an enemy in one deed appears as a friend in another deed of a later date.

Both the *pāḍi kāval* and *nilamaittiṭṭu* point to the military functions of the chiefs in a typical feudal polity. Besides, we have further evidence to show this military role. We have numerous references to the army divisions of the different chiefs. They include a *paḍaittalaivan* of a Śambuvaraya,[140] the *sēnai* of a Cēdirāya and an elephant-rider attached to it,[141] the *agambaḍi mudaligaḷ* (retainers) of Kadambarāyar,[142] Cēdirayar,[143] Vāṇa-ko Māgaḍaiperumāl,[144] Kāḍava Kōpperuñjiṅga[145] and Yādavarāya.[146] It is stated that there are even cases of Vēḷlaikkāra soldiers taking 'oaths of fealty' to the chiefs.[147] It is most likely that these armies were pressed into service in the expeditions of the Cōḻa rulers, as is clearly stated at least in two cases.[148] In one record, which is a typical *nilamaitfīṭṭu*, there is the statement that the two parties should stand together while both are in the service of the king or in the thick of *vaṇṇiyar valam* (which expression is interpreted as quarrels among the chiefs themselves).[149] The Tiruvālaṅgāḍu inscription of Rājādhiraja II dated 1175 AD refers to the armies (*ēḷagattār* and Maṟava 'regiments') of the chiefs Rājarāja Karkuḍimārāyan and Rājagambhīra Anju Kottai-nāḍālvān who helped the Cōḻa king against the Pāṇḍyas.[150]

In fact, it is in the matter of the military connections obtaining among these chiefs and between them on the one side and their overlords on the other that we are able to identify the exact nature of relationship in which they stood to one another. In spite of the limited scope of our records, we are able to delineate certain broad outlines in this regard. We have seen earlier in this chapter aspects of the military relations between the Pallavas and the chiefs within their 'sphere of influence'. Again, the military entanglements involving the Pāṇḍyas, the Āys and the Cēras have been brought out. But nowhere can the nature of such relationship be more clearly defined than between the Cēras and the Cōḷas, references to which have been made earlier in this chapter. In the ninth century, when the Cēra kingdom had just come into existence on the west coast, they had to contend with the still strong power of the Pāṇḍyas. It is in this context that the posthumous conferment jointly by

Śrīkanṭha Cōḻa of the Telugu Pottapi line and Śrikanṭha Ravi Cēra of certain titles and privileges on the Kadamba-Gaṅga chief, Vikki Aṇṇan by name,[151] has to be placed. Again, it is against the same background of a Cēra-Cōḻa *entente* that one has to see the complex relationship between the Cēras, Mūṣikas, Cēdis and Cōḻas that we disenssed above. A record from Tirunāmanallūr, giving details of a large number of Malayāḷi soldiers hailing from a large number of chiefly families in Kerala, acquires significance in this respect.[152] Members of chiefly families of Vaḷḷuvanāḍu, Neḍungālināḍu, Kiḻmalaināḍu, Veṇāḍu, etc., are found assisting the Cōḻa prince Rājāditya on the eve of the famous battle of Takkōḷam. This clearly brings out a three-tier relationship: the chiefly families in Kerala fulfilling their military obligation to their Cēra overlord and the latter, in turn, doing the same thing to his Cōḻa overlord. In the beginning of the following century when the tables were turned, we find the Cēras and Cōḻas fighting with each other. In that context, again, the Mūṣikas sent their forces in support of the Cēras. In fact, a whole 'war council' at the capital Mahodayapuram can be identified when six chiefs attest to the grant of privileges to a Jewish chief in the thick of the Cēra-Cōḻa war.[153] Similarly early in the twelfth century, another 'war council' consisting of the *sāmanta*s was convened by the Cēra Perumāḷ in the headquarters of one of the chiefdoms.[154] All this clearly points to the feudal nature of military obligations existing between the chiefs and their overlords.

It is a moot question if these chiefs paid any annual tribute to their overlords. As we have seen in a previous chapter, the *praśasti*s of the Pallavas and Cōḻas state that they received tributes from a number of vassals. There is no reason to dispute such statements, for, in the absence of the institution, the idea would not have been there. Of course, one may question whether a particular chief paid tribute to any particular king, especially in the absence of clear statements. But, considering the nature of our records which are for the most part records of temples dealing with some endowment or other kind of regulations, such statements regarding the payment of tribute to the overlords are not to be expected to figure in them. However, there are a couple of instances in the literature of the period. The Vaiṣṇava saint Tirumaṅgai speaks of 'those chiefs who do not pay tribute to Pallavas'[155] implying thereby that the practice of paying tribute to overlords prevailed at that time.

Similarly, Kulōttuṅga is said in the *Kaliṅgattupparaṇi* to be sitting in state in the palace at Kāñchipuram when one of his officers, a *tiru-mandira-ōlai*, informed him about the subordinate kings waiting upon him to pay tribute.[156] Granting that this typical piece of court poetry may have exaggerated things, the idea that subordinate chiefs paid tributes to their overlord is unmistakably seen there. So also, one has to believe that of the various forms of revenue collected at the local levels, some share reached the treasury of the kings through these local chiefs, especially from areas outside the directly administered regions in the kingdoms, although we do not know practically anything about the mode of revenue transfers. This is, however, suggested by a couple of cases in the Cēra kingdom brought out by M. G. S. Narayanan where fines for the default of dues are apportioned in one case between the king and the local chief in a 2:1 ratio and in another case between a local chief and a still lesser lord again in a 2:1 ratio.[157] There is no reason why the same arrangement did not work in the case of the revenue transfers as well, in which case it is nothing but the payment of tributes by the subordinate chiefs.

Summing up the discussion concerning the chiefs, it can be seen that to begin with they represented a continuation of the chiefs of an earlier period, living a life of cattle-raids and hero-worship, as seen from the earliest records in the Pallava country. Gradually one sees that the super-ordinate power of the newly emerging monarchical state is acknowledged by them. A further development is noticed as the Cōḻa rule is established in the Kāvēri valley, when a complex network of political and matrimonial relations is established among these chiefs and also between these chiefs and their Cōḻa overlords. The same situation prevailed in the Cēra kingdom also. But when the Cōḻa state expanded and consolidated itself by the close of the tenth century, the chiefs lost their political power, became part of the state system as royal functionaries and thus succumbed to the attempts at centralisation. About a century later, however, they gradually reappeared asserting a greater amount of power and independence and, by the closing years of the Cōḻa rule, it was these chiefs who were more powerful than the Cōḻa rulers themselves.

This fits in exactly with the pattern of a typical feudal polity. The chiefs are seen to be hierarchically arranged in relation to their overlord.

Even in the period from Rājarāja I to Kulōttuṅga, when chiefly rule in the Cōḻa country is not noticed, it could be seen that the neighbouring kings, such as the Cēras and Pāṇḍyas, stood in this kind of a relation to the Cōḻa overlord. Indeed, this hierarchy resembled the typical feudal pyramid. However, our presentation of polity as feudal is not based simply on the ostensible pyramidal structure: the whole gamut of relations is considered here. They include the military obligation of the chiefs to the overlords, their obligation to attend the overlord's courts and even to arrange for holding one in their own headquarters, the protection they received from the overlord, the annual tribute they paid to the overlord, the complex network of political and matrimonial alliance even within which the overlord retained a higher ritual status, and so on. When all this is considered against the background of the socio-economic reality taken up for discussion in the chapters to follow, this feudal character of polity will emerge with greater clarity.

## NOTES

1. E.g., M. G. S. Narayanan, *Political and Social Conditions of Kerala ..., op. cit.*, Chapters on 'Divisions of the Kingdom'.

2. K. A. Nilakanta Sastri, *The Pandyan Kingdom*, pp. 74–75; *The Colas*, pp. 126–28; 187–89; 259–60; 347–48; 372–75; 400–08; 429–32; T. V. Mahalingam, *South Indian Polity*, 321–28; M. S. Govindasamy, *The Role of Feudatories in Pallava History*, (Annamalainagar, 1975); *idem, The Role of Feudatories in later Chola History*, (Annamalainagar, 1979); M. Arokiaswamy, *The Kongu Country*, (Madras, 1956); V. Balambal, *Feudatories of South India 800–1070 AD* (Allahabad, 1978); etc.

3. R. Sathianathaier, 'Foreword' to Govindasamy, *The Role of Feudatories in Pallava History*, p. i.

4. Stein, 'The State and Agrarian Order ...', *op. cit.*, p. 83; *idem, Peasant State and Society ..., op. cit.*, pp. 112–17.

5. See discussion above, Chapter 3.

6. Stein, *Peasant State ...*, pp. 133–40 and diagrams on pp. 135 and 139.

7. See discussion below, Chapter 6.

8. For Āys and Vēls in Sangam literature, M. G. S. Narayanan, *Reinterpretations in South Indian History, op. cit.*, pp. 33–34 n.2; 36; n. 15; for Mūṣakas identified with Mūvas, *ibid*, pp. 63–64; 33–98; Adigamāns, Nilakanta Sastri, *History*

*of South India*, pp. 122–23; for Koḍumbāḷūr, *ibid.*, 433. T. V. Kuppuswami, *Sangam Chieftains and Their Times*, Ph.D. Thesis, Kerala University, Trivandrum, 1976.

9. This inscription from Jambai in South Arcot which is a label, speaks of Atiyāman Neḍumān Añji described in Sangam literature and describes him as Satiyaputō.

10. See discussion above, Chapter 1.

11. R. Nagaswami, (ed.) *Cengam Nadukarkal* (Madras, 1972).

12. *Ibid.*

13. *Ibid.*, nos. 1971/69; 1971/68.

14. M. D. Sampath, 'Hero Stone Inscriptions from Dharmapuri District' Mimeo.

15. *Ibid.*

16. 211 and 212 of1910.

17. Govindasamy, *Role of Feudatories in Pallava History*, pp. 2–25.

18. *E.I.* XI, p. 223, Ins.A.

19. Govindasamy, *Role of Feudatories in Pallava History*, p. 6.

20. Cf. discussion on the purpose of genealogy above, Chapter 2.

21. *Mysore Archaeological Reports*, 1913–14, Para 68–70.

22. *Ibid*, pp. 35–37.

23. Govindasamy, *Role of Feudatories in Pallava History*, pp. 10–11.

24. 584 of 1906; 164 of 1933–34; 187, 188, 196, 197, 229 and 230 of 1931–32. Also Govindasamy, *Role of Feudatories in Pallava History*, p. 16.

25. *E.C.*, IX, UK 9 (Rev. edn.)

26. *E.I.*, IV, no. 23, pp. 180–83.

27. Govindasamy, *Role of Feudatories in Pallava History*, pp.126, 127, 129; M.V. Krishna Rao, *The Gangas of Talkad* (Madras, 1936), pp. 11,63; B. Sheik Ali, *History of the Western Gangas*, (Mysore, 1976), pp. 44, 53, 92.

28. Govindasamy, *Role of Feudatories in Pallava History.*

29. See discussion in *ibid.*, pp. 68–70; K. G. Krishnan, *Studies in South Indian History and Epigraphy*, (Madras, 1981), Vol. I, pp. 133–38; Subbarayalu, *State in Medieval South India*, pp. 38–39, n. 3.

30. Above, n. 21.

31. T. V. Mahalingam, 'An Interregnum in Pallava History'. Originally published in *Journal of Indian History* (1963), reprinted in Mahalingam, *Readings in South Indian History*, pp. 59–71.

32. Govindasamy, *Role of Feudatories in Pallava History*, pp. 112–21.

33. *P.C.P.*, p. 21, II.24–25.

34. *S.I.I.*, XII, 78; *E.I.*, VII, 20 B and C.

35. Nagaswami, *op. cit.*, nos. 1971/46,47.

36. Rajan Gurukkal, *The Agrarian System and Socio-political Organisation under the Early Pandyas*, pp. 242 ff.

37. Nilakanta Sastri, *Pandyan Kingdom*, p. 74.

38. *Ibid.*, p. 75; 10 of 1899 and 421 of 1906.

39. M. G. S. Narayanan, *Reinterpretations in South Indian History*, pp. 24–40. For reference to earlier literature, *ibid.*, p. 33, n.1.

40. *Ibid.*, p. 36, n. 15.

41. *Ibid.*, pp. 26–28.

42. *T.A.S.*, I, pp. 1–14.

43. *T.A.S.*, I, XIII, pp. 197–200.

44. *T.A.S.*, I, XlI, A. pp. 187–93.

45. M. G. S. Narayanan's Ph.D. thesis, *op. cit.*, makes a detailed study of these chiefs in Kerala although he regards them as 'governors' and their territories as 'divisions' or 'districts' of the kingdom. The material for discussion in this section is taken largely from his work, which is acknowledged with gratitude.

46. For details, M.G.S. Narayanan 'Anatomy of a political alliance from Temple Records of Tirunavalur and Tiruvorriyur', *Journal of the Epigraphical Society of India*, Vol. V, 1978, pp. 24–31.

47. There are at least seven inscriptions from the territory of this chiefdom. Ramantaḷi, nos. 474 and 475 of 1926; Kannapuram, no. 476 of 1926; Tiruvaḍūr, nos. 477 and 478 of 1926; (actually forming only one record); Eramam, no. 523 of 1930; Pullur, no. 125 of 1963–64; Triccambaram, unnoticed and unpublished officially but copied by M. G. S. Narayanan and indexed as no. A 61 in *Index to Cera Inscriptions, op. cit.* Of these three are dated in Cēra regnal years and two quote the Muḻikkaḷam precedence (below Chapter 7). In fact, no. 523 of 1930 from Eramam is dated conjointly in the regnal years of Cēra Bhāskara Ravi and Mūṣika Kantan Kāri Varman, thereby showing in unmistakable terms the subordinate position of the latter to the former on account of the precedence.

48. Two manuscript copies of this *kāvya* were available in the manuscripts library, Trivandrum, nos. 20869 and 20870. Extracts and English summmary of its contents were published by T. A. Gopinatha Rao, *T.A.S.*, II, ii. pp. 87–113. Scholarly studies by K. V. Subrahmanya Aiyar, Chirakkal T. Balakrishnan Nayar, N. V. Krishna Varier, Ulloor S. Parameswara Aiyar and N. P. Unni have been published on various aspects of the *kavya*. For a historical study, M. G. S. Narayanan, *Reinterpretations in South Indian History*, pp. 58–65; Romila Thapar, 'The Mouse in the Ancestry', in S. D. Joshi (ed.), *Amrtadhara* (Delhi, 1984), pp. 427–34. The full text of the *kavya* as much as it survives has been

published with a Malayalam translation by K. Raghavan Pillai, *Mūskavaṁśam* (Trivandrum, 1983).

49. Narayanan, *Reinterpretations ..., op. cit.*, pp. 63–64; 83–98.

50. Raghavan Pillai, *op. cit.*, pp. 226–44, vv. 6–61.

51. *S. I. I.*, III, no. 113, M.G.S. Narayanan, *Political and Social Conditions ..., op. cit.*, Chapter on 'Early wars and alliances'.

52. Narayanan, *ibid.*

53. Raghavan Pillai, *op. cit.*, pp. 284–88, vv. 7–25.

54. For Srimūlavāsam as a Buddhist *Vihāra* in the Kerala country, M. G. S. Narayanan, *Cultural Symbiosis in Kerala, op. cit.*

55. Raghavan Pillai, *op. cit.*, p. 254, v. 96.

56. Gundert, ed., *Keralotpatti, op. cit.* There is the mention of an Udayavaraman who was a Mūṣika chief in a Kaṇṇapuram Inscription no. 476 of 1926. He may be either identical with, or an ancestor with the same name of the hero of the tradition.

57. *I.A.*, XX, pp. 235–90.

58. *T.A.S.*, II, iii, II.150–51.

59. Narayanan, *Political and Social Conditions ..., op. cit.*, Chapter on 'Divisions of the Kingdom'. This temple is famous for ancestral rites even today.

60. Above, n. 57.

61. *E.I.*, XVI no, 27.

62. *S.I.I.*, V. no. 784 and also an unpublished inscription from Ramanattukara, M.G.S. Narayanan, *Index to Cera Inscriptions, op. cit.*, C.14.

63. K. V. Krishna Ayyar, *The Zamorins of Calicut* (Calicut, 1938), *passim.*

64. *E.I*, III, p. 63 ff.

65. *T.A.S.*, V. no. 13.

66. No. 282 of 1969.

67. Krishna Ayyar, *op. cit.*, p. 10.

68. Gundert, ed., *op. cit.*

69. *S.I.I.*, V. no. 773 and 775; Narayanan, *Political and Social Conditions ..., op. cit.*, Chapter on 'Divisions of the Kingdom'.

70. *E.I.*, III, p. 68ff.

71. Above, n. 46.

72. *T.A.S.*, II, 7(H), pp. 42–44; *T.A.S.* VIII. P. 43 and 41. (Published as two separate records but actually forming parts of the same).

73. *T.A.S.*, VIII, no. 33 (v). See also n. 33 (viii).

74. Above, n. 46.

75. *T.A.S.*, III, no. 39. This mentions Paṉṟitturutti Yakkan Kuṉṟappolan as the chief of this *nāḍu*. The present writer has demonstrated elsewhere that the

Paṉṟitturutti family was a brahman family. Kesavan Veluthat, *Aryan Brahman Settlements of Ancient Kerala*, (unpublished M.A. dissertation, University of Calicut, 1974), Appendix II.

76. P. K. S. Raja, *Medieval Kerala* (Annamalainagar, 1968).

77. *Indian Historical Quartely*, IV, pp. 154–55.

78. Raja, *op. cit.*

79. *T.A.S.*, III, no. 47; II, iii, 1.351; etc.

80. Above, n. 46.

81. *T.A.S.*, V, no. 59, pp. 181–83.

82. *T.A.S.*, II, iii, II. 532–37.

83. *T.A.S.*, II, no. 7 (a) Also *T.A.S.*, II, no. 61; no. 7(B); *T.A.S.*, V, no. 57.

84. *T.A.S.*, V., no. 55.

85. *T.A.S.*, VIII, p. 43 and 41. (Actually forming parts of the same record). Narayanan, *Index to Cera Inscriptions*, A. 27.

86. *T.A.S.*, II, nos. 9 (I) and 9 (II).

87. *Ibid.*

88. *E.I.*, III, p. 68 ff.

89. Above, n. 46.

90. *T.A.S.*, IV, no. 1 *T.A.S.*, V. no. 13. The former record is interesting also for the fact that, issued by Śrīvallabhan Kōta, Chief of Vēṇadu in 973 AD, it is not dated in the regnal year of the then Cēra overlord, Bhāskara Ravi. This has been explained by M. G. S. Narayanan as a result of Bhaskara Ravi coming to the throne very early in his life and taking up the full reins only about eighteen years later. Narayanan, *Political and Social Conditions ...*, Chapter on 'Chronology'. This record would fall in the period of Bhaskara Ravi's minority, in his eleventh year.

91. *T.A.S.*, V. no. 13.

92. *E.I.*, XV, no. 5. The reason for their being described as Kerala kings is not clear. Hailing from a region near Karur, the ancient Cēra capital, would they have been related to, or confused with, the Cēras?

93. *S.I.I.*, XIII, 235, 298, 236.

94. *S.I.I.*, V. 682; XIX, 273.

95. *S.I.I.*, V. 670.

96. *S.I.I.*, V. 667.

97. *S.I.I.*, XIX, 378.

98. *S.I.I*, XIII, 208, 215, 344.

99. D. Thulasiraman, 'A Preliminary Report on Paḷaiyaṟai Excavations', *Tamil Civilization*, Vol. V, nos. 1 and 2, March–June 1987, pp. 118–23.

100. E.g., *S.I.I.*, VIII, 646.

101. *S.I.I.*, VIII, 616, 624, 627, 632, 668, 687, 694; XIX, 413, 414; *I.P.S.*, 23, 26, 30.

102. *S.I.I.*, VIII, 668, 601.

103. *S.I.I.*, VIII, 601.

104. *S.I .I.*, VIII, 668.

105. *Ibid.*

106. *Journal of Oriental Research*, pp. 8–9. II. 7–8. For other matrimonial alliances of the Vēḷs of Koḍumbāḷūr, Govindasamy, *The Role of Feudatories in Later Chola History, op. cit.*, pp. 16–20.

107. 370 of 1953–54.

108. 143 of 1912.

109. *S.I.I.*, VIII, nos. 4 and 754.

110. *S.I.I.*, III, 212.

111. *S.I.I.*, XIX, 80, 81.

112. Govindasamy, *Role of Feudatories in Later Chola History, passim.*

113. *Concordance*, 3325, 3623.

114. Subbarayalu, *State in Medieval South India*, pp. 49–50.

115. *S.I.I.*, XIX, 169.

116. Sastri, *Colas*, pp. 126–27.

117. Above, n. 46.

118. *S.I.I.*, VIII, no. 520; *E.I*, XV, no. 5.

119. Govindasamy, *Role of Feudatories in Later Chola History*, p. 34.

120. *S.I.I.*, XIX, 153.

121. *S.I.I.*, V. 671.

122. Govindasamy, *Role of Feudatories in Later Chola History*, pp. 17–22.

123. *Ibid.*

124. *Ibid.*

125. *E.I.*, VII, 20–d.

126. *S.I.I.*, V, 671.

127. *E.I.*, VII, 26–C.

128. Cf. Above, Chapter 3, Section on titles. This posting of erstwhile chieftains or members of chiefly families away from their traditional territory is significant because in the attempt to impersonalise state and government, Rājarāja and his immediate successors tried to avoid the development of vested local interests by these 'officers'.

129. *S.I.I.*, V, 1003.

130. No. 32 of 1952; *Concordance, 3960.*

131. *S.I.I.*, IV, 593.

132. *Concordance, passim.*

133. This corresponds with the tapering off of the officialdom in the Cōḻa state during this period. Above, Chapter 3.

134. Sastri, *Colas*, pp. 533–34; Mahalingam, *South Indian Polity*, pp. 246–47; Subbarayalu, *State in Medieval South India*, pp. 53–54.

135. *S.I.I.*, VIII, 285.

136. Subbarayalu, *State in Medieval South India*, p. 54.

137. Karashima, *South Indian History and Society*, p. 90 (Table 10).

138. *Ibid.*

139. Subbarayalu, *State in Medieval South India*, pp. 54–57.

140. *A.R.E.*, 1932–33, p. 66.

141. *S.I.I.*, VII, 890.

142. *I.P.S.*, 181.

143. *S.I.I.*, VIII, 124.

144. *S.I.I.*, VII, 1020.

145. *S.I.I.*, VII, 149.

146. *S.I.I.*, VIII, 84.

147. *A.R.E.* 1934–35, p. 61.

148. *S.I.I.*, VIII, 106; *A.R.E.*, 1934–35, p. 62.

149. *A.R.E.*, 1934–35, p. 62.

150. *E.I.*, XXII, 14.

151. *S.I.I.*, III, p. 89. See also M. G. S. Narayanan, *Political and Social Conditions ...*, Chapter on 'Early Wars and Alliances'.

152. Above, n. 46.

153. *E.I.*, III, p. 68ff.

154. *T.A.S.*, V, no. 13.

155. *Nālāyira Divya Prabandham*.

156. *Kaliṅgattupparaṇi*, Chapter 2, v. 314–42.

157. M. G. S. Narayanan, *Political and Social Conditions ...*, Chapter on 'Police and Revenue'.

# Four

# Aspects of Administration

Since the nature of administration is crucial to the understanding of the character of a political system, much of the discussion on the character of the state in medieval South India has centred on the question of what the administrative system was like. As stated earlier, K. A. Nilakanta Sastri and his followers have presented an elaborate picture of the administrative system in the Pallava, Pāṇḍya, Cō̤ḻa and Cēra states, neatly divided into 'central', 'provincial', 'local', etc.[1] On the other hand, the very existence of any such administration has been called into question by Burton Stein.[2] While there is no evidence to fall back on the nicely finished edifice of administrative structure as obtaining in the idealistic writings of Nilakanta Sastri, Minakshi and Mahalingam, the position taken by Stein is too much on the other extreme of the scale. In a previous chapter we have seen the existence of a large number of local landed magnates who were conferred royal titles and enlisted in the service of the king's government, thereby showing that there were a number of loyal functionaries acting on behalf of the state.[3] Their presence throughout the territory covered by the Cō̤ḻa rule is borne out by inscriptions. In this chapter we shall examine aspects of the work of such functionaries. In other words, we look into the question of how, and what kind of, 'administration' was carried out in the medieval states in south India. The present discussion would question the statement that it was 'not the case that evidence of the existence of a centralised, bureaucratised administrative structure prompted the reasonable question of what this administrative structure was for.'[4] For our purpose, however, we take up aspects of the functioning of such officialdom and of the fiscal, military and judicial administration. The basic assumption in doing so is that these three are the primary functions of the state in pre-modern times whether directly carried out or delegated. An examination of these three aspects, therefore, will throw light on the character of the state. We shall begin our discussion in relation to the Cōḻa state where our evidence is most copious and then proceed to the situation prevalent in the other states. This, however, does not mean that there was similarity in all the four cases.

## GENERAL

We have seen in a previous chapter the existence of a large number of offices and officials, who were drawn from among the landed magnates in the Cōḻa country and on whom the state had conferred royal titles and other privileges.[5] Although we are not very confident to describe these large number of state functionaries as constituting a 'bureaucracy' in the strict sense of the term, their existence is evidence enough to show that within the Cōḻa state, the political authority of monarchy functioned through delegating its power to these functionaries to a large extent. This reached its high watermark in that state under Rājarāja I and his immediate successors as we have seen in an earlier chapter when the authority of the local chiefs and the other local groups was eclipsed and the state penetrated even to the outlying areas directly through these functionaries. In this section, we shall examine aspects of the work done by these functionaries in the localities.

Our source of information for this purpose is inscriptions, mostly from temples and sometimes recording the grant of land to brahmans and other religious personages. This would give the impression that there was a preponderance of concern with temples in the matter of 'administration'; and the secular aspects are a matter of extrapolation. In fact, even the affairs of the temple looked into by the government such as the assessment and collection of revenue, auditing of accounts, redistribution of land and livestock, checking of the stock in temples, etc., were of a secular nature. This shows that there was a rationale for administration in the context of the state and society in medieval south

India, though its day-to-day function outside the temple is not clearly indicated in our records.

Royal inscriptions which are mostly grants dating from the reign of Uttama Cō̤ḻa (970–85 AD) mention a number of royal functionaries in connection with the execution of a document at various stages.[6] When the king pronounced an order, it was committed to writing by a functionary close to him, the *tirumandiraōlai* or *ōlai*. This would then be compared and checked (*oppiṭṭu*) by two or three *ōlai-nāyagams* before it was passed on for execution to the *adhikāri*. On occasions, there was the intermediary stage of the document being put up through the *naḍuvirukkai*. After the *adhikāris* endorsed the order in question to be registered in the [revenue] accounts (*variyil=iṭṭu=koḷka*), the *pu̱ravu-vari* department entered it in the proper registers and issued a copy of the order called *uḷvari* to the recipient. This was more or less the regular pattern in a large number of documents, except for minor variations up to the end of the reign of Virarājēndra (1070 AD) from when the procedure becomes simpler.[7] There is no reason to believe that this followed only a set formula without representing the reality, for in that case the function of such a formula is hard to explain.[8] However, these are cases concerned with the establishment at the centre.

The situation obtaining in the Pāṇḍyan records, if less elaborate, is comparable.[9] We find in that kingdom, apart from a number of *uttaramantrins*, functionaries such as *mandira-ōlai nāyagam, naḍu-nilai-nāyagam* (corresponding to *naḍuvirukkai?*), *ēi-mudal* (keeper of original orders?), *vāykkēḷvi, paṇṭārappottakam* (the keeper of the royal register) and *adhikāri*. Again, there are references to *pu̱ravu-vari* and *pu̱ravu-varik-kaṇtattār* in the Pāṇḍyan records answering to the land revenue department in the Cō̤ḻa case. Owing to the limited number and scope of the records in that kingdom during this period, we do not have as much quantifiable data there as in the case of the Cō̤ḻa empire. In the case of the Cēra kingdom, similarly, we come across *kōil adhikārikal* and *tiruvāy-kēlpan* who were both royal functionaries. In the chiefdoms under that kingdom, we come across the *adhikārar* in Ku̱rumpo̱rai-nāḍu and *adhikārar* in Veṇāḍu, the *mēnāyān* in Ku̱rumpo̱rai-nāḍu, etc.[10] Royal scribes are seen in both the Pāṇḍyan and Cēra records.[11] In the records of the Pallavas, there are similar references to *mātra*, and a *mantri-maṇḍala*.[12] Senior officers figuring as *āṇatti* (Skt. *ājñapti*) and *viṇṇappam*

(Skt. *vijñāpa*) occur in all the three situations of Pallava, Pāṇḍya and Cōḷa.[13] The *rahasyādhikṛta* figuring in one of the earlier Prakrit charters of the Pallavas has been identified with the *vāyil-kēlpār* figuring in the Kāśākkudi plates in the matter of functions.[14] A keeper of the treasury, known as the *kōśādhyaksa* in the Taṇḍantōṭṭam plates[15] identifiable with the *maṇikka-paṇḍāram-kāppān* in an Ulathur inscription,[16] both dating from the reign of Nandivarman II Pallavamalla, is also met within the Pallava kingdom. It appears, therefore, that in the matter of government at the centre the situation in the other states was comparable to, if not as elaborate as, the one obtaining in the Cōḷa country. It may be that what had evolved in a germinal form in the states of the Pallavas and Pāṇḍyas was adopted in the Cōḷa kingdom. The ramification of the machinery in the latter state was in answer to the elaboration and refinement which the institution of state received at the hands of the Cōḷas, especially in the period of and immediately after Rājarāja I.

There are other records which help in appreciating the actual process of the king's government in the localities through its functionaries. Again, we have of necessity to depend on the records from the temples for this purpose and extrapolate from there for possible information on other aspects of a more secular nature. An inscription of the early tenth century of an unidentified Parakeśarivarman from the South Arcot district refers to three functionaries collecting *mōṟam* (described as a tax) and *śuṅgam* (tolls) in Milāḍu and Vāṇako-pāḍi on behalf of two *kanmigaḷ* of the Perumāḷ.[17] There are at least a couple of records from the reign of Uttama where a *śrīkāryam* officer worked in a subordinate position to an *adhikāri*.[18] Similarly, another record of his reign speaks of a *śrīkāryam,* a *bhaṭṭa* title holder, working under a *kanmi* sporting a *mūvēndavēḷān* title, who was himself subordinate to another Brahmādhiraja, probably a *sēnāpati*.[19] An inscription from Tirukkāṭṭupaḷḷi in Tanjavur district dated in the thirteenth year of Rājarāja I speaks of an *uḍaiyān* title-holder who worked as *śrikāryam* under another *śrikāryam*, a *kiḻavan* title holder.[20] Another record of the same reign from Tirunāmanallur mentions a Vira-Cōḷa-*aṇukkan*, a *śrīkāryam*, under Mummuḍicōḷa-brahma-mārāyan, a *sēnāpati*.[21] Another *kanmi* of the same *sēnāpati* figures as collecting fines in a record from the same temple two years later (1006 AD).[22] A record from Mālūrpatṇa in the Bangalore district, dated 1008 AD, speaks of a *nāḍu-vagai* officer acting under the authority (*adhikāram*) of an *adhikāri*.[23] Rājarāja I in his twenty-eighth year ordered the copying of the inscriptions on the central shrine of a temple in Tirumaḻapādi (Tiruchirapalli district). Two *adhikāris*, Irumudicōḻa Mūvēndavēḷān and Mummuḍicōḻa brahmādhirājar, passed on a *niyoga* (order) to this effect to the local *sabhā* and a *paṇimagan* (servant, officer) who is described as 'governing the village' (*ūr āḷkiṉṟa*).[24] It can be gathered from what follows in the record, although it is mutilated, that a *sēnāpati* was supervising (*nāyagam*) the work on behalf of the *adhikāri* and that a soldier (*vil-vāḷ-koṇḍavar*) was acting on behalf of the *paṇimagan*. Another record of the same year from Tiruvilāṅgudi in the Kulattur taluk in Tiruchirappalli describes a *nāḍu-kaṇkāṇi-nāyagam* as a *kanmi* under a *sēnāpati*, a certain Muḍikonṭa Cōḻa Viḻupparaiyar.[25]

Similarly in the reign of Rājēndra I we have several such records where a two-or three-tier hierarchy of royal functionaries carries out acts and orders of the king's government in the localities.[26] So also we have at least one such instance from the reign of Rājādhirāja I.[27] There is a very interesting record dated 1116 AD from the reign of Kūlottuṅga I from Irumbanāḍu in the Tiruchirapalli district, showing the various stages through which passed a royal order concerning the settlement of boundaries of a *dēvadāna* land: the issue of the royal order (*tirumugam*) by the king, then the copy (*ulvari*) certified by the *puṟavu-vari* department, upon this the final order of execution (*kaḍaiyiḍu*) issued by the *maṇḍalamudali* which was carried out by the *nāḍu-kūṟu*.[28] However, such instances are few and far between in the period after Kūlottuṅga I suggesting a weakening of the Cōḻa imperial state and its penetration to the localities through its functionaries.[29]

The instances that we saw above indicate the presence of the state in the localities far and near as expressed through the functionaries among whom there was a hierarchy. There are other instances where the exact work done by these functionaries can be identified. A pre-Rājarāja Parakēsari inscription records that, following a command of a *nāḍu-vagai*, a defaulter paid off in gold the interest due to a temple.[30] There is the instance of a certain Veṇpaikkuḍināṭṭu-vēḷār, whose office is not, however, mentioned, visiting a village at the bidding of the king, Āditya I, to enjoin the *sabhā* there not to transact any business (*karaṇam*) on certain specified days and, when business is transacted on the other days, not to admit women to the hall.[31] State intervention in the affairs of the *sabhā* is amply demonstrated by the two famous Parāntaka inscriptions from Uttaramērūr, where, in the former record, a certain Tattanūr Mūvēndavēḷān and in the latter, a Karañcai-Koṇṭaya-Kramavitta-paṭṭan *alias* Cōmāci-pperumān figure as royal agents. It was in the presence of these royal agents, and at the instance of the monarch himself, that the *sabhā* made the celebrated 'constitutional arrangements' there.[32] That the decision was taken on the lines prescribed in the *dharmaśāstra* texts, however, shows that there was further restraint on the latitude that the *sabhā* enjoyed.[33] In the same category may be included the order of a Brahmādhirājar to the local *mūlaparuḍai* to get an inventory of the tax-free *dēvadāna* land held by a temple, which is recorded in an inscription of 987 AD at Śrīnivāsanallur.[34] A very interesting record from Uḍaiyāragudi in Tiruchirapalli district, dating from the same year, speaks of the confiscation and sale, by the *sabhā* of Vīranārāyaṇacaturvēdimaṅgalam, of the properties of some persons involved in the murder of Āditya II.[35] This procedure of the *sabhā* followed an order from the king, who had deputed two of his functionaries, Kōṭṭaiyur Brahmaśri-rājan and Pullamaṅgalattu Candraśēkhara-bhaṭṭan, to supervise its execution. Again, according to a Tiruviḍaimarudūr inscription of 1001 AD, when an accountant in a brahman village absconded without producing the proper accounts, his property was ordered to be confiscated. The order was issued by Rājarājamārāyar, who may be a *sēnāpati*, and who sent armed forces to execute it.[36] The local *sabhā* was intimidated and the members thereupon represented the matter to the official himself. He directed them to the *adhikāri*s (*adhikāramceyvār*). In the end, however, the *sabhā* sold the land of the defaulting accountant[37] and paid off the dues to the government. There are three inscriptions from three different places, two dated 1002 AD and the other 1003 AD, which refer to an *adhikāri*, Arumoḻi-Mūvēndavēḷān, who looked into the affairs of all these different places.[38] A *nāḍu-vagai*, assisted by the kaikkōḷa soldiers, are seen in an inscription from Sōmūr (Tiruchirapalli district) dated 1005 AD punishing the temple-priests by imposing a fine on them for their failure go to (*varā-viṭṭa-kuṟṟam*) the queen on the occasion of a solar eclipse.[39]

There are similar records of the reign of Rājēndra I when the stocks of a temple were checked against entries in the register,[40] when the ordering of rituals was made,[41] etc., by royal agents such as *nāḍu-kaṇkāṇi-*

*nāyagams* and *adhikāris.* In subsequent reigns in the same century, we have similar instances of royal officers regulating affairs of temples in different parts of the Cōḻa empire if at a reduced scale.[42]

The above instances are for the most part related to temples. However, they show the secular control that the temples were under and point clearly to the secular concepts of administrations. In fact, in the period before the growth of the Cōḻa state into imperial dimensions, the affairs of the temple were looked after by local committees such as *sabhā, pariṣad,* etc.[43] Even under the imperial Cōḻas, this practice continued, but with the significant difference that now there was the presence of the state interfering in the affairs of even these self-governing bodies. This, at any rate, should not be taken to mean that the state welded the whole of the territory into a single unit or that it acquired 'complete control' over it with a highly centralised bureaucracy. Far from that, our evidence is that the state identified and recognised the local magnates whom it enlisted in its service by conferring titles and assigning functions of the state in matters of administration. The fact that references to their interference even in local matters tapers off from the time of Kūlottuṅga I and after shows the further weakening of the state power. This falls in perspective when placed within the context of the re-emergence of the chiefs and chiefly rule from that time onwards as noticed in the previous chapter.[44]

## REVENUE ADMINISTRATION

A large number of terms indicating levies are met with in the records of our period. Conventional historiography tends to interpret these levies as 'taxes' although in the writings of Nilakanta Sastri, for example, there is no explicit statement that the revenues accruing from such levies went entirely to the state.[45] But even his detailed treatment of the problem, prudent and cautious as it is, does not dearly define either the nature of such levies nor the state's share of such levies. The situation is worse in the writings of those who follow Sastri; Appadorai, Mahalingam and Minakshi, by injudiciously mixing evidence from the Tamil inscriptions and the Sanskrit texts arrive at a highly idealised picture without correctly defining the nature of the revenue and the role of the state in it.[46] Burton Stein, who seeks to correct the conjectural nature in the understanding of the revenue system does not go far beyond: one kind of impressionistic speculation is substituted by another kind in his writing.[47] There has been yet another strain of scholarship in recent years attempting to analyse the evidence concerning such levies systematically and the results of such attempts have been made available to us.[48] In this section, we shall examine those aspects of revenue administration which have a close bearing on the nature of state in the four kingdoms taken up for consideration. Here also we shall be concentrating more on the Cō<u>l</u>a state for the simple reason of that state yielding more quantifiable data; wherever possible and necessary we shall go into the other cases as well, bearing of course in mind the qualitative differences in the various situations.

In a previous chapter dealing with the royal functionaries, we saw the existence of an elaborate 'land revenue department' which got ramified in the Cō<u>l</u>a empire by the time of Rājarāja I.[49] However, if we look at the records closely it will be clear that this 'department' had no function in the localities in the matter of either the assessment of taxes or their collection. In fact, this department obtained only at the centre in relation perhaps to the palace establishment Therefore, although there is an elaborate hierarchy in this department with as many as twelve rungs, the work done by this establishment would merit for it the description of a 'revenue secretariat' or 'revenue board', concerned with the maintenance of registers and accounts pertaining to land revenue.[50] It may be suggested that the mere existence of a 'land revenue department' of this description does not prove anything conclusively about the nature of the revenue system in a state.

However, we have other sources of information telling us about the existence of a number of levies which have been described as 'taxes' in conventional historiography. These myriad terms defied systematic analysis in the past; the advent of the computer has been very helpful in replacing speculative thinking of an impressionistic nature with systematic analysis.[51] That even this kind of systematic analysis could be used in the way exactly opposite to the suggestions led to by the analysis itself, as in the case of Burton Stein,[52] is a different matter altogether. In fact, Karashima has pointed this out and stated that the findings of their analysis 'support the view of those who admit the existence of the state administration, since the seven revenue terms appear frequently in both regions and throughout the Cōḻa period'.[53]

As stated earlier, there are hundreds of terms in the entire corpus of published Cōḻa inscriptions which indicate some levies charged from people. The names of these levies figure in the records more in the context of the remission than the actual collection of such imposts. In most cases, therefore, it is likely that rather than the *existence* of a particular impost, it was the *possibility* of any such impost that was excluded. This is suggested by the expression *eppērpaṭṭa* ('of whatever description') which is used in the end of such lists of immunities, usually in the sense of an *et cetera*. The analysis of the revenue terms in Cōḻa inscriptions undertaken by Karashima and Sitaraman shows that, out of the hundreds of expressions taken to be revenue terms, there are only twenty-seven with a frequency of more than ten occurrences; even out of them thirteen items figure exclusively in the Toṇḍaimaṇḍalam or Jayaṅgoṇḍacōḻamaṇḍalam area, three appear exclusively in the Cōḻamaṇḍalam area and only eleven appear in both the Cōḻamaṇḍalam and Jayaṅgoṇḍacōḻamaṇḍalam areas.[54] Even out of the ones figuring in both the areas, certain items have very high frequencies and are distributed throughout the rule of the Cōḻa dynasty. They are: *antarāyam* (73), *eccōṟu* (85), *kaḍamai* (65), *kuḍimai* (34), *muṭṭaiy-āl* (21), *taṭṭār-pāṭṭam* (27) and *veṭṭi* (117).

Even there, there is an interesting feature. In the case of *antarāyam, kaḍamai, muṭṭaiy-āḷ* and *taṭṭār-pāṭṭam*, there is a progressive increase in the number of occurrences as the Cōḻa rule progresses in time and in the case of *eccōṟu* and *veṭṭi*, which, incidentally, are the two expressions having the highest frequency (85 and 107 respectively), there is a progressive decrease in time. The implications of these phenomena can be taken up for discussion later.

In this context, it becomes necessary to have an idea of the exact nature of these levies. For, the distinction between tax and rent in the pre-modern context is generally vaguely understood. For instance, out of the seven most frequent and universal terms that we came across above, *eccōṟu* signified the obligation to feed the state functionaries[55] and *muṭṭaiyāl* and *veṭṭi* signified the obligation to render labour services.[56] These cannot be regarded as taxes. Similarly, in the case of other exactions as well, most except perhaps *antarāyam* and *tāṭṭār-pāṭṭam* were collected in kind, i.e. paddy. Even among them the most important impost, in terms of the proportion to the produce, namely, the *kaḍamai* (which amounted to forty per cent of the gross produce according to Nilakanta Sastri's calculation[57] and as much as fifty per cent according to R. Tirumalai[58]) was invariably collected in kind. To describe this as tax would miss the entire character of the surplus extraction. It can therefore be better described as rent. This is typical of a feudal formation. This inference can be supported by the fact that the other imposts such as *muṭṭaiyāḷ* and *veṭṭi* are better described as labour-rent in contradistinction with the produce rent, namely, *kaḍamai* discussed above. *Eccōṟu*, which has its counterpart in one of the Cēra inscriptions in the *iravu-coru*[59] and in the thirteenth century Malayalam commentary of the *Arthaśāstra* in the *irannūṇ*,[60] signified the obligation to feed royal functionaries, which is rightly likened by M. G. S. Narayanan to the practice of billetting in medieval Europe.[61]

As noted earlier, the most important due that we come across in the Cōḻa inscriptions is the *kaḍamai*.[62] Significantly in the pre-Rājarāja period of Cōḻa rule there is only one clear reference to this levy,[63] if we leave out an inscription of an unidentified Rājakēsari.[64] In the period between the accession of Rājarāja I and Kūlottuṅga I there are only five references to the *kaḍamai*,[65] if we leave out the Rājakēsari inscription referred to above. Even among these five, only two are from the Cōḻamaṇḍalam region, the others being from the Chingleput and North Arcot districts. It is only in the period after Kūlottuṅga I that we have more and more references to this levy, that too, in the post-Kūlottuṅga III period the frequency goes up to the figure of 43.5.[66] This makes the suggestion unmistakable that this impost became more and more popular in the later years of the Cōḻa rule. If *kaḍamai* meant the primary due on land or land revenue fastened on the land and charged upon the occupant,[67] would the above analysis mean that this came to be increasingly collected only towards the second half of the Cōḻa rule? The evidence we have is to the effect that at least in that name this was collected only towards the second half of the Cōḻa rule. However, there is evidence in the earlier Cōḻa records concerning the assessment and either collection or exemption of revenue in kind accruing from land.

Expressions such as *puṟavu, iṟai, kaḍan* or *kāṇikkaḍan* and *opāti* (skt. *upādhi*) were used to describe levies on land which the occupant was obliged to pay.[68] It was in place of *kaḍan* or *kāṇikkaḍan* that the expression *kaḍamai* was used in later times. Most instances we have suggest that this due was collected in terms of paddy. This would suggest that the most important demand on land was in the form of a rent.

Karashima has undertaken a similar systematic analysis of land revenue assessment during the Cōḻa rule[69] with the help of the Tanjavur Bṛihadiśvara temple inscriptions of the twenty-ninth year of Rājarāja I[70] and Gaṅgaikkoṇḍacōḻapuram inscription of Vīrarājēndra.[71] These records, both of which are very lengthy and copious, pertain to whole villages granted to the two temples by these monarchs. In the case of the land granted to the Tanjavur temple, the charter of which is in an excellent state of preservation, the rate of revenue described as *kāṇikkaḍan* is generally 100 *kalam* of paddy per *vēli* of land and in a few cases where assessment is made in gold, it is generally ten *kaḻañju* of gold per *vēli* or a little less.[72] There is no means to check the grade of the land in terms of productivity—single crop, double crop, wet land or dry land. However, judging from the uniform rate of assessment one can assume that all the forty villages granted to the great temple by the great monarch belonged to the same category.

Coming to Gaṅgaikkoṇḍacōḻapuram, we have more detailed information on the classification of land in spite of the highly damaged nature of the record. There, different categories of land such as double crop land, single crop land, dry land, wet land, garden land of different descriptions, etc., are specified, giving the exact extent of each category in every village granted.[73] Significantly, the rate of assessment in the Gaṅgaikkoṇḍacōḻapuram grants is highly fluctuating and much less in comparison with the Tanjavur grants, with an average rate of less than fifty *kalams* of paddy per *vēli*. The reason for this, however, is not known. It may be that while the Bṛihadiśvara temple was endowed, Rājarāja I chose only such villages which produced a uniform rate of revenue, which selection may not have been possible half a century later for Vīrarājēndra.

One significant aspect of these two records is that out of the fifteen villages recorded in the second part of the Gaṅgaikkoṇḍacōḻapuram inscription, fourteen were the ones which had been granted to the Tanjavur temple.[74] However, the Gaṅgaikkoṇḍacō̤lapuram record does not speak of the revocation of the earlier grant before the new assignment was made. Would it mean that, after Gaṅgaikkoṇḍacō̤lapuram became the more favoured temple and the capital of the Cō̤las, the obligation to the Tanjavur Bṛihadiśvara temple was not redeemed by the assessees upon which those villages were re-allotted to the Gaṅgaikkoṇḍacō̤lapuram temple? We do not know.

However, one thing stands out clear and unmistakable from this analysis of revenue assessment in the Cō̤la state: the details of revenue can be known more from the alienation of such rights than from their actual collection by the state. The assumption need not be made that before such alienation the collection had been made by the state.[75] Thus it could be that superior rights in land were created by the state and such rights were transferred to the assignees.[76] In the numerous other cases of land revenue assessment examined by Y. Subbarayalu, the assessment is made by the local groups such as the *ūr* and *nāḍu*.[77] What happens is perhaps that the right to assess and collect revenue, which was enjoyed by the local groups, is appropriated or usurped by the state and a fresh assessment is made, the benefits of which are alienated to, for example, a temple.

This is exactly the pattern that we see in the case of other beneficiaries of land grants as well. In the large number of instances that we have in the records of early medieval south India pertaining to eleemosynary grants such as *brahmadēyam, dēvadānam, pa̤l̤liccandam*, etc., what we see is the transfer of these fiscal rights.[78]

'Tax-free' in such cases did not mean that the peasant was not expected to pay his dues; on the other hand, the grantee was given the right to collect revenues from the primary producer, in many cases on his own terms.[79] R. Tirumalai has convincingly argued that the expression *kuḍi nīkki* and *kuḍi nīṅgā*, indicating two alternative types of tenures on which such eleemosynary grants were made, did not involve the physical eviction or otherwise of the peasants respectively. On the other hand, what they meant was that in the former case the assignee had the right to fix the terms of tenancy with the peasants while in the latter case such terms were pre-existing and unextinguishable.[80] This would support our argument further that the exactions that we come across in the records have to be seen more as various forms of rent and other feudal levies and not as tax. It is in this context that the problem of *eccōṟu* or the billetting of state functionaries in the villages and *veṭṭi* or labour rent decreasing with the progress of Cōḻa rule has to be examined.

The relation that we saw between *veṭṭi* which is labour rent *par excellence* and *kaḍamai*, which is produce rent paid in kind, is one of inverse proportion: the occurrence of *veṭṭi* goes on decreasing as the Cōḻa rule progresses and that of *kaḍamai* increases. In other words, labour rent gets increasingly replaced by produce rent in kind. In the classical analysis of the genesis of ground-rent in the capitalist mode of production, Karl Marx has characterised labour rent as the primeval form of surplus labour.[81] Labour which is over and above what is absolutely essential for the maintenance and reproduction of the labourer himself is directly appropriated by the 'owner' of the means of production. In the case of rent in kind, the difference is that it is the fruit of such surplus labour that is appropriated from the direct producer, presupposing 'a higher stage of civilisation'.[82] 'The transformation of labour rent into rent in kind', however, writes Marx, 'changes nothing from the economic standpoint in the nature of ground-rent.'[83] The mode of production, therefore, remains the same.

Again, it is significant that *veṭṭi*, although its frequency is less, continues to obtain even towards later stages of the Cōḻa rule when *kaḍamai* becomes the dominant form of produce rent. This is natural, for, according to Marx,[84] 'To whatever extent rent in kind is the prevailing and dominant form of ground rent, it is furthermore always more or less accompanied by survivals of the earlier form, i.e., of rent paid directly in labour, corvée-labour, no matter whether the landlord be a private person or the state.'

We may conclude by saying that the form which surplus extraction took in medieval south India, therefore, is a good indicator of the mode of production which prevailed there: 'The specific economic form, in which unpaid surplus-labour is pumped out of direct producers, determines the relationship of rulers and ruled ...'[85] The increase with time in the items on which revenue imposts were levied also indicates the combined nature of agricultural and industrial family labour 'as is often the case in the Middle Ages.'[86]

The situation in the other states that we have taken up also is not very different. In the case of the Cēra kingdom, however, the most important form of produce rent paid in kind, named *āṭṭaikkōḷ* ('the annual levy') is sanctified as *raksābhoga* 'a fee for protection'.[87]

This discussion of the revenue administration in the early medieval south Indian states can be concluded by some observations on the mode of collection of land revenue as well. The bulk of our evidence is to show that such exactions were made locally. It was the local groups such as the *ūr, nāḍu, sabhā* and *nagaram* that made the assessment and collection of the different levies. This is clear evidence of the fact of the decentralised revenue system. On occasions we also see local chiefs, 'feudatories', making the collections. On the whole, we get the picture of a decentralised system of the fiscal administration, typical of a feudal politico-economic formation.

## MILITARY AND POLICE

Conventional historiography has been very eloquent about the military organisation of early medieval south India. Much has been written about the huge standing army with numerous regiments and an equally huge navy with innumerable ships.[88] This picture is in part the result of a credulous interpretation of the *praśasti* documents and in part a concomitant of the wrong conception of the nature of the state. When the state was conceived as a highly centralised, top-heavy steam-roller, naturally the conception of an army becoming of that state would only be consistent with the understanding. When the *praśasti* literature is accordingly looked at, it lends itself to the kind of generalisation about a huge standing army and countless ships.

The fact of the matter, however, is that the nature of our evidence does not allow for any such generalisation. Its purpose is limited and does not include a detailed assessment or even mention of aspects of civil and military administration. Thus the historian, in dealing with the problem, is likely to be carried away either by the rhetoric in the inscriptional literature about the conquests that a king made or by the near absence of any statement concerning a military organisation in the so-called operational part of the documents. It goes without saying that the one course is as dangerous as the other. Rejecting the existence of a professional army in the Cōḻa Empire was the pitfall into which Burton Stein led himself.[89] Therefore, one has to piece together scattered and, for the most part, inadvertent pieces of information from the documents in order to get a picture of the military organisation in medieval south India. The references in the records to a large number of military engagements and defence are sufficient to show the existence of armies in medieval South India, although they do not tell us anything about the mode of its recruitment, organisation and maintenance. References to a number of military officers, such as *sēnāpati*s and *daṇḍanāyakam*s in the records of the Cōḻa state also fall into the same category.[90] Even so is the mention of a number of 'regiments' in the Bṛhadiśvara temple records of Rājarāja I and other records of earlier and later dates.[91] One will, therefore, have to look at other sources to see the character of the military force in this period.

The military force of the Cōḻa Empire, about which there exists extensive literature, is said to have consisted of about seventy 'regiments' of a territorial army and 'numberless' ships of a naval force.[92] The supposition, that 'Chola armies were exclusively or even dominantly central forces', has been rightly questioned by Burton Stein.[93] But he posits that the territorial *nāḍu* units and professional associations like those of the Kaikkōḷar maintained armies of their own on a parallel to what may have been the military force of the king at the centre. This follows an obvious misreading of the expressions there: the various *nāṭṭuppadais, paḍai*s from the *nāḍu*, are taken to mean the *paḍai*s of the *nāḍu* and the *kaikkōḷappaḍai, paḍai* consisting of the kaikkōlas, is taken to mean *paḍai* maintained by the kaikkōlas.[94] A parallel, for the sake of illustration of this point, would be the Madras Regiment and the Jat Regiment of the Indian Army in modern times: these are not independent forces of the Madras Presidency or the Jat community. The analogy, however, is not meant to be extended further. Thus, we will have to reassess the nature of these forces.

Again, a reassessment of the statements about the naval forces of Cōḻas will also be necessary. It is questionable if there was a navy at all. The evidence presented in support of this naval force consisting of 'numberless ships' is the Śrīlaṅkan expedition of Rājarāja I, and Śrī Vijaya expedition of Rājēndra I. While we do not reject the military involvement in this, we do question the expression 'navy' used to describe forces carried across the sea, much as a unit of the army air-lifted today does not qualify itself to be called 'Air Force'. Another argument to support the idea of the Cōḻa navy is this: 'The overthrow of the Cēra fleet at Kāntaḷūr Śālai may well be taken to mark the definite establishment of Cōḻa power in this period in the territorial waters of Southern India'.[95] Kāntaḷūr Śālai, figuring in the expression 'Kāntaḷūr-śālai-kalamaṟuttaruli' found in the Cōḻa *meykkīrtis*, has lent itself to different interpretations ranging from a feeding hall to a fleet of ships at the hand of epigraphists and historians.[96] But the dust kicked up by this debate seems to have settled with M. G. S. Narayanan offering the interpretation, with the help of a large number of inscriptions and literary works, that Kāntaḷūr Śālai was among the many educational institutions in south India training brahman students both in the academic and military sciences, an institution similar to the *ghaṭikā*s and that its destruction by the Cōḻa monarch would mean curtailing the potential prowess of the enemy.[97] This rules out the idea of the 'destruction of the *kalam* at Kāntaḷūr Śālai' being a naval engagement. Hence our concern in this section will be with the different aspects of the military force in early medieval south India.

M. G. S. Narayanan has made an excellent study of the institution of 'companions of honour' in south India, bringing to bear on it an integrated use of epigraphical sources, foreign accounts and indigenous literature.[98] He has shown that there was a group of trusted body-guards attached to the king. The *uḍankūṭṭam*, which Nilakanta Sastri took as 'the nearest approach to a council of ministers' in the the Cōḻa state,[99] the *Teṉṉavan āpattudavigaḷ* in the Pāṇḍyan kingdom whom both Nilakanta Sastri and T. V. Mahalingam identify with the 'king's Barons who had great authority in the kingdom',[100] described by Marco Polo, the *uḍan ceṉṟa paḍai vīrar* who are described in the *Periyapurāṇam* to have followed Cēramān Perumāḷ even in death[101]—all these have been identified and presented by Narayanan as constituting a body of trusted body-guards of the king, moving at close quarters with him and wielding great influence on him. Elaborating further, he has shown that the several 'hundred organisations' such as the *munnūṟṟuvar, ainūṟṟuvar, aṟunūṟṟavar, eḻuṉūṟṟuvar*, etc., attached to the feudatory chiefs in the Cēra kingdom and assigned the duty of protection of land and other religious endowments[102] and identified by writers on the history of Kerala in the past as democratic organisations,[103] were the counterparts of such companions at the level of the chiefly territories.[104] The survival of these bodies well into modern times in the form of *cāvēr* (suicide squads) is also brought out by him. He has also shown that the 'Thousand' or *Āyiram* attached to the Cēra king signified the same institution, a numerical designation of the *uḍan ceṉṟa paḍaivirar* figuring in the *Periyapurāṇam*. He argues further, convincingly, that these bodies, variously known as the *Uḍan-kūṭṭam*, the *teṉṉavan Āpattudavigaḷ* and the *āyiram* in the Cōḻa, Pāṇḍyan and Cēra records respectively were the counterparts of the *garuḍa*s figuring in contemporary Kannada records and the group called *āsanna*s, *mūlapuruṣa*s, *daśavargika*s, etc., in the *śāstra* literature in northern India.[105]

It is possible to extend this argument and apply this insight to a large number of other situations in south India. The descriptions of the character of the Vēḷaikkarar soldiers referred to in the Cōḻa and Pāṇḍyan records are exactly in the same pattern as these 'companions of honour' described in the accounts of foreign writers like Abu Zaid and Marco Polo and native authors like Cēkkiḻār. 'They pledged themselves to certain duties, failing which they would voluntarily undergo certain penalties, which in most cases was death.'[106] Mahalingam has rather intuitively identified them with *Teṉṉavan āpattudavigaḷ* mentioned above, which identification seems to be quite in order.[107] The *cēvagar* or *sēvakar*, the *akampaṭi mudaligaḷ* and *parivāram*, mentioned in various parts of south India in relation to military and police function, make sense when seen in this light.[108] To this group may perhaps have belonged specialists like *kudiraiccēvagar* (cavalrymen) and *ānaiyāṭkal* (those who fought on elephant).[109] A number of archers (*villigaḷ, aṇukkar*) also may be thought to have formed part of these forces.[110] So also the statement in the Grāmam records that Veḷḷan Kumaran was a *Camū-nāyaka* and *mūlabhṛtya* falls in perspective when examined against this background.[111] Among the number of Malayāḷi soldiers who assisted the Cōḻa prince Rājāditya in the battle of Takkolam was Malaiyāḷa *parivārattu sēvakan* Tirunkkuṉṟappoḻa Centa Kumaran, obviously a member of the *parivāram* (retinue) and a *sēvaka* (servant) of the Malayāḷa [king].[112] It is significant that he figures in the context[112] of a battle involving the Cōḻas and Rāṣṭrakūṭas to which the Cēras sent their forces consisting of soldiers from the different chiefly territories in Kerala in support of the Cōḻas, for it will bring out the hierarchy of political relations involved there. The amount of personal loyalty exhibited by these 'companions of honour' points to the other aspect of its feudal character—fealty.[113]

Thus, it appears that the 'standing army' of the kings in early medieval south India consisted of these companions of honour. Since they were hereditary men as brought out by the evidence, the question of their 'recruitment' does not arise very prominently. The mode of their payment is also fairly clear: they were assigned land in lieu of this protection. We have seen in a previous chapter that the royal functionaries in the Cōḻa state were drawn from among the landed magnates, and those with a military character were no exception. The numerous instances of *pāḍi-kāval* shown in a previous chapter could be cited here in support of the argument that it was in land that the military services were remunerated. Similarly, we have a number of *paṇiccavirutti* (service tenure for soldiers) in the inscriptions from the Cēra kingdom.[114] One may conclude by saying that this typically feudal kind of military organisation was the character of the medieval south Indian coercive power—the king's personal body-guards such as the *uḍankūṭṭam*, the *teṇṇavan āpattudavigaḷ* or the *āyiram* at the centre backed up by similar forces of the feudatory chiefs in the locality.

This 'standing army' may have been supplemented by mercenary soldiers recruited from among peasants and artisans. In fact, the references to *nāṭṭuppaḍai* and *kaikkōḷapadai* mentioned above may be treated in this manner. So also, the *valaṅgai-vēḷaikkārar* perhaps formed such groups of soldiers mustered from among the peasants and those belonging to the *iḍaṅgai*, from among the artisans, as *valaṅgai* and *iḍaṅgai* have been looked upon as 'root paradigms' to indicate these groups respectively.[115] The occurrence of at least four *sēnāpati*s in the Cōḻa inscriptions with the *uḍaiyān* title indicating land-ownership is perhaps suggestive of this.

There are a few *brahma* title-holders among the *sēnāpatis*, indicating thereby that even brahmans distinguished themselves in the military profession, something which was outside the *varṇa* tradition. In connection with our discussion of the problem of the 'destruction of the *kalam* at Kāntaḷūr Śālai', we saw that Kāntaḷūr Śālai was an institution of education for brahman students where training was offered, among other things, in the art of warfare. A large number of such institutions called *śālai* offering instruction to brahman students called *chātras* (*Tamil-cāttirar*; Prakrit: *caṭṭas*) are seen in south India.[116] Even in the great 'college' at Eṇṇāyiram, the senior students were called *chātras* and the curriculum there closely resembled the one offered at Pārthivapuram, a *śālai* in south Travancore, which is explicitly stated as 'modelled on the lines of Kāntaḷūr [śālai].[117] As the *chātras* or *caṭṭas* are identified as brahman students, so the *bhaṭṭas* are identified as their teachers, and their presence in the educational institution is ubiquitous. In fact, the present writer has shown elsewhere that the elusive groups of *caṭṭas* and *bhaṭṭas* seen in the inscriptions of northern India in the Gupta and post-Gupta periods can be explained in this light.[118] Thus it appears that the *brahma* and possibly *bhaṭṭa* title-holders among the *sēnāpatis* and *daṇḍanāyakams* were groomed in such paramilitary training centres.

Our understanding of the army in early medieval south India presents the following picture: a standing army consisting of the companions of honour at the centre and similar troops provided by the chiefly families in the localities; the supplementary forces of specialists consisting of horsemen, elephant riders, archers, etc., and the mercenary militia mustered from among the peasants and artisans; and finally brahman leaders proficient in the art of warfare trained in professional educational centres. This would conform to the pattern of a decentralised polity with no monopoly over coercive power; but this does not agree with the picture of a multiplicity of centres, each wielding power in an equal manner.

## ADMINISTRATION OF JUSTICE

It is accepted that one of the major functions of state is the administration of justice, which includes the making and implementation of law. An examination of this aspect throws further light on the character of the state in the early medieval south Indian kingdoms taken up for study here. Conventional literature has brought together a wealth of information on this aspect of the problem although it refuses to place that information in an over-all framework. Nilakanta Sastri appears to have appreciated the rather local and generally communal nature of the judicial administration[119] while Mahalingam confuses the ideal and the actual, and mixes up evidences drawn from prescriptive manuals and descriptive inscriptions as also from situations in the early Christian centuries and those in the late mid-second millennium AD, allowing for no change at all. Burton Stein, significantly, ignores the whole question in his study of the nature of the Cōḻa state, whereby not only are the impressive data on this question pushed under the carpet but also a major aspect of the state function.

In discussing the judicial administration, scholars like Nilakanta Sastri and Minakshi have referred to an institution called *dharmāsana* which is taken to mean a 'king's court of justice'[120] and 'an organised judicial body or law court'[121] respectively. However, a contextual examination of the records which mention this institution would show it to have had a different character. In a Tiruvoṟṟiyūr inscription of the time of Nṛipatuṅgavarman the *sabhā* of Maṇali is found closely in association with the *dharmāsana* which receives a fine.[122] Similar cases are met with in records from the time of Aparājita[123] and Kampavarman.[124] In the Cōḻa records there is mention of *dharmāsana-bhaṭṭa*s, who are said to have assisted the court.[125] Even here, it is clear from an Uttaramērūr inscription dated 994 AD that the *rājadvāra* was distinct from the *dharmāsana*.[126] This record states that fines could be incurred at the royal court, the *dharmāsana*, or the *vari*. In fact, Subbarayalu has brought out that 'in all places the *dharmāsana* is found mentioned only in the *brahmadēya* village'.[127] This would help in the identification of the *dharmāsanabhṭṭa*s as well. Another body of 'judicial officers of the villages' is identified by Nilakanta Sastri in *niyāyattar*, deriving the expression perhaps from *nyāya*.[128] However, he does not pursue the matter further. Again a contextual examination of this expression shows that it was meant to indicate the retinue of a king as, for example, in the case of the Tanjavur inscription of Rājēndra I[129] or the Pallavarāyanpēṭṭai inscription of Rājādhirāja II.[130] Subbarayalu favours the derivation of the word from *nyāsa* after Hultzsch;[131] but we would suggest that it may well be derived from *nikāya*; Sastri, in fact, suggests this in the context of the Pallavarāyanpēṭṭai inscription[132] although he does not reconcile the contradiction between his two positions.

It would appear, therefore, that there was no central court of justice as was assumed by the conventional historians. In fact, the many instances involving processes of judicial administration quoted by Nilakanta Sastri and Mahalingam themselves show that this aspect of state function was generally carried out locally. A large number of instances are available, and an examination of a few typical cases will clarify the matter further. Cēkkiḻār's story of Śiva appearing before Sundaramūrtti Nayanar in the guise of a brahman and claiming that Sundaramūrtti was his bond slave, the contest of this claim by Sundaramūrtti and the settlement of the issue by the *sabhā* of Tiruveṇṇainellūr has been quoted extensively by Nilakanta Sastri and reproduced, like most other cases, by Mahalingam.[133] The trial of the plaintiff and the defendant, the production of a document in support of the plaintif's claim, the examination of the exhibit and the final decision of the *sabhā*—all these are of great interest here. So also, the *sabhā* acting as a judicial body, the dominance of senior and learned brahmans there on the occasion, and the role of the *karaṇattān* in comparing the records—this is a picture which emerges as clearly in the inscriptions as in this literary piece. It is stated in this context that in considering proof for a claim, the order of preference shall be usage (*āṭci*), documents (*āvaṇam*) and testimony of eyewitnesses (*ayalār-taṅgal-kāṭci*). R. S. Sharma has shown[134] that these are precisely the kind of evidences prescribed in the *Dharmaśāstra*s with the *rājāsāśana*, left out in the present context as evidently irrelevant, being the most effective and forceful. In fact, the present writer has shown elsewhere the close similarity between the constitution and proceedings of the *sabhā* on the one side and prescriptions regarding these aspects in the *Dharmaśāstra* literature.[135]

J. D. M. Derrett has made an extensive study of a couple of inscriptions from the later Cōḻa period from Uyyakoṇḍān which records a clear case of the *bhaṭṭa*s in a *sabhā* invoking at length the prescriptive texts of the *Dharmaśāstra*s in determining the caste status of certain artisans.[136] The details presented by Derrett show how the law presented in the *Dharmaśāstra*s was adopted and implemented in the particular cases in south India under the Cōḻas, which fell outside the area where these *śāstra*s were conceived. An article by M. G. S. Narayanan brings out clearly this extension and application of the *śāstraic* law in the case of the Cēra kingdom in Kerala where he has brought out the significant fact that in the conduct of the *sabhā* and the zealous safeguarding of its interest as a corporate body, the *śāstraic* concept of *mahāpātakas* was invoked.[137] R. Tirurnalai has brought out a significant case, where the decision of the Māhēśvarar of Tirukkāḷūr concerning the succession of property through the female line on the extinction of the male line was recognised and this found its way into one of the later *śāstra* texts.[138] All this would show that legal procedure in the brahman *sabhās* in south India followed the prescriptions in the *Dharmaśāstras*. Moreover, these and numerous other instances also show that judicial administration which is supposed to be a major aspect of state function was carried out by these corporate bodies at the local level, thereby indicating a considerable erosion of state power, characteristic of the feudal formation. In fact the present writer has shown that if the land grants in northern India present the charters of the alienation of administrative, fiscal and judicial rights, the inscriptions of south India in our period present the picture of these rights being enjoyed at the operational level by those groups who received such grants—the actual mechanics of feudal forces at work.[139]

A similar point is underscored by a number of other instances of legal action involving people of the non-brahman community.[140] In all these instances, as Subbarayalu has ably brought out, the 'judicial proceedings ... were communal or local in nature.'[141] Although we do not find the same amount of sophistication and refinement as in the case of the judicial proceedings of the brahmanical *sabhās*, even these instances show that the central government or the king's government had little, if any, role in such matters. But there are other instances where, for the execution of a decision, generally a punishment, the coercive power of the local chief or the king himself was resorted to. In fact, there are even instances where the king exercised an original jurisdiction in the matter of settling cases of a civil and criminal nature. These instances of the state power being invoked as a last resort also point to the fact that ultimate authority still rested with the king in the matter of the administration of law. The king is supposed to be the law-maker, but in the typical feudal set up, legislation did not take place in the strict sense of the term. In the case of India, it was only the adaptation and implementation of *dharma*, already available in *Dharmaśāstras* texts. As pointed out by Marc Bloch, the king was the supreme judge.[142] That is what is suggested by the precedence of *rājaśāsanas* over local custom, documentary proof and witness.

In this chapter, we have made an examination of certain aspects of administration in the early medieval states of south India. We saw that in matters of local administration, evidence of which comes largely from the regulation of property and other affairs of the temple, the state attempted to penetrate into the localities and subvert local autonomy through royal functionaries. This penetration and subversion reached a high stage when an effort at centralisation was made in the Cōḻa state under Rājarāja I and his immediate successors; but that effort did not meet with enduring success in the later years as we see the fading off of evidences of this penetration following the last quarter of the eleventh century. As regards the revenue administration, one of the strongest indicators to the character of the state, it is seen that the most important form which the extraction of surplus took was that of a rent and not a tax, the distinction between the two being generally vaguely understood in the context of the discussion of the character of the state in early medieval south India. In the case of this rent, it has been shown that *veṭṭi*, a form of labour rent, was the more popular form in the earlier years of our period and that it got gradually replaced by *kaḍamai*, a form of produce rent generally paid in kind. This substitution of the most primeval form of surplus extraction ('the labour rent') with a slightly more sophisticated form ('the rent in kind'), however, did not make any qualitative difference so far as the mode of production was concerned. We also saw that, by the creation or recognition of various shades of rights over the means of production enjoyed by a class of intermediaries, the incidence of this surplus extraction was becoming heavier and heavier on the primary producer.

The nature of the military organisation as we saw is as different from the conventional discourse on the subject as it is from the recent American scholarship. Judicial administration, too, presents the picture of a rather localised, decentralised and communal system. Both these aspects, showing little centralisation and large amounts of local initiative, authority and power, point to a system where state power was enjoyed to a great extent by the local chiefs and the dominant local groups. However, the fact that both the coercive power and the judicial machinery were ultimately subject to the control of the king at the centre should not be overlooked in appreciating the significance of these aspects bearing on the character of the states. Thus, what has been looked at either as a centralised polity or, alternatively, as a polity with numerous foci of power subject only to a 'ritual hegemony' of the centre would present itself as a polity with a great deal of decentralisation, but more or less pyramidally arranged with the king in the centre at the top, the local chieftains below him, the locality groups still lower and the units of social and economic organisation at the bottom. This is typical of the feudal pattern. In order to appreciate this further, one has to look into the deeper reality of the social structure, to which we shall turn in the following chapters.

## NOTES

1. K. A. Nilakanta Sastri, *The Pandyan Kingdom*, pp. 74–83; *idem, The Colas*, pp. 445–545; C. Minakshi, *Administration and Social Life under the Pallavas*, pp. 45–153; M. G. S. Narayanan, *Political and Social Conditions of Kerala* ..., Chapters on 'Nature of Monarchy', 'Divisions of the Kingdom', 'Local Bodies', 'Police and Revenue', Mahalingam, *South Indian Polity.*

2. Stein, 'The State and Agrarian order....' *op. cit.; idem, Peasant State and Society ..., op. cit.*, pp. 254–64.

3. Above, Chapter 2.

4. Stein, *Peasant State and Society ..., op. cit.*, p. 257.

5. Above, Chapter 2.

6. See e.g., Nilakanta Sastri, *Colas*, pp. 466–72; Subbarayalu, *State in Medieval South India*, pp. 184–85. See also *S.I.I.*, III, 142, 151, 205; *S.I.I.*, IV, 259; *E.I.*, XXII, 34; *T.A.S.*, I, pp. 164–68; etc.

7. Subbarayalu, *loc. cit.*, also above, Chapter 2.

8. Cf. above, Chapter 3, n. 22; *Contra* Nilakanta Sastri *Colas*, p. 469.

9. Rajan Gurukkal, *The Agrarian System ..., op. cit.*, pp. 221–30.

10. *E.I.*, XVI, no. 27, Also above, Chapter 4.

11. Gurukkal, *op.cit.*, pp. 230 ff; *E.I.*, III, p. 68ff; nos. 477 and 478 of 1926.

12. Above, Chapters 2 and 3; Minakshi, *Historical Sculptures ..., op.cit.*

13. Above, Chapter 3.

14. Minakshi, *Administration and Social Life, op. cit.*, pp. 66–67.

15. *Ibid.*, pp. 67–68; *TPCP*, p. 208 and 1.18.

16. No. 17 of 1889.

17. *S.I.I.*, XIX, 351. Though *Perumāḷ* could mean both the deity in a temple and the king, in this context the reference is to the king as will be clear from the following instances.

18. *S.I.I.*, XIX, 92(A), 162.
19. *S.I.I.*, III, 140.
20. *S.I.I.*, VI, 3.
21. *S.I.I.*, VII, 988.
22. *S.I.I.*, VII, 998.
23. *E.C.*, IX, p. 132.
24. *S.I.I.*, V, 652.
25. *I.P.S.*, *90.*
26. *S.I.I.*, VIII, 745; *S.I.I.*, IV, 293; *S.I.I.*, V, 449, *S.I.I.*, XVII, 319; *S.I.I.*, V, 65; *E.C.*, X, K1. 109 (A); *S.I.I.*, VI, 33.
27. *S.I.I.*, VIII, 33.
28. *I.P.S.*, 126.
29. Above, Chapter 3.
30. *S.I.I.*, VIII, 580 (A).
31. *S.I.I.*, XIII, 312. It is interesting that this practice of keeping the temples where the *sabhā* usually met out of bounds for women continued in Kerala well into the modern times although its significance has not been realised. A number of stories explaining this practice exist in relation to, for example, old temples such as Tiruvalla, Tṛipraṅgoḍe, Alattūr, etc., while such a ban does not exist in the case of less prosperous temples such as Tirunāvaya, Guruvāyūr, etc. The latter ones, incidentally, are more famous for their 'spiritual' heritage.
32. *S.I.I.*, VI, 283; 284.
33. Kesavan Veluthat, 'The *Sabhā* and *Pariṣad* in Early Medieval South India: Correlation of Epigraphic and Dharmaśāstraic Evidences', *Tamil Civilization*, Vol. III, nos. 2 and 3, pp. 75–82.
34. *S.I.I.*, XIII, 3.
35. *E.I.*, XXI, 27.
36. *S.I.I.*, V, 723.
37. The expression used is *peruvilai*, meaning an auction. Land is not presented generally as a saleable commodity in the records of this period.
38. *S.I.I.*, VII, 843; *S.I.I.*, XVII, 243; *A.R.E.*, no. 28 of 1919.
39. *S.I.I.*, IV, 391.
40. E.g., *S.I.I.*, VII, 891.
41. E.g., *S.I.I.*, VIII, 68.
42. *S.I.I.*, III, 57; *S.I.I.*, VIII, 4; *E.C.*, X, Sd., 92; *S.I.I.*, V, 473, etc.
43. See below, Chapter 7.
44. See above, Chapters 3 and 4.
45. Nilakanta Sastri, *Colas*, pp. 520–45.
46. A. Appadorai, *Economic Conditions ...*, *op. cit.*, Vol. 2, pp. 661–732;

Mahalingam, *South Indian Polity, op. cit.*, pp. 153–99; Minakshi, *Administration and Social Life, op.cit.*, pp. 88–105.

47. Stein, *Peasant State and Society ...*, pp. 258–64.

48. Noboru Karashima, *South Indian History and Society, op. cit.*, pp. 69–130.

49. Above, Chapter 3.

50. Cf., Subbarayalu, *State in Medieval South India*, pp. 199–200.

51. Above, n. 48.

52. Stein, *Peasant State and Society ...*, pp. 260–64.

53. Karashima, *South Indian History and Society*, p. xxiii.

54. *Ibid.*, pp. 72–73, Table 8.

55. Cf. Subbarayalu, *State in Medieval South India*, p. 205.

56. Cf. Nilakanta Sastri, *Colas*, p. 529. This is a Tamilised form of Sanskrit *viṣṭi*. Other expressions which denoted such labour dues include *vedinai, muṭṭaiyāḷ, sēvagam, amañji*, etc.

57. Nilakanta Sastri, *Colas*, p. 533.

58. R. Tirumalai, *Land Grants and Agrarian Reactions in Cola and Pandya Times*, (Madras, 1987), p. 172.

59. *T.A.S.*, II, no. 9.

60. This is the Malayalam expression of Sanskrit *praṇaya* in the *Arthaśāstra*, which means the practice of offering food to the officers of the state. Nilakanta Sastri, *Colas*, p. 520.

61. Narayanan, *Political and Social Conditions of Kerala ...*, Chapter on 'Police and Revenue'.

62. Nilakanta Sastri, *Colas*, pp. 522 f; Appadorai, *op. cit.*, Vol. 2, p. 681; Mahalingam, *South Indian Polity*, pp. 158–72; Subbarayalu, *State ...*, p. 206. For a discordant note, Stein, *Peasant State and Society ...*, pp. 258–64.

63. *S.I.I.*, Vol. III, no. 150. Even this record comes from the reign of Uttama Cōḻa (970–985 AD), immediately before Rājarāja I.

64. *S.I.I.*, IV, 516.

65. *S.I.I.*, V., 861, *S.I.I.*, VII, 467; *S.I.I.*, VIII, nos. 68 and 681; *I.P.S.*, *36*.

66. Karashima, *South Indian History and Society*, Table 8.

67. Tirumalai, *op. cit.*, pp. 87–93.

68. Cf. Subbarayalu, *State in Medieval South India*, pp. 205–06.

69. Karashima, *South Indian History and Society*, pp. 94–105.

70. *S.I.I.*, II, nos. 4 and 5.

71. *S.I.I.*, Vol. IV, no. 529.

72. Karashima, *South Indian History and Society*, Table 11, pp. 100–01.

73. *Ibid.*, Tables 12, 13, 14 and 15. 102–05.

74. *Ibid.*, p. 95.

75. One of the major criticisms against the idea that the grant of administrative, fiscal and judicial rights along with the grant considerably decentralised state power is that in such a position there is the assumption of such rights originally enjoyed by a central authority; Cf Stein, '*The State and Agrarian Order....*' *op. cit.*, p. 88, Hermann Kulke, 'Fragmentation and Segmentation versus Integration? Reflections on the Concepts of Indian Feudalism and the Segmentary State in Indian History', *Studies in History*, Vol. IV, no. 2 (1982), p. 237.

76. Cf. Marc Bloch, 'Feudalism' in *International Encyclopaedia of Social Sciences*'.

77. Subbarayalu, *State in Medieval South India*, pp. 208–19.

78. *P.C.P. passim; T.P.C.P., passim*; etc.

79. This is clear from the context of the numerous records granting such 'tax–free' land where many imposts were still fastened on the land.

80. Tirumalai, *op. cit.*, pp. 93–98.

81. Karl Marx, *Das Capital*, Vol. III (Moscow edn, 1974), p. 790.

82. *Ibid.*, p. 794.

83. *Ibid.*

84. *Ibid.*

85. *Ibid.*, p. 791.

86. *Ibid.*, p. 795.

87. Narayanan, *Political and Social Conditions ...*, Chapter on 'Police and Revenue'.

88. Nilakanta Sastri, *Colas*, pp. 453–60; Mahalingam, *South Indian Polity*, Chapter 6, pp. 254–309, etc.

89. Cf. Stein, '*The State and Agrarian Order ...*', *op.cit.*, pp. 75–76; *Peasant State and Society ...*, pp. 256–57, etc.

90. Above, Chapter 3.

91. *S.I.I.*, II, Introduction, p. 9.

92. Mahalingam, *South Indian Polity*, pp. 264–65; 285–86.

93. Stein, 'The Segmentary State....', *op.cit.*, p. 12.

94. *Ibid.*, p. 13; *idem*, 'State and Agrarian Order....' p. 75.

95. Sastri, *Colas*, p. 459; Mahalingam, *South Indian Polity*, p. 286.

96. For a summary of the controversy in which stalwarts such as E. Hultzsch, V. Venkayya, S. Desivinayagam Pillai and K. A. Nilakanta Sastri took part, M. G. S. Narayanan, 'Kantalur Salai—New Light on the Nature of Aryan Expression to South India', *Proceedings of the Indian History Congress*, (Jabalpur, 1970), pp. 125–36.

97. *Ibid.*

98. M. G. S. Narayanan, *Reinterpretations in South Indian History*, pp. 99–112.

99. Sastri, *Colas*, p. 473.

100. Sastri, *Colas*, pp. 454–55; Mahalingam, *South Indian Polity*, pp. 66, 267.

101. *Periyapuraāṇam*, 'Veḻḻānaiccarukkam', pp. 703–04.

102. Above, Chapter 4; Narayanan, *Political and Social Conditions ...*, Chapter on 'Police and Revenue'.

103. Cf. Logan, *Malabar*, I, pp. 131–32; II, App. XII, p. xxxii; V. Nagam Aiya, *Travancore State Manual* I, p. 225; K. P. Padamanabha Menon, *History of Kerala*, I, p. 252; etc.

104. Narayanan, *Reinterpretations ...*, pp. 107–10; *idem*, 'The Hundred Organisations and the Rise of Nayar Militia in Medieval Kerala', *Proceedings of the Indian History Congress* (Burdwan, 1983).

105. Perhaps the group of *Tuḻilālgl* or *Tuḻilasanda* met with in Kannada sources of this period were the counterparts of the *Vēḷaikkārar*. S. Settar, 'Tuḻilālgaḷ', (in Kannada), *Sādhane*, Vol. IX, no. 3, July–September, 1980. (Bangalore University). This would also offer a clue to the meaning of the expressions such as *Vēḷaikkārar, tuḻilālga, sēvaka*, all of which literally mean 'servants'. [*velai* = *tuḻil* (*toḻil*) = *sēvana* = service]

106. Quoted in Mahalingam, *South Indian Polity*, p. 266.

107. *Ibid.*, p. 267.

108. *Ibid.*

109. Sastri, *Colas*, p. 454.

110. *Ibid.*

111. M. G. S. Narayanan, 'The Anatomy of a Political Alliance from Temple Records of Tirunavalur and Tiruvorriyur', *op. cit.*, p. 28.

112. *Ibid.*

113. Mahalingam, *South Indian Polity*, pp. 65–67; pp. 265–68 has brought out details to show this although he has not himself drawn this conclusion.

114. Narayanan, *Political and Social Conditions ..., op. cit.*, Chapter on 'Economic Conditions' under 'Land Tenure'.

115. Arjun Appadurai, 'Right and Left Hand Castes in South India', *The Indian Economic and Social History Review*, Vol. XI, nos. 2 and 3 (1974), pp. 216–60.

116. For a detailed study, see, S. Gurumurthy, *Education in Early South India*, (Madras, 1978).

117. *T.A.S.*, I, i. pp. 1–14.

118. Kesavan Veluthat, 'The Caṭṭas and Bhaṭṭas: A New Interpretation' in *Proceedings of the Indian History Congress* (Aligarh, 1975).

119. Sastri, *Colas*, pp. 473–80.

120. *Ibid.*, p. 474.

121. Minakshi, *Administration and Social Life ...*, p. 71.

122. No. 162 of 1912.

123. 161 and 190 of 1912.

124. 189 of 1912.

125. Sastri. *Colas.* p. 474.

126. *E.I.*, XXII. no. 32.

127. Subbarayalu, *State in Medieval South India*, p. 222.

128. Sastri, *Colas*, p. 513.

129. *S.I.I.*, II. 11–19; 65, 66.

130. *E.I.* XXI. p. 31.

131. Subbarayalu, *State in Medieval South India*, p. 174.

132. Sastri, *Colas*, p. 357.

133. *Ibid.*, pp. 474–76; Mahalingam, *South Indian Polity*, pp. 220–22.

134. R. S. Sharma, 'Raja-śāsanas', *Indian History Congress*, Calicut. 1976.

135. Kesavan Veluthat, 'The *sabhā* and *pariṣad* in Early Medieval South India: Correlation of Epigraphic and *Dharmaśāstraic Evidences*', *Tamil Civilization*, Vol. 3. nos. 2 and 3. pp. 75–82.

136. J. Duncan M. Derrett, 'Two Inscriptions Concerning the State of Kammāḷas and the Application of Dharmaśāstra·. Prof. K. A. Nilakanta Sastri 80th Birthday Felicitation Volume (Madras. 1971). pp. 32–56. See also *idem.*, 'The Concept of Duty in Ancient Indian Jurisprudence: The Problem of Ascertainment'. in W. Doniger O' Flaherty and J. D. M. Derrett. (eds.). *The Concept of Duty in South Asia* (New Delhi. 1978). pp. 18–66.

137. M. G. S. Narayanan, 'Socio-economic Implications of the Concept of Mahāpātaka in the Feudal Society of South India', *Indian History Congress.* Calicut.1976.

138. R. Tirumalai. *Land Grants and Agrarian Reactions in Cola and Pandya Times* (Madras, 1987). pp. 11–12. Tirumalai refers to an inscription from Tirukkāḷūr *S.I.I*, III. no. 210. where a certain *Vyavasthā* was arrived at and cites the Smṛti-candrikā of Devaṇṇabhatta, a late text (Vol. III. Part II. p. 682) in the Mysore (1916 ed.) where it was sanctified.

139. Above. n. 135.

140. Subbarayalu. *State ...*, pp. 222–24.

141. *Ibid.*, p. 222.

142. Marc Bloch, *Feudal Society*, Vol. II, p. 372.

Five

# The Ūr and the Nāḍu

In the previous chapters we discussed the form of polity in early medieval south India by examining the image of the monarch and the organisation of his government in the kingdoms. A correct appreciation of the structure of polity and the position of the monarch within it can be made only by examining its basic building blocks in society. Conventional scholarship in the subject has largely failed to take note of this point. Topics like *ūr, nāḍu, brahmadēyam* and *nagaram,* taken up for discussion here, have been treated at varying lengths by historians in the past; but they were generally looked upon at best as organs of the government and not as units of social organisation constituting the base of the political structure. Even where this social aspect is appreciated, the organic relationship between the form of government and the social order is largely overlooked or wrongly understood. Our treatment takes the position that the particular form of state which came into existence under the Pallavas and Pāṇḍyas in South India and which was elaborated and modified under the imperial Cōḻas was organically related to a certain socio-political framework resulting from the interplay of a variety of forces at work.

By the close of the sixth century AD, the historical scene in south India is illumined by epigraphy, literature and archaeology. This sudden emergence of newer and richer forms of historical evidence denotes that this part of the country had already entered a new stage of historical development, with economic, social and political forms that were substantially different from an earlier period. Now we have a landscape which is studded by clearly identifiable peasant settlements in areas irrigated by rivers or tanks, a number of brahmanical agrarian corporations, and structural temples dedicated to Agamaic deities such as Śiva and Viṣṇu and a few mercantile centres here and there. Society had been getting stratified in a graded hierarchy with the *jāti* formula as its rationalising principle. This society found its religious ideology in the devotional *bhakti* cult which both legitimised and strengthened the emerging social formation.[1] It was in this milieu that the monarchies of the Pallavas and Pāṇḍyas and the Cēras and Cōḻas flourished. Therefore, an examination of the social foundations of these states would entail consideration of these different factors.

As noted earlier, a prime factor in south Indian history was an expanding agrarian order, which had established itself firmly by the beginning of the seventh century AD. Owing to the nature of our sources, i.e., inscriptions from temples in the main, the information we have is largely one-sided and presents the picture of the temples and other brahmanical settlements as the most powerful institutions commanding property in land. In reality this need not have been the case. The side-light provided by those very records, shows that there was a very strong non-brahman section controlling land, consisting of peasant proprietors and even huge landed magnates. But the lacuna in our sources does not permit any detailed discussion of these sections and hence it is understandable that the existing literature makes either scanty mention of these groups or detailed discussions of a speculative nature. For our purposes we start from the situation in the Cōḻa kingdom, where records are the most copious, and from there proceed to the situations in the other kingdoms. It is by no means assumed that there was identity in all these cases.

The Copper Plate records of the Cōḻas take into consideration the following four major categories of notables in making a grant:[2]

I The *nāṭṭār*

II The *brahmadēyakkiḻavar*,

III (1) *dēvadāna*

(2) *paḷḷiccanda-*

(3) *kaṇimuṟṟūṭṭu*

(4) *veṭṭāppēṟu-ūrkaḷilār*, and

IV The *nagarattār.*

The *nāṭṭār* were the spokesmen of the *nāḍu* locality; the *brahmadēyakkiḻavar* were the land-owning brahmans of the *brahmadēya*, and the *nagarattār* were the members of the *nagaram* organisations of traders. The identity of the third group is also clear from the fact that the *ūrkaḷilār* are described as belonging to the different kinds of eleemosynary villages, viz., the *dēvadāna, paḷḷiccanda, kaṇimuṟṟūṭṭu* and *veṭṭāpēṟu*, although about the exact nature of the latter two kinds of villages there is some dispute.[3] The one group that is strikingly absent in the list is the *veḷḷānavagai ūrār*, which has been presented by historians as a numerous and powerful group in medieval south Indian society.[4] Y. Subbarayalu has computed that the above eleemosynary types of villages constituted only a fraction of the total number of villages on record and argues on its basis that the first category, namely the *nāṭṭār*, were 'none other than the representatives of the *veḷḷānavagai* villages'.[5] However, the question remains as to why the locality group of *nāṭṭār* alone and not the spokesmen of the peasant village, *ūr*, find mention among the list of notables there, especially when even those of the relatively insignificant ones like those of the *kaṇimuṟṟūṭṭu* and *veṭṭāppēṟu* lands (which, according to Subbarayalu, did not even form a whole village) have a place. One will have to believe that the *nāṭṭār* subsumed the *ūr* villages, as the former was a congeries of the latter. An inscription from Kīranūr speaks of the *ūrōm* of five different villages as constituting the *nāḍu* assembly there, which is a clear instance to support this inference.[6] In fact, Subbarayalu states that the village was 'the fractional element of the *nāḍu*. It was a fraction of the society that the *nāḍu* represented; it had its relation with the governmental activities only as a part of the *nāḍu*.'[7] However, in discussing the constitution of a *nāḍu*, Subbarayalu takes up cases of *veḷḷānvagai* villages with membership ranging from four to thirty, although according to his calculation the representation of the spokesmen of the *ūr*s in the *nāḍu* gathering is, on the average, two.[8] He rejects the argument of Nilakanta Sastri that the *nāḍu* was constituted by the representatives of each of the villages in it (both *brahmadēya* and *non-brahmadēya*) coming together.[9] The basis of Professor Sastri's argument is that, of the twenty-seven 'accountants' signing the Larger Leiden grant of Rājarāja I, there were ten representing the *brahmadēya*s and sixteen, the *non-brahmadēya* villages, the remaining one being that of the grant village itself.[10] All these together are taken to constitute the *nāṭṭār* of

Paṭṭinakkūṟṟam. This, however, need not be necessarily so. The grant being addressed to the *brahmadēyakkiḻavar* as well as the *nāṭṭār*, it can be justly pointed out that the ten brahman signatories represented the *brahmadēya*s in their own right and not as constituents of the *nāḍu*. It, therefore, follows that the *nāṭṭār* were the spokesmen of the *veḷḷānvagai* villages which formed the locality group representing the territorial unit of the *nāḍu*. In the few cases where the identity of the members of the *nāḍu* is known, there are no Brahmans.[11]

Y. Subbarayalu has taken up about 240 inscriptions from all over the Tamil country which relate to the activities of the *veḷḷānvagai* villages and their corporate bodies.[12] Obviously, this is a very small fraction of the total number of epigraphical records available for the period; and even among them, only one-third, i.e., about eighty, contain any useful detail regarding this body. Despite these shortcomings the historian can make out certain broad outlines regarding the composition and functioning of the corporate bodies of the *veḷḷānvagai* agrarian settlements.[13]

The relative scarcity of records pertaining to the *veḷḷānvagai* settlements has been explained by scholars as only natural: unlike the brahman settlements or the trading corporations or other special types of villages such as the *dēvadānam, paḷḷiccandam, kaṇimuṟṟūṭṭu* and *veṭṭāppēṟu*, there was nothing extraordinary about the *veḷḷānvagai* villages that had to be recorded.[14] In other words, the activities in these villages followed too routine a course to demand recording. Alternatively, it may be that the *ūr* represented a largely non-literate society which did not bother about recording its proceedings, for such records as we have of the *ūr* come from temples relating to a different group which had a literate tradition.

Noboru Karashima has undertaken detailed studies of the character of village settlements of peasants in the Cōḻa country with the help of two Tanjavur inscriptions of Rājarāja I and a Gaṅgaikkoṇḍacōḻapuram inscription of Virarājēndra.[15] He suggests that the *veḷḷānvagai* villages included habitation sites, cremation grounds, drinking water sources, irrigation channels, cultivated lands, pasture lands, etc. Even the residential areas are said to have consisted of the following: (1) the quarters of the *ūr* landholders/cultivators (*ūr-nattam/ūr-irukkai*), (2) that of the *kammāṇa*s or artisans (*kammāṇacceri*) and (3) that of the *paṟaiya*s or agricultural labourers (*paṟaicceri*). Karashima has elsewhere suggested, on the basis of a comparative study of *brahmadēya* and *non-*

*brahmadēya* villages, that stratification had not clearly emerged in the *non-brahmadēya* villages.[16] However, the evidence from the Tanjavur and Gaṅgaikkoṇḍacōḻapuram inscriptions, though of a later period, would point to the contrary. There were clearly three strata with the landholders/cultivators at the top, the artisans in the middle and the agricultural labourers at the bottom. Those who occupied the top position in the non-brahman villages appear to have enjoyed parity with the brahmans in an economic sense on account of their control of the land and hence to have been in an almost equally commanding position. These owner-cultivators were generally known by the expression *kāṇiyuḍaiyār* and the tenant-cultivators, by the expression *uḻukuḍi*. On occasions, both were indiscriminately referred to as *kuḍimakkaḷ*, which suggests to Subbarayalu that there was not always marked differentiation between the owner-cultivators on the one side and the tenant-cultivators on the other.[17] Both were *veḷḷāḷas.*

There are a few records which throw light on the corporate body of the *ūr.* Since the habitation sites of the *ūr* landholders were known as *ūr-nattam* or *ūr-irukkai* (literally the residential area of the *ūr*), it appears that the corporate body, also known by the term *ūr* or *ūrār* (those of the *ūr*) or *ūrōm* (we of the *ūr*), consisted exclusively of those who lived in such quarters, i.e., the landholders. Among the inscriptions dealing with the *ūr*, about seventy cases provide evidence regarding the strength of the corporate body called the *ūr.*[18] A few inscriptions give the impression that there were only one or two members in the body, but on closer examination it will be seen that most of such cases are taken from records of collective gatherings of many villages, the one or two members being the representatives rather than the entirety of the respective villages. There are nineteen such cases. Twenty-four *ūr* bodies have members ranging from three to five; fifteen, from six to ten; six, from eleven to fourteen; two, nineteen; two, twenty-three; one, twenty-five and one, twenty-nine. These data very strongly suggest that most villages had the *ūr* with less than ten members; the number of effective landholders in a village may have been just as many. In fact, Subbarayalu has calculated that landholders held land in extent ranging from two to ten *vēlis*.[19] He has also suggested, on the basis of two Tanjavur inscriptions of Rājarāja I that villages varied in extent in the more fertile areas from five to hundred *vēlis.*[20] This makes the suggestion, that the strength of the *ūr* body was generally less than ten, plausible.

Unlike the brahman *sabhās* which represented the *brahmadēya* villages, the *ūr* does not appear to have had many other restrictive qualifications except ownership of property. Again, since the *ūr* was a corporate body concerned with the management of landed property, viz., the sale of land, the gift of land, exemption of tax dues on land, etc., only the landholders had any place there. There are very explicit statements to the effect that only the members of the *ūr* paid tax on land, which is further indication of the fact that all the landholders of a village were members of the body of the *ūr.*

The computerised concordance of the names in the Cōḻa inscriptions provides further information. As noted in an earlier chapter, the names figuring in Cōḻa inscriptions have various segments arranged in an almost regular pattern.[21] One of the more frequent segments is associated with a title, *uḍaiyān. Uḍaiyān* is a title which in most cases is preceded by the name of a village. This literally means that the holder of the village name + *uḍaiyān* title is the owner or possessor of the particular village; but since we see more than one *uḍaiyān* associated with the same village, this meaning cannot simply apply. Therefore it is suggested that wherever a title with the village name + *uḍaiyān* pattern occurs, the reference is to one who held or possessed some land in the particular village.

Records from the Tanjavur, Tiruchirappalli and parts of South Arcot districts, i.e., of the Cōḻamaṇḍalam area, show a regular increase in the occurrence of names with the title *uḍaiyān* as one of the segments from the ninth to the thirteenth centuries.[22] Thus in Tanjavur district we have 11.4 per cent names with the *uḍaiyān* title out of the total personal names in the pre-Rājarāja I period; 12.7 per cent for the period from Rājarāja I to Adhirājēndra, 16.4 per cent for the period from Kulōttuṅga I to Rājādhirāja II and 22.9 per cent for the period from Kulōttuṅga III to Rājēndra III. Similarly for Tiruchirapalli district, the figures are 4.4 per cent, 14.9 per cent, 17.5 per cent and 17.7 per cent respectively for each of the above four periods. Again for South Arcot district we have a similar progression with the figures seven per cent, 14.9 per cent, 20.5 per cent and 19.9 per cent. This appears to be a clear indication of an increase in the number of landholders in the Cōḻamaṇḍalam area. However, in Toṇḍaimaṇḍalam or Jayaṅgoṇḍacōḻamaṇḍalam, consisting of the North Arcot, Chingleput, Chittur and Nellur districts, such regularity cannot be seen.[23] One reason may be that long before that region became part of the Cōḻa state, there already existed a well-established peasant community under the Pallavas, leaving little scope for further expansion.

The titles *kiḻān* and *kiḻavan*, as noted earlier, are similar in meaning.[24] There are about thirty published Cōḻa inscriptions in which the names of the members of the *ūr* are given. It is seen that in most cases the members held one of the titles viz., *uḍaiyān, kiḻān* or *kiḻavan*; in a few other cases there are *vēḷān*s and *pēraraiyan*s, both indicating, in different ways, possession of some land. It is interesting that in two cases we have brahmans, one holding the title *kiḻavan*[25] and another Pallavan Brahmātarāyar who is explicitly stated as 'ruling the *ūr*' (*ūr āḷkiṟṟa*).[26] The role of the former is not clear; that of the latter, with his title Brahmātarāyan and his being described as ruling the *ūr*, appears to be more than that of an ordinary member of the *ūr*. Generally, therefore, the statement that the *ūr* formed a corporate body consisting of the non-brahman landholders in a village stands confirmed by an analysis of the results of the statistical examination of personal names in the inscriptions.

Since it is suggested that the *ūr* consisted of landholders, the nature of land-ownership among the members of the *ūr* needs some elaboration. Noboru Karashima has argued with the help of a few records of land transfer that land ownership in the non-*brahmadēya* villages was collective, in contrast to the individual ownership in *brahmadēya* villages.[27] The picture does not stand ostensibly altered from the analysis of the computerised *Concordance*. Of the different cases relating to land transfer involving members of the *ūr*, none is concerned with the sale of land by a member of the *ūr* in his individual capacity.[28] But since these are records relating to the *ūr* as a corporate body, this is only natural. Karashima has himself brought out other cases where, even in records pertaining to members of the *ūr*, a border land of the land sold is described to have been held by members of the *ūr* in their individual capacity.[29] Further, Subbarayalu has pointed out that individual ownership of land among non-brahman landholders was increasing in the period during and after the tenth century AD.[30] Subbarayalu's paper shows a shift in the nature of land ownership in the course of time, a point stressed by Karashima elsewhere. It has been suggested that this is too hasty a conclusion, given the nature of our records.[31]

In the records of the other regions taken up for study, the situation in relation to *ūr* is more or less similar. The existing literature on the Pallava kingdom is not quite sufficient to say that the picture stands altered in that region. In fact, since that region formed part of the Cōḻa Empire in the tenth century and after and since the picture there in this period was not significantly different from the rest of the Cōḻa Empire, there is no reason why a different picture should be postulated about that area. And that is what is indicated by the extant records of the Pallava kingdom from the seventh through the ninth centuries.[32] As for the Pāṇḍyan kingdom, the student is now in a better position, thanks to the research of Rajan Gurukkal.[33] Gurukkal has marshalled evidence to suggest that the picture we have in the records of the Pāṇḍyan kingdom, if less elaborate, is not any less clear. Even there, the smallest and the most enduring unit of agrarian settlement was the *ūr.* Regional differences in detail, however, were there: thus while the place name generic, *irukkai*, in the Cōḻa country denoted the habitation sites as we have seen above, that in the Pāṇḍyan country stood for a whole village. Otherwise the pattern appears to be the same, both in relation to the settlement and the assembly of its spokesmen. In the case of the Cēra kingdom, however, the evidence we have is far less copious. There we do not come across such non-brahman groups at all, the expressions such as *ūr* and *ūrār* being used to denote the brahman settlements and their assembly respectively. M. G. S. Narayanan's study of the history of the Cēra kingdom has ably brought out the relatively less developed character of the non-brahman peasant agricultural organisation there,[34] which stands confirmed by later studies undertaken by Rajan Gurukkal[35] and the present writer.[36] The less fertile character of the soil and the totally different settlement pattern in that region may have been responsible for this. This, however, affected the pattern of social evolution in that part of the country in a big way: a greater amount of brahmanical influence is noticed there in all aspects of social life as well as in the details of political structure.

If the *ūr* is considered as the fractional element of the *nāḍu*, then the whole formed by the aggregate of such elements is the *nāḍu*. This conception of the relationship between the two groups follows the conventional, constitutive, view of the *nāḍu*, according to which the village was the basic unit of administration and several such villages constituted a *nāḍu*.[37] This is one picture of the *nāḍu* in conventional historiography as it is seen from below, as it were. There is another, in a way contradictory, picture from above which presents the *nāḍu* as an administrative division, the subdivisions of which were the villages.[38] There may be differences in detail such as whether the *nāḍu* consisted only of the *veḷḷānvagai* villages or other kinds of villages such as the *brahmadēya, dēvadāna*, etc., also, but generally either of these has been the image of the *nāḍu* presented by the conventional historians.

In recent studies, however, the picture has been significantly altered. There has been a major shift in the emphasis. The 'eternal village', conforming to the archetypes created by British administrator-historians and supported by Indian nationalist writers, appears to have lost its significance. Burton Stein suggested this in a vague manner[39] and Noboru Karashima has elaborately dethroned the eternal village,[40] both consecrating, as it were, the *nāḍu* in its place. Their scholarship, thus, appears to recognise the *nāḍu* as a more important factor in the understanding of society and polity in medieval south India. The student of the history of localities and local groups under the Cōḷas is under an eternal debt of obligation to the penetrating research of Y. Subbarayalu on the political geography of the Cōḷa country.[41] He has shown that, like the expression ūr, *nāḍu* also denoted both a locality and an assembly of the spokesman of that locality. The *nāḍu* as a territory was a grouping of the *veḷḷānvagai* villages, i.e., the agrarian settlements. There is no way to define precisely the boundaries of the territory of a *nāḍu* although statements describing particular villages as belonging to particular *nāḍu*s would help us identify the territory covered by such *nāḍu*s. They had no natural boundaries such as a river. In fact, there were *nāḍu*s lying on either side of a stream or a watercourse, including the Kāvēri in one case.[42] This suggests that at least in those cases importance was given to a source of irrigation as central to the locality, a point which supports the idea that the *nāḍu*s formed spontaneous natural groupings of agrarian settlements. Further, the *nāḍu*s were widely disparate in their size, varying from a handful of square miles to a few hundreds and comprising villages varying from one to as many as forty. These facts, together with the lack of uniformity among the *nāḍus*, suggest strongly against the idea of their being artificial divisions. The few cases of rearrangements of *nāḍus* by the regrouping of villages among them singularly lack in evidence of governmental interference in such matters.[43] The nomenclature of the *nāḍu* too is indicative of this: it mostly followed the name of a village, which was usually a toponym.[44] On the other hand, the *vaḷanāḍu* units, which were clearly administrative divisions of an artificial nature, had natural boundaries; they were named after one of the titles of the Cōḻa ruler; there was less disparity among them in size.[45]

The situation in the other regions appears to conform to this suggestion. In the Pallava kingdom we come across a locality called *kōṭṭam*, which is at times taken as a unit bigger than the *nāḍu*. But in all other respects, the *kōṭṭam* answered to the *nāḍu*.[46] In that region, the question of artificial units such as the *vaḷanāḍus* does not arise at all under the Pallavas for the simple reason that they were administrative units contrived by the Cōḻa imperial government under Rājarāja I and after, by whose time Toṇḍaimaṇḍalam or Jayaṅgoṇḍacōḻamaṇḍalam, the erstwhile Pallava territory, had been integrated as part of the Cōḻa empire. In the Pāṇḍyan kingdom, too, Rajan Gurukkal has demonstrated that the *nāḍus* had similar characteristics as they had in the Cōḻa country, spontaneous groupings of agrarian village communities.[47] Again, like in the Cōḻa country, when units like the *vaḷanāḍus* begin to appear in the tenth century, they are clearly administrative divisions of an artificial nature, with a name or title of one of the Pāṇḍyan rulers or their Cōḻa overlords prefixed to the name of each *vaḷanāḍu*.[48] In the Cēra kingdom, as in many other cases, we do not have the counterparts of the *nāḍu* or *kōṭṭam* units in the rest of south India. We do come across an expression *nāḍu* in terms such as Kōlattunādu, Ēṛalanāḍu, Vaḷḷuvanādu, Vēṇādu, etc., which stood for territorial divisions; but they denoted whole territories under chiefly rule, answering to the *pāḍi* or *viṣaya* in the Cōḻa country.[49] Again, the pattern of settlement may have been responsible for this variation here; but its implication, in the absence of the aggressive non-brahman peasant localities in the rest of the Tamil country, was far-reaching for the nature of socio-political organisation there.

If thus the spontaneous, evolutionary, character of the *nāḍu* is appreciated, then the increase in the number of *nāḍu* units as pointed out by Subbarayalu can be understood more meaningfully. He feels that the fact of more and more *nāḍus* being mentioned in the inscriptional records dating from the period after the ninth century is evidence for the proliferation of such *nāḍus* settlements,[50] a statement which is rejected by Burton Stein who believes that it shows 'not a new existence, but a new recognition of Chola overlordship' in these *nāḍus*.[51] But by extending Stein's own logic, this can be questioned: the first mention of anything in a record is as little evidence for its 'new recognition' as it is for its recent origin! The point is about the spontaneity as well as the evolutionary nature of these units. It was in the more fertile regions that the earlier *nāḍus* are situated while the later ones appear in the less fertile regions on the fringes of the settled agrarian society, thus presenting the picture of a gradual agrarian expansion. Again, the more densely populated *nāḍus*, which comprised larger number of villages, were in the more fertile regions and the more sparsely populated ones, which consisted of smaller numbers of villages, were in the less fertile regions.

Burton Stein assumes that the *nāḍus* existed 'long before' the Cōḻa empire.[52] He believes that the neolithic farming communities in the plains and uplands were the bases of these groups and that by the early centuries of the Christian era, even the *nāḍu* units were crystallised as is clear (to him) from the early Tamil literature.

A major confusion has crept in here with respect to both the archaeological and literary evidence. While we have evidence, from the neolithic levels, of the knowledge of agriculture from excavations, for example, at Paiyampalli, there is nothing on record to suggest that well-organised farming communities existed there at that time.[53] Again, even though pockets of agrarian settlements can be identified in what is usually called Sangam literature, the evidence there is far too inconclusive to suggest that the peasant localities in early medieval south India represented a direct, unbroken, continuation from the ancient times. The evidence he presents in favour of this argument is based on references to a number of *nāḍus* found in that literature:[54] he fails to recognise that the twelve dialect zones in the didactic/prescriptive sections, which are demonstrably late compositions, use the term *nāḍu* in the sense of territory, country, etc.,[55] much in the same way as this word was used in Kerala and Karnataka in the medieval period. Thus expressions like Kuṭṭanāḍu, Kuḍanādu, Pūḻināḍu, etc., figuring in

Sangam literature, should not be understood in the same way as the *nāḍus* in early medieval times in the Cōḻa country. In the latter case, they were groupings of peasant settlements with a corporate identity.

As pointed out earlier, most *nāḍus* derived their names from the names of one of the villages within them. But beyond this 'name-giving' aspect, there was nothing special about that village to qualify it as the 'centre' of the *nāḍus*, its 'headquarters'. 'There is not a single inscription', writes Subbarayalu, 'which would connect even vaguely the activities of the *nāḍu* assembly with some chief village or the activities of the government with the same.'[56] There are at least eleven *nāḍus* where the 'chief village' was a *brahmadēya*.[57] It is not possible that a *brahmadēya*, where administrative, fiscal and judicial powers were alienated, could have been created in a place which was an administrative headquarters. Indeed, centres such as Uṟaiyur, Paḻaiyāṟai, Tiruvāmūr, Chidambaram and Kāñcīpuram did not have any *brahmadēya* or other free-hold places within them. Burton Stein believes that the 'name-giving' village was the earliest peasant settlement of a *nāḍu*, its 'inner core', which attracted subordinate settlements around it and thus welded together the peasant group of the locality.[58] This idea of an 'inner core' and an 'outer pulp' (as it were) is not warranted by the evidence of the *nāḍus* which in reality were homogeneous entities. This 'name-giving' village may have been the earliest settlement in a locality; but there is nothing to suggest that it had a primacy in the *nāḍu* in any other respect.

These *nāḍus*, which are understood by Stein with an 'inner core' in a primary village and subordinate settlements gathered around it, are taken by him as discrete units of ethnic, social and economic organisation.[59] In fact, these are looked upon as the atomic aspects of the segmentary organisation in medieval south India. Its salient features according to him were: (1) restricted marriage and kinship networks, (2) narrow territorial social coalitions beyond kinsmen and (3) locally based agrarian relationships, political and religious affiliations and loyalties.[60] While the possibility of the *nāṭṭār* being related to one another in an affinal or agnatic way is not denied here, our evidence shows that it was their common interests as prominent landholders that brought them together and gave them their corporate identity and character. The concern with landed property, agriculture and the management of surplus is prime in the documents and even a suggestion of their bonds being based on kinship loyalties is not found there. In fact, the period between the close of what is described as the Sangam Age, which is usually put at the third-fourth centuries AD, and the beginning of the period of our study had witnessed the break-up of such loyalties based on kinship and marriage and the emergence of new loyalties based on economic and social differentiations.[61] By the ninth and tenth centuries and after, with large extents of land cleared and larger sections of population transformed as peasants, bringing about marked differentiation in society, the clannish loyalties had no place in society as a major organising principle.

Stein appears, in fact, to be begging the question. He writes:[62]

> In the absence of effective, continuous, extra-local, non-peasant authority over agrarian relationships and over the distribution of the products of the land, it was only through secure relationships with those local groups which controlled the land that benefits could be obtained by groups without such control.

Stein assumes here his main thesis of the absence of extra-local, non-peasant authority over the distribution of the products of the land and then makes that his premise on which to base his argument about the territorially segmented character of society, which argument itself is the major premise of the book, the larger purpose of which is to prove the absence of extra-local, non-peasant authority of an effective and continuous nature!

Another factor which Stein regards as important with respect to territorial segmentation in the southern peninsula is the absence of conquests.[63] It is argued that there have not been any major conquests in this region in historical times and hence there was no major change in society. This not only assumes that war and conquests bring about major social changes; but it also ignores the ability of changes in the means and relations of production to lead to such changes. And, surprisingly, Stein legitimises his whole argument in this matter swearing by Kosambi[64] who would, in actual fact, consider history as the 'presentation ... of successive developments in the means and relations of production.'[65] Again, apparently thinking in circles, Stein concludes that this changelessness was preserved and protected by the segmentary character of society.

Stein makes a distinction among three types of *nāḍus*, although he does not cite any evidence either primary or secondary to support his distinction.[66] The differences relate generally to their internal organisation and their connection with other localities. There were *nāḍus* which were horizontally divided ('vertically segmented' in Stein's words) with an elaborate hierarchy with political chiefs at the top (of course, below the Cholas according to the diagram on p. 135), brahman ritual specialists below them, the dominant peasantry of the *nāḍu* still lower, followed by the lower peasantry and dependents in the next stratum, the artisan-traders further down and the landless labourers at the bottom. Such *nāḍus* are designated as 'central *nāḍus*', although the term 'central' has admittedly no spatial connotation about it. They obtained in the fertile plains, where agriculture was easiest and most profitable. A second type of *nāḍu* is stated to have been found in those tracts of the lowlands or in the large interior uplands above the Tamil plain lacking reliable sources of water for extensive irrigated agriculture. For want of the necessary surplus, there were fewer of the hierarchical elements found in the 'central' *nāḍus*. Here society was vertically divided (or, 'horizontally segmented' in Stein's words). Stein makes an important distinction between the 'central' and 'intermediate' *nāḍus*. While the 'central' *nāḍus* were closely linked to a ruling dynasty, for the most part Cōḻa, in the 'intermediate' *nāḍus* the sovereignty of other dynasties was recognised. Further, the brahmanical institutions were fewer in the intermediate *nāḍus*. Although 'intermediate' *nāḍus* are stated to have been horizontally segmented giving little scope for differentiation, etc., the diagram on p. 139 shows hierarchy nonetheless, if on a less elaborate scale than in the 'central' *nāḍus*. He also distinguishes a third type of *nāḍu* in those parts of south India which were least hospitable to sedentary agriculture or even to mixed agricultural and pastoral activities. These were scattered *nāḍu* localities without any differentiation whatsoever. They are designated as the 'peripheral' *nāḍus*, which are stated to have displayed the strongest tribal characteristics.

However, these distinctions are not supported by any kind of evidence in Stein's treatment.[67] It would appear that he is speculating too much here in order to form the premise on which he seeks to base his arguments about the segmentary nature of the Cōḻa state. In reality, evidences we have about the *nāḍu* as a territorial unit and about the *nāṭṭār* as a corporate body are far less exhaustive than would support this kind of classification.

In the conventional literature on the subject of the corporate body of the *nāṭṭār*, also known, like the *ūr*, by the term *nāḍu* itself, is treated as a sort of territorial assembly which functioned in the territorial unit known by the name *nāḍu*. The assembly is either looked at as consisting of the representatives of each of the villages coming together or by the more influential residents of the unit.[68] It is also stated that the assemblies of *brahmadēya, paḷḷiccandam, kaṇimuṟṟūṭu*, and *veṭṭāpēṟu* villages and the *nagara* were subject to the administrative control of the *nāḍu*. However, our view of the *nāḍu* differs from these positions. The part played by the *nāḍu* in the administration of the country is not denied; but the view that it was an organ of the government, constituted for the purpose, is explicitly rejected here. In our view, the *nāḍu*s were pre-existing groupings of the peasant settlements with a spontaneous character and these groupings were identified and made use of by the state under the Pallavas, Pāṇḍyas and Cōḷas for purposes of government. In the records of the Cēra kingdom, however, this locality group is strikingly absent. This may be explained by the totally dissimilar character of the settlement pattern there, where nucleated settlements as they obtained in the Tamil speaking regions did not obtain and where the settlements were of a dispersed nature.

As stated earlier, the *nāḍu* was a grouping of the *veḷḷānvagai* villages in a locality. This is amply clear from the Kīranūr inscription of 1310 AD mentioned above, which speaks of the *ūrōm* of the villages Nāñjil, Peruñcēvūr, Viṟaikkuḍi, Chunaiyakkuḍi and Oḍuvūr as qualified for the *nāḍu* of Vaḍa-Chiṟuvāyil-nāḍu: '*nāṭṭukkuccamainda-Nāñcil-ūrkkuc-camainta-ūromum; peruñcēvūr-ūrkkuccamainta-ūrōmum*', etc.[69] A Mannarguḍi inscription of 1239 AD states that the *nāṭṭavar* of the *Taniyūr* (generally a *brahmadēya* and less frequently a temple excluded from the jurisdiction of *nāḍu* within the territories of which it was located and constituting practically a *nāḍu* in its own right) Rājādhirājacaturvēdimaṅgalam represented to a gathering of the local *sabhā*s and the *nāṭṭavar* of five other *nāḍu*s that 'they could not carry on their agricultural profession (*veḷḷāmaic-ceydu-kuḍiyirukka-ppokutillaiyenru*)' due to the exacting nature of the tax collectors.'[70] This brings out the fact that the *nāṭṭār* consisted of the *veḷḷāḷas.* Further, in all other available cases the signatories to the transactions of the *nāḍu*s belong to the *veḷḷāḷa* community and they in most cases bear the *vēḷān* title.[71]

The *nāḍu*, thus, being a grouping of agricultural settlements, the *nāṭṭār*, the spokesman of those groupings, had agriculture as their prime concern. It was the *nāṭṭār* who were addressed in the Pallava, Pāṇḍya and Cōḷa copper plates granting land; and it was they who acted on the order by delimiting the boundaries, resettling the occupants and implementing the grant in other ways. This shows the ultimate acquiescence of the *nāṭṭār* to the writ of the king who appears to have reserved the right to create superior rights in land, either by removing earlier occupants or by subjecting them to the new superior rights of the donees.

Among the other functions performed by the *nāṭṭār*, we see that they took care of the management of irrigation in many cases.[72] There are a number of cases where the *nāṭṭār* donated landed property, mostly to temples.[73] The *nāṭṭār* also figure as custodians of some charities made by others, in the same way that the *panmāhēśvara*s and *śrīvaiṣṇava*s figure in some other records relating to land owned by temples.[74] There are cases, rare though, where the *nāḍu*s receive and administer endowments from private individuals by making a remission on the tax on the piece of land donated in lieu of a specified amount of money which they took as a capital deposit.[75] The donations that the *nāḍu* made to temples etc. are put under the category of tax-free land described as *naṭṭiṟaiyili*.[76] The *nāḍu* undertook to pay the tax on account of such land to the state.[77] The *nāḍu* appears to have collected a due for defraying the expenses incurred on such acts.[78] Such levies were known as *nāḍāṭci, nāṭṭu-viniyōgam* or *nāṭṭu-vyavasthai*. There are also records relating to transactions of temple lands including leasing and sale with the involvement of the *nāṭṭār.* [79]

From the records stating that the *nāḍu* undertook to pay the taxes on lands made tax-free or *naṭṭiṟaiyili*, it is clear that it was the *nāḍu* which assessed and collected tax on land. There are other records which say that the *nāṭṭār* were responsible to pay the tax to the king's agents, *kōmaṟṟavar.*[80] These records suggest that the king's agents made regular demands and collections of such dues from the *nāḍu*s. There are more cases where the spokesmen of the *nāḍu*s themselves acted as agents of the state.[81] Thus in a record of 1267 AD, the *mudaligaḷ* who are clearly royal agents are stated to be 'the *mudaligaḷ* belonging to the *nāḍu*' (*nāḍu* *uḍaiya mudaligaḷ*);[82] a Tirumayam inscription describes a *daṇḍanāyakam* as 'of this *nāḍu*' (*in-nāḍ-uḍaiya*);[83] the earliest of this category appears to have been a Tiruvāmāttūr record of 917 AD which mentions a certain Cōḻa-Śikhāmani Pallavaraiyan as one who acquired the local *nāḍu* (*in-nāḍu-peṟṟa*).[84] It follows that the major land owners of a locality who formed the group known as the *nāḍu* were recognised by the state as its agents for administrative purposes. All this is clear evidence of the king's control over the *nāḍu* units, typical of a feudal political structure in which a local magnate or corporate group as a fictitious individual is recognised as the agent of the state.

There are clearer statements in some other records to show the close link between the groups of the locality called the *nāḍu*s on the one hand and the royal government on the other; in fact it would appear that the former was the local expression of the latter.[85] This is clear from the fact that in questions related to land revenue, the chief source of royal revenue, it was the *nāṭṭār* who mattered most. As the *nāṭṭār* were the dominant land-owners and hence the important taxpayers, so also they came in as the handiest groups with whom the royal government could have negotiations over the assessment and settlement of land revenue. Thus, it is recognition of this commanding position of these groups of landed magnates by the royal government that is expressed in the fact of their being addressed in making a grant of land. Further, expressions such as *nattup-puṟavu, nāṭṭu-vari* and *nāṭṭuk-kaṇakku*, the first two indicating the land revenue account of the *nāḍu* and the revenue account of the *nāḍu* in general respectively, and the third meaning both these accounts collectively as also the person in charge· of those accounts,[86] clearly show that the *nāḍu* was the basic revenue unit. The revenue demands and collection from a village were settled in relation to the *nāḍu* locality within which it was situated. When an *ūr* made remissions of tax, corresponding deductions were made in the dues from the *nāḍu* as well.[87] When the dues from a temple were diverted by a king for instituting certain services in that temple, this was caused to be entered in both the *variyilārkaṇakku* (the revenue account of the royal government) and the *nāṭṭuk-kaṇakku*,[88] emphasising the significance of the *nāḍu* as an integral part of the state system with its local autonomy.

Burton Stein states that 'no contemporary documents speak of the *nāḍu* in terms the Chola governmental structure or function.'[89] This is simply not the case. The instances examined above are themselves indicative of this function, with the *nāḍu* taking an active part in the revenue administration of the state. We have further evidence of officers or the king's agents concerned with the *nāḍu* and its administration. We have at least three different categories of royal agents: the *nāḍu vagai ceyvar*, the *nāḍu kūṟu ceyvar* and the *nāḍu kaṇkāṇi nāyagam* or *nāḍu kaṇkāṭci*. Stein takes them as functionaries of the *nāḍu* itself concerned with the maintenance of accounts and assessment.[90] We have shown in a previous chapter that these were clearly agents of the royal government in the *nāḍu* localities and that they were not employed by the *nāḍu* groups.[91] To maintain that they were the employees of the *nāḍu* groups would imply two things: (a) the existence of specialised administrative staff appointed and maintained by the local groups which would certify to the segmentary nature of the Cōḻa state and (b) the relative lack of penetration of the 'central government' to the localities which would, again, indicate a weak centre in a segmentary state.[92] In reality, however, the evidence we have does not support this position with its implications. Hence, the idea that the *nāḍu* localities formed 'subordinate foci of power' does not stand the scrutiny of the evidence concerning 'specialised administrative staff'. Closely related to this position taken by Stein is his interpretation of the significance of *madhyasthan* and *madhyasthan-karaṇaṭṭān* in the Larger Leiden Plates. This has been rightly questioned by Jha and Ramaswamy. Besides, it has been shown that this term gets increasingly replaced by clearly identifiable royal agents in the post-Rājarāja I period, which detail clearly fits into the pattern of an increasing penetration of royal power in the localities.

On account of the nature of our sources which are highly biased in favour of the temples, these officers are seen in relation to the temples; but one may reasonably believe that they did not exclusively relate to the religious institutions. Their function was not religious in character. An inscription of 1116 AD of Kulōttuṅga I is very interesting in this respect.[93] Here, a *nāḍu kūṟu* settled the affairs of a new *dēvadāna* and arranged for the services in the temple out of the income from the land. He did it, expressly under the authority of a *tirumugam* (royal order) from the king, of the *uḷvari* (a duplicate entry made in the tax register) of the *pur̤avuvariyār* (an officer of the land revenue department), and of a *kaḍaiyīḍu* (deed of execution) of the *maṇḍaḷamudaligaḷ*. This is a clear instance of the king's government penetrating into the *nāḍu* through its agents at various levels.[94] These officers were also charged with the work of checking and auditing the accounts of temples in the localities.[95] A *nāḍu vagai* officer is even found to be present in a meeting of the *sabhā* of a *brahmadēya* village.[96] We find the *nāḍu kaṇkāṇi* officers also in a similar role. In a Tiruviḷaṅguḍi inscription dated 1013 AD, a certain Chikāruḍaiyān Tāyan Aḍigaḷ is clearly stated to be in the locality in charge of the *nāḍu kaṇkāṇi nāyagam* office as a subordinate (*kanmi*) of the *sēnāpati*, Mudikoṇḍacōḻa Viḻupparaiyar by name.[97] There are instances of the *nāḍu* officers, both *nāḍu vagai* and *nāḍu kaṇkāṇi nāyagam*, being transferred from place to place.[98] Again, instances of the same officer who was in charge of more than one *nāḍu* are also met with.[99] This shows clearly that these officers, though acting *in* the *nāḍus*, were not part of the corporate group of the *nāṭṭār* and that they were agents of the royal government.

A very important aspect about the *nāṭṭār* as agents of the king's government is brought out by a very recent and illuminating study by James Heitzman.[100] Heitzman takes up five study areas within the Cōḻa state for intensive study of the problem of state formation in south India.[101] Out of these five areas, the Pudukkottai area to the south, which is the most outlying among them and ecologically the least hospitable to rice cultivation, has the largest number of references to the *nāṭṭār* groups in relation to governmental functions, in spite of the fact that this area has yielded fewer inscriptions than the other areas.[102] In the other areas, two, Kumbakonam and Tiruchirappalli, which have yielded larger number of inscriptions, have fewer references to the *nāṭṭār* groups.[103] In the case of the other two, viz., Tirukkoyilur in South Arcot district and Tirutturaippundi in Tanjavur district, the former was in an intermediary zone under the chiefly rule of the Malaiyamāns and, following the pattern that we have seen in a previous chapter, the period of Rājarāja and his immediate successors found a greater penetration of the Cōḻa king's government there in the form of the royal functionaries present in the inscriptions.[104] In the case of the latter, which represented the tail-end of the irrigation channels and which has been described by Heitzman as a 'political backwater', the situation was comparable to that which obtained in the other two areas in the core territories.[105]

Again, in the Pudukkottai area, which has the maximum number of references to the *nāṭṭār*, most of these references are noted to be of either the pre-Rājarāja or post-Virarājēndra periods.[106] This suggests the very important fact that state function in the more outlying areas was carried out by and through the *nāṭṭār* groups as much as it was done directly in the core regions and by the chiefly families in the intermediate regions of Cōḻa political authority and that in the period of Rājarāja and his immediate successors, there was a greater attempt at centralisation which aimed at steamrolling the entire territory into a single political system. This finding in relation to the period 985–1070 AD is exactly in the same pattern that we have seen in two earlier chapters:[107] of a greater penetration of the state through its functionaries and a ramified 'revenue department' and a corresponding eclipse of chiefly rule wherever it prevailed. In other words, the evidence we have about the *nāḍu* also conforms to the situation obtaining in relation to other aspects of the governmental structure. This, however, will have to be further elaborated.

Though thus subject to the administrative control of the state's agents, the *nāṭṭār* still were a cohesive group of landowners within a locality. From the large number of records pertaining to the group called *nāḍu* examined by Subbarayalu, there is no evidence to suggest that there was a head, a leader, a president, of this group.[108] It functioned collectively. As in identifying a 'chief village', as an 'inner core' of the *nāḍu* and distinguishing among three types of *nāḍu,* so in attributing a leader to the *nāṭṭār*, Stein is not backed by any evidence. His purpose is clear:

> The deltaic portion of Chola-mandalam can be designated the central area of the central domain of the Chola segmentary state. It was here that the power of the kings from Rajaraja I to Kulottunga I was concentrated; this was their *nāḍu*; they were the leaders of its *nāṭṭār.*[109]

In reality, however, the evidence we have is far from sufficient to support this position. For one thing, there is nothing on record to show that there was a chief, a president to the *nāṭṭār* group. Stein grants such a position to the holders of the titles such as *uḍayāns, araiyans, mūvēndavēḷāns*, etc., always equating them with the so-called feudatories.[110] This, as we have seen in a previous chapter, is not warranted.[111] They were landed magnates with a different character altogether. In fact, among the very few cases where the personal identity of the members of the *nāḍu* assembly is known, most held one of these titles, many sporting the same title, which, by extending Stein's logic, would suggest that there were too many chiefs in one *nāḍu*. And none of them is described as the chief or presiding member of the group.

If, thus, there was no chief among the *nāṭṭār*, that will have major implications for the understanding of the nature of state under the Cōḻas. The identity of the Cōḻa rulers as one among the chiefs of the many *nāḍus* as Burton Stein would have it, is lost in favour of a more conservative picture of their being rulers of a monarchical state. Secondly, in the absence of chiefs in the *nāḍus*, they would no longer answer to the description of being replicas of the political system obtaining in the centre; that is to say, the major argument concerning the segmentary nature of the Cōḻa state is proved to be invalid.

Thus, it would follow from the examination in this chapter that the smallest identifiable peasant community in south India in this period was the *ūr* or the agrarian village. But it was not the spokesmen of the *ūr* villages that were taken into consideration in the copper plate charters and other records for purposes of land settlements, etc., this recognition being reserved to the larger locality group, viz., the *nāḍu*. These *nāḍu* groups are seen as pre-existing groupings of peasant settlements, spontaneously come together. They were recognised by the state in medieval south India under the Pallavas, Pāṇḍyas and Cōḻas as its agents to carry out the royal writ as in the case of the settlement of land, creation of a superior right over it, assessment of revenue and so on. As the state grew and sought to centralise authority and power, the autonomy and aggressiveness of these groups dwindled, and we see direct penetration of the state through its officialdom into areas where the *nāḍu* and its spokesmen, the *nāṭṭār*, functioned as the state agents even in the more peripheral regions of the Cōḻa state. This is a picture which is in conformity with other aspects of polity in south India that we have outlined in the previous chapters–a polity with a largely decentralised character, attempting at a certain point in time to achieve a degree of centralisation which, however, was foiled by the centrifugal forces of a typically feudal nature. Again, our findings in this chapter would suggest that the details do not agree with the formulation of a segmentary state with subordinate foci of power which are replicas of the centre, with a chief and a specialised administrative staff repeating at each of such foci.

## NOTES

1. For a brief discussion and references to the details of literature on this transition and the historical processes involved in it, see Chapter 1.

2. Usually these are the addressees in royal charters. See e.g., Tirumālpuram inscription of Uttama Cōḻa (984 AD), *S.I.I.*, III. no. 142. II. 2–8; Larger Leiden Plates of Rājarāja I (1006 AD), *E.I.*, XXII, no. 34, p. 243, ll. 2–4. The Tiruvalaṅgādu Plates of Rajendra adds *Paḻavaṟa-śālābhogam* to the third group: *S.I.I.*, III, no. 205, p. 402, 1.15. The Paḻḻankoil (Cōḻa) grant of c. tenth century uses these expressions in the first person plural: *TASSI*, 1958–59, pp. 103, 107; and the Anbil plates, both in the first and third persons in two different contexts: *E.I.*, XV, no. 64, II. 124ff; 130ff.

3. *Dēvadāna* was the village or land the income from which went to the maintenance of a temple and *paḻḻiccandam*, to a Jain centre. In the case of *veṭṭāppāṟu* and *kaṇimuṟṟūṭṭu*, however, there is no clear indication as to their significance. Nilakanta Sastri suggested both to represent service tenures. *The Colas*, p. 507. Subbarayalu, however, believes that all the four, and the *śālābhogam*, included as a fifth category in the Tiruvalaṅgaḍu grant, were eleemosynary villages or lands: *Political Geography* ..., p. 34. K. V. Subrahmanya Aiyar, while editing the Larger Leiden Plates, identified *kaṇimuṟṟūṭṭu* as an income right to those who were called *kaḍigaiyārs* or announcers of time *E.I.*, XXII p. 231. Burton Stein quotes a personal communication from the epigraphist K. G. Krishnan suggesting this to refer to payment to non-brahman scholars. Stein, *Peasant State and Society* ..., p. 232. *Veṭṭāppāṟu* may be land recently cleared and brought under the plough. c.f. T. N. Subrahmanyan, *South Indian Temple Inscriptions*, 'Glossary', and *Tamil Lexicon*.

4. Sastri, *Colas*, pp. 492–94; Mahalingam, *South Indian Polity*, pp. 368–69; *idem*, *Readings* in *South Indian History*, (Delhi, 1977), pp. 94–104; etc.

5. Subbarayalu computes that out of the 1300 and odd villages of which we have evidence, about 250 were *brahmadēyas*, a fifty *dēvadānas*, and a few

*paḻḻiccandams.* Neither the *kaṇimuṟṟūṭṭu* nor the *veṭṭāppāṟu* is known to have constituted whole villages. *Political Geography* ..., p. 34. Burton Stein, however, believes that these four categories of lands were under the control of the *ūrar* or *ūrgaḷilār. Peasant State and Society* ..., p. 144.

6. *IPS*, no. 546.

7. Subbarayalu, *Political Geography*, p. 89.

8. *Ibid.*, p. 37–38.

9. Sastri, *Colas*, p. 504.

10. *Ibid*, Burton Stein interprets this passage in the Larger Leiden Plates to derive quite a different meaning: the whole argument, strangely, leads him to the position that 'the dominant landed groups ... sought to remain aloof from divisions within the locality'. *Peasant State* ..., p. 121.

11. *Concordance, passim*, under SB 210.

12. Y. Subbarayalu, 'The Place of Ur in the Economic and Social History of Early Tamilnadu, 750–1350' paper presented to the ICHR Seminar on South Indian History, Madras University, February, 1977.

13. The excellent studies of Subbarayalu, *ibid*, and *idem*, *Political Geography ... and Karashima, South Indian History and Society* are cases in point.

14. Subbarayalu, 'The place of Ur ...' *op. cit.*, cf. Marc Bloch, *Feudal Society*, vol. I, pp. 109–20.

15. Karashima, *South Indian History and Society*, pp. 40–55.

16. *Ibid*, pp. 3–15.

17. Subbarayalu, 'The Place of Ur ...', *op.cit.*

18. *Ibid.*

19. *Ibid.*

20. *S.I.I.*, II. nos. 4. 5. See Subbarayalu. 'The Place of Ur ...', *op.cit.*, n. 8.

21. See Chapter 3.

22. *Concordance*, Appendix 3. pp. xlv–xlvii.

23. *Ibid.*

24. See Chapter 3.

25. *S. I. I.*, IV. no. 327.

26. *Ibid.*, III. no. 156.

27. Karashima, *South Indian History and Society*, pp. 3–15.

28. *Concordance*, under FN 010, 030, 031.

29. Karashima, *South Indian History and Society*, pp. 7–9. Also *Concordance*, under FN 090.

30. Y. Subbarayalu. 'Transfer of land in the Kaveri Valley', a paper presented in the *Indian History Congress*, 37th Session, Calicut. 1976.

31. M. G. S. Narayanan, Presidential Address in *South Indian History Congress*, Mysore, 1985.

32. Cf. Minakshi, *Administration and Social Life under the Pallavas*, p. 143.

33. Rajan Gurukkal, *The Agrarian System and Socio-political Organisation under the Early Pandyas*, c. AD 600–1000. (unpublished Ph.D. thesis, Jawaharlal Nehru University, New Delhi, 1984). pp. 105–077; 258–60.

34. M. G. S. Narayanan, *Political and Social Conditions of Kerala under the Kulasekhara Empire, op. cit.*, Chapter on 'Local Bodies'.

35. Rajan Gurukkal, 'The Socio-economic Milieu of the Kerala Tempie: A Functional Analysis'. *Studies in History*, vol. II. no. 1 (1980). Also *idem*, M.Phil. Thesis, Jawaharlal Nehru University, New Delhi. 1978.

36. Kesavan Veluthat, *Brahman Settlements in Kerala*, esp. pp. 52–67.

37. Nilakanta Sastri, *Colas.* pp. 465, 503–04.

38. Mahalingam, *South Indian Polity*, p. 369.

39. Stein, *Peasant State and Society ...*, pp. 90–140. esp. p. 106.

40. Karashima, *South Indian History and Society*, Introduction. pp. 40–55.

41. Subbarayalu, *Political Geography ..., op.cit.*

42. *Ibid.*, p. 22 and Map 10.

43. *Ibid.*, pp. 21–25; 28–29.

44. *Ibid.*, p. 31; list of *nāḍus* with village contents in the end of the book, which is not paginated. For a similar situation in the Pandyan country, Gurukkal. *The Agrarian System ..., op. cit.*, pp. 105–07.

45. Subbarayalu, *Political Geography ...*, pp. 56–71.

46. Minakshi, Administration and Social Life...., *op. cit.*, Subbarayalu, *State in Medieval South India*, Chapter on 'Territory'.

47. Gurukkal, *The Agrarian System ..., op. cit.*, pp.107ff.

48. *Ibid.*

49. Narayanan, *Political and Social Conditions ..., op. cit.*, Chapter on 'Divisions of the Kingdom'.

50. Subbarayalu, *Political Geography ...*, p. 21.

51. Stein, *Peasant State and Society ...*, pp. 97–98.

52. *Ibid.*, pp. 99–100.

53. For Paiyampalli, *Indian Archaeology: A Review* (1964–65), pp. 22–23; (1967–68) pp. 26–30.

54. Stein, *Peasant State ...*, p. 107.

55. Subbarayalu, *Political Geography*, p. 31.

56. *Ibid.*

57. *Ibid.*, p. 32.

58. Stein, *Peasant State ...*, pp. 104–05.

59. *Ibid.*, Chapter 3, *passim.*

60. *Ibid.*, p. 101.

61. For discussion, see Introduction to the First Edition.

62. Stein, *Peasant State* ..., p. 102.

63. *Ibid.*, p. 100.

64. *Ibid.*, n. 19.

65. D. D. Kosambi, *An Introduction to the Study of Indian History*, 2nd edn., (Bombay, 1975), p. 1.

66. Stein, *Peasant State* ..., pp. 134–40.

67. In the entire section in *ibid.*, pp. 134–40, there are only two footnotes, both of them irrelevant to the question of categorisation of *nāḍus*!

68. Sastri, *Colas*, pp. 503–04; Mahalingam, *South Indian Polity*, p. 369.

69. Above, n. 6.

70. *S. I. I.*, VI, nos. 50 and 58.

71. *Concordance*, under SB 210.

72. E.g., *IPS, 28.*

73. *S. I. I.*, XVII, nos. 503; 534, 539; *ARE* 234 of 1924.

74. *S. I. I.*, VIII, nos. 576, 719; XIII, nos. 281 (A), etc.

75. *I. P. S*, no. 36. This practice of commuting the tax on a piece of land for all time to come and receiving a capital deposit, the interest accrued on which was considered as in lieu of the tax, was known as *iṟai-kāval* the capital deposit being known as *iṟai-dravyam:* Sastri, *Colas*, p. 509.

76. Subbarayalu, *Political Geography* ..., p. 39.

77. *S. I. I.*, XVII, no. 549.

78. *S. I. I.*, XVII, nos. 143,462,540 etc.

79. *I. P. S.*, nos. 266; 287; 343; 367; 374.

80. *I. P. S.* 196; 375.

81. Thus, fitting into the pattern we saw in chapter 3 where the more important landed magnates were identified by the state and made use of as its agents, here also the corporate body is made use of as the state agents.

82. *I. P. S.*, no. 370. *Nāḍu=uḍaiya=mudaligal* may be literally translated as the *mudaligl* who 'possessed' the *nāḍu*; but as in the case of the titles with a village name + *uḍaiyān* pattern, this has to be identified as a *mudaligal* who possessed some land in the *nāḍu*. Alternatively it can also mean the *mudaligal* of the *nāḍu*.

83. *I. P. S.*, no. 340.

84. *S. I. I.*, VIII, no. 739.

85. In fact, in most cases the penetration of the state to the localities was through these bodies, although the role of royal agents themselves, as we saw in a previous chapter 3, was of equal importance.

86. Subbarayalu, *Political Geography* ..., p. 41.

87. *I. P. S.*, 267.

88. *S. I. I.*, XVII, no. 135. Also, no. 143.

89. Stein, *Peasant State and Society* ..., p. 96.

90. *Ibid.*, p. 111.

91. Above, chapter 3.

92. Stein, *Peasant State and Society* ..., p. 265.

93. *I. P. S.*, no. 126.

94. *S. I. I.*, VI, no. 33.

95. *S. I. I.*, VII, no. 988.

96. *ARE*, no. 262 of 1912.

97. *I. P. S.*, no. 90.

98. Above, Chapter 2. Also Subbarayalu, *Political Geography* ..., p. 44.

99. Subbarayalu, *Political Geography* ..., p. 44.

100. James Heitzman, 'State Formation in South India, 850–1280', *The Indian Economic and Social History Review*, vol. XXIV, no. 1 (March 1987), pp.35–61.

101. Map 1 and *ibid.*, p. 40.

102. Table 1 on *ibid.*, p. 41. For the nature of land; n. 47 on p. 53 for the distribution of references to *nāṭṭār.*

103. *Ibid.*, p. 53, n. 47.

104. *Ibid.*, pp. 52–53. For our own treatment, above, Chapter 3.

105. *Ibid.*, p. 39.

106. Thirteen total references to *nāṭṭār* occur in records prior to 985, seventeen in those after 1178. The time between the accession of Rājarāja I and that of Kulōttuṅga I (985–1070) saw only five references to this group. *Ibid.*, p. 53, n. 49.

107. Above, Chapters 3 and 4.

108. Subbarayalu, *Political Geography* ..., p. 39.

109. Stein, *Peasant State and Society* ..., p. 286.

110. *Ibid.*, pp. 111–17.

111. Above, Chapter 2.

# Six

# The Brahmadēyam and the Nagaram

In the list of notables with which we began our treatment of the dominant sections of society in the previous chapter, we have discussed the agrarian settlements of the *ūr* villages and their grouping in the *nāḍu* localities. In this chapter we take up the remaining two categories, viz., the *brahmadēyam* and the *nagaram*. The fact that both of them were corporations of a relatively exotic nature within the locale of their existence would justify their being discussed together: the *brahmadēyam*s were groups of brahman settlers in the peasant localities who were granted property and were formed into corporations of land-owners while the *nagaram*s were organisations of traders settled in trading centres. They functioned as corporations looking after their interest of trade and artisanal production and even landed property.

## THE BRAHMADĒYAM

In the existing historical literature there is no paucity of information regarding the *brahmadēyams.* In fact, a major chunk of the epigraphical material from early medieval south India pertains to the *brahmadēyam*s and their *sabhās*, with the result that there is a spate of literature exaggerating their importance to such an extent that the other groups such as the *ūr, nāḍu* and *nagaram* have been drowned in the flood, as it were.[1] In the previous chapter we have tried to present a somewhat clearer picture of the *ūr* and *nāḍu*, based on the recent researches in this area. Burton Stein has introduced the idea of an alliance between the brahman settlers and the peasantry of the locality, apart from making a restatement of things which are already known.[2] We shall see below that the formulation of a brahman-peasant alliance cannot hold much water. There is another element introduced by Stein: the individual brahman living in ordinary peasant settlements. While he may have been a real entity, his role in polity was minimal except in certain cases where he was a military or civil functionary. It is more of the corporate bodies of brahman settlements known as the *sabhā* and its various ancillaries such as the *gaṇa, pariṣad*, etc., that the sources have to speak in connection with the social and political organisation in the localities.

It was these corporate bodies which gave expression to the landowning groups of the brahmans in the temple-centred settlements. To begin with, in the period of the Pallavas and early Pāṇḍyas, that is to say by the seventh century, the *brahmadēyams* were getting established in the more fertile tracts of the Pālār, Peṇṇār, Kāvēri and Vaigai basins. The factors responsible for this growth have not been clearly brought out by existing scholarship. There are statements suggesting a higher level of civilisation including organisational ability, a new technology, the calendar wisdom, etc., as responsible for this phenomenon.[3] None of these appears to solve the problem fully. In our discussion of the historical background to the emergence of the Pallava, Pāṇḍya, Cēra and Cōḻa states, we have seen that long before the rise of these states, there had come into existence numerous peasant settlements in the more fertile river valleys.[4] There is, however, no indication as to how far the chiefly houses in those periods had an initiative in the creation of such settlements. Nor is there any means to know the nature of the organisation in these pockets of agrarian settlements surrounded by large tracts of non-agrarian land and people. Indicators in contemporary and near contemporary sources suggest that these pockets were exposed to marauding tribes from the less settled and less developed regions. A cohesive force, which would have integrated the peasant communities, was lacking. It is in this context that one has to place the emergence of the brahman settlements in the agrarian tracts, endowed with superior rights over land and the entailing command over the cultivating peasantry.

The earliest evidence that we have about the creation of such a brahman settlement or *brahmadēyam* is contained in the newly discovered and very important Pulankurichi inscription of about the fifth century AD.[5] It speaks of the creation of a new settlement of brahman landholders together with their *kuṭis*. Various kinds of land such as wet land, dry land and garden land are mentioned in the record as well as the superior right (*miyāṭci*) of the *brahmadeyakkiḻavar* over the land and the subordinate rights (*kārāṇ-kiḻamai*) of the settler-tenants. Although in the Pāṇḍyan kingdom the copper plate records registering the grant of land to brahmans date only from the eighth century AD, it has been demonstrated with the help of place names figuring in inscriptions of an earlier period that *brahmadēyams* existed in that region in a much earlier period.[6] In fact, the earliest known copper plate record of the Pāṇḍyas, namely the Vēḷvikuḍi copper plate of Neḍuñjaḍaiyan (767–811 AD), purports to be the renewal of an earlier grant of the same village which had been given to an ancestor of the donee of the record.[7] Whether the claim in this particular record is correct or not, it is clear that the tradition of granting land to brahmans and creating *brahmadēyams* existed before Neḍuñjaḍaiyan himself. One of the claims made by most Pāṇḍyan rulers in *praśasti* literature is that they created *brahmadēyams* in large numbers apart from performing other charitable acts.[8]

In the same period, the Pallava kingdom in the north was going through a similar experience. It is from the Pallava kingdom that we have the earliest instances of land grants in the deep south. The earliest records of the Pallavas, namely, the Mayidavōlu plates and the Hīrehaḍagaḻḻi plates, both in Prakrit, assigned to the third or fourth century AD, are themselves charters of such grants to Brahmans.[9] Even the Sanskrit charters of the Pallava rulers of a slightly later period have the same purport.[10] However, these records are from the Andhra region. By the time we come to the reign of Siṁhavarman, we start getting bilingual charters in Sanskrit and Tamil, recording grant of land to brahmans, except in the case of the Paḻḻankōil plates of Siṁhavarman making a grant to a Jain teacher.[11] In fact, this shift from the Prakrit-Sanskrit charters to the bilingual Sanskrit-Tamil records indicates a major shift in the geographical locale and the economic base of that dynasty. It has been argued that this can be identified as signalling the beginnings of the forces of state formation in the Toṇḍaimaṇḍalam region.[12]

The Kūṟam plates of Paramēśvaravarman (669–690 AD) record the consecration of a Siva temple in a pre-existing *brahmadēya* village of

108 *caturvēdi* Brahmans.[13] Another record of the same ruler, contained in the Unne Guravayapāḷaiyam plates, speaks of the grant of a village to a certain Dēvaśarman, the purpose of the grant being stated as the enhancement of the longevity and health of the donor.[14] A similar purpose is stated to be behind the grant of land to a certain Sōmayajin Kumāramaṇḍaśarman made by Narasimhavarman II (690–728–29 AD).[15] Later records such as the Udayēndiram plates,[16] the Pullūr plates,[17] the Taṇḍantōṭṭam plates[18] and the Paṭṭattāḷmaṅgalam plates[19] of Nandivarman II Pallavamalla speak of the creation of large settlements with 108 brahmans each settled in both Udayacandramaṅgalam and Nayadhirāmaṅgalam, 214 listed in the surviving parts of the Taṇḍantōṭṭam plates settled in Dayāmukhamaṅgalam and 16 brahmans in Pattattāḷmaṅgalam. It is interesting that the last mentioned record speaks of a pre-existing *brahmadēya* there. What follows is that the practice of inviting brahmans from outside and establishing them in large settlements was well under way in the Pallava kingdom by the seventh and eighth centuries AD. The same point is underlined by the existence of a much larger number of *brahmadēya* villages as known from place names figuring in contemporary records although the original charters of their creation have not come down to us.[20]

By the beginning of the ninth century, the territory covered by the Cēra kingdom on the west coast had been already studded with a large number of brahman settlements.[21] The brahman settlers there, unlike their counterparts in the rest of Tamiḻakam, cherished the Paraśurama tradition together with brahmans of the Koṅkan and Kanarese coasts. This has been shown as indicating a southward migration along the west coast, the southernmost major settlement in Kerala being the latest. Tradition embodied in the Kannada chronicle *Grāmapaddhati* and the Malayalam chronicle *Kēraḷotpatti* has it that the brahmans were established in the *Paraśurāmakṣetra* in sixty-four village settlements lying between Gōkarṇa in the north and Kanyākumāri in the south.[22] Epigraphic and literary evidences have helped the identification of most of the settlements located on the Kerala coast to the south of the Chandragiri river which are thirty-two in number according to the same tradition.[23] All these thirty-two settlements on the Kerala coast were well established by the time of the emergence of the later Cēra kingdom of Mahōdayapuram, early in the ninth century. In fact, the Vāḻapalli copper plate of Rājaśēkhara (*circa* 812 AD)[24] pertains to two *upagrāmas* (subsidiary settlements) of Tiruvalla, which is one of the southernmost and hence the latest, of the traditional brahman settlements of Kerala.[25] Curiously, the original charters creating these grants have not come down to us. It is likely that the immigrant brahman groups along the west coast settled down in the relatively undeveloped river valleys in Kerala and established their authority there on their own, and that they opened up the land for cultivation by transforming the local population, which was still at a tribal level, into peasant communities. At any rate, the entire landscape was covered by a rather closely knit network of brahman settlements by the time the Cēra state of Mahōdayapuram had been established.

In the Cō̤la country the experience was almost parallel. Long before the emergence of the Cō̤las of the Vijayālaya line in the middle of the ninth century, huge brahman settlements had been already established there. The Taṇḍantōṭṭam plates and the Paṭṭattāḷmaṅgalam plates of Nandivarman II Pallavamalla mentioned above are only two examples of the Pallava initiative in creating large brahman settlements in the Cō̤la country. Place names such as Simhaviṣṇucaturvedimaṅgalam, Videlviḍugucaturvedimaṅgalam, etc., are further indication of the same fact. By the time the Cō̤las established themselves around Tanjavur in the middle of the ninth century, the Kāvēri valley had a large number of populous and prosperous brahman settlements in it. The land grants of the later Cō̤la rulers, the richest example of which is provided by the Karantai plates of Rājēndra I settling as many as 1080 brahmans in Tribhuvanamahādēvicaturvēdimaṅgalam,[26] continued a tradition which had been already in vogue in the Pallava and Pāṇḍya territories.

To begin with, these settlements must have found themselves pockets of an exotic element in a strange situation. With the efficient management of landed property and the entailing control over the peasant population subject to it, through the organisational ability evidenced in the functioning of their corporate bodies known as the *sabhā* or *mahāsabhā* and with their superior ideological force, it was possible for them to sustain themselves in the new situation and promote themselves further. This made them the most dynamic and progressive force in contemporary society. In an era of the expansion of agrarian settlements and the transformation of huge chunks of tribal population to settled peasant communities, a force capable of helping society to absorb the shock of such a sudden change required all the dynamism necessary to characterise it as the most positive element. It was this role of the brahmanical settlements in the agrarian villages that made them the most active force in contemporary society. This historic role of the brahmans was reflected in their function of providing the rational explanation of social organisation. In the new agrarian society that had come into existence with different shades of right in land and stratified accordingly in hierarchy, this rationalising principle took the form of *jati*.[27] *Jati* as a paradigm of social organisation was already well established in the ideas and institutions of northern India with which the brahman settlers were very familiar through the *Dharamaśāstra* texts. When the semi-tribal population was transformed into peasants and other occupational groups, they were accommodated into the hierarchically oriented society as so many *jatis.* Occupying the highest rung in this *jati* hierarchy, the brahmans were able to dictate the pattern of society, once this rationalising principle had been accepted by the upper classes in society.

The stratification of society which was so rationalised was provided with ideological sanction, too, through the religious institutions and movements. Most *brahmadēyam*s revolved around a temple and that institution was the nerve-centre of many social activities. A whole new ideology was disseminated from the temple through the exposition of the *purāṇa*s and *itihāsa*s, through the various forms of art and through spreading the philosophy of *bhakti*. All these helped in legitimising the principle of social stratification and its epitomised expression in the *varaṇāśrama-dharma*. Accordingly, the brahman priest and the 'kṣatriyised' ruler occupied the highest position in society. This helped strengthening and validating the newly formed monarchies. Thus the state, which was the creation of the upper classes in the stratified society, received its legitimacy at the hands of these new ideologues. This role of the brahmans may have made the chieftains and kings invite more of them to settle in different parts of their territories. That this entailed the curtailment of a major chunk of revenue to the state need not have been a major deterrent: for one thing, in many cases it is not clear whether the land granted to the brahmans had actually yielded any revenue to the state previously and secondly, the ideological legitimacy provided by the settlers to the stratified social order and the state was of much greater significance than the paltry revenue.

In some of the records pertaining to the *brahmadēyams* there is the statement that the major *brahmadēyams* in the Cōḻa country were *taniyūrs*. This expression means literally a 'separate village'. There are references to a large number of *taniyūrs* described as situated within a *nāḍu*. Thus Tiruveḷḷaṟai, which was a *brahmadēyam*, was a *taniyūr* in Vaḍavaḻināḍu.[28] Tribhuvanamahādēvicaturvēdimaṅgalam was stated to be situated in Viḻupparaiyanāḍu[29] and, in a later record, in Mātturnāḍu;[30] Rājādhirājacaturvedimaṅgalam, Vīranārāyaṇacaturvēdimaṅgalam and Perumbāṟṟappuliyūr in Cuttamali-valanāḍu;[31] etc. Although they were located in these *nāḍus*, they are seen to have been completely independent of the jurisdiction of the *nāḍus*. For instance, these villages carried out the administration of revenue and justice on their own without reference to the *nāḍus*. It is seen that many agrarian villages were attached to a *taniyūr*. Y. Subbarayalu has pointed out that the powers of the *nāḍu* were superseded by the spokesman of the *taniyūr*.[32] One of the *taniyūrs* mentioned above, Perumbāṟṟappuliyūr (modern Chidambaram), was not a *brahmadēyam* but was under the control of a temple.[33] This, however, did not make any qualitative difference so far as the status of that *taniyūr* was concerned: instead of the *sabhā*, it was the *mūlaparuṣai* which carried out the administration there.

This position of importance in society that the brahman settlers acquired on account of their land control and the other factors mentioned above was zealously maintained through the well-knit organisations of the *sabhā* or *mahāsabhā*. In the early decades of the present century, when inscriptions pertaining to such bodies were discovered and published, they were hailed as popular democratic assemblies. While this is understandable in the context of the nationalist enthusiasm of Indian scholars at that time, there is no reason why such stereotypes should be carried on. It is only a matter of common sense that in the context of early medieval Indian society democracy is out of question. An examination of some aspects of the constitution, functioning and procedure of these bodies will bring this out clearly. Since there is a spate of literature already existing on the problem of the organisation and administration in the brahman settlements in medieval south India, we shall touch upon only those aspects which will bring out the characteristic features of these bodies.

The celebrated Mānūr inscription of Māṟañcaḍaiyan registers a resolution of a *mahāsabhā* laying down the qualifications of its members.[34] It is stated that only the 'children' of those who own shares in the property of the village and those who are proficient in the *mantrabrāhmaṇa* inclusive of one *dharma* and who have good antecedents shall be eligible for membership in the *sabhā*. Only one membership shall be allowed for one share. If one were to acquire shares by way of purchase, gift or dowry he shall be admitted provided he satisfies the other requirements. No half or quarter or three-quarters of a membership shall be provided for. In the case of those who acquire shares by purchase, one whole *vēda* with its *pariśiṣṭa*s had to be studied for eligibility. Only such full members shall be eligible for the different committees of the *sabhā*. Filibustering of the proceedings of the *sabhā* was discouraged by imposing a fine on those who obstructed the proceedings. The nature of the business transacted by the *sabhā* or its jurisdiction is not, however, discernible from this record.

In the same category of records may be included the two famous Parāntaka inscriptions from Uttaramērūr.[35] They have been quoted too often to bear one more quotation. The general vein of these records which lay down the eligibility to the various committees (*vāriyam*) of the *sabhā* is similar to that of the Mānūr record quoted above except for minor differences in detail. The insistence on ownership of property, educational qualifications and good conduct is common to the records from both the places. Similar specifications obtained in less celebrated records as well, such as an inscription of the eleventh year of Rājarāja I from Uttamacōḻacaturvēdimaṅgalam.[36] A similar record comes from Talaināyar dated in the seventh year of Kulōttuṅga III where similar qualifications of age, property and education are prescribed by a royal order for the executive committee of the *sabhā* of Kulōttuṅga Cōḻantanināyakacaturvēdimaṅgalam.[37] An inscription from Airāṇikkaḷam in Kerala, while speaking about those who abrogate the decisions of the *sabhā*, states that they shall lose their membership and their property, and shall be equated with one who had slain one's father and the teacher who taught one the *Vēda*s, thereby implying that membership in the *sabhā* was restricted to those who owned property and those who were proficient in the *Vēdas*.[38]

The business transacted by these bodies is equally interesting. For the most part it was the management of the landed property and the reallocation of the funds and the live-stock of the temple that was looked after by these bodies. Rent was collected regularly. Land was leased out methodically and accounts of all incomes and expenditure were maintained systematically. The day-to-day service in the temples occasionally formed the concern of the *sabhā* and there are records speaking about the *sabha*'s jurisdiction over temple servants 'from priest to sweeper'.[39] In fact, the large number of inscriptions from all over south India dating from the medieval period are replete with references to the day-to-day working of such bodies.

The follow-up of the decisions of the *sabhā* was done in an equally systematic manner. The records say that those who violated the decision of the *sabhā* would forfeit their membership of the *sabhā*, lose their property and incur such other losses in society.[40] In fact, a large number of records state that such abrogators would be equated with those who have slaughtered cows, those who have slain their father, those who have slain their teacher and those who have been involved in incest with their mother. This equation of violating the decisions of the *sabhā* with one of the *mahāpātaka*s, which were abhorred by the *śāstra* texts, had been looked upon by earlier historians as a mere moral stricture.[41] Recently M. G. S. Narayanan has brought out the implications of invoking the idea of the *mahāpātaka*s as amounting to social ostracism by which an individual lost all his property and his place in society which, apart from a social banishment, was a veritable material loss.[42] These aspects of the follow-up action of the *sabhā* show how zealously the corporate interest of the body was safeguarded against individual interests and idiosyncracies. This explains the insistence on the full attendance of members expressed by the phrase *kuṟaivu-tirttukūṭi* and on unanimity expressed by the phrase *avirōtattāl*.[43]

The copper plate charters creating the *brahmadēya* settlements do not speak about the constitution of bodies such as the *sabhā* or the *mahāsabhā* even in cases where huge *brahmadēyam*s are created as in cases registered in the Pullūr plates (108 brahmans) or Karantai plates (1080 brahmans). However, the Vēḷvikuḍi plates assume the pre-existence of a *sabhā*, for it states that the reallocation of the land granted was made with the concurrence of the *sabhā*.[44] Similarly, the Daḷavāypuram plates too recognise the earlier existence of a *mahāsabhā* there in the same manner.[45] None of these records shows that the formation of the corporate body of the brahmans owed its authority to a royal charter. Therefore, the sanction, rationale and authority of these bodies will have to be looked for elsewhere.

Even if the records creating the *brahmadēyams* are not articulate about the authority behind the constitution of the managerial bodies of the brahmanical agrarian corporations, the details available in the innumerable inscriptions of south India point to this authority in a clear manner. As we have seen above, the documents pertaining to the management of the property of a temple on which the settlement generally centered give us information about the organisation, procedure, functioning and follow-up action of such managerial bodies as the *sabhās* and their organs such as the *vāriyam, pariṣad, gaṇa etc.*[46] With their insistence on the qualifications of property, education, good conduct etc., these bodies can clearly be seen to have been of an exclusively communitarian character with the management of property as their prime concern. All these details are seen to follow, to the last letter, prescriptions in the *dharmaśāstra* literature.[47] Qualifications of property and education for membership, provisions for full attendance in the meetings, the presence of a king's deputy, unanimity in the decisions and the details of the follow-up actions–all these followed very closely the *dharmaśāstraic* rules prescribed for bodies like the *sabhā* and *pariṣad*.

In the epigraphical records of northern India in the Gupta and post-Gupta period, where these *śāstraic* rules most probably had their origins, one does not get such detailed information regarding the actual working or even the existence of such bodies. Indeed we do not have records from northern India of the nature of the south Indian inscriptions. It may be suggested that in the epigraphs of southern India we have the practical instances of the theoretical exposition contained in the *śāstra* texts. J. D. M. Derrett has brought out how two inscriptions concerning the status of Kammāḷas present an example of how the *dharmaśāstra* texts were referred to and made use of as guides in deciding questions of a social nature.[48] This is not, as Derrett imagines, a unique case of a *vyavasthā* on the typical *dharmaśāstra* lines; the numerous other inscriptions explicitly claim to be *vyavasthā*s and show clearly how the *dharmaśāstra* texts were followed in the corporate bodies in southern India. Thus it may be suggested that in the epigraphs of southern India we have evidence to show that the authority and sanction behind bodies such as the *sabhā* and *pariṣad* were the *dharmaśāstra* texts. In other words, at the hands of the land owning brahmanical upper class, the *raison d'etre* of their corporations was none other than the sanction behind their own conception of polity with the *varṇśāramadharma* norms of social stratification which ultimately protected their own interests.

This should not, however, give the impression that everywhere in south India the uniform pattern of organisation obtained without any variation whatsoever. The case of such settlements in Kerala, although they followed the general pattern of their counterparts elsewhere in south India, presents certain major variations. This has to be explained by two major factors. For one thing, the ecology of Kerala is different from that of the rest of the Tamil country.[49] Rural settlements in that region are dispersed in contrast to the nucleated villages in the rest of south India. In fact there is no 'village' in Kerala in the strict sense of the term.[50] In the absence of such a core for a settlement and given the peculiar pattern of settlement in Kerala, the brahman settlements, known as *grāma*s, tended to be invariably temple-centred. Although the activities of the *sabhā*s in other parts of South India also generally centred on a temple, this identification of a brahman settlement with a temple did not obtain anywhere else.

Another factor which possibly distinguished the brahman settlements in Kerala was that they constituted the final links of a long chain of migration from the north along the west coast with a Prakrit-Kannada-Tulu preponderance in their traditions.[51] Therefore, differences in the character of the organisation of the settlements and their influence on the rest of society are to be expected in a broad way.

Apart from the invariably temple-centred nature of the brahman settlements there are other aspects also which make the brahman *grāma*s of Kerala distinct from the *brahmadēya*s in the rest of south India. *Agrahāra*s do not occur there at all. We have reference to a number of *upagrāma*s or subsidiary settlements affiliated to the larger and more prosperous original settlements of Kerala. There are also references to the grant of parts of the estates of members of royal family or the family of the local chiefs to major brahman settlements such as Tiruvalla,[52] Ceṅgannūr[53] Airāṇikkaḷam[54] and Aviṭṭattūr.[55] There is the tradition, which is supported by epigraphic and literary evidences, that the entire brahman community in Kerala was represented by four major *grāma*s situated near the capital of the Cēras in Mahōdayapuram, namely, Paṟavūr, Mūḻikkaḷam, Airāṇikkaḷam and Iriñjālakkuḍa, and that each of these *grāma*s in turn was represented in the capital city by two celibate brahmans with their seats in the temples of Neṭiya Taḷi, Mēlttaḷi, Kiḻttaḷi and Ciṅgapuram Taḷi respectively.[56] These brahmans figure as members of the Cēra court in what is known as the Nālu Taḷi.[57] In fact, in the traditional account of the foundation of the Cēra monarchy in Mahōdayapuram, the statement is to the effect that it was these councillors or *taḷiyātiri*s who established the Perumāḷ on the throne.[58] Such a clear indication that the entire brahman community was the power behind the throne is not given by records from other parts of south India.

A similar feature is found in following the precedent of one of the major settlements, viz., Mūḻikkaḷam, as a model for the functioning of the temple-centred brahman settlements all over Kerala.[59] Mūḻikkaḷam, it has been shown above, was one of the four major brahman *grāma*s of Kerala with its representatives forming part of the Cēra king's permanent council. It was also situated very close to the capital of the Perumāḷ, Mahōdayapuram. A *vyavasthā*, variously referred to as Mūḻikkaḷa-*kaccam*, Mūḻikkaḷa-*vyavastai*, Mūḻikkaḷa-*ccavattai*, Mūḻikkaḷa-*ttoḻukkam* etc., is quoted at least from end of the ninth century till the end of the reign of the last Cēramān Perumāḷ and in records from Pullūr in the Kasaragod district in the north to Tirunandikkara in Trivandrum district in the south.[60] The text of the original *vyavasthā* has not come down to us. Historians had tried to interpret the *vyavasthā* of Mūḻikkaḻam as intended to protect the interest of the tenants of temple properties against the caprices of the temple trustees.[61] But a systematic contextual examination of references to this in the records undertaken by M. G. S. Narayanan has shown that it was more the interest of the corporate groups of brahman landlords that was sought to be protected by such rules and precedents, much in the same way as the *śāstra* prescriptions did.[62]

This integral nature of the brahman community in entire Kerala with its zealous guarding of the class interests as property owners had its impact on the local chieftains and the king himself on a scale larger than in the rest of south India. In Kerala, there were a larger number of local chieftains who claimed the kṣatriya status,[63] there was a greater importance for the temple establishment in general and, most important of all, there did not exist the powerful and aggressive groups of the *nāḍu* or *nāṯṯār* unlike in the rest of south India.[64] Apart from the peculiar settlement pattern in that region, the relatively less developed nature of peasant agriculture before the advent of the brahman settlements also may have been responsible for these phenomena.

Even with regard to the *brahmadēya* settlements in the rest of south India one should not assume homogeneity everywhere. In the existing scholarship this assumption appears to be implied by a process of what Nilakanta Sastri describes as 'historical averaging' in another context.[65] Thus Uttaramērūr or Mānūr or Eṇṇāyiram or Tribhuvani or Tiruvāḍutuṟai or Tiruvalla are discussed at great length suggesting thereby that what obtained there was repeated elsewhere. This need not really have been the case. There certainly were settlements which were less populous and, indeed, far less prosperous. The command they had over the surrounding rural population also was correspondingly less than what may have been the case in the more important settlements. For instance, the elaborate records we get from these more important settlements bear testimony to the complex nature of the settlements often revolving around temples which had, or later acquired, hagiographical importance.[66] They also show the fact that such temples were prime centres of education, both religious and secular, with their fame reaching far and wide. These centres of the brahman settlements in temples were also the focal points in an elaborate network of relations among the different social groups including traders, artisans and pastoralists, apart from the cultivators. This kind of a varied and complex role need not be assumed in the case of all the brahman settlements everywhere in south India, some of which were small pockets within native surroundings.

Nor need the temple-centred brahman settlements be assumed to have continued throughout the period in the same influential position which they enjoyed in the early phase of, say, the Cōḻa rule. A record from Uttaramērūr itself offers an interesting case.[67] This inscription relates that when a temple in a nearby village demanded repayment of a loan advanced to the *mahāsabhā* of *Uttaramērūr*, the latter, being without funds, transferred to the former its share of income from a neighbouring village, Veṇṇakkuṭṭanallūr. There are even records of *brahmadēyams* being converted into *veḷḷānvagai villages* by royal order and then donated to temples as *dēvadāna* or *tirunāmattukkāṇi* or *tiruviḍaiyāṭṭam* (land donated to temples as offerings).[68] The case of Paḷaiyanūr recorded in the famous Tiruvalaṅgādu plates is of interest in this respect.[69] There are other similar cases in the Pāṇḍyan and Cōḷa records of the twelfth and thirteenth centuries.[70] This would suggest that by this time the *brahmadēya* settlements had already fulfilled their historical mission and started bowing out, as it were, in favour of the temple which, in altered form, had now started to occupy centre stage. This surmise is further supported by the fact that less and less *brahmadēyams* were created in the period after the middle of the eleventh century while more and more temples came to be established and existing ones got expanded further and further in this period.

The above discussion brings out the role of the brahman settlements in early medieval south India. Beginning as pockets of an exotic population, these settlements gradually sent roots in society through the effective manipulation of agrarian resources and accelerating the process of social stratification in such a way as to best suit their interests. The magic of religion institutionalised in the temple helped in propagating an ideology which was most helpful to rationalise and maintain this kind of social stratification. The most important feat of the brahmanical establishment was to provide the rationalising principle of the *varṇāśramadharma* and accommodating the peasants and artisans in the *jāti* formula, both of which was sanctified and legitimised by the ideologies of *dharma* and *bhakti*. Their position so consolidated, it was maintained by the excellent organisation of their corporate bodies in the *sabhā, pariṣad* etc. However, there were regional variations with a greater brahmanical influence on the chiefly and royal families in the Cēra kingdom and with equally competing and strong strata of non-brahman landholders and cultivators in the Cōḷa and Pāṇḍyan kingdoms. The assumption of uniformity in all the places is also questionable, as also the continuity of the *brahmadēya* settlements throughout the period of our study in a position of uniform importance. At any rate, it can be seen that the role of the *brahmadēyas* in sanctifying the particular type of social stratification which was the *raison d'etre* behind the early medieval south Indian states cannot be exaggerated.

## THE NAGARAM

The fourth and final category of notable groups figuring in the copper plate records, with which we began our discussion, is the *nagarattār* or 'men of the *nagaram*'. In comparison with the *brahmadēyams*, there is very little evidence about the composition, organisation and administration of the *nagaram*. The conventional historical literature fails to provide a framework for the study of these institutions in early medieval south India, although available inscriptional details are brought out in the work of, for example, Nilakanta Sastri[71] and Appadorai.[72] In recent years, however, there has been a new spurt of interest on this problem. Among the more important publications are the monograph by Kenneth R. Hall[73] and a few articles by R. Champakalakshmi,[74] B. D. Chattopadhyay,[75] Mary Meena Abraham,[76] R. Sumathi,[77] *et al.*

All these scholars do not share the same frame of reference; nor is the same height of conceptual rigour to be expected in all their works. For instance, Hall presents formidable data regarding the *nagaram* organisations in medieval south India but by adhering to a particular orientation in the history of medieval south India in an 'unreasoned and tenacious' manner, his effort becomes rather misdirected.[78] Hall appears to envisage two domains of trade: that between localities and those involving long distance maritime exchanges. Following the model of networks and centres, originally constructed by William Skinner for rural China,[79] Hall identifies one marketing centre in each *nāḍu* locality which was also a connecting link between the villages in the *nāḍus* on the one side and higher marketing centres like *mānagaram eṟivirapaṭṭinam* and coastal ports. In trying to situate the *nagaram* in Cōḻa polity, Hall argues that the state made use of these relatively autonomous groups in the integration of the political system of medieval south India. Both the empirical validity and the theoretical soundness of the neat pattern of politico-economic relationships have been called into question by B. D. Chattopadhyaya[80] and R. Vanaja.[81]

The work of R. Champakalakshmi on the urban processes in early medieval Tamil Nadu lays greater stress on the empirical data. She is free from the constraints of the particular orientation to which Hall is committed. In an overview of urban processes which she makes[82] and also the case study of the twin city of *Kuḍamūkku-Paḻaiyāṟai*,[83] Champakalakshmi makes a down-to-earth study of the inscriptions and archaeological material available for tackling the problem of urbanisation in medieval south India. The part played by the urban centres and their autonomous groupings in the polity of the early medieval period has been clearly brought out in another more recent paper of hers.[84] In fact, the data that she has brought together challenges the findings of Hall, especially his almost obsessive equation of one *nāḍu*=one *nagaram*. In a recent exposition of an overview of urban centres in early medieval India, B. D. Chattopadhyaya too has tried to provide certain insights against which the problem of urbanisation in early medieval South India can be examined.[85] We shall make a brief examination of some of the documents below with a view to bringing out the role of the *nagaram* in the socio-political organisation of medieval south India.

Like in other corporate bodies, the membership of the *nagaram* was restricted among certain sections of the population. A Cidambaram inscription speaks of the creation of a *nagaram* which was settled by *viyāpārigal, veḻḷāḷar, saṅkarapāḍiyār, cāliyar,* and *paṭṭinavar* as well as 'all other people of the *nagaram* including *taccar* (carpenters), *kollar* (blacksmiths), *taṭṭār* (goldsmiths) and *kōliyar* (leather-workers).[86] It is not, however, clear whether all these settlers formed the *nagarattār.* In a Cōḻapuram record (Kalahasti, Chittoor Dt.), we find six signatories to a decision, of whom five were *ceṭṭi*s and the sixth indicated his association with *saṅkarapāḍi.*[87] These and other records show that the *nagaram* was a separately designated area inhabited primarily by men of the trading community and others who earned their living largely by commercial and artisanal activities and also that the corporate body of *nagarattār* was constituted only by the merchants of the locality. The way in which these bodies functioned is also demonstrated by the records brought together by Hall.[88] It appears that like the *sabhā* and the *ūr,* it was a corporate body managed by a committee formula, with the *nagaravāriyam* as the most important among them. We also hear about a *mānagaramāḷvān* in Kāñcīpuram,[89] who was associated with the annual supervision committee, *āṭṭaivāriyam* in that place, reminding us of the *samvatsaravāriyam* of Uttaramērūr and other places. Officers concerned with the *nagaram*, such as the *nagarakkaraṇattān* and *nagarakkaṇakku* are also met with in the records.[90] We see, again like the rural corporations such as the *ūr* and *sabhā*, the *nagaram* possessing communally owned land called *nagarakkāṇi*.[91] Instances of the establishment of *nagarams* by acquiring land and house sites are also on record. Assignment of land, purchase of land, union of several hamlets, lease of land and house sites, etc., coupled with a responsibility to pay levies or provide certain specified goods and services to the local community in creating a *nagaram* are all found in the records.[92] The *nagaram* is shown to have been held collectively responsible for the collection of land revenues from its domain and to have handled its internal assessments and collections in such manner as it saw fit, thereby showing that the *nagaram's* administrative rights over its own affairs were comprehensive. This is indicated, as usual, in the assignment by the *nagaram* of dues to the local temples. These dues included *antarāyam* (a royal levy on local bodies), *kaḍamai* (a levy fastened on land), *kuḍimai* (a levy on occupancy of land), *kōyiṟṟamappēṟu* (a due payable to the *kōyiṟṟamar* or king's agents) and *nagaraviniyōgam* (a local levy to support *nagaram* expenditures: cf. *nāṭṭuviniyōgam*) apart from different kinds of market cesses and duties.[93] A Koṅgukoṇḍacōḻapuram record shows that the local *nagaram* was expected to pay the king's revenue agents 23,000 *kalam* of paddy on cultivated lands and 1000 *kāśu* of gold on dry lands.[94] There are numerous other instances of the *nagaram* collecting land revenue.[95] This compares with the situation obtaining in other local bodies such as, for example, the *nāḍu*. We have seen in the previous chapter that the *nāḍu* as a corporation of landowners in a locality was recognised by the state as an agent of the state for purposes of the assessment and collection of revenue and the settlement of other administrative matters.[96] What was happening there was that state functions were carried out by the *nāḍu*, which could be easily described as a clear example of the feudal principle. There the state power was enjoyed by the local groups. Evidence concerning the *nagaram* suggests that in regions where this body existed, the state powers and functions were either granted to or appropriated by the *nagaram* in a comparable manner. This would also bring out the function of the *nagaram* in the political organisation of medieval south India.

In Mammuḍicōḻapuram, the *nagaram* collected the fees for *pāḍi kāval*.[97] In fact, the *nagaram's* proprietory as well as jurisdictional right over neighbouring agricultural land is eminently brought out by many records, in a manner comparable to that of the *sabhā* whose members, nonetheless, did not presumably take part in primary agricultural operations. There are even instances of the *nagaram* assigning land on service tenure, as shown by the cases of a *nagarakkaṇakkan* at Jambai, South Arcot,[98] and a carpenter at Nārttāmalai.[99] The profits of individual merchants are stated to have been invested in land, as indicated by another Nārttāmalai record which relates the transfer of the *nagaram's* superior right over a plot of land to two merchants of the *nagaram* for 68,000 *kāśsu* of gold.[100] All these show that basically land was considered to be a permanent investment, the symbol of prestige, and point to the basic nature of economy and society which was largely landbased.[101]

This projection of the concern of the *nagaram* with land and agrarian relations is not to minimise the non-agrarian aspect of its pre-occupation with artisanal production and trade. In fact the *nagaram* is to be seen primarily as a marketing centre, coordinating the exchange of agricultural surplus and other locally produced commodities. The *nagaram*, to be sure, is seen at its best in its role as coordinating artisanal production and facilitating exchange. The *rathakāra* inscriptions studied by J. D. M. Derrett amply illustrate this.[102] The importance of the way in which the weavers in Kāñcīpuram, the oil mongers, potters and smiths everywhere, apart from merchants of articles produced far and near, were brought into the orbit of the *nagaram* can never be exaggerated. In the localised economy of the age, however, even these activities will have to be seen as a recycling of local resources within the locality. It is characteristic of the pre-capitalist socio-economic formation that there should be a combination of agriculture and home industry. The industrial aspect never freed itself from the agrarian entanglements and therefore failed to take off to any other form.

If the *nagaram* is thus seen as conforming to the feudal pattern which was obtaining in economy and society, it is not hard to appreciate the feudal character of the *nagaram* in the political organisation also. Some of the *nagarams* were assigned *taniyūr* status which involved the independence of the *nagaram* within the territorial limits of a *nāḍu*.[103] We have seen above that such independent status was assigned to the major *brahmadēyams* also (for example Rajadhirajacaturvedimangalam and Uttaramērūr). This would show that as much as the *brahmadēyams*, the *nagarams* too were accorded an amount of local autonomy within the *nāḍu*. Further, the creation of new *nagarams* under royal patronage, the evidence of which is seen in Kollam, Muyirikkōḍu, Uṟaiyūr, Nāgapaṭṭānam, Kāñcīpruam, Nārttāmalai (Nagarattārmalai), Pirāṇmalai, etc. would show that the *nagaram* played a role comparable in its own way to that of the *brahmadēyams* in integrating society in the new form of polity that had emerged in south India in the early medieval period. The recognition of these *nagarams* as representing a major section of society and their being made use of for purposes of administration by the state as its agents would indicate the character of these groups forming part of a feudal power structure.

Thus the above discussion of the *brahmadēyam* and *nagaram* brings out a significant aspect of the social structure in early medieval south India. Both of them represented pockets of social groups which were more or less different in character from the rest of the agrarian groups in the peasant localities. The former shared with the rest of the dominant peasantry the interest in agrarian land and the surplus from it; the latter, although they may have belonged to the same ethnic groups as the peasants, differed from them in their interest in that their character was generally that of the traders. Both the *brahmadēyam* and the *nagaram* with their local autonomy in the *taniyūr* settlements shared between them the role of integrating society, if in different ways. It was this role that the rulers identified and it was on this account that both were liberally encouraged and patronised. In the political structure of early medieval south India, both enjoyed comparable places although the place of the *brahmadēyam* in society, for reasons discussed above, proved to be more crucial in the period under study and in the centuries to follow.

## NOTES

1. In the lengthy chapter (XVIII) on 'Local Government', Nilakanta Sastri, *Colas*, pp. 486–519, devotes a little more than a quarter of a page to the *ūr* (p. 492), about one-third of a page to the *nagaram* (p. 503) and about two pages to the *nāḍu* (pp. 503–05), the remaining portion being generally concerned with

the *brahmadēya* villages. This is typical of the imbalance, doubtless on account of the nature of sources.

2. Stein, *Peasant State and Society....*, Chapters 2 and 3.

3. Cf. Kesavan Veluthat, *Brahman Settlements in Kerala, op. cit.*, pp. 5–6.

4. Above, Introduction to the First Edition.

5. A transcription of this inscription has not been yet officially published. R. Nagaswami reported the discovery with his own reading which is not very convincing. R. Nagaswami, 'An Outstanding Epigraphical Discovery in Tamil Nadu', *Proceedings of the Fifth International Conference Seminar on Tamil* (Madurai, 1981). I am indebted to Dr M. R. Raghava Varier for permitting me to examine his eye-copy of the record which to my mind is more dependable. I also thank Dr T. K. Venkatasubrahmanyan who was kind enough to help me inspect the record *in situ*.

6. Gurukkal, *Agrarian System ..., op. cit.*, pp. 81–83.

7. *P. C. P.*, pp. 29–31, II. 108–141.

8. Above, Chapter 1.

9. *T. P. C. P.*, pp. 356–60; 361–68.

10. *Ibid., passim.*

11. *Ibid.*, pp. 26–29.

12. R. Champakalakshmi, 'Introduction', *Studies in History*, Vol. IV, no. 2, (1982), pp. 161–66.

13. *T.P.C.P.*, pp. 45–53.

14. *Ibid.*, pp. 71–73, esp. p. 72, I. 17.

15. Rēyūru Copper plates, *T.P.C.P.*, pp. 83–86, esp. p. 85, II. 16–17.

16. *T. P. C. P.*, pp. 124–32.

17. *Ibid.*, pp. 186–96.

18. *Ibid.*, pp. 207–23.

19. *Ibid.*, pp. 240–45.

20. Minakshi, *Administration and Social Life ...*, p. 143, gives a list of the *brahmadēyas* which existed in the Pallava kingdom.

21. Veluthat, *Brahman Settlements in Kerala*, pp. 3–7.

22. *Ibid.*, pp. 21–38; M. G. S. Narayanan and Kesavan Veluthat, 'A History of the Nambudiri Community in Kerala' in Fritz Staal (ed.), *Agni*, Vol. II, pp. 256–78.

23. Veluthat, *op. cit.*

24. *T. A. S.*, II, no. 2, pp. 8–14.

25. V. Raghavan Nambyar, 'Annals and Antiquities of Tiruvalla', *Kerala Society Papers* (1929), pp. 57–94.

26. Cp. 57 and 58 of 1949–50; *A.R.E.* 1929–30, pp. 3ff.

27. For a detailed discussion, see below, Chapter 7.

28. *S.I.I.*, IV, nos. 537 and 538.

29. No. 176 of 1919.

30. Nos. 190 and 198 of 1919.

31. For Rajadhirājacaturvedimaṅgalam, *S. I. I.*, Vol. VI, nos. 48, 52, 58, 59, 60. For the other two villages, Subbarayalu, *Political Geography*, p. 92.

32. Subbarayalu, *Political Geography*, p. 94.

33. *S.I.I*, Vol. VIII, no. 43.

34. *E.I.* XXII, pp. 9–11; K.A. Nilakanta Sastri, *South India and South-East Asia*, (Madras, 1978), pp. 9–18.

35. *S.I.I.*, Vol. VI, nos. 283, 284.

36. Nos. 240 and 241 of 1922; Sastri, *Colas*, p. 497.

37. 148 of 1927; *ARE.*, 1927, II, 28; Sastri, *Colas*, p. 497.

38. *Bulletin of the Ramavaram Research Institute*, IX, II, p. 134.

39. E.g., *T. A. S.*, VI, no. 52, p. 64.

40. For details, Veluthat, *Brahman Settlements in Kerala*, pp. 52–67.

41. Mahalingam, *South Indian Polity*, pp. 350–81; Elamkulam, P. N. Kunjan Pillai, *Janmisampradāyam Kēraḷathil* (Kottayam, 1959) pp. 39–40; etc.

42. Narayanan, 'Socio-economic Implications of the Concept of Mahapataks in the Feudal Society of South India', Indian History Congress, Calicut, 1976.

43. E.g., Sastri, *Colas*, p. 506; Veluthat, *Brahman Settlements in Kerala*, p. 57.

44. *P. C. P.*, p. 31, II. 138–39.

45. *Ibid.*, p. 114. I. 222.

46. Sastri, *Colas*, pp. 486–519; Mahalingam, *South Indian Polity*, pp. 350–81; Veluthat, *Brahman Settlements*, pp. 52–67.

47. Kesavan Veluthat, 'The Sabhā and Pariṣad ...', *op. cit.*

48. Derrett, 'Two Inscriptions ...', *op. cit.*

49. For an interesting comparative study of the settlement patterns in the two different regions and the implications thereof, Joan P. Mencher, 'Kerala and Madras: A Comparative Study of Ecology and Social Structure', *Ethnology*, V, ii (University of Pittsburg, Pennsylvania, April 1996, pp. 136–71.

50. V. K. J. Menon, 'Geographical Basis of the Distribution and Pattern of Rural Settlement in Kerala', *Journal of the M.S. University of Baroda*, II, pp. 41–54.

51. Veluthat, *Brahman Settlements ...*, pp. 3–5; Narayanan and Veluthat, 'A History of the Nambudiri Community in Kerala' in Staal ed., *Agni, op. cit.*, Vol. 2, pp. 256–59.

52. *T. A. S.*, II, iii, pp. 131–207. This is a lengthy inscription in which a large number of gifts to the Tiruvalla temple, and various decisions of the temple committee, all made on different occasions, are recorded.

53. *E.I.*, IX, pp. 234ff.

54. This is an unpublished record discovered by the present writer on the *namaskāramaṇḍapa* of the Umāmahēśvara temple, Airāṇikkuḷam, Trichur district, Kerala. I thank Professor M. G. S. Narayanan and Dr Raghava Varier for their help in deciphering the record, the estampage of which is kept in the Department of History, University of Calicut.

55. *I. H. Q.*, IV, no. 1, pp. 154–55.

56. Above, Chapter 3.

57. *Ibid.*

58. Narayanan, *Political and Social Conditions ..., op. cit.*, Chapter on 'Early Wars and Alliances'.

59. Elamkulam P. N. Kunjan Pillai, *Janmisampradāyam Kēraḷattil*, pp. 28–35; Narayanan, *Political and Social Conditions ...*, pp. 325–40; Veluthat, *Brahman Settlements ...*, p. 58; etc.

60. *Ibid.*

61. Kunjan Pillai, *loc. cit.*

62. Narayanan, n. 58.

63. Above, Chapter 4.

64. Above, Chapter 6.

65. Nilakanta Sastri, *Studies in Cola History and Administration*, p. 74.

66. Cf. M. G. S. Narayanan and Kesavan Veluthat, 'Temples in South India', Paper presented to the Symposium on the Socio-Economic Role of Religious Institutions in India, Indian History Congress, Bodh Gaya, 1981.

67. No. 68 of1898; Sastri, *Studies in Cola History and Administrations*, p. 128.

68. No. 327 of 1916; no. 74 of 1931–32; no. 260 of 1939–40; etc.

69. *S.I.I.*, III, 205, Tamil portion, II. 19–25.

70. Above, n. 66.

71. Sastri, *Colas*, Chapter on 'Economic Conditions'.

72. Appadorai, *Economic Conditions of Southern India, op. cit.*

73. Kenneth R. Hall, *Trade and Statecraft in the Age of Colas* (Delhi, 1980).

74. R. Champakalakshmi, 'Growth of Urban Centres in South India: Kudamukku-Palaiyarai, the Twin-city of the Colas', *Studies in History*, Vol. I, no. 1 (1979); *idem*, 'Urban Processes in Early Medieval Tamilnadu', in Sabyasachi Bhattacharya and Romila Thapar (eds.), *Situating Indian History* (Delhi, 1986); *idem*, 'Urbanisation in South India: The Role of Ideology and Polity', Presidential Addresses, Section I, Indian History Congress (Srinagar, 1986).

75. B. D. Chattopadhyaya, Review of Hall, n. 73, *op. cit., idem*, 'Urban Centres in Early Medieval India; An Overview', in Sabyasachi Bhattacharya and Romila Thapar (eds.), *Situating Indian History; idem, Coins and Currency Systems in South India* (New Delhi, 1977); etc.

76. Mary Meena Abraham, *The Ayyovole Guild of Early Medieval South India*, Unpublished M.Phil. dissertation, New Delhi, 1978.

77. R. Sumathi, *Trade and its Impact on Early Tamils: the Chola Experience*, Unpublished M.Phil. Thesis, Jawaharlal Nehru University, (New Delhi, 1984).

78. Chattopadhyaya, Review of Hall, n. 71, *op. cit.*

79. G. William Skinner, *Marketing and Social Structure in Rural China* (Ann Arbor, 1974).

80. Above, n. 75.

81. R. Vanaja, 'Trade and Statecraft in the Age of the Colas,' a review article, *Studies in History;* Vol. IV, p. 2; July–December, 1982, pp. 321–33.

82. Champakalakshmi, 'Urban Processes in Medieval Tamilnadu', *op. cit.*

83. *Idem*, 'Growth of Urban Centres in South India ...', *op. cit.*

84. *Idem*, 'Urbanisation in South India: the Role of Ideology and Polity', *op. cit.*

85. Chattopadhyaya, 'Urban Centres in Early Medieval India: An Overview', *op. cit.*

86. *S.I.I.*, IV, 223.

87. *S.I.I.*, XVII, no. 326. All the six signatories are, however, described as *Viyāpārigaḷ* ('traders').

88. Hall, *op. cit.*, Chapters 3 and 4.

89. *S.I.I.*, III, pp. 268–76, Hall, *op. cit.* p. 56, n. 40.

90. No. 285 of 1959–60; *S.I.I.*, III, 15, 16, 18; *S.I.I.*, I, 40; *S.I.I.*, V, 592; etc. Also Hall, *op. cit.*, p. 56.

91. No. 264 of 1943–44; also Hall, *op. cit.*, p. 55.

92. See Hall, *op. cit.*, p. 56 and nn. 46–53.

93. S.*I.I.*, XVII, no. 463, Hall takes *Kōyiṟṟamappēṟu* as 'a royal tax payable to temples'; *op. cit.*, p. 57; but we have shown that the *Kōyiṟṟamar* were kings' agents and hence our explanation. Above, Chapter 3.

94. No. 388 of 1939–40.

95. No. 431 of 1954–55; *S.I.I.*, IV, 377, etc.

96. Above, Chapter 5.

97. No. 204 of 1908.

98. No. 100 of 1906.

99. *I.P.S.* 200.

100. *Ibid.*, 170.

101. For the pattern of traders investing on land in the context of feudal Europe, Henri Pirenne, *Economic and Social History of Medieval Europe* (London, 1936, 1972), pp. 85–86.

102. Derett, 'Two Inscriptions ...,' *op. cit.*

103. Champakalakshmi, 'Urbanisation in Medieval Tamilnadu', *op. cit.*, Tables II, III, IV.

Seven

# Social Parameters
## Stratification and Ideology

In the two previous chapters we examined the dominant local groups in early medieval south India such as the *ūr, nāḍu, brahmadēyam* and *nagaram*. We saw that in the royal charters and other records it was these who owned or controlled land and other means of production that were taken into consideration. In any pre-modern, pre-capitalist society, it is indeed such groups that show themselves prominently in the historical records. But the deeper reality of social relations can be gauged with a certain amount of accuracy even by looking at these aspects of upper class life. In the present chapter we shall examine not only the kind of complex relations existing among these dominant groups but the entire social structure so that a picture of the differentiation in that society can be brought out. It will also help us in understanding the factors which sustained such stratification. Our analysis would also entail consideration of the ideology which lent sanction and legitimacy to this stratification which it sought to maintain in an unaltered form. Questions regarding the nature of state and the power structure of that state can be raised and answered with greater confidence within the context of this social stratification.

In our discussions in the two previous chapters it has been brought out that agriculture was the most important form of production in early medieval south India. This is not, however, to deny the existence of artisanal and trading activities; nor do we undervalue the importance of pastoral activities in this period. The former was generally geared to the needs of a largely closed agrarian society where the artisanal activities did not rise above the level of what is described as 'petty production'. In the case of the latter, existing scholarship has largely failed to appreciate the importance of pastoralism in this period which is brought out by evidence of the donation of livestock in large numbers to temples, the occurrence of shepherds with a high frequency in the records, etc. But this activity represented survivals from a very ancient past, and there is little evidence and less scope for any marked social stratification on the basis of production and distribution caused by this factor in a predominantly agrarian economy. Therefore, in taking up the social stratification of early medieval south India for discussion, the best indicator would be the structure of land relations.

South Indian historians in the past have generally tended to view society in early medieval south India as generally smooth, free from any contradictions. In fact, Nilakanta Sastri would go as far as to glorify the 'political spirit of the time ... [which] aimed at securing the harmony of classes, rather than their equality',[1] and the 'healthy society ... which was free from the glaring economic oppression of one class by another.'[2] He seldom recognised the contradiction between these statements on the one side and the rich empirical data he had himself marshalled in the monograph about the class distinctions and contradictions on the other. The situation is not any better in the case of later studies by Appadorai, Minakshi and Mahalingam.[3] In Appadorai's work, which is on the economic conditions of southern India in the first half of the second millennium AD, one would naturally expect a picture of class differentiation and contradiction, but in vain.

Recent American scholarship which starts with the avowed purpose of offering a corrective to the kind of historiography represented by Nilakanta Sastri does not make the position any better. For instance Burton Stein in his major work on peasant state and society in medieval south India characterises society in the Pallava and the succeeding Cōḷa ages as organised into a large number of peasant localities and culture.[4] Naturally one would look for a picture of the structured relationship within such a highly developed peasant society. But the whole work is professedly about 'peasants without lords'.[5] Perhaps Stein is right in characterising his own work as 'somewhat perverse in theoretical and historiographical senses'[6] in a very literal way! On the one hand, Stein is indifferent to the rich data on the differentiation within the peasantry in making the assumption of a world of peasants without lords. He seems to push under the carpet the subject nature of a major chunk of peasantry while describing the relationship between the brahmans and peasants as an alliance which was somewhat contradictory in actual fact as we shall see below. True, it was one of cooperation if we take it in the sense that in every situation of oppression there has to be the cooperation of the oppressed! The conception of an undifferentiated, monolithic, peasantry obviously springs from perverse theoretical position and a total indifference to data.

However, there is a happy development in recent years represented by the work of a few Asian scholars, Noboru Karashima, Y. Subbarayalu, M. G. S. Narayanan, D. N. Jha, R. Champakalakshmi and Rajan Gurukkal among them.[7] This is not to say that every one of them shares the same frame of reference and the same set of assumptions: they are not, however, burdened by the kind of 'commitment' that Stein and Hall have taken up for themselves. The detailed, down-to-earth, analyses made by these scholars on aspects of the economy and society help the student in identifying the major social parameters, so that one is able to situate the medieval south Indian state within the socio-economic context.

The copper plate records of the Pallavas and Pāṇḍyas in the seventh and eighth centuries provide information on the various shades of rights on land and concomitantly the position of different sections in society depending upon the nature of right that one enjoyed on a particular piece of land. As we have seen in a previous chapter, most of the Pallava copper plates record the grant of land to brahmans.[8] Inevitably, they are related to the creation and transfer of certain superior rights over land. This is expressed in the case of a few Pallava records by the expression *kuḍi nīkki*[9] which means literally removing the earlier occupants. The same idea is conveyed by another expression *mun-peṟṟārai māṟṟi*[10] found in a couple of other Pallava records. Both these signify that the recipients of the land were at liberty to evict the earlier occupants of the land and settle it with new occupants of their own choice. However, R. Tirumalai has convincingly argued with the help of formidable data that these expressions need not signify the eviction of the earlier occupants in a physical sense.[11] On the other hand, he suggests, it may indicate the extinction of the existing rights of the occupants over the land that was granted. It is also significant that, apart from the handful of records speaking of land where the earlier occupants were either removed or their earlier rights were extinguished, the vast majority of Pallava charters do not speak about the fate of the earlier settlers. This would suggest that what was granted to brahmans was relatively unsettled land where all the rights were given to the donees.

The land grants of the Pallavas, therefore, indicate the beginnings of a structured relationship in the matter of land rights. In many cases there is no mention at all of the earlier occupants on the land indicating thereby that the donees were granted unsettled land.[12] Here it is clear that what was granted was to be enjoyed by the donees, with the right to get the land cultivated with the help of tenants if they wanted to. In the other records which do speak of the pre-existing occupants, it is invariably either by removing them physically or by extinguishing their rights over the granted land that the grant was made. Even here the prevailing situation is as if there was the state at the top enjoying an overall suzerainty and final right over the land and the occupant-tenant at the bottom who cultivated the land with one stratum of intermediary, i.e., the donees of the grant. On them were conferred not only the right to get the land cultivated and its rights enjoyed but also other fiscal and administrative rights such as the collectionof numerous imposts and the maintenance of law.[13]

As we come to the situation obtaining in the Pāṇḍyan kingdom, we have a clearer picture of a more evolved system of land rights, thanks to the excellent study of the agrarian system and sociopolitical organisation under the early Pāṇḍyas undertaken by Rajan Gurukkal.[14] Most land grants of the Pāṇḍyas are concerned with the creation or maintenance of a *brahmadēyam, dēvadānam* or *paḷḷiccantam*. They speak of the conferment of two kinds of rights: the *mīyāṭci* and the *kārāṇmai*. These two expressions indicate, respectively, the superior possessive right and the right to cultivate. The phrase in the Pāṇḍyan records, *kārāṇmai mīyāṭci uḷḷaḍaṅga* in the Tamil portions and *kārāṇmai mīyāṭci yutam* in the Sanskrit portions, indicating the right to cultivate the land and/or get it cultivated, is an exact translation of the expression *karṣayataḥ karṣāpayataśca* occurring in the same context in inscriptions from northern India.[15] Below these two shades of rights, there appears to have been a third one, namely, that of occupancy (*kuṭimai*). In a stone inscription from Ambasamudram, it is clearly stated that the *mīyāṭci* alone was transferred with the *kārāṇmai* retained by the earlier tenants of the land.[16] It is explicitly stated in the record that the land in question was to be a *mutal kuṭi nīṅṅā dēvadānam*, a *dēvadānam* where the earlier occupants were not to be disturbed. This shows that *kuṭimai* or occupancy right differed from *kārāṇmai*. There are expressions such as *āḷaḍaṅga* (literal meaning: 'including the men') found in the grants indicating the transfer of agrestic labourers also along with land. This is a clear evidence of labour tied to soil, in the same way as we have in the Sanskrit charters from northern India expressed by part of the phrase *dhanajanasahitā*.[17] This stipulation not to disturb the earlier occupants and their tenurial rights over land is in contrast to the statement that we saw in the case of the Pallava records where the expression *kuḍi nīkki* is invariably used wherever there is mention of the earlier occupants, meaning either that the earlier occupants were evicted or that their rights were terminated. In the Pāṇḍyan records, therefore, one can see the further evolution of land rights into the next stage. In certain records from the Pāṇḍyan kingdom the expressions *mērpāti* and *kīḻpati* are used in the place of *mīyāṭci* and *kārāṇmai* respectively.[18] This is sufficient to dispel the misunderstanding created by Stein with regard to the expressions *mēlvārm* and *kiḻvārm* in the Cōḻa records.[19]

This discussion of the land rights in Pāṇḍyan records helps in the reconstruction of the structured relationship concerning land with various shades of tenurial rights. With the help of a diagram, Rajan Gurukkal has demonstrated this hierarchy with the *kuṭi*s (occupants) at the bottom of the scale and the king at the top and a graded hierarchy of intermediaries placed between the two. This class of intermediaries consisted of, according to Gurukkal, the chiefs, the *nāḍu*, the *ūr* and *dēvadānam* or *brahmadēyam* as the case may be, and the *kārāḷar* (*the* cultivating tenants) in that descending order.[20]

The situation in the Cēra kingdom is comparable. M. G. S. Narayanan's research into various aspects of the history of Kerala in this period has brought out a detailed picture of the structured relations in the matter of land obtaining in the Cēra kingdom.[21] In a study of the traditional land system in Kerala undertaken by Professor Narayanan and the present writer, the following representation is given with the help of a diagram:[22] The Perumāl or the king was at the top. He had his own land known as *cērikkal* (something of a demesne land) in which there were the *kārāḷar* or tenants and *kuṭiyāḷar* or the occupants. Below the *kārāḷar* were the labourers attached to land known as *aṭiyāḷar.* A portion of the *cērikkal* land may have been granted as *virutti* or service tenure to religious and secular functionaries but the pattern of *kārāḷar kuṭiyāḷar-aṭiyāḷar* relationship remained the same in such pieces also. In other areas where the local chieftains obtained, even they had the *cērikkal* (demesne) land and had granted *virutti* tenures carrying with it the same pattern of subject peasantry. In certain cases between the *kārāḷar-kuṭiyāḷar-aṭiyāḷar* peasantry on the one side and the local chief or the king himself on the other, there were the significant group of intermediaries in the brahman settlements owning right over land as either *brahmasvām* (brahman's property) or *dēvasvam* (god's property) and marginally the trading groups in the *nagarams*. Thus we get the picture of a stratified peasantry which was itself subjected to several tiers of intermediaries with superior rights. Although the number of records available in the case of the Cēra kingdom is as limited as they are in the case of the Pallava and Pāṇḍyan kingdoms, the picture of land relations obtaining there represents a slightly more complex and presumably more evolved structure. However, there is a major difference in Kerala: we do not come across the strong non-brahman peasant proprietors who characterise the agrarian structure of the rest of south India.

Coming to the situation in the Cōḻa country we are in a much better position on account of the vast amount of evidence and the varied literature on the subject. Long before Nilakanta Sastri had published his studies on Cōḻa history, K. M. Gupta had completed a study of the land system in South India between 800 and 1200 AD.[23] Starting from Gupta till the most recent publication of R. Tirumalai on land grants and agrarian reactions in Cōḻa and Pāṇḍya times, a vast body of literature has grown around this topic. Among them the most significant ones, either for the new light they shed or for the refreshing questions they raise, are those by D. N. Jha,[24] Y. Subbarayalu,[25] N. Karashima,[26] Dharma Kumar[27] and R. Tirumalai.[28]

The systematic analysis of epigraphic material undertaken by Noboru Karashima presents a pattern of the evolution of tenurial rights on land. In the studies of earlier historians and those who follow their frame of reference, it is the land relations in the *brahmadēya* type of villages that had received greater attention. Karashima takes up the question in relation to the non-*brahmadēya* villages also.[29] This is important in two respects. For one thing, since the non-*brahmadēya* villages were more ancient than the *brahmadēya* villages, they have a greater significance in a study of the historical development of tenurial rights over land. Secondly, as we have seen, since the non-*brahmadēya* villages far outnumbered the *brahmadēyams*, the basic determinant of the social relations will have to be looked for in the production relations in the non-*brahmadēya* villages. In a comparative study of the nature of landed property in a non-*brahmadēya* village and a *brahmadēyam*, undertaken with the help of nine inscriptions from the former and twenty-one from the latter, Karashima argues that private property was not as well developed in the non-*brahmadēya* as it was in the *brahmadēya* villages.[30] Land was held in common by the community in the non-*brahmadēya* villages. In the case of the *brahmadēya* villages there was individual landholding and the landholders were different from the cultivators. This would suggest that in the beginning of the Cōḻa rule, individual holding of land by non-brahman peasant proprietors was not fully developed. This is supported by further studies made by Karashima and Subbarayalu.[31] In a tabulated presentation of details available in the 260 Cōḻa inscriptions registering sale of land, Subbarayalu has brought out the increasing proportion of non-brahman individuals selling land in the four periods of Cōḻa rule in a 1.5: 4.2: 7.7: 3.7 ratio in percentage. This would show that in the earlier periods of Cōḻa rule individual landholding was not common in the non-brahman villages while it became increasingly prevalent in the later years of Cōḻa rule. This is very much in conformity with the pattern of the distribution of the titles of landholders such as *uḍaiyān, kiḻān, vēḷān, mūvēndavēḷān* in the respective periods, which goes on increasing as the Cōḻa rule progresses in time.[32]

The fact of individual non-brahman landowners being on an increase in the later periods of Cōḻa rule is further supported by Karashima's examination of a large number of inscriptions recording the sale or donation of land to the Jambukēśvaram temple in Tiruchirapalli.[33] This has brought out significant information about the growth of huge landed magnates owning whole villages in certain cases. Karashima has brought out, significantly, that patterns of landholding in the same village underwent a transformation of this kind. He seeks to explain this phenomenon in the light of two economic factors: 'First, accumulation of wealth brought by the imperialistic expansion of Chola power during the reigns of Rājarāja I and Rajendra I, which was distributed to the people of the heart of the Chola country, the Lower Kavery Valley. Second, an increase in agricultural productivity was made possible by the introduction of new agricultural techniques such as the construction of dams, the maintenance of water tanks and channels etc.'[34] It may also be that grant of land on a large scale to secular functionaries of the state on service tenure helped in this process. In a further analysis of more inscriptional details, Karashima has laid bare the pattern of some people accumulating large extents of land and becoming big, locally influential, landlords and others losing possession of their land and slipping into the position of tenants and landless cultivators.[35] He has rightly identified in this pattern 'the emergence of a new agrarian order'. Though he is 'still unable to say whether this means the appearance of a feudal system or not, this new agrarian order seems to have brought changes in the relations of many communities belonging to the locality.'[36]

This discussion will dispel any doubts about whether or not there existed private property in land in this period in south India. The weighty evidence presented by Karashima in relation to non-*brahmadēya* villages and non-brahman peasant proprietors has its counterpart in the information concerning individual brahman landowners as well as their corporate bodies such as the *sabhā, pariṣad*, etc., looking after the *brahmadēya* and *dēvadāna* properties. It is well known that temples had developed into huge landed magnates in this period.[37] In the circumstances, to still support the notion of the Asiatic mode of production with its basis on the absence of private property in land is to close one's eyes towards reality.[38] At the same time to say that absolute property existed in land will have to ignore the various shades of right that different sets of people enjoyed on the same piece of land, a situation of what is called multiplexity of rights.[39] That would entail consideration of the structured relationship based on land rights as gleaned from the Cōḻa records.

As in the case of the land rights existing in the Pāṇḍyan kingdom, records granting land to *brahmadēyams* in the Cōḻa country too speak of land being granted with the rights of both *kārāṇmai* and *mīṭāṭci*. As we saw above, these were the rights to cultivate the land and get it cultivated. Another distinction that one notices in land rights, mostly in the case of non-*brahmadēya* villages, is the almost opposing bipolarity of *kārāṇmai* and *veḷḷāmai*. From the contexts in which the expression *veḷḷāmai* occurs, it would appear that this was the right which could be more or less compared with peasant proprietorship. *Veḷḷāmai*, literally 'the state of being a *veḷḷala*' is interesting as it is presented as a binary opposite of *kārāṇmai*, literally 'the state of being a *kārāḷa*'.[40] However, the facts of the existence of peasant proprietors and of the increase in the strength and number of such peasant proprietors has been noted above.

Again, *kārāṇmai* is seen to be of two different kinds in the situation in the Coḷa country as elsewhere. These are expressed by the phrases *kuḍi nīkki* and *kuḍi nīṅgā*. As we have seen above, the former represented a tenure where either the previous settlers were physically removed or their rights were extinguished in favour of the new grantees. In the latter case, *kuḍi nīṅgā*, the previous settlers were not to be disturbed. Burton Stein has strangely translated the expression *kuḍi nīṅgāya* to mean an arrangement where 'the previous cultivators are said to have been removed from the land and village at the time of being granted'.[41] R. Tirumalai has shown that even in *kuḍi nīkki* tenures there was not necessarily a physical eviction of the earlier occupants involved but only a renewal of the terms of occupancy rights.[42] However, this form of tenure may have meant greater latitude to the new class of intermediaries placed above them, for it is only natural that demands should be enhanced at the time of the renewal of the terms. The same argument is made by Dharma Kumar in her separate study of Cōḷa property rights.[43]

Another element that we come across in the records relating to agrarian relations is the agrestic labour. Given the nature of our records concerned with the upper classes, details about the agrestic labourers are hard to come by. In relation to the villages granted to the Bṛihadīśvara temple in Tanjavur by Rājarāja I and those granted to the Gaṅgaikoṇḍacōḷapuram by Virarājēndra, it has been shown that in the former list, where 40 villages are involved, 19 had a *paṟaicceri* (separate residential quarters of the *paṟaiya*s who were the agrestic labourers) each and in the latter list involving seven villages there was one, apart from the residential quarters of other communities and occupational groups.[44] Many records speak of the transfer of land together with the labourers attached to it (*āḷaḍaṅga*).[45] If one can go by the indicators in the records which are heavily biased in favour of the upper sections in society, it would appear that these labourers who present themselves to have had a bonded nature occupied the lowest rung in the hierarchy of land rights. By all indications it was these sections who were made use of in redeeming the obligation to pay the service rent, namely *veṭṭi*.

The following structural representation of the complex relationship obtaining in the world of agrarian relations may be made by way of summarising our discussion of the nature of land rights in the Cōḻa country. The king was at the top of the hierarchy with his right, which was exercised occasionally, to appropriate the title to grant land both settled and unsettled and also to create superior rights over it.[46] There were different kinds of hierarchies below him. On the one side there was the large number of *nāḍu* groups which were themselves congeries of peasant villages known as the *ūr.* Each of these villages had a number of magnates who had a share in the arable land there. To begin with they shared common property in the village, but as time progressed individual peasant proprietors also rose there. Most of them had their land cultivated by labourers attached to their land but it is probable that in certain cases between them and the labourers there was another tier of sub-tenants. In another hierarchy below the king were the local chiefs. Either below every chief or directly under the king were the huge landed magnates who came to sport bombastic titles and functioned as the state's agents in the Cōḻa political structure. Below these magnates were their tenants, below them the occupants and still below them the agrestic labourers. Again directly below either the king or one of the chiefs were the different kinds of eleemosynary villages such as the *brahmadēyam, dēvadānam, paḻḻiccandam, śālābhōgam, kaṇimuṟṟūṭṭu* and *veṭṭāppēṟu.* In these the tenurial pattern was the same: the *kārāḷa* (tenants), *kuḍi* (occupants) and *paṟaiya* (labourer) placed one below the other.

This structured relationship of land rights in early medieval south India, beginning in a rudimentary form under the Pallavas and getting elaborated by the time we come to the age of the Cōḻa state, is seen extending specially to cover the whole of south India. This compares well with the picture of land rights in early medieval north India as outlined by R. S. Sharma.[47] Again, this strikes a favourable comparison with the situation in medieval Europe as brought out by Marc Bloch:[48]

> The tenant who–from father to son, as a rule–ploughs the land and gathers in the crop; his immediate lord, to whom he pays dues and who, in certain circumstances, can resume possession of the land; the lord of the lord, and so on, right up the feudal scale–how many persons there are who can say, each with as much justification as the other, 'That is my field!'

Although one need not cling to the idea of the absence of private property in land as the protagonists of the Asiatic mode of production would,[49] one cannot be very assertive about the existence of absolute proprietorship over land as Dharma Kumar has tended to do in a recent study.[50]

Burton Stein describes this society as a peasant society. His conception which is highly eclectic is shown to have been taken from economists, sociologists and anthropologists of varying ideological positions such as Chayanov, Eric Wolf, Marshall Sahlins and Theodore Shanin.[51] He completely misses the subject nature of peasantry. His theoretical assumptions constrain him to stretch the evidences to such an extent as to force him identify an alliance between the brahmans and peasants.[52] In reality, however, the case was far from being such an unchanging monolith. We have seen that varying shades of relationship existed between the brahmans (themselves not an undifferentiated lot) on the one hand and the different levels of peasantry on the other, varying in different points of time. But, stratification within peasantry is one thing which Stein does not recognise at all. As pointed out by D. N. Jha, to speak of massive peasant support to brahmans, one will have to ignore the solid evidence that out of the entire corpus of published Cō̱ḻa inscriptions, which are largely concerned with arrangements about land, there are only seven identifiable cases of veḻḻāḷa peasants granting land to brahmans.[53] The picture that we have seen above is that of a structured relationship where the landowning class, both brahman and veḻḻāḷa, occupied the upper strata exploiting the surplus in agriculture produced by cultivating tenants and agricultural labourers. It is the untenable theoretical position, backed by a distortion of evidence that has led Professor Stein to close his eyes towards this picture which seems to be more realistic.

The picture of social stratification that we reconstructed pertains to the world of production and distribution in the field of agriculture. This kind of a hierarchy generally obtained in the field of other activities of production such as trade and the artisanal occupations also. Even there largely the same kind of a hierarchy obtained as has been brought out in the case of the Cēra kingdom by M. G. S. Narayanan,[54] and Cōḻa empire by R. Champakalakshmi[55] and Y. Subbarayalu.[56] The traders and artisans, as we saw in a previous chapter, were eager to invest in land, typically in the way in which the same thing happened in medieval Europe as brought out by Henri Pirenne.[57] This is understandable in view of the dominance of agriculture over other forms of economic activities. Hence, the hierarchy even in non-agrarian production relations sought to emulate that in the field of agrarian relations.

Such a structured society with a graded hierarchy of infinite variations in status based on the extent of control over the means and relations of production found its expression in the *jāti* formula. Based on the near total absence of caste designations for those other than brahmans named in the temple records of the Cōḻas, B. Suresh has argued that the caste system had not yet set.[58] This confusion is comparable to a similar situation in the case of the Cēra records from Kerala where, again based on the absence of caste suffix, P. N. Kunjan Pillai argued that several temple committee members were non-brahmans.[59] In the latter case the researches of M. G. S. Narayanan and the present writer have shown that this is a clear misunderstanding.[60] Even in the case of the Cōḻa country, Subbarayalu has shown that a large number of occupational groups identified in so many words as belonging to different castes make their appearance in the records.[61]

This *jāti* formula, which was the rationalisation of social stratification, had the contact with the brahman caste as the point of reference in fixing the social and ritual status, the assumption there being that the brahmans were the highest caste. But in reality we see that the veḻḷāḷa caste, which is identified significantly as of the śūdra *varṇa*, is seen to be enjoying a status almost equal to that of the brahman caste on account of the control of land they had. For instance, in making important decisions concerning land revenue and allied matters, these two groups are always mentioned together in a premier position. An inscription from Uttaramērūr, recording a decision of the *sahhā* relating to fines to be collected from different castes, gives the following order: brahman, Śivabrahman, kaṇakkar, veḻḷāḷa and others.[62] The equal prominence of brahman and veḷḷāḷa is brought out by a couple of records from Mannarudi,[83] one dated 1118 AD and the other 1239 AD. However, the fixing of the ritual status was always with reference to the contact with the brahmans. An inscription of Rājarāja I dated 1002 AD orders that the landholdings of the members of all castes below the brahmans (*brāhmaṇarkku kīḻpaṭṭa jātikaḷil*) should be sold away in the particular brahman village.[64] This reference certainly includes the veḷḷāḷas who were the most prominent landholders.

There is a major lacuna in our sources that we do not get a true picture of the caste hierarchy because of the fact that the inscriptions in the temples do not identify the large number of persons mentioned in them by their castes. This is only natural considering the purpose of those records. Thus, while the statistical method may be very systematic, in view of the above difficulty in relation to the sources, there is the likelihood that one is misled by the results of such analyses. For instance, Y. Subbarayalu has calculated that in the Cōḻa inscriptions, the highest frequency of caste obtains in the case of the cattle-keepers or *maṉṟādi*s (228/663) while the brahmans (110/663), veḷḷāḷas (76/663), and others occupy a much lower position.[65] If one were to follow such pattern blindly, the conclusion might be that the cattle-keepers were more than twice as important as the brahman and three times as the veḷḷāḷas! But when it is realised that a large number of temple inscriptions are concerned with the endowment of livestock for the maintenance of 'perpetual lamps', the role of a large number of individual cattle-keepers entrusted with the upkeep of such animals can be appreciated.[66] It is not as if pastoralism was three times as strong as agriculture! However, even this methodology is far superior to the kind of impressionistic, speculative, argument of Suresh and Kunjan Pillai mentioned above.

We have seen that the brahmans occupied the highest position in the *jāti* hierarchy. This is only natural. For one thing *jāti* was a brahmanical paradigm at least in the historical context in south India. Secondly, they were not only among the most powerful in terms of economic resources but also the custodians of religious ideas and institutions centering on the temples. Second only to the brahmans in the ritual status were the veḷḷāḷas who on account of their land control occupied an equally influential position in society. Irfan Habib has marvelled that the veḷḷāḷa peasants were not accorded the vaiśya status.[67] This is unnecessary. By the period of our study, the *varṇa* principle had become at best a mere theoretical construct irrespective of the question whether or not it ever had any real significance as a representation of social stratification even in northern India. Secondly, the vaiśyas, like the kṣatriyas, even as a category have not migrated in numbers to south India, and hence one cannot expect a network of the group representing the vaiśya *varṇa* there as in the case of northern India. Thus it is natural that these peasants of all grades were designated to the residual category of the śūdras. At the same time not all of them were subjected to the kind of disabilities that the śūdras in northern India had been[68] for the obvious reason that the veḷḷāḷa peasantry constituted a major force as the owners of the means of production. In fact, many of them were granted the status of *sat-śūdra*s, a curious category by the standards of the *varṇa* formula. This is evidence enough to show that although the social stratification expressed itself in the *jāti* formula, the determinant factor was neither caste nor the various shades of connection with the priestly class. On the contrary it was the control of the means of production in the case of both agriculture and trade that decided the status. This would call into question Romila Thapar's statement that 'what was immutable in Indian society was ... caste.'[69]

Burton Stein states that the community of what he has identified as the political chiefs consisting of the title-holders of the *uḍaiyān-araiyan-mūvēndavēḷān* variety, to whom he attributes political authority and warrior power, were not designated as kṣatriyas.[70] These magnates, we have seen, belonged to the veḷḷāḷa community. Even in the case of the so-called feudatories, there is no kṣatriya claim made in the Cōḻa country.[71] The kṣatriya category as a whole, like the vaiśya category, did not exist on any considerable scale in south India and hence did not form part of the upper class there. But it was necessary to convert the rulers, as it were, to kṣatriyahood, given the character of the upper class and its ideology of social organisation in the *varṇāśramadharma*.[72] Thus, even if the kṣatriya caste did not exist as a social category, there were innumerable claims made by and on behalf of the ruling families to kṣatriyahood. In the case of the Cēra kingdom we have seen that even some of the local chieftains claimed this status.[73] Certain other chiefly houses in late medieval Kerala started claiming the status of a *sāmanta* caste, since it was too late to stake their claims to kṣatriyahood.[74] Stein assigns this general absence of the kṣatriya category in south India to his obsessive idea of the brahman-peasant alliance.[75] Here, not only does he confuse the numerous landed magnates with political chiefs but also assumes that there might have been a numerous kṣatriya group had it not been for this alliance, the evidence of which is, however, elusive.

In accommodating the semi-tribal population that was getting transformed into peasants and other occupational groups such as traders and artisans in the hierarchically oriented society as so many *jāti*s, the model that was followed was that which was prescribed in *dharmaśāstra* literature. Two interesting inscriptions examined at length by J. D. M. Derrett throw significant light on this aspect.[76] One of the inscriptions dated 1118 AD from Uyyakoṇḍān Uḍaiyar in the Tiruchirapalli taluk registers the proceedings of a gathering of brahman *bhaṭṭa*s to consider the status of such artisans and craftsmen as smiths, carpenters, stone-cutters and masons.[77] It is stated that the brahmans, after considering authorities including Yājñavalkya, Gautama, Kauṭilya, Baudhāyana and others, decided that these artisans could be designated as *rathakāras*, this being an *anulōma* caste supposed to be born of a *māhiṣya* male and *karaṇa* female, *māhiṣya* himself being the offspring of a kṣatriya male by a vaiśya female and *karaṇa*, the offspring of a vaiśya male by a śūdra female. It is very interesting that the legal fiction of *saṅkīrṇajāti* which permitted a wide variety of permutations and combinations was invoked in accommodating the newly transformed group into the *jāti* formula. This offered immense possibilities of clearly defining the social and ritual status on the graduated scale of hierarchy. It is significant that the names of the *rathakāra*s in question all end with the title *ācārya*, which is a title used by carpenters, masons, etc., in south India to this day.

Another record claims a legendary origin for a group of *kanmāḷar* (artisans), attributing it to Viśvakarman, son of Brahmā and father-in-law of the Sun.[78] Details of the achievements of Viśvakarman are given, with some famous *ācārya*s of the lineage, so that the claim to respectability gains further support. In the similar group could be included a record from Tirukkaṇṇapuram, Tanjavur, describing the local *Paṭṭanavar* weavers to have supplied cloth to 'gods, kings and people in general' and assigning them a Sanskritic title, *utkṛṣṭāyogapa'*,[79] *āyōgava* being a mixed caste of the *pratilōma* variety in the *dharmaśāstra* literature.[80] These instances also show that on different occasions different *jāti* status was attributed to similar occupational groups. However, as a whole, this resulted in the acceptance of the formula of the *varṇāśramadharma* for explaining social stratification and glossing over the contradictions there. Once this formula was generally accepted, the tribes who lived in the twilight zone of settled society were being brought into its pale and assigned to particular castes. Instances of the Paḷḷi, Curutimān, Nattamān, Kaḷḷar, Maṟavar etc., are interesting cases in point who are described in so many words as *jāti*s in records after the tenth century AD.[81]

A major aspect that is generally discussed in connection with the castes in early medieval south India is the dual division of the castes into the left hand and the right hand castes (*iḍaṅgai* and *valaṅgai*). Writers on south Indian history have recognised the existence in the age of the Cōḻas, of these two antagonistic divisions, the feuds between whom in later centuries were extremely notorious in certain parts of south India. For instance, the several *valaṅgai terinda vēḷaikkarar*, or the 'select regiments of the right hand division', referred to in the Tanjavur inscriptions of Rājarāja or the *iḍaṅgaivari* meaning a levy on the left hand division have been noticed by scholars from the days when these records were edited and published.[82] It has been generally accepted that while the communities included in the left hand division represented largely artisanal and trading communities, those who were designated to the right hand division were generally agrarian in nature.[83] The beginnings of the unhappy relationship between the two divisions can perhaps be noticed from the time of the later Cōḻa rulers as recorded in a Kulōttuṅga inscription.[84] However, this mutually opposing character of the two divisions need not be projected to the days of their origin although in the seventeenth century and later 'their feuds filled the streets of Madras with blood'.[85] A recent study by Noboru Karashima and Y. Subbarayalu has brought out numerous instances where both the divisions came together for common purposes in the fifteenth century.[86]

About the origins and the nature of these divisions we are totally in the dark. Brenda Beck has made an extensive study of the *iḍaṅgai-valaṅgai* divisions in her work on the peasant society in Kongu.[87] G. Oppert had tried to explain the positional appellation of left and right to these communities as indicating the relative degree of purity and pollution.[88] In Arjun Appadorai's analysis he introduces the cultural conception of 'root paradigms' after Victor Turner to explain the basically contending character between the left and the right castes.[89] In the context of the Cōḻa society, however, none of these models appears to be very satisfactory, for, the evidence we have of these divisions in that period is far too little to permit any such generalisation.

Burton Stein devotes a whole chapter to the discussion of the right and left hand castes in his work on the Cōḻa state.[90] He looks upon them as supra-local associations of the artisan and peasant castes. Again he appears to stretch the aspect of opposition between the two divisions, read into the evidence with retrospective effect, to such an extent as to identify in them the balanced and opposed elements which is a characteristic necessity of the idea of pyramidal segmentation in the anthropological literature on the problem. His detailed treatment of the two divisions and the lengthy speculative exercise on their origins, therefore, is another instance of the slender base on which he builds up his argument. In reality, however, it seems that the original, down to earth, understanding of the early scholars that the *iḍaṅgai* represented the artisanal and trading communities and that the *valaṅgai* represented the agrarian communities still appears to be the maximum that can be said about them in the Cōḻa period.[91] That a categorisation of the various communities came into existence in course of time on the basis of the different professions which each of them undertook and that those among them who were related to agricultural production claimed a superior status may suggest that the predominantly agrarian society sought to subordinate to it the other forms of petty production.

Irfan Habib has raised the important question: 'given the structure of the caste system, who were its chief beneficiaries?'[92] The truistic answer that it was the brahmans has been often given by historians including Kosambi and sociologists like Dumont. However, Habib has tried to look at the economic consequences of caste in a different way:[93]

> By its repression of the menial castes, it cheapened labour available for agriculture. At the village level, by providing especially for the services of hereditary village artisans and servants, it reduced the necessary expense on the tools, goods and services that the peasant needed. By thus reducing the portion of agriculture needed for the peasant's subsistence, it enlarged the surplus product, out of which the

> revenues of the ruling class came. At the same time through hereditary skill-transmission, caste cheapened artisan-products, and thus reduced wage-costs generally. The primary economic consequence of the caste system was, then, a substantial enlargement of the income of the ruling class from both agriculture and crafts.

Thus, within the existing social formation the standardisation of stratification through the *jāti* formula became very handy for the upper classes in society for their interest of the maximisation of revenue. This is, however, not to suggest that a crude application of such a calculated material interest was adopted in a mechanical way. On the contrary, the acceptance of this formula of social stratification by all sections of society was achieved by subtler means which included a particular religious ideology which went a long way in validating the stratified social order.

Such a social order came into existence through a process of gradual evolution. As seen in a previous chapter, one major element which went a long way in standardising this stratified society was the brahman settlements established in the fertile tracts of south India.[94] This coincided with a number of parallel and related developments such as the growth and consolidation of the new monarchies, the flowering of the early temple movement, the emergence of prosperous trade and artisan guilds, the eruption of acrimonious brahman-Buddhist-Jain disputes and finally the establishment of an all-embracing caste system. M. G. S. Narayanan and the present writer have demonstrated that the *bhakti* movement in south India contained an attempt to sanctify and legitimise this new social order with all its complexities.[95] The hierarchy of social relationships obtaining in the microcosm of the mundane world was projected to the macrocosm of the spiritual world where the complex relationship among the chief deity, his consorts, the innumerable subsidiary deities, a whole army of temple functionaries including musicians, dancing girls, story-tellers, actors, garland makers and priests existed. It has been shown that the elaborate parallelism between their services in the temple and the services in the palace reflected not so much the royal connotation as the feudal connotation of fealty. 'The plurality and coexistence of different deities, each deity occupying the position of the lord for his devotees was as much recognised in the *bhakti* movement as the plurality and the coexistence of the lords, each lord singularly commanding loyalty from his immediate vassal.'[96] However, once the new social order came to be established with a firm footing and the institution of state was ramified by the ninth century, the *bhakti* movement became part of the establishment. To begin with the movement functioned as a strong prop which helped society and state to get established. This was reinforced in the succeeding period by the proliferation and expansion of temples in a big way. The intellectual dissent which was part of the *bhakti* movement gradually gave in by the beginning of the tenth century when the temple movement became part of the establishment. One does not hear of new *bhakti* saints after the middle of the ninth century; instead, their place was taken by the long list of *ācārya*s, all of whom were brahmans and scrupulous ritualists. Naturally enough, the forward urge of the *bhakti* cult came to an end. Its place was taken by the temples and the *maṭha*s which became the bastions of brahmanical orthodoxy. It is in this context that one has to appreciate the ideology represented by the *bhakti* movement as a veritable material force. It was this force which gave the sanction and legitimacy to the social order in early medieval south India. Even non-brahman movements like the *Śaivasiddhānta* and savants like the *Siddhar* could only conform to this deeply entrenched social order validated by the ideology represented by the temple.

## NOTES

1. K. A. Nilakanta Sastri, *Colas*, p. 508.
2. *Ibid.*
3. Appadorai, *Economic Conditions of Southern India, op. cit.*; Minakshi, *Administration and Social Life ..., op. cit.*; Mahalingam, *South Indian Polity.*
4. Stein, *Peasant State and Society ...*, p. 67, *et passim.*
5. *Ibid.*, Preface.
6. *Ibid.*
7. For details above, Introduction to the First Edition.
8. Above, Chapter 6.
9. *T. P. C. P.*, p. 29, I. 53; p. 166, I. 107; p. 187, II. 20–21.,
10. *T. P. C. P.*, p. 166, I. 106; p. 187, I. 20.
11. R. Tirumalai, *Land Grants and Agrarian Reactions in Cola and Pandya Times* (Madras, 1987), pp. 93–98.

12. Out of the thirty copper plate grants edited by T. N. Subramanyan, *T. P. C. P.*, only the three records quoted above, n. 9, speak of the earlier occupants.

13. *T. P. C. P.*, *passim*. See Minakshi, *Administration and Social Life ...*, although she does not appreciate the significance of this alienation.

14. Gurukkal, *Agrarian System ...*, pp. 109–25.

15. *Cf.* Kosambi, *Introduction to the Study of Indian History* (Bombay 1956, 1975), p. 323.

16. *S.I.I.*, XIV, no.. 95.

17. *Cf.* D. C. *Sircar, Indian Epigraphical Glossary.*

18. Gurukkal, *Agarian System ...*, p. 113, n. 2.

19. Stein, *Peasant State and Society ...*, pp. 167–68.

20. Gurukkal, Diagram on p. 135.

21. Narayanan, *Political and Social Conditions ...*, *op. cit.*, Chapter on 'Economic Conditions' under Land Tenures.

22. M. G. S. Narayanan and Kesavan Veluthat, 'The Traditional Land System of Kerala: Problems of Change and Perspective', Paper presented at the Logan Centenary Seminar on Land Reforms in Kerala, Calicut, 1981.

23. K. M. Gupta, *The Land System of South India between about 800 and 1200* AD, (Lahore, 1933). Completed as a Ph.D. thesis in 1926, London University.

24. E.g., D. N. Jha, *Studies in Early Indian Economic History* (Delhi, 1980).

25. Y. Subbarayalu, *op. cit.*

26. Karashima, *op. cit.*

27. Dharma Kumar, 'Private Property in Asia? The Case of Medieval South India', *Comparative Studies in Society and History*, vol. 27, no. 2, April, 1985.

28. Tirumalai, *op. cit.*

29. Karashima, *South Indian History and Society*, pp. 1–35.

30. *Ibid.*, p. 12.

31. *Ibid.*, pp. 15–35. Subbarayalu is quoted to have personally communicated to Karashima the findings of an unpublished study. *Ibid.*, p. 182. n. 17. Also Table 2 on p. 14. Also Subbarayalu. *State ...*, p. 101.

32. Above. Chapter 2.

33. Karashima. *South Indian History and Society*, Chapter 2.

34. *Ibid.*, p. 20.

35. *Ibid.*, pp. 26–27.

36. *Ibid.*, p. 31.

37. Jha, *Studies in Early Indian Economic History*, pp. 74–89.

38. This is what Kathleen Gough appears to be doing. Gough, 'Modes of Production in South India', *op. cit.*

39. Dharma Kumar, *op. cit.*

40. *Kārāḷa* is generally translated as peasant, tenant, etc., the etymology not being clear. Is it possible to derive it from *karṣaka* in Sanskrit? In that case he would be the cultivating tenant which indeed he appears to have been. *Kār* in the Dravidian languages signifies black and *veḷ*, white; would therefore veḷḷāḷa be treated as a binary opposite of *kārāla*, a symbolic dichromatism?

41. Stein, *Peasant State and Society* ..., p. 168. n.74.

42. Tirumalai, *op. cit.*, pp. 95–98.

43. Dharma Kumar, *op. cit.*

44. Karashima, *South Indian History and Society*, pp. 44–45. Chart 1.

45. This is a common feature in the Pāṇḍya, Cēra and Cōḷa records.

46. Above, Chapter 3.

47. *Indian Feudalism*, 2nd edn. *passim.*

48. Bloch, *Feudal Society*, I. p. 116.

49. *Above*, n. 38.

50. Dharma Kumar, *op. cit.*

51. Jha, 'Relevance of Peasant State and Society ...', *op. cit.* pp. 74–75.

52. Stein, *Peasant State and Society* ..., Chapters 2 and 3.

53. Jha, 'Relevance of Peasant State and Society ...', *op. cit.*, pp. 78–79.

54. Narayanan, *Political and Social Conditions* ..., *op. cit.*

55. R. Champakalakshmi, *op. cit.*

56. Y. Subbarayalu, *op. cit.*

57. Pirenne, *loc. cit.*

58. Suresh, *Historical and Cultural Geography* ..., *op. cit.*, p. 315 quoted in Stein, *Peasant State and Society* ..., p. 103.

59. Elamkulam P. N. Kunjan *Pillai, Janmisampradayam Kēraḷattil, op. cit.*, pp. 18–50.

60. Narayanan, *Political and Social Conditions* ..., *op. cit.*, Chapter on 'Police and Revenue' and Social Systems', Veluthat, *Aryan Brahman Settlements of Ancient Kerala.* (Unpublished M.A. Dissertation. Calicut University. 1974). Appendix II.

61. E.g., Subbarayalu. *State* ..., Chapter 6. esp. Table on p. 86.

62. *E.I.*, XXII. no. 33.

63. *S.I.I.*, VI, no. 57; nos. 48, 50, 58.

64. *Ibid.*, V, no. 1409.

65. Subbarayalu, *State* ..., p. 86.

66. Above, Chapter 3.

67. Irfan Habib, 'The Peasant in Indian History', Presidential Address, Indian History Congress, Kurukshetra, 1982.

68. For the disabilities of the *śudras* in the context of northern India, R. S. Sharma, *Sudras in Ancient India*, 2nd edn (Delhi, 1980), *passim.*

69. Romila Thapar, *A History of India*, Vol. I (Harmondsworth, 1966), p. 77. Thapar takes a position different from, for example, Kosambi, *Introduction to the Study of Indian History*, *op. cit.*, pp. 313–14; Survira Jaiswal, 'Caste in the Socio-Economic Framework of Early India', Presidential Address, Section I, Indian History Congress, Bhuvaneswar, 1977.

70. Stein, *Peasant State and Society* ..., pp. 70–71.

71. Above, Chapter 3.

72. Above, Chapter 1.

73. Above, Chapter 3.

74. *Ibid.*

75. Stein, *Peasant State and Society*, pp. 70–72. He apparently forgets that the brahmans stood to gain if their allies were of a higher caste!

76. Derrett, 'Two Inscriptions ...', *op. cit.*

77. No. 479 of 1908. *ARE.* 1909, p. 94.

78. No. 57 of 1909. *ARE.* 1910, para 60.

79. No. 508 of 1922. See also 208 of 1918 for another instance of the weavers being accorded a special status.

80. *Manu*, X, 16.

81. For a list of the different *jāti*s, *S.I.I.*, VII, 118. Also Subbarayalu, *State* ..., pp. 84–111.

82. *S. I. I.*, II, Introduction.

83. Sastri, *Colas*, pp. 550–52.

84. *ARE.*, 1936–37, para 27. Also Sastri, *Colas*, p. 551.

85. Sastri, *Colas*, p. 550.

86. Noboru Karashima and Y. Subbarayalu, 'Valaṅgai, Idaṅgai, Kāṇiyāḷar and Irājagarattār: Social Conflict in Tamilnadu in the 15th century', in D. N. Jha (ed.), *Feudal Social Formation in Early India*, Delhi (1987), pp. 285–310.

87. Brenda E. F. Beck, *Peasant Society in Konku*, (Vancouver, 1972).

88. Gustav Oppert, *On the Original Inhabitants of Bharatavarsa or India* (Reprint, Delhi, 1972), p. 62.

89. Arjun Appadurai, 'Right and Left Castes in South India', *The Indian Economic and Social History Review*, XI, nos. 2 and 3 (1974), pp. 216–60.

90. Stein, *Peasant State and Society* ..., pp. 173–215.

91. Above, n. 83.

92. Irfan Habib, *Interpreting Indian History* (Shillong, 1985), p. 19.

93. *Ibid.*, p. 20.

94. Above, Chapter 6.

95. M. G. S. Narayanan and Kesavan Veluthat, 'The Bhakti Movement in South India', *op. cit.*

96. *Ibid.*

# Eight

# Conclusion
## Towards a Model

An attempt has been made in the foregoing pages to examine, on the one hand, the image that royalty projected of itself and, on the other, the various aspects of the power structure in the four monarchical states of early medieval south India. The examination of the self-image of royalty brings out several aspects which went into the making of this image–origin myths, dynastic traditions, genealogies, etc. through which the dynasty in general claimed greatness. These aspects also included the presentation of an individual king as having acquired the kṣatriya status, as a *cakravartin*, as a warrior hero, as a protector and fountainhead of all *dharma*, as a munificent donor, as a divine figure, as a patron of arts and culture and finally as of an attractive mien.

The origin myths of the *itihāsa-purāṇa* type suggest that in spite of the clear non-Sanskritic origins of these dynasts, they participated vicariously, as it were, in a pan-Indian tradition of the origin of dynasties. This points to the commonness of the political culture that was evolving in early medieval India which sought legitimacy through what Romila Thapar calls legitimation by descent.[1] This was emulated in the southern regions and the preponderance of Sanskritic ideals there would indicate the influence of the brahmanical sections of the population. Again in the case of the dynastic traditions conforming to the *kāvya-śāstra-nāṭaka* pattern we see that the function was of validating the entire dynasty as of respectable traditions. The same point is underscored by the genealogical portions of the court literature concerning both the remote and the recent past. While accounts of the former helped in claiming an ideological legitimacy for the ruling dynasty, the latter was perhaps aimed at seeking political validation. So also the innumerable claims made to kṣatriya status sought to establish a title to power and authority within the framework of an upper class which had accepted the theory of *varṇāśramadharma* as the organising principle in society. The ideals of the *cakravartin* and the warrior hero helped in seeking the same political validation. This military-political aspect of kingship justified his wielding the coercive power, both for the maintenance of the ideal social order and for purposes of defence and aggrandisements. The positive role of the king in economic and social transformation is brought out by the donor image especially in relation to land. Again, the attributes of divinity, invoking religious symbolism, attempt to legitimise secular power while claims about scholarship, patronage, beauty, etc. provide a cultural dimension to the image.

We have seen that such an image of the ruler was necessary to legitimise and validate the new form of state which had come into existence in the seventh and eighth centuries in south India and which got refined, elaborated and ramified in the late ninth and the tenth centuries. That would naturally raise the question as to why this particular means of legitimation was adopted by the rulers and as to why there should have been any legitimation at all. In the understanding of political theorists, every new or changed form of state requires its own legitimacy.[2] Therefore, if the states in medieval south India sought legitimacy in ways different from those in the earlier periods, it would naturally follow that the kind of state that came into existence in south India in this period was different from the ones that existed there, such as they were.

## I. A CENTRALISED EMPIRE?

This leads us to the major question, what was the nature of state in early medieval south India? In recent years this question has been increasingly engaging the attention of scholars. In fact, ever since the study of early medieval south India was started in the twenties of the present century, questions about the administrative system, provincial and local government, judicial and military administration, etc. had been discussed at great length. They received comprehensive treatment and a certain level of standardisation at the hands of Professor K. A. Nilakanta Sastri in the late 1920s and early 1930s. Sastri presented the picture of a rather highly centralised empire in the Cōḻa country bulwarked by an efficient bureaucracy and sustained, on the one side, by a comprehensive revenue system and, on the other, by a strong coercive power consisting of 'numerous regiments' and 'number less ships'.[3] The glory of such a polity was identified in the cultural expressions such as the arts, architecture and literature of the period which were munificently patronised by the rulers. Within this polity Nilakanta Sastri also identified a large number of autonomous villages, the understanding of the vitality of which was to a great extent his own contribution. This idyllic picture of the village communities was in part the result of the imperialist discourse on the nature of Indian village communities.[4] To accommodate the two rather contradictory aspects of polity, namely, imperial centralisation and local autonomy, Professor Sastri had the following formula: 'the national state, represented by the king's government, enveloped and sustained the groups together'[5] or '... between an able bureaucracy and the active local assemblies ... there was attained a high standard of administrative efficiency and purity, perhaps the highest ever attained by the Hindu state.'[6] Nilakanta Sastri has been successful in locating changes in the nature of monarchy from time to time although this kind of a realistic appreciation is lacking in the writings of those who followed him–Minakshi, Appadorai and Mahalingam.

This is not to say that Nilakanta Sastri's conception of the nature of state in medieval south India is faultless. On the contrary, it is wrought with contradictions and unwarranted assumptions, his own attempts to gloss over such weaknesses making matters only worse. For instance, in spite of his assertions to the contrary, the highly centralised state cannot be reconciled with the presentation of the autonomous and vital local groups. Again, the empirical validity of both these constructs as well as the assumptions behind them has been questioned in the previous chapters.

Instead of viewing the king as one who concentrated in himself all the authority and power of the state, we have seen that he was enjoying the position of an overlord, a suzerain, over a large number of local chiefs, local magnates and local groups. In the matter of the bureaucracy, of which Nilakanta Sastri makes rather too much, the evidence at hand is that the important landed magnates in the localities were identified and made use of by the king as his agents. In fact, it is very doubtful whether the expression 'bureaucracy' can be used to describe these functionaries at all. So also in the matter of revenue administration, far from being a centralised system of taxation where the entire revenue went to the state exchequer, the picture that we have traced is of an arrangement where feudal rent was collected and enjoyed by various levels of a graded hierarchy of intermediaries placed between the state and the producers. The military organisation, too, presents a similar picture: a select band of the king's companions of honour strengthened in times of necessity by similar forces from the chiefly territories owing allegiance to the king and the militia drawn from among the peasants and the artisans apart from some specialists. Administration of justice also tells a similar story: it was carried out generally locally and followed usage and custom standardised in the manuals of social conduct. Such a polity cannot be described as a centralised state.

Nilakanta Sastri's conception of the state in medieval south India, however, had held the ground for at least four decades and Indian scholars who wrote during this period followed him rather blindly. This historiographical tradition was seriously shaken when Burton Stein came out with his critique of this 'conventional historiography'.[7] Perhaps the most enduring contribution of Stein to south Indian historiography is the administration of this shock which shook Clio awake from the slumber of complacency although in doing so he has resorted to exaggerations and even misquotations as we have noted above. This historiographical critique was promptly followed by his own alternative model for explaining the state in medieval south India.

## II. A SEGMENTARY STATE?

This model of the segmentary state, originally constructed by Aidan Southall to explain the Alur society in East Africa, is more anthropological than historical.[8] Based on the idea of pyramidal segmentation advanced by John Middleton and David Tait,[9] the model at times has the characteristics of the segmentary lineage advanced by Marshall Sahlins[10] and the segmented society proposed by Robert Wiebe.[11] Implicit in the model of segmentary society as understood by Stein in the case of medieval south India is the assumption of a non-stratified peasant society, this concept itself being indebted to the neo-populist discourse starting with A. V. Chayanov as well as to such economists, sociologists and anthropologists as Marshall Sahlins, Theodore Shanin, Eric Wolf and others.[12] Within this peasant society which is presented as having come together on bonds of kinship and marriage, Stein identified numerous vertically divided segments. These segments are sought to have been sustained by the balance due to opposition of elements within itself, e.g. the left hand and the right hand castes.

The segmentary state, as adapted to the south Indian situation by Stein is presented to have had the following characteristics:[13]

(1) a dual sovereignty consisting of actual political sovereignty and what is called 'ritual hegemony'
(2) multiplicity of 'centres', each of them exercising political control over a part, or segment, of the political system encompassed by the state but one of them having primacy over the others as a source of ritual hegemony
(3) 'specialised administrative staff' operating at and within the segments and not exclusively the primary centre; and
(4) the distinction of subordinate levels or 'zones' of the segmentary state with a pyramidal organisation which, in contrast with hierarchical forms of political organisation, have a series of relationships between the centre and the peripheries of any particular segment as a replica in miniature of that between the primary centre and the periphery of the entire state.

Each of these characteristics is loaded with assumptions which fail to stand the scrutiny of evidence. We shall take up below each of the above aspects of the segmentary state in some detail to demonstrate Stein's Procrustean exercise.

(1) *Dual Sovereignty:* In distinguishing two kinds of sovereignty, one of the political variety and the other of the ritual kind, Stein is misled by a false distinction between *kṣatra* and *rājadharma* introduced by Robert Lingat.[14] What is sought to be distinguished by Lingat, in reality, is one aspect of the image of royalty from another, as we have seen in our treatment of the self-image of royalty. The ideal of the king as a

warrior-hero, a *cakravartin* and a kṣatriya, all making claims to worthy ancestry is as much part of this image as that of the king as a donor, and a fountain-head and protector of *dharma* which held the ideal moral order. In arguing that the former set of attributes or claims represented real political authority and the other, a ritual hegemony, Stein follows the confusion that 'conventional historiography' had in mixing up the ideal with the actual and thereby presenting a blurred picture, although his purpose is professedly to correct this. The attempt to elaborate on the ritually incorporative character of the kingship and the attempt to read a lot of meanings into the attributes of divinity claimed for the king in Indian tradition confuse the ideal for the actual. We have seen in our discussion of the image of royalty that there are aspects which lent colour to the portrait of the monarch, and the portrait itself was among the apparatuses of legitimising the new form of state.

If these aspects of the image of royalty in medieval south India are identified as representing the 'ritual sovereignty' in the segmentary state, real political sovereignty is located separately in the segments of the macro-region in the *nāḍu* divisions each with its own chiefs, corporate bodies and all the other details. In each of these segments the chiefs or the 'little kings' exercised political authority as much as the Cōḻas did in their *nāḍu* segment in the Kaveri delta, the only difference in Stein's understanding being that the latter's ritual hegemony was accepted by the other chiefs. Among the more important means of getting this ritual hegemony accepted were, according to Stein, the 'royal Śiva cult' and the patronage of *brahmadēyams*, both of which are presented to have been begun from the time of Rājarāja I. It is well known that the worship of agamaic deities such as Śiva and Viṣṇu had been quite popular long before the establishment of the Cōḻa Empire in south India and that the predecessors of Rājarāja had patronised these sects in a big way. This is not to deny the role of religion as a political tool or the importance of the temples of Tanjavur and Gaṅgaikoṇḍacōḻapuram in the cultural devise of political integration of the Cōḻa empire; but to isolate one aspect of the agamaic religion which formed part of the techniques of ideological legitimation and to exaggerate it beyond all proportions is not sustainable.

Stein's argument about how the *brahmadēyams* were used in the political world for purposes of extending the ritual hegemony of the rulers too is untenable. It is well known that from the time of the establishment of the south Indian states in the Tamil country, the *brahmadēyams* had played a major role, an aspect which is sufficiently understood by Stein himself in a rather lengthy chapter on the Coromandel brahmadēya village. To assert that it was after Rājarāja came across the organisation of the *brahmadēyas* in Kerala following his invasion of South Travancore, signified by the expression *Kāndaḷūrśālai-kalamaṟuttaruḷi*, is to contradict oneself. What is most interesting is to regard the great Cōḻa monarch to have been inspired by the Huzur Office Plates of the Āy Chief Karunandaḍakkan in organising such *brahmadēyams* in the Cōḻa country. As a corollary to this, Rājarāja is also said to have studied the colophons to the Tamil poetical work *Patiṟṟuppattu* which, we are made to believe, were available only in Travancore, and on the model of which he styled his *meykkīrttis* or inscriptional preambles.

(2) *Multiplicity of Centres:* Closely related to the idea of dual sovereignty is that of the multiplicity of centres. As we have seen in an earlier chapter, such centres in Stein's understanding are the large number of *nāḍu* divisions, each of which has been rightly regarded as a peasant locality. However, Stein's treatment of these *nāḍu* divisions is loaded with too many assumptions. They are looked upon as the atomic aspects of the segmentary organisation in medieval south India. The salient features of these units were, according to him, restricted marriage and kinship networks, narrow territorial social coalitions beyond kinsmen and locally based agrarian relationships, political and religious affiliations and loyalties. We have seen that our evidence would not support any of these assumptions.[15] It would appear that Stein is begging the question.

Each of these *nāḍu* divisions is described as having been characterised by almost every detail entitling it to be presented as a microcosm of the macrocosm of the Cōḻa state. They include a political chief, an 'inner core' at the centre of every *nāḍu*, military units under its command and such other aspects as are necessary to qualify each of these divisions to be a state in itself. What Stein identifies as the chiefs are in reality a large number of landed magnates, on whom royal titles were bestowed such as *mūvēndavēḷan, araiyan* etc., and a large number of whom are met with in the same *nāḍu* divisions. We have demonstrated that these landed magnates were identified and made use of by the Cōḻa state as its agents. Similarly, the assumption of an 'inner core' and an outer pulp in the homogeneous *nāḍu* units is unsupported. Again in the case of the existence of military units under the command of the different *nāḍu* divisions, we have seen that there is nothing on record to warrant this assumption. It would appear that Stein is distorting evidence in order to fit it into his neat pattern.

(3) *Specialised Administrative Staff:* The same difficulty besets Stein's supposition about the 'specialised administrative staff' in the Cōḻa state. On the one side, he vehemently rejects the idea of the existence of such a staff, what Nilakanta Sastri calls a bureaucracy. On the other hand, he seeks to identify functionaries such as *nāḍu kūṟu, nāḍu vagai, nāḍu kaṇkāṇi nāyagam*, etc., as forming part of the specialised administrative staff of the *nāḍu* units. We have seen above that these functionaries at the *nāḍu* level were as much the agents of the king's government, as were the *adhikāris, ōlaināyagams*, etc. at the centre. Thus, Stein's idea of the different segments having their own staff of administrative personnel if at a reduced scale in comparison with the centre does not have any empirical validity.

(4) *Pyramidal Organisation:* The segmentary state as understood by Stein in the case of medieval South India comprises different subordinate levels of zones organised in a pyramidal fashion. In this, the relationship between the centre and the peripheral units is the same as the relationship between the prime centre and all peripheral focusses of power, but in a reduced form. There is, however, a contrast which this organisation has with hierarchical forms of political organisation where, even though subordinate levels of organisation exist, executive authority is of different kinds at the different levels. In elaborating this aspect Stein makes use of his distinction among different kinds of *nāḍus* with reference to the seat of the Cōḻa political power. They are the central *nāḍus*, the intermediary *nāḍus* and the peripheral *nāḍus*. However, as we have noted in one of the above chapters, this classification is not supported by adequate evidence.

The very idea of pyramidal segmentation cannot be applied to the highly evolved political systems of medieval south India. This conception is proposed to explain tribal situations as has been done by Middleton and Tait and Sahlins as well as by Southall in the context of the Alur society. In trying to apply this model to a stratified society of a predominantly agrarian nature, one will naturally have to distort and misrepresent evidence. For one thing, Stein does not recognise the massive evidence of social stratification within peasantry, he being concerned with a world of 'peasants without lords'. Following this, he postulates a brahman-peasant alliance which the evidence does not warrant. Looking for the balancing and opposed elements to complete the picture of a pyramidally segmented society, Stein is at pains to identity such a relationship between the *iḍaṅgai* and *valaṅgai* castes. On the whole, therefore, the segmentary state model proposed by Burton Stein for explaining the socio-political situation of early medieval south India fails to inspire confidence.

## III. THE ASIATIC MODE OF PRODUCTION?

In spite of the 'decent burial' given to the time-(dis)honoured concept of the Asiatic Mode of Production, which is a refined Marxian variant of Oriental Despotism, by scholars like D. D. Kosambi, Irfan Habib, R. A. L. H. Gunawardana, Hindess and Hirst, Bipan Chandra, Perry Anderson and others,[16] an attempt has been made recently by Kathleen Gough to resurrect and use it in the context of the state in early medieval south India.[17] To be sure, she considers a refined variant of the construct of the Asiatic Mode of Production itself, following the work of D. Ribeiro.[18] Accordingly she describes the Cōḻa state as an 'archaic state', the characteristics of which are generally those of the Asiatic Mode of Production with little or no private property, the identity of tax and rent, the existence of large scale irrigation works managed by the state, the prevalence of slavery on a large scale and finally a despotic ruler. The data-base of Gough is so outdated that she does not consider even the works of Nilakanta Sastri, being familiar only with a work completed in 1926.[19] In the context of Kerala, which area is also taken up for consideration, Gough is not familiar with most of the historical research undertaken in the twentieth century. It goes without saying, therefore, that a generalisation based on such outdated information cannot hold much water. Moreover, we have seen in our examination in the previous chapters that most of the characteristics listed above did not simply exist except perhaps the inter-changeability of tax and rent which is as much characteristic of any other pre-capitalist socio-economic formation. Therefore, the idea of Asiatic Mode of Production is not worthy of consideration as an alternative to explain polity and society in medieval south India.

## IV. AN EARLY STATE?

Another model that has been proposed recently as an explanation for the Cōḷa state in medieval south India is that of the 'Early State'. This model is made use of by Y. Subbarayalu[20] and later by James Heitzman to explain in the Cōḷa state.[21] Originally derived from the model proposed by Henry Claessen and Peter Skalnik, the early state has been used to explain a wide variety of political systems.[22] After analysing twenty-one case studies, Claessen and Skalnik define the 'early state' as a centralised socio-political organisation for the regulation of social relations in a complex stratified society divided into at least two basic strata, or emergent classes–viz., the rulers and the ruled–whose relations are characterised by political dominance of the former and tributary obligations of the latter, legitimised by a common ideology of which reciprocity is the basic principle.[23]

They distinguish three different varieties of the early state, namely the inchoate, the typical and the transitional. The model itself, which tries to generalise on a vast variety of systems ranging from early Pharaonic Egypt (3000 BC) well into modern times in the Jimma and Kachari in the twentieth century including the Mauryan state in India,[24] is a category which seeks to include too much and hence fails to explain anything. Recently Jerome Jacobson has argued that the Harappan state too can be described as an 'early state'.[25] In the case of the Cōḷa state, although Subbarayalu would take the Cōḷa state 'tentatively' an 'early state', he is himself aware that' it is difficult to explain the historical process of the Cōḷa state by applying the classificatory criteria of the 'early state'.[26] Even Heitzman, who does not, significantly, acknowledge Subbarayalu in this matter, is not very sure: the Cōḷa polity according to him was an 'early state' only in the sense that 'its agrarian base and the political power of its elites were in an early stage of expansion'.[27]

Thus, we see that none of the existing explanations of the nature of state in early medieval south India is successful in explaining the phenomenon. We shall propose our own view of the state below.

## V. THE FEUDAL STATE

The hypothesis of feudalism has not been systematically tested in the context of the historical situation of early medieval south India. True, there have been casual suggestions and loose applications of the feudal jargon in the context of this part of the country in this period. Thus Nilakanta Sastri and Mahalingam would speak of 'feudatories' in early medieval south India.[28] They know about the 'king's barons'; they also speak of 'oath of fealty'.[29] Similarly M. S. Govindasamy and V. Balambal have written books on the role of feudatories in Pallava history and Cōḻa history in south India.[30] But in none of these works there is a rigorous formulation of the concept of feudalism. Nor do they bring out the interplay of the various forces, where economy, society and polity will have to be looked at in their totality. This is not to deny the importance of their contributions; but when conceptualisation in historiography was at its infancy in south India, pioneers could not bring to bear upon their work a consistency of arguments everywhere.

Noboru Karashima has suggested that at least the later years of the Cōḻa rule could be described as feudal although his suggestion is also rather tentative.[31] More recently Karashima has made a detailed exposition especially in relation to the post-Cōḻa period.[32] But in none of his writings has he attempted a systematic application of the feudal model to the situation obtaining in early medieval south India as a whole.

In a joint study of the *bhakti* movement in south India, M. G. S. Narayanan and the present writer had attempted a systematic application of the idea of feudalism to the socio-economic formation obtaining in South India in the early medieval period.[33] In the present study we seek to elaborate and extend it to other aspects which were not covered in the previous study. In doing so we are conscious of the reservations expressed by scholars about the applicability of the idea of feudalism to the Indian context.

It was D. D. Kosambi who first sought to apply systematically the idea of feudalism in the context of Indian history in the fifties of the present century.[34] Kosambi's understanding of a dichotomy between feudalism as a product of administrative action ('feudalism from above'), and feudalism as an evolution at the local levels ('feudalism from below'), when propounded, was actually pioneering. Before scholars had started questioning this kind of unnecessary bifurcation, his cue had been taken for elaboration and refinement, in this particular case by R. S. Sharma.[35] Sharma demonstrated with the help of land grants how the alienation of land and along with it the administrative, judicial and fiscal rights considerably eroded state power and placed a graded hierarchy of intermediaries between the state and the actual producers.[36] The symptoms of the genesis of this formation were identified by Sharma in the late Gupta and immediate post-Gupta periods in the history of northern India. At the back of this, however, Sharma identified two major factors: (a) a crisis in society and (b) a decline of trade and decay of the urban centres. The former was identified in the pathological fear of the Kali Age, references to which abound in texts dating from the Gupta and immediate post-Gupta periods.[37] Sharma has argued that this indicated a situation where the existing social formation failed to contain the newly emerging means and relations of production. Following Sharma, B. N. S. Yadava has added further material to Sharma's thesis that the references to the Kali Age indicated a transition from pre-feudal to feudal forms.[38] Again, R. S. Sharma himself has tried to map and locate the decline of trade and decay of the urban centres in the Ganga valley.[39] The concomitant economic change caused a total reorientation in the systems of production and distribution where, instead of salary, land as service tenure was increasingly preferred. In a most recent study Sharma has worked out the process of urban decay in various parts of India from the fourth to the tenth centuries AD.[40] Now, with major economic changes and social crises, a transition to a new formation around the middle of the first millennium AD is generally accepted by scholars in the case of north India.

However, this should not be taken to mean that the 'feudal India' thesis is unanimously accepted by the academia.[41] Immediately after

Sharma delivered his lectures on Indian feudalism in the University of Calcutta, but before they were available in print, D. C. Sirkar edited and published a series of articles.[42] He also brought out other publications questioning the validity of the idea of feudalism in the context of India. Even more serious are the objections raised by Harbans Mukhia.[43] Mukhia assumes the existence of a relatively autonomous peasantry with more or less complete control over the means of production. The absence of the archetypal manor in India is also held out by Mukhia. Burton Stein, too, rejects the viability of the feudal thesis in the context of early medieval India, although his work is concerned with south India.[44] Stein has also argued that to speak of the erosion of state power as a result of the parcelling out of authority as well as land, one will have to assume that the state enjoyed all such powers in the first instance.[45] This argument is shared by Hermann Kulke.[46]

Sharma has himself ably shown that peasantry in early medieval India was subjected to several disabilities and servility and that to speak of a free peasantry in this context would be opposed to evidence.[47] The absence of the manorial system or of the fief as a 'legally constituted political sub-region'[48] need not be taken as a serious objection for, that is not one of the essential features of feudalism. The idea of having all rights concentrated at the centre of the state as a precondition for alienating them does not appear to be sustainable. In fact, in most cases it is the superior right which was created *de novo* that was granted along with land which carried with it several administrative and judicial rights.

At any rate the application of the model of feudalism in the context of south India will have to define clearly what is meant in this context by feudalism. It is well known that there is a vast variety of definitions of the concept of feudalism. In his classic study of the feudal society in medieval Europe, Marc Bloch has identified the following 'fundamental features of European feudalism':

> A subject peasantry; widespread use of the service tenement (i.e., the fief) instead of a salary, which was out of the question; the supremacy of a class of specialised warriors; ties of obedience and protection which bind man to man and, within the warror class, assume the distinctive form called vassalage; fragmentation of authority, leading to disorder; and in the midst of all this, the survival of other forms of association,

> family and State, of which the latter, during the second feudal age, was to acquire renewed strength–such then seem to be the fundamental features of European feudalism.[49]

F. L. Ganshof, who has been described as the doyen of the students of feudalism, has defined feudalism with the emphasis laid on the aspects of dependence and hierarchy. According to him:

> Feudalism may be conceived as a form of society possessing well-marked features which can be defined without difficulty. They may be summarised as follows: a development pushed to extremes of the element of personal dependence in society, with a specialised military class occupying the higher levels in the social scale; an extreme subdivision of the rights of real property; a graded system of rights over land created by this subdivision and corresponding in broad outline to the grades of personal dependence just referred to; and a dispersal of political authority amongst a hierarchy of persons who exercise in their own interest powers normally attributed to the State and which are often, in fact, derived from its break-up.[50]

While there is little to differ from these classic understandings, another more recent definition sounds more acceptable. Enriched as much by a first-hand knowledge of the Japanese experience as by the empirical studies and theoretical refinement on European feudalism, the one offered by Noboru Karashima is more succinct and, also, more in the Marxist tradition. According to him feudalism is understood theoretically to have had the following four characteristics:[51]

(1) the basic direct producers are not slaves but peasants who own the means of production themselves,

(2) local magnates, who possess superior rights to the land that the peasants cultivate, subdue the peasants under their control and extract surplus produce by means of extra-economic coersion [*sic*],

(3) political power assumes a hierarchical structure which is sustained by land grants among the ruling class and also by a certain ideology, and

(4) commodity production is not generalised but limited only to the surplus portion which is appropriated by the exploiting class.

We shall examine these aspects below:

(1) The basic direct producers in a feudal system own the means of production themselves in a very technical sense.[52] They are not themselves 'owned' by others in the sense of the slaves being owned by their masters. In the context of the situation in early medieval south India, we have in the *kuṭi*s the primary producers. In the previous chapter we saw that the *kuṭi*s in large numbers were at the bottom of the graded hierarchy of those who enjoyed a certain amount of right over land.[53] These *kuṭi*s were not strictly speaking bonded in the same way as a peasant in the feudal society was not. We have seen changing fortunes of the *kuṭi*s—some developing into huge landed magnates and some others getting reduced to the position of landless labourers. That did not, however, change the pattern of relations in the system of production and distribution.

We have also seen the existence of a sizeable force of labour almost comparable to the serfs in the feudal context. There are a number of instances where the labourers are transferred along with land at the time of the land being sold, mortgaged or gifted. This nature of the labourer being tied down to the piece of land on which he works strikes a favourable comparison with classical serfdom. Closely linked with this bonded nature of labour is the practice of collecting rent in the form of labour itself. In our examination of the revenue administration we have seen the significant fact of the existence of the *veṭṭi* (Skt. *viṣṭi*) which may be compared to corvée in medieval Europe. The significance of the labour-rent such as *veṭṭi* and *muṭṭaiyāḷ* gradually being replaced by a produce-rent, payable in kind, has also been brought out.[54] In the classical discussion of the genesis of capitalist ground-rent, Karl Marx has characterised this phenomenon of produce-rent gradually overtaking labour-rent as typically feudal, where, in spite of the greater sophistication in the latter instance, there is no difference at all in the mode of production.[55]

(2) The possession of superior rights by local magnates over land as well as the extra-economic coercion by which those magnates extract surplus from the primary producer are among the foremost characteristics of the feudal mode of production. In the case of medieval south India both these characteristics are found. Apart from the political chiefs known to existing historiography as 'feudatories'

and members of the royal families who owned large extents of land, there were other landed magnates, both individuals and institutions. We have seen in our discussions of the titleholders and the evolution of property rights that a large number of landed magnates existed in the Cōḻa country especially in the period of and after Rājarāja I.[56] In certain cases such individuals are stated to 'own' whole villages. We have seen that such magnates, sporting titles such as *uḍaiyān, vēḷān, kiḻān, araiyan, mūvēndavēḷan* etc., often prefixing the name or title of a Cōḻa king to this title (e.g., Mummuḍicōḻamūvendavēḷār), were enlisted in the service of the state as its functionaries.[57] Often they had to be far from the area where they owned their land, as has been indicated by a large number of instances. This is the situation as it obtained in the Cōḻa country. In the absence of data as copious as in the Cōḻa Empire, one is not as clear about the situation in other parts of south India. But there is no reason to believe that such individual peasant proprietors did not exist in those regions as well.

Among the landed magnates in south India the greater importance should actually be given to the large number of institutions.[58] They included the *agrahārams* of brahmans holding land as their common property (*brahmadēyam*); temples holding land as *dēvadānam*, Jain and Buddhist centres holding land as *paḷḷiccandam*; educational institutions known as *śālai*s enjoying land as *śālābhogam*. There were also other eleemosynary tenures known as *veṭṭāppēṟu, kaṇimuṟṟuṭṭu* etc., the exact import of which is not clear to us; but that they were also landholdings of a particular variety amounting to being landed magnates is beyond doubt. Given the situation with such a wide variety of landed magnates controlling production, the system can certainly bear comparison with a feudal system, especially when the fact of their subjecting peasantry and extracting surplus from them through extra-economic coercion is taken into consideration.

Since these landed magnates, both individuals and institutions, were not directly engaged in production, they enjoyed only certain superior rights over the land which the peasants cultivated. In our discussions concerning the managerial groups and concerning the land rights, we have seen that a variety of shades of right were created over land.[59] In certain cases such rights were granted to the magnates by the state and in certain other cases such rights of the magnates were recognised by the state. Such landed magnates with superior rights over the peasants exercised various administrative, judicial and fiscal rights over the actual cultivators. In fact, we have seen that the administrative and judicial machinery in early medieval south India was highly decentralised with a large amount of power exercised by these individuals and institutions. In the case of revenue, there was a virtual inter-changeability of tax and rent typical of the precapitalist formation. Even this revenue was extracted by invoking law, religion, force, etc.[60] This points to the extra-economic nature of coercion in extracting surplus from the primary producer which is typical of a feudal formation. Again, stratification within peasantry and its subject nature are points which have been underlined by our study.

(3) A hierarchically oriented political structure sustained by both land grants and a certain ideology is another characteristic feature of feudalism. In the political structure of early medieval south India we have seen a pyramidally organised hierarchy. Ideally it looked like the typical feudal pyramid with the king at the top, with the feudatory chieftains immediately below him, with the local groups of *nāḍus, brahmadēyams* and *nagarams* either below them or directly below the king, the tenants and cultivators below these groups and finally the landless labourers at the bottom. In the matter of administrative functions in areas directly under the king, he managed affairs through 'his men' who were recruited from among the landed magnates. In areas under the control of the feudatories, the situation was similar but even there the state tried to penetrate both through the state functionaries and, in the case of the Cōḻa state under Rājarāja I and immediately after him, through even converting these feudatory chieftains into state functionaries for a time. The affairs of the relatively autonomous groups such as the *nāḍu, brahmadēyam, nagaram*, etc., were also subject to the overall authority of the state functioning at the centre.

In the matter of military organisation a similar hierarchy has been observed. Apart from the fact of individual soldiers taking oaths of fealty to their lord as in the case of the *vēḷaikkārar*, we have seen that the coercive power in medieval south India consisted of a band of trusted 'companions of honour' around the king supplemented by similar forces of the feudatory chieftains and a few specialists in different branches of the art of warfare. There are also references to mercenaries taken from among peasants and artisans. A kind of exaction made in the countryside known as *pāḍikāval* which was a fee for the protection of the country collected by the chieftains, land assigned on service tenure to soldiers known as *paṇiccavirutti*, etc., point to the military aspect of the feudal character of polity in south India. The numerous 'pacts' entered into among the different feudatory chieftains, known as *nilamaitīṭṭu*, show in unmistakable terms the feudal character of equality amounting to peerage among the chieftains on the one side and, on the other, the lord-vassal relationship between the king and the chieftains.

The picture presented by aspects of judicial administration is not different. Although the king was theoretically the source of all law in the typical feudal pattern, in actual practice law meant the regularisation of local customs and usage. Administration of justice was generally carried out by local groups such as the *ūr, brahmadēyam, nagaram*, etc., with a highly local and communal character. In certain cases that we have seen, there are instances of legislation being effected through the decision of such corporate groups and then being reduced to standard legal practices at a later point in time. This shows the decentralised nature of judicial administration with the king certainly reserving the final authority at least in the case of the brahman villages.

This hierarchically oriented political structure in almost every aspect was sustained by a graded hierarchy in society which itself was a reflection of the varying shades of land rights. In fact, we have seen in a previous chapter that this hierarchy expressed itself in the paradigm of *jāti*. *Jāti*, it has been shown, suited the interests of the differentiated society in an ideal manner. The fact of this graded hierarchy with infinite variations in social and ritual status being ramified in this period points to it being most acceptable in the context of the feudal society in south India. Although the *jāti* had its origins in an earlier period and in another context, the mutations it underwent during the feudal age, with the provision for *saṅkīrṇajāti* was most suited to the contemporary social formation. Such a structure, we have seen, was held together by the ideology of *varṇāśramadharma* and *bhakti*. The ideology of *bhakti*, we have shown elsewhere, was the projection of the temple cult. The deity-devotee relationship, etherialised in *bhakti*, was a translation of the lord-vassal relationship into the religious jargon. In fact, the social function of religious architecture, sculpture and painting in this period will be worth analysing from this point of view.

(4) In the feudal set-up commodity production is always under the tutelage of agriculture, a situation which has been described by Karl Marx as petty-production. It does not involve production addressed to the market. Such commodity production as existed was limited only to the surplus and was promptly appropriated by the exploiting class. This is clearly noticeable in the case of medieval south India. We do come across artisanal activities such as weaving, oil pressing, etc. Most of the artisanal products, however, were consumed by those who did not re-cycle the produce into the economy: kings, queens, chieftains, temples and other magnates. Thus, in spite of the existence of some amount of commodity production, it did not break the barriers of the closed rural economy of feudal south India.

A similar picture is presented by the evidence of trade also. True, there was trade, both local and long-distance, in south India during the period under study. But such trade was always marginal to economy and society. Again, we have seen the traders investing in land, a point which underscores the predominance of agriculture. A similar character existed in the case of the urban centres also. Many towns, which pre-existed the period with which we are concerned, showed symptoms of decline during our period. Others were what are described as 'temple towns', not co-ordinating artisanal and trading activities in a big way.

On the whole, therefore, it would appear that the best description of society and polity in medieval south India would be that it was feudal. However, in saying this one need not assume that there was a one-to-one correspondence between the archetypal feudalism of, say, France and that of south India. The adjective in *Indian* feudalism as R. S. Sharma has elaborated is significant; we will qualify our usage further as *South Indian* feudalism in the context of this study. We do recognise some possible limitations of this model for explaining state and society in medieval south India. For instance, it is true that south India had not experienced an earlier classical society in the pre-feudal phase nor is there evidence of a clearly identifiable slave mode of production in a period anterior to that of our study. But if one accepts the argument of Amalendu Guha, one can postulate the emergence of a feudal formation directly out of tribal bearings.[61] Similarly, it is not necessary to postulate the transformation of slaves into serfs or the substitution of the former by the latter, as a pre-condition for the formation of a feudal society. It is true that the forces that brought about the transition into a feudal society in this part of the country have not been isolated and analysed by historians; nor have we taken up such problems in the limited context of our present study. It may be that the earliest form of state in this part of the country took the feudal form, given the character of socio-economic forces working here and the ideology which legitimised them. Thus, if one is not dogmatic about a unilinear pattern in historical development, the model of south Indian feudalism may be proposed to explain the political and social conditions in early medieval south India.

## NOTES

1. Romila Thapar, 'Legitimation Politique et Filiation: le Varna Kshatriya en Inde du Nord', *op. cit.*

2. Cf. Lawrence Krader, 'The State in History', *Studies in History*, IV, 2, pp. 167–80.

3. Sastri, *Colas*, pp. 447–48, *et passim.*

4. *Ibid.*, p. 486.

5. *Ibid.*, p. 488.

6. *Ibid.*, p. 514.

7. Stein, 'State and Agrarian Order ...', *op. cit.*

8. Stein, 'The Segmentary State ...', *op. cit.*; *idem, Peasant State and Society....* The idea of Segmentary State is borrowed from Aidan Southall, *The Alur Society, op. cit.*

9. Middleton and Tait develop the idea of territorial segmentation in John Middleton and David Tait, *Tribes Without Rules* (London, 1958).

10. Marshall D. Sahlins, 'The Segmentary Lineage: An Organization of Predatory Expansion', *American Anthropologist*, LXIII, No. 2 (1961), pp. 332–45.

11. Rober H. Widebe, *The Segemented Society* (New York, 1975).

12. D. N. Jha, 'The Relevance of Peasant State and Society....', *op. cit.*, pp. 74–75.

13. Summarised from Stein, *Peasant State and Society ...*, p. 274.

14. Robert Lingat, *The Classical Law of India*, translated from the French, with additions, by J. Duncan M. Derrett (New Delhi, 1973), pp. 207–37.

15. Above, Chapter 5.

16. Above, Chapter 1, n.l.

17. Kathleen Gough, 'Modes of Production in Southern India', *Economic and Political Weekly*, Annual Number, February, 1980.

18. Darcy Ribeiro, *The Civilisational Process* (Harper Torchbooks, 1968).

19. K. M. Gupta, *The Land System of South India between about 800 and 1200 AD*, (Lahore, 1933), originally submitted as a Ph.D. thesis to London University, 1926.

20. Y. Subbarayalu, 'The Cola State', *op. cit.*

21. J. Heitzman, 'State Formation in South India', *op. cit.*

20. H. J. M. Claessen and Peter Skalnik (ed.), *The Early State* (The Hague, 1978).

23. *Ibid.*, p. 640.

24. Sundarsan Seneviratne, 'The Mauryan State', in Claessen and Skalnik (ed.), *op. cit.*, pp. 381–402.

25. Jerome Jacobson, 'The Harappan Civilization: An Early State', in Jerome Jacobson (ed.), *Studies in the Archaeology of India and Pakistan* (New Delhi,1986).

26. Subbarayalu, 'The Cola State', *op. cit.*, p. 304.

27. Heitzman, *op. cit.*, p. 61.

28. Above, Chapter 3.

29. Above, Chapter 4.

30. Above, Chapter 3.

31. Karashima, *South Indian History and Society*, Introduction.

32. Noboru Karashima, 'Nayaka Rule in North and South Arcot Districts in South India during the sixteenth Century', *Acta Asiatica*, 48 (1985), pp. 1–26.

33. M. G. S. Narayanan and Kesavan Veluthat, 'The Bhakti Movement in South India', *op. cit.*

34. Kosambi, *Introduction to the Study of Indian History, op. cit.*, Chapters 9 and 10.

35. R. S. Sharma, 'The Origins of Feudalism in India', *Journal of the Economic and Social History of the Orient*, I, Part 3 (1958) and *idem., Aspects of Political Ideas and Institution in Ancient India* (Delhi, 1959), esp. Chapter on Gupta Polity are the two earliest attempts where Sharma tested the idea of Feudalism. This was taken up for elaboration in a series of lectures given to the University of Calcutta. Sharma, *Indian Feudalism* (Calcutta, 1965), Sharma has further refined and developed this concept in his later studies.

36. Sharma, *Indian Feudalism* 2nd edn. (Delhi, 1980). 1980).

37. R. S. Sharma, 'The Kali Age: A Period of Social Crisis', in S. N.

Mukherjee (ed.), *India: History and Thought* (*Essays in Honour of Professor A.L. Basham*) (Calcutta, 1982).

38. B. N. S. Yadava, 'The Accounts of the Kali Age and the Social Transitions from Antiquity to Middle Ages', *Indian Historical Review*, V, no. 182 (July 1978: January 1979).

39. R. S. Sharma, 'Decline of Trade and Decay of Urban Centres in Gangetic Valley in the Gupta and Post-Gupta Times', *Proceedings of the Indian History Congress* (Muzaffarpur, 1972).

40. R. S. Sharma, *Urban Decay in India* (Delhi, 1987).

41. A major section of historians such as Romila Thapar, Irfan Habib, B. D. Chattopadhyaya and a few others are still not sure about the exact way in which early medieval India could be classified, although they recognise the mid-first millennium AD as having witnessed a change in the entire socio-political formation.

42. D. C. Sircar (ed.), *Land System and Feudalism in Ancient India* (Calcutta, 1966); *idem, Studies in the Society and Administration of Ancient and Medieval India* (Calcutta, 1967); *idem, Studies in Indian Coins* (Delhi 1968); *idem, Landlordism and Tenancy in Ancient and Medieval India as Revealed by Epigraphical Records* (Lucknow, 1969); *idem, Political Administrative System of Ancient and Medieval India* (Delhi, 1974) etc. All these objections, however, have been effectively met by R. S. Sharma, 'Indian Feudalism Retouched', *Indian Historical Review*, II, ii (1974).

43. Harbans Mukhia, 'Was There Feudalism in Indian History?', Presidential Address, Section II. Indian History Congress, Waltair, 1979.

44. *Ibid.*, Stein, 'State and Agrarian Order ..., *op. cit.*, summarily rejects the viability of feudalism as a category to explain the formation.

45. *Ibid.*

46. Kulke, 'Fragmentation and Segmentation ...', *op. cit.*

47. R. S. Sharma, 'How Feudal was Indian Feudalism', *Journal of Peasant Studies*, vol. XII, no. 4 (February, 1984).

48. D. N. Jha, 'Introduction', in D. N. Jha (ed.), *Feudal Social Formation in Early India* (Delhi, 1987) has effectively countered this argument.

49. Marc Bloch, *Feudal Society*, II, p. 446.

50. F. L. Ganshof, *'Feudalism'*. 3rd edn, (London, 1979), p. 1.

51. Noboru Karashima, *'Nayaka Rule ...'*, *op. cit.*, p. 2, n. 6.

52. *Cf.* Marx, *Capital* III (Moscow, 1971), pp. 190–91; Maurice Dobb, *Studies in the Development of Capitalism*. (London, 1963), pp. 35–36.

53. Above, Chapter 7.

54. Above, Chapter 4.

55. *Ibid.*

56. Above, Chapter 2.

57. *Ibid.*

58. Above, Chapters 5, 6 and 7.

59. *Ibid.*

60. Perry Anderson, however, considers extra-economic coercion not typical of the feudal formations. Anderson. *Lineages ..., op. cit.*, pp. 403–04. But Marx is very clear about this. *Capital*, III, pp. 790–91.

61. Amalendu Guha, 'Tribalism to Feudalism in Assam: 1600–1750'. *Indian Historical Review.* I, I (March 1974). In a booklet prepared by M. G. S. Narayanan, A. P. Ibrahim Kunju, M. P. Sreekumaran Nair, M. R. Raghava Varier and the present writer for the Department of Public Relations, Government of Kerala, this idea is suggested, too. M. G. S. Narayanan, *et al., Kerala Through the Ages* (Trivandrum, 1976), Section I, 'From Tribalism to Feudalism'.

# Select Bibliography

## PRIMARY SOURCES


*Administrative Reports of the Archaeological Department of Cochin.*

*Administrative Reports of the Archaeological Department of Travancore.*

*Annual Reports of the Mysore Archaeological Departments*, Bangalore, 1905–56.

*Annual Reports on (South Indian) Epigraphy, 1887–.*

Anonymous, *Pāṇḍyar Ceppēḍukal Pattu*, Madras, 1966.

*Bulletins of the Rama Varma Research Institute*, Trichur.

*Damilica, Journal* of the State Department of Archaeology, Madras, 1970.

*Epigraphia India* (*E.I*), 1892–.

*Indian Antiquary*, 1872–1923.

Gopalacharyar, K. (ed.) *Nālāyira Divya Prabandham*, Madras 1959.

Gopalaier, A. (ed.) *Nandikkalambagam*, Madras, 1927.

*Inscriptions (Texts) of the Pudukkottai State Arranged According to Dynasties*, Pudukkottai, 1929.

Karashima, Noboru 'A Bibliography of South Indian Epigraphy', *Journal of Asian and African Studies*, no. 6, Tokyo, 1973.

Krishnamacharlu, C.R. *List of Inscriptions Copied by the Office of the Superintendent for Epigraphy*, Delhi, 1941.

Krishnamacharyar, E. (ed.) *Guruparamaparāprabhāvam*, Madras, 1927.

Nagaswami, R. *Seminar on Inscriptions*, Madras, 1966.

———. *Tañjaipperuvuḍaiyār Kōil Kalveṭṭugaḷ*, Madras, 1969.

———. (ed.) *Kanniyākumari Kalveṭṭugaḷ*, Madras, 1972, 1979.

———. *Seminar on Hero Stones*, Madras, 1974.

Nilakanta Sastri, K. A. (ed.) *Foreign Notices of South India*, Madras, 1939.

Puliyurk-Kesikan (ed.) *Kaliṅgattupparaṇi*, Madras, 1958.

Raghavan Pillai, K. (trans. and ed.) *Muṣikavamśam*, Trivandrum, 1983.

Ramachandran Chettiyar, C. M. (ed.) *Koṅgudeśarājākkaḷ*, Madras, 1950.

Sircar, D. C. *Indian Epigraphy*, Delhi, 1965.

———. *Indian Epigraphical Glossary*, Delhi, 1966.

*South Indian Inscriptions*, 24 Vols, 1891–1981.

Srinivasa Aiyar, K. R. (ed.) *Inscriptions in the Pudukkottai State*, Pudukkottai, Part I, 1941; Part II, 1946.

Subramaniyam, K. (ed.) *Periya Purāṇam*, Srivaikuntam, 1974.

*Studies in Epigraphy (Bharatiya Purabhilekha Patrika); Journal of the Epigraphical Society of India*, Mysore, 1974–.

Subrahmanyan, T. N. (ed.) *South Indian Temple Inscriptions*, Madras, vol. I, 1953; Vol. II, 1954, Vol. III, Part I, 1955; Vol. III, Part II, 1957.

Subrahmanyan, T. N. (ed.) *Thirty Pallava Copper Plates*, (*T.P.C.P.*), Madras, 1966.

*Transactions of the Archaeological Society of South India*, Madras, 1955.

*Travancore Archaeological Series*, 9 Vols., 1910–1941.

Unni, N. P. (ed.) *Mattavilāsam*, Trivandrum, 1974.

## SECONDARY WORKS

Abraham, Mary Meena. *The Ayyavole Guild of Early Medieval South India*, Unpublished M.Phil. dissertation, Jawaharlal Nehru University, New Delhi, 1978.

Altekar, A. S. *The Rashtrakutas and Their Times*, Poona, 1936.

Anderson, Perry. *Passages from Antiquity to Feudalism*, London, 1974.

Anderson, Perry. *Lineages of the Absolutist State*, London, 1974.

Appadorai, A. *Economic Conditions of Southern India AD 1000–1500*, 2 vols., Madras, 1936.

Appadurai, Arjun. 'Right and Left Hand Castes in South India', *The Indian Economic and Social History Review*, Vol. XI, nos. 2 and 3, 1974, pp. 216–60.

Arokiaswamy, M. *The Kongu Country*, Madras, 1956.

Balambal, V. *Feudatories of South India: 800–1070 AD*, Allahabad, 1978.

Balasubrahmanyan, S. R. *Early Chola Temples*, Delhi, 1974.

———. *Middle Chola Temples*, Delhi, 1975.

Banerjee, Diptendra. 'Lawrence Krader and the Asiatic Mode of Production', a review article, *Society and Change*, Vol. II, no. 1, Oct.-Dec. 1980, pp. 99–113.

———. 'In Search of a Theory of Pre-capitalist Modes of Production', in Diptendra Banerjee (ed.) *Marxian Theory and the Third World*, New Delhi, 1985, pp. 13–39.

______. 'Marx and the "Original" Form of Indian Village Community' in Diptendra Banerjee (ed.), *Marxian Theory and the Third World*, New Delhi, 1985, pp. 133–171.

Beck, Brendra E. F. *Peasant Society in Konku*, Vancouver, 1972.

Bendix, Reinhard (ed.), *State and Society: A Reader in Comparative Political Sociology*, Boston, 1968.

Bhandarkar, R. G. *Vaisnavism, Saivism and Minor Religious Sects*, 1928, Reprint, Varanasi, 1965.

Bhattacharya, N. N. *Ancient Indian Rituals and Their Social Content*, Delhi,1975.

Bloch, Marc. *Feudal Society*, 2 vols., translated from the French by L.A. Manyon, London, 1961, 1982.

______. *French Rural History: An Essay on Its Basic Characteristics*, Translated from the French by Janet Sondheimer, London, 1966.

Breman, Jan. *The Shattered Image: Construction and Deconstruction of the Village in Colonial Asia*, Amsterdam, 1987.

Chackochan, P. L. *Historical and Cultural Geography of Venadu, Travancore,* C. AD *1124 to 1729*, Unpublished Ph.D. Thesis, Deccan College, Pune, 1980.

Champakalakshmi, R. 'New Light on the Chola Frescoes of Tanjore', *Journal of Indian History*, Golden Jubilee Volume, 1973.

______. 'Archaeology and Tamil Literacy Tradition', *Puratattva*, Vol. VIII, 1975–76.

______. 'The Bhakti Movement and Religious Persecution in Tamilnadu', *Proceedings of the Indian History Congress*, Calicut, 1976.

______. 'Religious Conflict in the Tamil Country: A Re-appraisal of Epigraphic Evidence', *Journal of the Epigraphical Society of India*, 1979, V.

______. 'Growth of Urban Centres in South India: Kuḍamūkku-Paḻaiyāṟai, the Twin-City of the Colas, *Studies in History*, Vol. I, no. 1, 1979.

______. 'Peasant State and Society in Medieval South India: A Review Article', *Indian Economic and Social History Review*, XVIII, nos. 3–4,July-Dec. 1981, pp. 411–26.

Champakalakshmi, R. 'Introduction', *Studies in History*, Vol. IV, no. 2, 1982.

______. 'Urban Processes in Early Medieval Tamilnadu', in Sabyasachi Bhattacharya and Romila Thapar (eds.) *Situating Indian History*, Delhi, 1986.

______. 'Urbanisation in South India: The Role of Ideology and Polity', Presidential Address, Section I, *Proceedings of the Indian History Congress*, 47th Session, Srinagar, 1986.

______. *Trade, Ideology and Urbanization: South India 300* BC *to* AD *1300* (Delhi, 1996)

———. 'From Devotion and Dissent to Dominance: The Bhakti of the Tamil Alvars and Nayanars', in Champakalakshmi and S. Gopal, (eds.) *Tradition, Ideology and Dissent: Essays in Honour of Romila Thapar*, New Delhi, 1996, pp, 135–163.

———., Kesavan Veluthat and T. R. Venugopalan, (eds.) *State and Society in Pre-modern South India*, (Thrissur, 2002)

Chandra, Bipan 'Karl Marx: His Theories of Asian Societies and Colonial Rule' in Marian O'Callaghan (ed.) *Sociological Theories, Race and Colonialism*, UNESCO, 1980.

Chattopadhyaya, B. D. 'Trade and Urban Centres in Early Medieval North India', *Indian Historical Review*, Vol. I, no.l, 1974.

———. 'Origin of the Rajputs: Political, Economic and Social Processes in Early Medieval Rajasthan', *Indian Historical Review*, III, no. 1, 1976.

———. 'Political Processes and Structure of Polity in Early Medieval India', Presidential Address, Section, I, *Indian History Congress*, Burdwan, 1983.

———. *Coins and Currency Systems in South India*, New Delhi, 1977.

———. Review of Hall, *Trade and State Craft in the Age of the Colas*, in *Indian Historical Review*, Vol. X, nos. 1–2, July 1983 to Jan. 1984, pp. 186–89.

———. 'Urban Centres in Early Medieval India: An Overview', in Sabyasachi Bhattacharya and Romila Thapar (eds.) *Situating, Indian History*, Delhi, 1986.

Claessen, Henri, J. M. and Skalnik Peter (eds.). *The Early State*, The Hague, 1978.

———. and Skalnik Peter (eds.). *The Study of State*, The Hague, 1981.

DeCasparis, J. G. 'Inscriptions and South Asian Dynastic Traditions' in R.J. Moore (ed.) *Tradition and Politics in South Asia*, New Delhi, 1979.

Derrett, J. D. M. 'Bhū-bharaṇa, Bhū-pālana, Bhu-bhojana: An Indian Conundrum', *Bulletin of the School of Oriental and African Studies*, Vol. XXII, I, 1959, pp. 108–23.

———. 'Two Inscriptions Concerning the Status of Kammalas and the Application of Dharmasastra', *Professor K. A. Nilakanta Sastri 80th Birthday Felicitation Volume*, Madras, 1971.

Desai, Devangana. 'Art under Feudalism in India', *Indian Historical Review*, I, no. 1, 1974.

Dirkes, Nicholas B. 'Political Authority and Structural Change in South Indian History' in *Indian Economic and Social History Review*, Vol. XIII, no. 2, 1976.

Dorairangaswami, M. A. *The Religion and Philosophy of Tevaram*, Madras, 1958.

Dumont, Louis. *Homo Hierarchicus*, Delhi, 1970.

Fox, Richard G. (ed.) *Realm and Region in Traditional India*, Delhi, 1977.

Frykenberg, R. E. (ed.) *Land Control and Social Structure in Indian History*, Madison, 1969.

Frykenberg, R. E. Review of Stein's *Peasant State and Society in Medieval South India* (Typescript).

Ganesh, K. N. *Some Aspects of the Agrarian Structure in Early Medieval Venad*, Unpublished M.Phil. dissertation, Jawaharlal Nehru University, New Delhi, 1979.

Ganshof, F. L. *Feudalism*, Third English Edition, London, 1979.

Gopalan, R. *History of the Pallavas of Kanchi*, Madras, 1928.

Gopinatha Rao, T. A. *History of Srivaisnavas*, Madras, 1917.

Gough, Kathleen. 'Modes of Production in Southern India', *Economic and Political Weekly*, Annual no., Feb. 1980.

Govindasamy, M. S. *The Role of Feudatories in Pallava History*, Annamalainagar, 1975.

Govindasamy, M. S. *The Role of Feudatories in Later Chola History*, Annamalainagar, 1979.

Guha, Amalendu. 'Tribalism to Feudalism in Assam, 1600–1750', *Indian Historical Review*, Vol. I, no. 1, Mar. 1974.

Gunawardana, R. A. L. H. 'The Analysis of Pre-Colonial Social Formation in the Writings of Karl Marx' *Indian Historical Review*, Vol. II, no. 2, 1976.

Gundert, Hermann (ed.) *Kēraḷōlpatti*, Mangalore, 1881.

Gupta, K.M. *The Land System of South India between About 800 and 1200 AD*, Lahore, 1933.

Gurukkal, Rajan. *The Socio-economic Role of Temples in Medieval Kerala*, Unpublished M.Phil dissertation, Jawaharlal Nehru University, New Delhi, 1977.

______. 'The Socio-Economic Milieu of the Kerala Temple: A Functional Analysis', *Studies in History*, Vol. II, no. 1, 1980.

______. The *Agrarian System and Socio-Political Organisation under the Early Pandyas, c. AD* 600–1000, Unpublished Ph.D. thesis, Jawaharlal Nehru University, New Delhi, 1984.

______. 'Non-Brahmana Resistance to the Expansion of the Brahmadeyas: The Early Pandya Experience', *Proceedings of the Indian History Congress*, Annamalainagar, 1984.

______. 'Non-Brāhmaṇa Resistance to the Expansion of Brahmadeyas: The Early Pāṇḍya Experience', PIHC (Annamalaingar, 1994), pp. 181–84.

______. 'Antecedents of State Formation in South India' in R. Champakalakshmi, Kesavan Veluthat, Rajan Gurukkal, and T. R.Venugopalan, (eds.) *State and Society in Pre-modern South India*, (Thrissur, 2002), pp. 39–59.

———. 'Did State Exist in Pre-Pallavan Tamil Region?' in Proceedings of the Indian History Congress, Amritsar, 2002, pp. 138–150

———. Social Formations in Early South India, New Delhi, 2010.

Gururaja Rao, B. K. *Megalithic Culture of South India*, Mysore, 1972.

Habib, Irfan. 'An Examination of Wittfogel's Theory of Oriental Despotism', *Enquiry*, old series, 1962.

———. 'Problems of Marxist Historical Analysis', *Enquiry*, New Series, Vol. III, no. 2, 1969.

———. 'The Peasant in Indian History', Presidential Address, Indian History Congress, Kurukshetra, 1982.

———. 'Classifying Pre-Colonial India', *Journal of Peasant Studies*, Vol. XII, nos. 2 and 3, Jan.-Apr., 1985.

———. *Interpreting Indian History*, Shillong, 1985.

Hall, Kenneth R. *Trade and Statecraft in the Age of the Colas*, Delhi, 1980.

Hart III, George L. 'Ancient Tamil Literature: Its Scholarly Past and Future' in Stein (ed.) *Essays on South India*, Delhi, 1975.

———. *The Poems of Ancient Tamil: Their Milieu and Their Sanskrit Counterparts*, Berkeley, 1975.

Havighurst, A. F. (ed.) *The Pirenne Thesis: Analysis, Criticism, Revision*, Farnborough, 1958.

Heesterman, J. C. 'Power and Authority in Indian Tradition' in R. J. Moore (ed.), *Tradition and Politics in South Asia*, New Delhi, 1979.

Heitzman, James. 'State Formation in South India, 850–1280', *The Indian Economic and Social History Review*, Vol. XXIV, no. 1, Mar. 1987, pp. 35–61.

Herlihy, David. *The History of Feudalism*, New York, 1970.

Hilton, Rondey (ed.) *Transition from Feudalism to Capitalism*, London, 1976.

Hindess, Barry and Paul Q. Hirst *Pre-Capitalist Modes Production*, London, 1975.

Indrapala, K. 'Some Medieval Mercantile Communities of South India and Ceylon', *Journal of Tamil Studies*, Vol. II, no. 2, Oct. 1970.

Jacobson, Jerome. 'The Harappan Civilization: An Early State', in Jerome Jacobson (ed.) *Studies in the Archaeology of India and Pakistan*, New Delhi 1986, pp. 137–73.

Jagadisa Aiyar, P. V. *South Indian Temples*, Madras, 1920.

Jagadeesan, N; and S. Jeyapragasam (eds.) *Homage to a Historian: A Festschrift*, Madurai, 1976.

Jaiswal, Suvira. 'Caste in the Socio-Economic Framework of Early India', Presidential Address, Section I, Indian History Congress, Bhuvaneswar, 1977.

Jayaswal, K. P. *Hindu Polity*, 5th ed., Bangalore, 1978.

Jha, D. N. *Studies in Early Indian Economic History*, Delhi, 1980.

———. 'Relevance of 'Peasant State and Society to Pallava-Cola Times', *Indian Historical* Review, VIII, no. 1–2 July 1981–January 1982, pp. 74–94.

———. (ed.) *Feudal Social Formation in Early India*, Delhi, 1987.

Joveau-Dubreuil, G. *Pallava Antiquities*, Vol. I, London 1916; Vol. II, Pondicherry, 1918.

———. *Dravidian Architecture*, Madras, 1917.

———. *The Pallavas*, English Translation, Pondicherry, 1917.

Kailaspathi, K. *Tamil Heroic Poetry*, London, 1968.

Kanakasabhai, V. *The Tamils Eighteen Hundred Years Ago*, Madras, 1904.

Kane, P. V. *History of Dharmasastras*, 5 vols., Poona, 1935–56.

Karashima, Noboru. *South Indian History and Society: Studies from Inscriptions, AD 850–1800*, Delhi, 1984.

———. 'Introduction' *Acta Asiatica*, 48, Tokyo, 1985, pp. iii–xiv.

———, and Y. Subbarayalu. 'Valaṅgai, Idaṅgai, Kāṇiyāḷār and Irājagarattār: Social Conflict in Tamilnadu in the 15th Century' in D. N. Jha, (ed.), *Feudal Social Formation in Early India*, Delhi, 1987, pp. 285–310.

———, Y. Subbarayalu and Toru Matsui. *A Concordance of the Names in the Cola Inscriptions*, 3 vols, Madurai, 1978.

———. *South Indian Society in Transition: Ancient to Medieval*, New Delhi, 2009.

Kasinathan, Natana. 'Pulankuricci Inscription, A Re-look', *Tolliyal Karuttaraṅku*, Madras, 1983.

Kennedy, Richard S. 'The King in Early South India as Chieftain and Emperor', *Indian Historical Review*, Vol. III, no. 1, 1976.

Kominsky, E. A. *Studies in the Agrarian History of England in the Thirteenth Century*, Oxford, 1956.

Kosambi, D. D. *An Introduction to the Study of Indian History*, Revised edn. Bombay, 1975.

———. *The Culture and Civilisation of Ancient India in Historical Outline*, Delhi, 1972.

Krader, Lawrence. *Formation of the State*, New Jersey, 1968.

———. *The Asiatic Mode of Production*, Assen, 1975.

———. 'The State in History', *Studies in History*, Vol. IV, no. 2, 1982.

Krishna Ayyar, K. V. *The Zamorins of Calicut*, Calicut, 1938.

Krishna Rao, M. V. *The Gangas of Talkad*, Madras, 1936.

Krishnan, K. G. *Studies in South Indian History and Epigraphy*, Madras, 1981.

Krishnan, K. G. (ed.) *Karandai Tamil Sangam Plates of Rajendrachola*, New Delhi, 1984.

Krishnaswami Aiyangar, S. *Early History of Vaishnavism in South India*, Madras, 1920.

———. *Ancient History of Deccan*, Madras, 1920.

———. *Evolution of Hindu Administrative Institutions in South India*, Madras, 1929, 1932.

———. *Ancient India and South Indian History and Culture*, 2 vols., Poona, 1941.

Kula, Witold. *An Economic Theory of the Feudal System*, London, 1976.

Kulke, Hermann. 'Fragmentation and Segmentation *versus* Integration? Reflections on the Concepts of Indian Feudalism and the Segmentary State in Indian History', *Studies in History*, Vol. IV, no. 2, 1982.

Kumar, Dharma. 'Private Property in Asia? The Case of Medieval South India', *Comparative Studies in Society and History*, Vol. 27, no. 2, April 1985.

Kunjan Pillai, Elamkmulam P. N. *Kerala Bhāṣayuṭe Vikāsapariṇāmaṅgaḷ*, Kottayam, 1953.

———. *Kēraḷa Caritrattiṉṟe Iruḷaḍañja Ēṭukal*, Kottayam, 1953.

———. *Janmisampradāyam Kēṟḷattil*, Kottayam, 1961.

———. *Caritrattiṉṟe Paśćāttalattil*, Kottayam, 1963.

———. *Cila Kēraḷa Caritrapraśnaṅgaḷ*, Kottayam, 1963.

———. *Studies in Kerala History*, Kottayam, 1971.

Kuppuswami, T. V. *Sangam Chieftains and Their Times*, Unpublished Ph.D. Thesis, University of Kerala, Trivandrum, 1976.

Leshnik, Leon S. *South Indian 'Megalithic' Burials: The Pandukal Complex*, Wiesbaden, 1974.

Lingat, Robert *The Classical Law of India*, Translated from the French, with additions, by J. Duncan M. Derrett, New Delhi, 1973.

Logan, William. *Malabar Manual*, 3 vols, Madras, 1886.

Mahadevan, Iravatham. 'Corpus of the Tamil Brahmi Inscriptions' in R. Nagaswami, (ed.) *Seminar on Inscriptions*, Madras, 1966.

———. Tamil Brahmi Inscriptions, Madras, 1970.

Mahalingam, T. V. *South Indian Polity*, Madras, 1955.

———. 'An Interregnum in Pallava History', *Journal of Indian History*, Vol. XLI, 1963.

———. *Kancipuram in Early South Indian History*, Bombay, 1969.

———. *Readings in South Indian History*, Delhi, 1977.

———. *Early South Indian Palaeography*, Reprint, Madras, 1974.

Maloney, Clarence. 'Dynastic Drift: A Process of Cultural Universalisation', in *Professor K. A. Nilakanta Sastri Felicitation Volume*, Madras, 1971.

Marr, J. A. *The Eight Anthologies: A Study in Early Tamil*, Madras, 1987.

Marx, Karl. *The Capital*, 3 vols., Moscow Edition, 1974.

Mencher, Joan P. 'Kerala and Madras: A Comparative Study of Ecology and Social Structure', *Ethnology*, Vol. V, no. 2, University of Pittsburg, Pennsylvania, Apr. 1966, pp. 136–71.

Menon, V. K. J. 'Geographical Basis of the Distribution and Pattern of Rural Settlement in Kerala', *Journal of the M.S. University of Baroda*, Vol. II, pp. 41–54.

Middleton, John and David Tait. *Tribes without Rulers*, London, 1958.

Minakshi, C. *Administration and Social Life under the Pallavas*, Madras, 1938. 2nd edn. with revisions and additions, Madras, 1977.

______. *The Historical Sculptures of the Vaikunthapperumal Temple, Kanchi*, Memoirs of the Archaeological Survey of India, no. 63.

Mukhia, Harbans. 'Was There Feudalism in Indian History?' Presidential Address, Section II, Indian History Congress, Waltair, 1979.

Nagam Aiya, V. *Travancore State Manual*, Trivandrum, 1904.

Nagaswami, R. (ed.) *Ceṅgam Nadukarkaḷ*, Madras, 1972.

______. (ed.) 'An Outstanding Epigraphical Discovery in Tamilnadu' *Proceedings of the Fifth International Conference Seminar on Tamil Studies*, Madurai, 1981.

Nandi, R. N. 'Feudalisation of the State in Medieval South India, *Social Science Probings*, March, 1984.

______. 'Some Social Aspects of the Nalayira Divya Prabandham', *Proceedings of the Indian History Congress*, Calicut, 1976.

______. 'Growth of Rural Economy in Early India', Presidential Address, Section I, Indian History Congress, Annamalainagar, 1984.

______. *Social Roots of Religion in Ancient India*, Calcutta, 1986.

Narayana Ayyar, C. V. *Origin and Early History of Saivism in South India*, Madras, 1920.

Narayanan, M. G. S. 'Kāntaḷūr Śālai—New Light on the Nature of Aryan Expansion to South India', *Proceedings of the Indian History Congress*, Jabalpur, 1970, pp. 125–36.

______. *Political and Social Conditions of Kerala under the Kulaśēkhara Empire, c. 800–1124* AD, Unpublished Ph.D. thesis, University of Kerala, Trivandrum, 1972.

______. *Cultural Symbiosis in Kerala*, Trivandrum, 1972.

______. *Keralacaritrattiṉṟe Aṭisthānaśilakal*, in Malayalam, Calicut, 1972.

______. *Aspects of Aryanisation in Kerala*, Trivandrum, 1973.

______. 'The Vedic-Sastraic-Puranic Element in Tamil Sangam Literature', *Proceedings of the Indian History Congress*, Aligarh, 1975.

______. 'Socio-Economic Implications of the Concept of Mahāpātaka in the Feudal Society of South India', *Proceedings of the Indian History Congress*, Calicut, 1978,

______. *Reinterpretations in South Indian History*, Trivandrum, 1977.

______. 'Cattle Raids in Sangam Literature', *Proceedings of the Indian History Congress*, Bhubaneswar, 1977.

______. 'Anatomy of a Political Alliance from Temple Records of Tirunavālūr and Tiruvoṟṟiyūr', *Journal of the Epigraphical Society of India*, Vol. V, 1978.

______. 'Historiography: Trends and Prospects', Presidential Address, Section I, *Proceedings of the Indian History Congress*, Hyderabad, 1978.

______. 'The Hundred Groups and the Rise of Nayar Militia in Kerala', *Proceedings of the Indian History Congress*, Burdwan, 1983.

______. 'The New Plunder Theory and the Nature of Cola Imperialism', Indian History Congress, 45th Session, Annamalainagar, 1984.

______. 'New Trends: A Case Study of the Chola Times', Presidential Address, Socio-Economic History, South Indian History Congress, V Session, Mysore, 1985.

______. 'A Critique of the *History of South India* and a Prosposal for a New Conceptual Frame', Paper presented to the VII Session of the South Indian History Congress, Madras, 1987.

______, and Kesavan Veluthat. 'The Bhakti Movement in South India' in S. C. Malik (ed.), *Indian Movements: Some Aspects of Dissent, Protest and Reform*, Simla, 1978.

______. 'The Traditional Land System of Kerala: Problems of Change and Perspective', Paper presented to the Logan Centenary Seminar on 'Land Reforms in Kerala', Calicut, 1981, Unpublished.

______. 'Temples in South India', a paper presented to the symposium on the Socio-Economic Role of Religious Institutions in India, Indian History Congress, Bodh Gaya, 1981.

______. 'A History of the Nambudiri Community in Kerala' in Frits Staal (ed.) *Agni*, Vol. II, Berkeley, 1983.

______. 'Peasants in Early Tamilakam', in H. V. Sreenivasamurthi, B. Surendra Rao, Kesavan Veluthat and S. A. Bari, (eds.) *Essays on Indian History and Culture: Felicitation Volume to Professor B. Sheik Ali*, New Delhi, 1990.

______. 'The Mauryan Problem in Sangam Works in Historical Perspective', *Journal of Indian History*, Vol. 53, no. 2, 1975

______. *The Vedic, Puranic, Sastraic Elements in Tamil Sangam Society and Culture*, PIHC, Aligarh, 1975.

______. *The Warrior Settlements of the Sangam Age*, PIHC, Kurukshetra, 1982.

Nilakanta Sastri, K. A. *The Pandyan Kingdom: From the Earliest Times to the Sixteenth Century*, London, 1929, 2nd impression, Madras, 1972.

______. *Studies in Cola History and Administration*, Madras, 1932.

______. *The Colas*, 2nd edn, Madras, 1955, 1975.

______. *A History of South India*, 3rd edn., Madras, 1966.

______. *Development of Religion in South India*, Delhi, 1975 rpt.

______. *South India and South-East Asia*, Mysore, 1978.

O'Flaherty, Wendy Doniger, and J. D. M. Derrett (eds.). *The Concept of Duty in South Asia*, Delhi, 1978.

Oppert, Gustav. *On the Original Inhabitants of Bharatavarsa or India*, rpt, Delhi, 1972.

Padmanabha Menon, K. P. *History of Kerala*, 4 vols., Ernakulam, 1924–1937.

Pillay, K. K. *Social History of the Tamils* I, Madras, 1975.

Pirenne, Henri. *Economic and Social History of Medieval Europe*, London, 1936, 1972.

Polanyi, Karl. 'The Economy as Instituted Process' in Polanyi, et al. (eds.) *Trade and Market in Early Empires*, Glencoe, 1957.

Radha, K. K. *Kulaśēkhara Āḷvār and the Advent of Vaiṣṇavism in Kerala*, Unpublished M.A. Dissertation, University of Calicut, 1976.

Raghava Varier, M. R. *Jainism in Kerala*, Unpublished M.Phil. Dissertation, Jawaharlal Nehru University, New Delhi, 1977.

Raghavan Nambyar, V. 'Annals and Antiquities of Tiruvalla', *Kerala Society Papers*, 1929, pp. 57–94.

Raghottam, Venkat. 'Rajendra Cola's Raid on Sri Vijaya in AD 1025: A Study of the Political and Economic Dimensions of the Plunder Dynamic in Eleventh Century Tamilnadu', *Tamil Civilization*, Vol. I, no. 2, 1983.

Rai, G. K. 'Forced Labour in Ancient and Early Medieval India', *Indian Historical Review*, Vol. II, no. 1, 1976.

Rajamanikkam, M. *The Development of Saivism in South India AD 300–1300*, Dharmapuram, 1964.

Raman, K. V. *Some Aspects of Pandyan History in the Light of Recent Discoveries*, Madras, 1978.

Ramaswamy, Vijaya. 'Peasant State and Society in Medieval South India', A Review Article, *Studies in History*, Vol. IV, no. 2, 1982, pp. 307–19.

Raychaudhury, Tapan and Irfan Habib (eds.) *The Cambridge Economic History of India I*, Delhi, 1984, Reprint.

Ribeiro, Darcy. *The Civilizational Process*, Harper Torch books, 1968.

Sahlins, Marshall D. 'The Segmentary Lineage: Organization of Predatory Expansion', *American Anthropologist*, Vol. LXIII, no. 2, 1961, pp. 332–45.

Sahu, B. P. 'Conception of Kali Age in Early India: A Regional Perspective', *Trends in Social Science Research*, Vol. 4, No.1, 1998.

Sampath, M. D. 'Hero Stone Inscriptions from Dharmapuri District', Unpublished paper, 1976.

Satyanarayana, K. *Studies in the History and Culture of the Andhras*, New Delhi, 1975.

Seneviratne, Sudrasan. 'The Mauryan State', in H. J. M. Claessen and P. Skalnik (eds.) *The Early State*, The Hague, 1978, pp. 381–402.

Settar, S. 'Tuḻilāḷgaḷ (in Kannada), *Sādhane*, IX, 3, July–Sept. 1980.

Shanmugam, P. *The Revenue System of the Colas, 850–1279*, Madras, 1987.

Sharma, R. S. 'The Origins of Feudalism in India', *Journal of the Economic and Social History of the Orient*, Vol. I, Part 3,1 958.

———. Aspects of Political Ideas and Institutions in Ancient India, Delhi, 1958, 3rd edn, 1991.

———. 'Decline of Trade and Decay of Urban Centres in Gangetic Valley in the Gupta and post-Gupta Period', *Proceedings of the Indian History Congress*, Muzaffarpur, 1972.

———. 'Indian Feudalism Retouched', *Indian Historical Review*, Vol. 2, no. 2, 1974.

———. 'Rajaśāsana: Meaning, Scope and Application', Indian History Congress, Calicut, 1976.

———. *'Indian Feudalism*, 2nd edn., Delhi, 1980.

———. *Sudras in Ancient India*, 2nd edn, Delhi, 1980.

———. 'The Kali Age: A Period of Social Crisis', in S. N. Mukherjee (ed.) *India: History and Thought, Essays in Honour of Professor A. L. Basham*, Calcutta, 1982.

———. *Material Culture and Social Formations in Ancient India*, Delhi, 1983.

———. 'How Feudal was Indian Feudalism', *Journal of Peasant Studies*, Vol. 12, no. 2, Feb. 1984.

———. *Urban Decay in India*, AD *300–1000*, Delhi, 1987.

Sheik Ali, B. *History of the Western Gangas*, Mysore, 1976.

Shungoonny Menon, P. *History of Travancore from Earliest Times*, Trivandrum, 1878.

Sircar, D. C. (ed.) *Land Systems and Feudalism in Ancient India*, Calcutta, 1966.

———. *Studies in the Society and Administration of Ancient and Medieval India*, Calcutta, 1967.

———. *Studies in Indian Coins*, Delhi, 1968.

———. *Landlordism and Tenancy in Ancient and Medieval India as Revealed by Epigraphical Records*, Lucknow, 1969.

———. *Political and Administrative System of Ancient and Medieval India*, Delhi, 1974.

Sivathambi, K. *Studies in Ancient Tamil Society*, Chennai, 1998.

Skinner, G. William. *Marketing and Social Structure in Rural China*, Ann Arbor, 1974.

Soundararajan, K. V. *South Indian Temples*, Delhi, 1966.

Southall, Aidan. *Alur Society: A Study in Processes and Types of Domination*, Cambridge, 1956.

Spencer, George W. *The Politics of Expansion: The Chola Conquest of Sri Lanka and Sri Vijaya*, Madras, 1983.

______. 'Religious Networks and Royal Influence in Eleventh Century South India', *Journal of the Economic and Social History of the Orient*, Vol. XII, no. 1,1969, pp. 42–56.

______. 'The Politics of Plunder: The Cholas in Eleventh Century Ceylon', *Journal of Asian Studies*, Vol. XXXV, 1976, pp. 405–19.

______. 'Heirs Apparent: Fiction and Function in Chola Mythical Genealogies', *Indian Economic and Social History Review*, Vol. XXI, no. 4, 1984.

Sreedhara Menon, A. *A Survey of Kerala History*, Kottayam, 1969.

Staal, et.al. *Kerala Through the Ages*, Trivandrum, 1976.

Stein, Burton. 'The State and Agrarian Order in Medieval South India' in Stein (ed.) *Essays on South India*, Delhi, 1975.

______. (ed.) *Essays on South India*, Delhi, 1975.

______. (ed.) *South Indian Temples*, Delhi, 1975.

______. 'The Segmentary State in South Indian History' in Fox (ed.) *Realm and Region in Traditional India*, Delhi, 1977.

______. *Peasant State and Society in Medieval South India*, Delhi, 1980.

______. *All the King's Mana*, Madras, 1984.

______. 'Politics, Peasants and the Deconstruction of Feudalism in Medieval India', *Journal of Peasant Studies*, Vol. XII, nos. 2 and 3, 1985.

Subbarayalu, Y. *Political Geography of the Chola Country*, Madras, 1973.

______. *The State in Medieval South India*, Unpublished Ph.D. thesis, Madurai Kamaraj University, 1976.

______. 'Transfer of Land in Kaveri Valley', Paper presented to the Indian History Congress, 37th Session, Calicut, 1976.

______. 'The Place of Ur in the Economic and Social History of Early Tamilnadu, 750–1350', Paper presented to the ICHR Seminar on South Indian History, Madras University, 1977.

______. 'The Cola State', *Studies in History*, Vol. IV, no. 2, 1982, pp. 265–306.

______. 'The Peasantry of the Tiruchirapalli District from the 13th to 17th centuries', *Studies in the Socio-Cultural Changes in Villages in Tiruchirapalli District, Tamilnadu, India*, Part I, Tokyo, 1983.

______. Presidential Address, Section IV, Indian History Congress, Burdwan, 1983.

———. 'Pottery Inscriptions of Tamilnadu: A Comprehensive View', in R. Kalaikkovan et al., (ed.) *Airāvati: Felicitation Volume in Honour of Iravatham Mahadevan*, Chennai, 2008, pp. 209–248.

———. 'Visāki and Kuvaran: Historical Implications of Names in the Tamil Brahmi Inscriptions', in K. Indrapala (ed.) *Early Historic Tamilnadu c. 300 BCE to 300 CE: Essays Commemorating Prof. K. Kailasapathy on the Twenty-fifth Anniversary of his Death*, Colombo and Chennai, 2009, pp. 95–122.

———. *South India under the Cholas*, New Delhi, 2012.

Subramanya Aiyar, K.V. Historical Sketches of Ancient Dekhan, Madras, 1917.

———. 'The Largest Provincial Organisation in Ancient India', *Quarterly Journal of the Mythic Society*, Bangalore, Vol. LXV, 1954–55; LXVI 1955.

Subrahmanyan, N. Sangam Polity, Bombay, 1966.

———. A Review of Karashima, *South Indian History and Society*, in *Indian Historical Review*, Vol. X, nos. 1–2, July 1983 to Jan. 1984.

———. *Pre-Pallavan Tamil Index*, Reprint, Madras, 1990

Sumathi, R. *Trade and Its Impact on the Early Tamils: The Chola Experience*, Unpublished M.Phil. Dissertation, Jawaharlal Nehru University, New Delhi, 1984.

Sundara, A. Early Chamber Tombs of South India, Delhi, 1975.

Suresh, B. *Historical and Cultural Geography and Ethnologoy of South India with Special Reference to Cola Inscriptions*, Unpublished Ph.D. Thesis, Deccan College, Poona, 1965.

Swaminatha Iyer, U. V. *En Kathai* (Tamil) translated into Malayalam, Sahitya Academy, Trichur, 1966.

Terray, Emmanuel. *Marxism and 'Primitive Societies'*, London, 1972.

Thapar, Romila. *A History of India*, Vol. I, Harmonsdsworth, 1966, 1974.

———. *Ancient Indian Social History*, Delhi, 1978.

———. 'The Mouse in the Ancestry' in S. D. Joshi (ed.) *Amrtadhara: Professor R. N. Dandekar Felicitation Volume*, Delhi, 1984.

———. *From Lineage to State*, Bombay, 1984.

———. 'Legitimation Politique et Filiation: Le Varna Kshatriya en Inde du Nord', *Annales*, no. 4, July-Aug. 1984, pp. 783–97.

———. 'Black Gold: South Asia and the Roman Maritime Trade', *Journal of the South Asian Studies Association*, New South Wales, 1992, Vol. XV, No.2, (New Series), pp. 13–14.

Tirumalai, D. 'A Preliminary Report on Palaiyarai Excavations', *Tamil Civilisation*, Vol. V, nos. 1–2, 1987, pp. 118–23.

Tirumalai, R. *Land Grants and Agrarian Reaction in Cola and Pandya Times*, Madras, 1987.

Tokei, Ference, *Essays on the Asiatic Mode of Production*, Budapest, 1979.

Trautmann, Thomas R. 'Traditions of Statecraft in Ancient India', in R.J. Moore (ed.) *Tradition and Politics in South Asia*, New Delhi, 1979.

Vanaja, R. 'Trade and Statecraft in the Age of Colas', A Review Article, *Studies in History*, Vol. IV, no. 2, July-Dec. 1982, pp. 321–33.

Vanamamalai, N. 'Consolidation of Feudalism and Anti-feudal Struggles during Chola Imperialist Rule', *Proceedings of the Second International Conference Seminar of Tamil Studies*, II, Madras, 1968.

Veluthat, Kesavan. *Aryan Brahman Settlements of Ancient Kerala*, Unpublished M.A. Dissertation, University of Calicut, 1974.

______. 'The Cattas and Bhattas: A New Interpretation', *Proceedings of the Indian History Congress*, Aligarh, 1975.

______. *Brahman Settlements in Kerala* AD *1100–1500*, Unpublished M.Phil Dissertation, Jawaharlal Nehru University, New Delhi, 1978.

______. *Brahman Settlements in Kerala: Historical Studies*, Calicut, 1978.

______. 'Royalty and Divinity: Legitimisation of Monarchical Power in South India', *Proceedings of the Indian History Congress*, Hyderabad, 1978.

______. 'The Temple-base of the Bhakti Movement in South India', *Proceedings of the Indian History Congress*, Waltair, 1979.

______. The Status of the Monarch: A Note on the Rituals Pertaining to Kingship and Their Significance in Tamil Country (AD *600–1200*) *Proceedings of the Indian History Congress*, Kurukshetra, 1982.

______. 'The Sabha and Parisad in Early Medieval South India: Correlation of Epigraphic and Dharmasastraic Evidences', *Tamil Civilisation*, Vol. III, nos. 2 and 3, 1985, pp. 75–82.

______. 'The Progress of Epigraphical Studies in Kerala: The Last Two Decades', *Tamil Civilization*, Vol. V, nos. 1 and 2, 1987.

______. *The Early Medieval in South India*, New Delhi, 2009

Venkatesan, P. 'A Study of the Office Called Naduvirukkum in the Central Administration under the Colas', *Tamil Civilization*, Vol. 3, nos. 2 and 3, 1985.

Vijayam, T. M., *The Panas in Sangam Literature* (M.Phil. Dissertation, Calicut University, 1986).

Wiebe, Robert H. *The Segmented Society*, New York, 1975.

Yadava, B. N. S. 'Some Aspects of the Changing Order in India during the Saka-Kusana Age', in G.R. Sharma (ed.) *Kushana Studies*, Allahabad, 1968.

______. *Society and Culture in Northern India in the Twelfth Century*, Allahabad, 1973.

______. 'Immobility and Subjection of Indian Peasantry in Early Medieval Complex', *Indian Historical Review*, Vol. I, no. 1, 1974.

______. 'Problems of the Interaction between Socio-Economic Classes in the Early Medieval Complex', *Indian Historical Review*, Vol. III, no. 1, July, 1976.

______. 'The Accounts of the Kali Age and the Social Transitions from Antiquity to Middle Ages', *Indian Historical Review*, Vol. V, nos. 1 and 2, July 1978—January 1979.

______. 'The Problem of the Emergence of Feudal Relations in Early India', Presidential Address, Section I, Indian History Congress, Bombay, 1980.

Zvelebil, Kamil, The Smile of Murugan, Leiden, 1973.

# Index